Mr. Kazin's concern with literature does not preclude his interest in other things; CONTEMPORARIES includes reflective essays on travel in Russia, Germany, Israel, Puerto Rico; five essays on Freud and the significance of psychology in modern life and culture; an inquiry into politics and society. The final section, "The Critic's Task," concerns itself with the critic's function within a popular and an academic context, and with critical theory and principles.

Books by Alfred Kazin

ON NATIVE GROUNDS
A WALKER IN THE CITY
THE INMOST LEAF
CONTEMPORARIES

Editor:

THE PORTABLE WILLIAM BLAKE
F. SCOTT FITZGERALD: THE MAN AND HIS WORK
THE STATURE OF THEODORE DREISER
(WITH CHARLES SHAPIRO)
MELVILLE'S *Moby-Dick* (RIVERSIDE EDITION)
RALPH WALDO EMERSON: A MODERN ANTHOLOGY
(WITH DANIEL AARON)
THE OPEN FORM: ESSAYS FOR OUR TIME

Contemporaries

Alfred Kazin

An Atlantic Monthly Press Book
LITTLE, BROWN AND COMPANY

Contemporaries

BOSTON • TORONTO

LIBRARY OF CONGRESS CATALOG CARD NO. 62-10528

SIXTH PRINTING

Acknowledgment: The author wishes to thank the following for permission to reprint copyrighted material:

Dell Publishing Co., Inc., for Alfred Kazin's Introduction for their Laurel Dreiser series, © copyright, 1959, by Alfred Kazin; Doubleday and Company, Inc., for "The Background of Modern Literature" by Alfred Kazin, from AN OUTLINE OF MAN'S KNOWLEDGE OF THE MODERN WORLD, edited by Lyman Bryson. Copyright © 1960 by Catherine McGrattan Bryson, Executrix of the estate of Lyman Bryson, reprinted by permission of Doubleday and Company, Inc., and published by McGraw-Hill Book Company; Houghton Mifflin Company, for the Introduction to MOBY-DICK by Herman Melville; Random House, Inc., for Mr. Kazin's essay reprinted from SELECTED STORIES OF SHOLOM ALEICHEM, by permission of Random House, Inc., © 1956 by Alfred Kazin; Wayne State University Press, for "William Faulkner: The Stillness of LIGHT IN AUGUST," copyright 1958 Wayne State University Press; *Psychoanalysis and Psychoanalytic Review* for Mr. Kazin's "Psychoanalysis and Literary Culture," Volume 45, Numbers 1 and 2, Spring-Summer 1958, © copyright 1958; seven lines from "Howl" by Allen Ginsberg, © 1956 & 1959 by Allen Ginsberg, by permission of City Lights Books; 250 words from NIGHT by Elie Wiesel, © Les Editions de Minuit, 1958, English translation © MacGibbon and Kee, 1960, reprinted by permission of Hill and Wang, Inc.; six lines from "The Second Coming" by W. B. Yeats, reprinted with permission of The Macmillan Company, Mrs. W. B. Yeats and Macmillan & Co. Ltd. from THE COLLECTED POEMS OF W. B. YEATS, © 1924 by The Macmillan Company, © 1952 by Bertha Georgie Yeats; 240 words from "In Haste" from THE OLD COUNTRY by Sholom Aleichem © 1946 by Crown Publishers, Inc., used by permission of the publisher.

ATLANTIC–LITTLE, BROWN BOOKS
ARE PUBLISHED BY
LITTLE, BROWN AND COMPANY
IN ASSOCIATION WITH
THE ATLANTIC MONTHLY PRESS

Published simultaneously in Canada
by Little, Brown & Company (Canada) Limited

PRINTED IN THE UNITED STATES OF AMERICA

To Edmund Wilson

Acknowledgments

MOST OF THESE ESSAYS appeared first in the following publications, and are republished here with their permission: the *Reporter*, the *Atlantic Monthly*, *Harper's*, the *American Scholar*, the *New Republic*, the *New York Times Book Review*, *Partisan Review*, *Commentary*, the *Griffin*, the *New Yorker*, *Psychoanalysis and the Psychoanalytic Review*, the *New Leader*. "The Background of Modern Literature" appeared first in *An Outline of Modern Knowledge*, edited by Lyman Bryson, and is republished here by permission of Doubleday and Company; "Ishmael and Ahab" is the introduction to the Riverside Press edition of *Moby-Dick*, and is republished here by permission of Houghton Mifflin Company; "Dreiser: The Esthetic of Realism" is the general introduction to the novels of Theodore Dreiser published by Dell Publishing Company, and appears here by their permission; "The Stillness of *Light In August*" was written for *Twelve Original Essays on Great American Novels*, edited by Charles Shapiro, and is republished here by permission of Wayne State University Press; "Sholom Aleichem: The Old Country" was written as an introduction to the Modern Library edition of *Selected Stories of Sholom Aleichem*, and is republished here by permission of Random House.

The author also wishes to thank the following for permission to use excerpts: Basic Books, for *The Letters of Sigmund Freud*; Farrar, Straus and Cudahy, for *Life Studies* by Robert Lowell, and for *Gimpel the Fool* by Isaac Bashevis Singer; Alfred Knopf, Inc., for *Borstal Boy* by Brendan Behan; David McKay Company, Inc., for *Warrior's Rest* by Christiane Rochefort; Random House, Inc., for *Light in August* by William Faulkner, *The Legacy of the Civil War* by Robert Penn Warren, and *Breakfast at Tiffany's* by Truman Capote; Charles Scribner's Sons and Macmillan and Company, Ltd., for *Homecoming* by C. P. Snow; The Viking Press, for *Henderson the Rain King* by

Saul Bellow, and for an excerpt from *Herzog* by Saul Bellow as it appeared in *Esquire;* and Little, Brown and Company, for "Because I Could Not Stop for Death" from *The Complete Poems of Emily Dickinson,* edited by Thomas H. Johnson.

In addition to these formal acknowledgments, I should like to express my personal gratitude to the many editors and publishers who invited me to contribute these essays and who then assisted me to realize my own intentions. I owe many kindnesses to the staff of the *Reporter,* in which so many of these literary articles first appeared.

I am particularly grateful to Mr. Robert B. Silvers for his editorial advice and for his invaluable help in arranging the order of these essays.

Contents

I

The Background of Modern Literature

Ever since the end of the eighteenth century, when great poets like Goethe and Blake denounced experimental science as partial and inconclusive, the distinctively modern writers have been those who have claimed that literature gives us a more direct and more comprehensive access to reality than science can. It is not knowledge as such, or even the power over nature that can be won through knowledge, that the modern writers have questioned; it is knowledge gained by scientific method. Wordsworth says disapprovingly that we murder to dissect, and Whitman condescendingly turns his back on the "learn'd astronomer" to look up "in perfect silence at the stars." Poe cried out in his sonnet "To Science" that science had robbed the world of its magic, and later in the nineteenth century the great French visionary poet Arthur Rimbaud, himself in the tradition set up in France by disciples of Poe, protested that "our pale reason hides the infinite from us." As early as the seventeenth century, the particular concern of the *modern* writer is typified by that genius in both mathematics and literature, Blaise Pascal, who wrote that the heart has its reasons — which reason cannot know. Yet the spell of even scientific knowledge is so great that Goethe made investigations in botany and optics, realistic novelists from Balzac to Zola have conceived of fiction as a branch of biology, and in the twentieth century an extraordinary poet and would-be mathematician, Paul Valéry, wrote certain poems as if he were preparing theorems.

Valéry's master, the Symbolist poet Stéphane Mallarmé, had already shown (on a hint from the stories of Poe) that the effects of one sense can be described as if gained through another. A sound can be expressed as a vision and each vowel in a word can suggest a different color. Through this doctrine of "synaesthesiae" Mallarmé had proclaimed that unity of the poetic imagination that had been broken ever since science had taught men to separate reason from intuition. One reason why Poe was such a profound influence on these French poets, starting from Baudelaire, is that he conceived of himself as a seer, a poet who was a genius at ratiocination. Those demigods of popular literature — the amateur detectives who are never at a loss for a solution — actually have their beginning in the fantasies and ambitions of Edgar Allan Poe, who may be said to have invented the detective story, and whose hero, C. Auguste Dupin, is the very type of the modern literary intellectual — an aristocrat temporarily down on his luck who lives alone, works by night, and, entirely by superior guesswork, has a knowledge of crime and the human heart that confounds the stupid representatives of the official police, with their reliance on common sense and laboratory methods.

This contempt for the official police on the part of poets who prize their independence is really a dramatization of the everlasting contempt that the Romantic writers — the first self-consciously modern group — felt for the conventional picture of the world and the conventional morality that narrowed the possibilities of man. Whether it is Goethe's Faust or Shelley's Prometheus or Melville's Captain Ahab, the characteristic heroes of the Romantics are those who know that reality is more mysterious and intangible than the ruling gods will admit — and who try to meet this reality on every side of their personal experience. The great insight of the Romantics — and of those who have become the fundamental type of modern writer in our day, Joyce and Proust and Yeats — is that the world which science seeks so laboriously to understand must be grasped through man, not despite him. A contemporary social scientist has contemptuously defined personality as "the index of inefficiency." But Yeats wrote in "The Tower" (1928) that "Death and life were not/Till man made up the whole." Where the scientists studied "the facts," unrelated and external to man, the modern writer, as early as the eighteenth century, took his stand on human consciousness as the key to reality.

It is this claim that explains the extraordinary inner consistency of modern literature from the fall of the Bastille to the fall of mechanistic conceptions in twentieth-century science, as it is this claim that explains the actual influence of literature on science. Although science and technology seem pre-eminent in our present culture, the really suggestive thing about the very greatest twentieth-century writers, like Proust, Joyce, Lawrence, Yeats, Mann, is that they have never felt outdone or outclassed by scientific investigation. Although literary people often complain that they feel isolated and anomalous in a world where scientists exert so much influence and get so much prestige, the greatest writers of our time have celebrated in literature man's increasing contact with the profundities of his own experience. In a book of startling encouragement to writers, *Science and the Modern World* (1925), Alfred North Whitehead, speaking from his immense prestige as a mathematician and philosopher, substantiated the criticism first made by the Romantic poets of mechanistic conceptions of the external world. In his tribute to Wordsworth, Whitehead noted that the philosophy which had reached its ultimate expression in the eighteenth-century dream of ordering human nature and society in a fixed mode, through reason, had a fatal weakness: "It involves a fundamental duality, with material on the one hand, and on the other hand mind. In between there lie the concepts of life, organism, function, instantaneous reality, interaction, order of nature, which collectively form the Achilles' heel of the whole system." And Whitehead added: "We are witnessing a conscious reaction against the whole tone of the eighteenth century. That century approached nature with the abstract analysis of science, whereas Wordsworth opposed to the scientific abstractions his full concrete experience. Wordsworth in his whole being expressed a conscious reaction against the mentality of the eighteenth century. What moved him was a moral repulsion. He felt something had been left out, and that what had been left out comprised everything that was most important."

In one form or another, much that had been left out by nineteenth-century science was brought back by modern literature. For the missing "life," "organism," "function," "instantaneous reality," "interaction," one could now fill in William James's radical empiricism, Henri Bergson's *élan vital*, Sigmund Freud's theory of the unconscious. Such men are not merely philosophers and psychologists but superb writers, whose greatest contributions to knowledge, as in *The Principles of Psychology* (1890), *Matter and Memory* (1896), *The Interpretation of Dreams* (1900), have not only exerted enormous influence on the modern movement in twentieth-century literature, but have themselves become classic parts of this literature.

In writers like James, Bergson, and Freud, modern literature and modern science have gone hand in hand, and despite the efforts of second-rate poets to cut themselves off from difficult subject matter and of second-rate psychologists to dismiss the insights gained by modern writers, literature and science have shown themselves in the best hands to be profoundly respectful of each other. Freud, who was a very beautiful writer—he was awarded the greatest German literary honor, the Goethe prize, even if he was steadily refused a Nobel Prize in science — typified the intelligence of an original scientist when he wrote, in a famous essay on Dostoevsky: "Unfortunately, before the problem of the creative artist, analysis must lay down its arms." The influence of Freud on modern literature and art, so overwhelming that no one can trace it completely, can be attributed to the belief that Freud had confirmed the creative role of the imagination, that necessary and valuable projection of human symbols upon the world, which Wordsworth, as early as 1798, had summed up as "the mighty world of eye, and ear — both what they half-create, and what perceive."

It is this identification of personal consciousness with the hidden areas of reality that explains why the language in modern poetry, which to so many readers seems unintelligible and even willfully so, is so often regarded by the poet as "ultimate" and irreducible in its truth. The poet regards his words not as signs or referents, but as direct images of the world. "Poetry is not written with ideas," said Mallarmé the Symbolist, "it is written with words." This could have been said by the Romantics as well, and one can find in so Romantic a poet as Whitman the same reliance on words whose import is mysterious and unknown to himself that one can find in the Symbolist poets. Where Symbolism broke with Romanticism was on the question of form, not belief. Romantics like Whitman assumed that the revelations they made in their poems were in line not only with their own unconsciousness but with the moral order of the world, and that the "rapt" inspiration of the poet was in perfect correspondence with God, society, science, and truth. The Symbolists — their idol, Poe, significantly insisted that a successful poem must be short and strict in form — did not think of themselves as nature's priests but as nature's alchemists: they were fabricators rather than "revealers." For them poetry was not in line with society but in opposition to it. A poem had to be not "open" but "closed": for the hermetic images on which the poem was founded were absolute in themselves, and the experience to be gained from the complex interweaving of human sensations together would finally be unstatable. By opposing sensation to conscious understanding, the poem to prose, the poet to society, the Symbolists diverted poetic imagination from the transcendental to the subjective. The implied despair of the outside world, of commonplace human experience, even of sexual love, became elements of which the poem was hardened in form, and what had been sponsored by Wordsworth, Hugo, and Whitman as revelation was now adored as magic. The typical Symbolist poets — Mallarmé in France, Stefan George in Germany — had cults around them which regarded them as "magicians," celebrating the mystery of the word. The religion of the individual genius which the Romantics had formed was based on the image of the poet as an oracle and great national leader: Emerson in America, Carlyle in Britain, Goethe in Germany, Dostoevsky in Russia. The poet was akin to God because he was the voice of God. The Romantics had emphasized "creativity" because they had wished to establish the value of originality, and this, founded on the image of Shakespeare, had meant an analogy between genius and nature. Even the most famous Romantic definition of Shakespeare's creative power — Keats's conception of "negative capability," that the poet in himself is nothing but becomes in turn all the personages he creates — implies that genius is as mysteriously re-creative of itself as nature is. But the cult of the *poet* among the Symbolists is significantly opposed to that of the *bard* among the Romantics; with the Symbolists the poet not only becomes the highest human being, but is privileged by understanding which he cannot share with anyone else and which, since it cannot even be *stated* in the poem itself (it is merely suggested), cannot be grasped at all outside the immediate experience of the poem.

Much of what is said in explanation of modern poetry is based on the doctrine of the Symbolists and is misleading when it is used to substantiate the particular achievement of *all* poetry. Because of the overwhelming success of modern poetry in the style of Eliot and Pound, their followers often speak of poetry as if it had always been a rite, as it was to the Symbolists. When Allen Tate declares that poetry gives us a higher form of knowledge than science does, a knowledge that is "complete" in itself, he is speaking of poetry as in itself a religious experience — which is what it was to the Symbolists, but is not to Eliot himself, as it was not to Dr. Johnson or to Shakespeare. Everyone knows Archibald MacLeish's famous lines: "A poem should not mean / But be." But since the victory of the specifically modern poetry that grew out of Symbolism, not everyone remembers that many a great poem before the nineteenth century — and in it — could both mean *and* be.

The particular emphasis which the Symbolists put on the being of a poem rather than its meaning grew out of their revolt against the narrow-minded science of the mid-nineteenth century. The quality of this period comes back to us when Matthew Arnold reports in his essay on *Literature and Science* that a young man in an English training college for teachers, having to paraphrase the passage in *Macbeth* beginning "Can'st thou not minister to a mind diseased?" turned this line into: "Can you not wait upon the lunatic?" Arnold commented in his official report as an inspector of schools that it would be a curious state of things if every pupil in English national schools knew in exact figures the diameter of the moon but thought that these two lines came to the same thing. In the heyday of nineteenth-century science, the poets reacted so strongly against the cocksure materialism of the scientists that they made a cult of experiences that could be only suggested, not represented or defined. Arnold collected the most affecting single lines of poetry and read them as if he were a priest reading his breviary. The Symbolists relied for their art entirely on the thaumaturgic power of words, which can affect us in the same way that we are affected by actual physical representations in the fine arts and by sounds in music.

« 2 »

If we look now at the way Symbolism triumphed—in the invigorating atmosphere of artistic "modernism" that just before World War I began to sweep everything before it—we can see that, as in all periods, the poetry which it ridicules and destroys, the poetry that has been too long in favor, confesses its weakness by proclaiming its "moral" intentions. A characteristic sign of creative weakness is talk about doing good. Such talk was particularly rife at the end of the nineteenth century, when the more "genteel" poets, in the now diffused poetic tradition of the Romantics — "Tennyson-and-water" — could not respond directly enough to the challenge offered by science and escaped into a religion of beauty. It was the period when the poets of the future, like Eliot and Pound, were as students significantly turning away from nineteenth-century English poetry to the hard, biting, eccentric poetry of Jules Laforgue and Tristan Corbière. Elsewhere, even the greatest poet of the future, William Butler Yeats, was still writing wistfully pastoral poems like "Innisfree," based upon his reading of Thoreau's *Walden;* it often seemed in those days that poetry had no future but would yield to fiction based on the documentary methods of those naturalistic novelists who were followers of Ernst Haeckel and Herbert Spencer.

Characteristically, it was in the poetry of the Symbolists and in the philosophy of James and Bergson that the challenge to mechanism was first made, thus living up to the boast of so many writers that literature is a swifter, more prophetic apprehension of reality. This is what Ezra Pound meant when he said that writers are the "antennae" of the race, but have to work against the "bullet-headed" many. In the late 1890s and early 1900s, however, the "antennae" were often invisible, a minuscule advance guard of literature. In literary circles in America, there was a sickly belief that poetry meant either roundelays or the hearty "athletic" verse that came in with Kipling and the celebration of imperialism. Though a remarkable group of young poets — Trumbull Stickney, William Vaughn Moody, George Cabot Lodge — had sprung up at Harvard in the 1890s, and had significantly been concerned in their verse dramas with the martyrdom of Prometheus, they soon gave up or died off; visibly killed, says their contemporary George Santayana, by the lack of air to breathe. At the time when Edwin Arlington Robinson was working in the New York subways and Stephen Crane's vinegary little poems were regarded as jokes, when Whitman was still indecent and the poetry of Emily Dickinson was "corrected" by her first editors, one saw the great tradition of the English Romantics reduced to an academic cult of beauty. The philosophical purposiveness which had sought God in nature was replaced by a worship of nature itself. The Georgians, as the more introverted cultists of nature were to be called in England — the genteel tradition, as it was later to be called in America when it was directly under attack — these represented that dependence on literature as consolation rather than as exploration of reality which was soon to mark off traditional poetry from that of the modern group. In the verse that was so soon to seem old-fashioned, the poet saw himself as a victim rather than as an observer, and it is this self-pity that peculiarly characterizes the literary tradition that succumbed to the devastating insights of twentieth-century poetry.

By contrast, the poetry of Eliot and Pound, which grew out of Symbolism, went back to Baudelaire's conception of the poet as a "dandy," an ironic observer of big-city life. Poetry in the hands of the Symbolists had become a little too arcane, too prone to cherish itself as a mystery. Eliot and Pound gave their poems a quality more immediately dry and biting, an ironic tang. Instead of the seclusion that had figured so largely in the Symbolists, the center of interest now became the self-mockery in "The Love Song of J. Alfred Prufrock" (1917), the ". . . muttering retreats / Of restless nights in one-night cheap hotels / And sawdust restaurants with oyster-shells." In Eliot's poem there were "Streets that follow like a tedious argument / Of insidious intent," and one felt in his early poems not only contempt for the genteel tradition of the Boston Brahmins, but the insidious emptiness of modern life, the loneliness and dinginess of big cities — which Eliot was able to realize with the sardonic dramatic emphasis that explains his power to reach so many people. But this was dramatic monologue in poetry as incongruous and flip as the distortions in the new paintings of Picasso and Braque. Eliot went beyond the trancelike effect of Symbolist poetry, so often weak in poetic power, to catch the unaccountability of modern experience. And to the prevailing sense of meaninglessness, which he suggested with such poignant irony in the actual texture of poems like "Prufrock," he added a startling genius for lines that made sense only because they laughed at sense, for epithets that clowningly reduced pompous or much-used words to their sickening banality. One of the French poets whom Eliot learned his manner from, Tristan Corbière, once appeared in Rome with a miter on his head, circles painted around his eyes, leading a pig decorated with ribbons. Eliot's early poetry had this deliberate provocation, this dramatic wit. In terms that by now have become the clichés of modern criticism, but that once were needed to describe the actualities of Eliot's verse, he emphasized paradox and ambiguity and tension. And though he himself gravely attributed his literary debts to the Jacobean dramatists, the seventeenth-century metaphysicals, and marginal figures in French poetry like Laforgue and Corbière, it was the immediate dramatic verve of this poetry, besides its content of fashionable hopelessness, that made it so tonic and effective.

« 3 »

Ezra Pound, who was actually the instigator of many of Eliot's experiments, was the leading spirit behind a movement that was influential in fiction as well as in poetry, and it was Pound who first campaigned for Henry James when he seemed to be undervalued at his death in 1916, as it was Pound who insisted, against the documentary methods of the realists, on the importance of style in the novel and the legacy of Flaubert. And significantly, it was through Pound's influence that original writers of fiction like James Joyce began to appear in American *avant-garde* reviews.

Pound's influence on fiction, though he does not write it himself, indicates the direction in which literary expression was moving. Some of the greatest twentieth-century novelists — Joyce, Hemingway, Lawrence, Faulkner — began as poets; of others — James, Conrad, Woolf, Proust — one feels that if they did not themselves write poetry, they certainly brought a poetic sense to the novel. Even the novelists of the nineteenth century who have been notable influences on the twentieth, like Melville, have been distinguished more for their poetic power, the freedom and originality of their language, their power to suggest the mythical and the supernatural in ordinary events, than for the kind of lifelike realization of commonplace events and ordinary people for which the great novelists of the nineteenth century were famous. The most influential figures in twentieth-century fiction are distinguished precisely by their feeling for language. Although even their admirers apologize for the stylistic crudities of Balzac or Dreiser, one thinks of certain passages in Proust, Joyce, or Lawrence as splendors of language in themselves. In some of the later novels of Virginia Woolf, like *The Waves*, and in Joyce's last book, *Finnegans Wake*, the language is central, not what is described; "ordinary" life, life as it is, rude and accidental, becomes a function of language. The contents of such books are the actual contents of the human mind — dreams, longings, memories, thoughts. The emphasis in modern fiction on "the stream of consciousness," on "interior monologue," on "point of view," on the organizing of events around a "foreground observer," as in the novels of Henry James — all illustrate how much in a modern novel is presented to us by a mind initially conscious of itself. The narrator, and central figure, in Proust's great novel, *Remembrance of Things Past,* lies in bed, gathering his dreams and memories around him, for Proust believed that "when a man is asleep, he has in a circle around him the chain of the hours, the sequences of the years, the order of the heavenly host." The whole of James Joyce's *Ulysses* takes place on a single day, the outward events reverberating in the interior thoughts of the characters. If Proust's novel begins in the sleeper's mind, *Ulysses* ends in the "night-thoughts" of a heartily sensuous woman falling asleep. And the world of man's unconscious that Proust and Joyce used as a bridge to the world of society becomes itself the ideal in the novels of D. H. Lawrence, for what Lawrence celebrates in the name of sex is actually that ideally unrestricted consciousness which makes us feel our primitive connection with the world.

The "poetic" reconquest of the novel has led to grand, even profound achievements. Certain complex works of twentieth-century fiction — *Ulysses, Remembrance of Things Past,* Franz Kafka's *The Castle,* seem to us as intellectually revealing as discoveries by Einstein and Rutherford and Planck. But the limitations of this emphasis on personal consciousness is that the "I" who is behind each of these books, who seeks to unite the free world of his consciousness to the ordinary world, is restricted to what can be grasped by *his* consciousness. In this theory of relativity, nothing can be reported which is not imagined by an observer, that is not initiated or expressed in a human mind: which means a glorification of contemplation and a minimizing of the actual world process. The self-conscious vision of the world which the Romantics inaugurated is symbolized by the fact that none of the great Romantic poets (or their descendants in the nineteenth century) was able to achieve a great drama. And grand in conception as Joyce's last work is, it represents art which is relatively stationary and inert, a picture rather than a story, lacking in the full sense of human conflict that we get from the great realistic novels of the nineteenth century. Such twentieth-century novels are usually defended on the basis of their intellectual wit rather than their literary power. The novels of Joyce and Virginia Woolf, so plainly triumphs of prophetic intelligence as well as of the ability to represent life powerfully, deepened the division of the reading public between highbrow and lowbrow. Where Dickens, Balzac, Dostoevsky wrote for the largest possible public, and figured before this public as national leaders as well as popular storytellers (a relation typified by Dickens's public justification, in the magazine which he himself edited, of his separation from his wife), the form in which even the great twentieth-century novelists have first appeared has proverbially been the little magazine, the coterie, the advance-guard fighting to establish the new literature. The great seminal figures in the modern movement — Gertrude Stein, Joyce, Eliot, Pound — remind one in their early days of old-fashioned conspirators and revolutionaries. And like modern revolutionaries, they were leaders and instigators, not brothers of those they led.

« 4 »

Yet if these writers have been right to distrust popularity, popularity has gone after them. The recent interest in literary criticism can be traced in large part to the position which certain critics in this country and in England — the New Critics — have taken up as explicators and interpreters of the difficult modern writers. There is no better instance of what the advance guard has been in modern literature than the success of the New Critics, who have been nearest to modern poetry, and who, without any effort at deliberate popularization, have been notable mediators between a remarkably complex group of writers and a public which — even in the universities — seems to know nothing of literature but what the critics can tell it.

The *effect* of the New Criticism, which one can now see institutionalized in American colleges, where "modern literature" has become the canon, tends to fit too well with the pragmatic temper of Americans. Undergraduates can get the same pleasure from taking apart a poem by Eliot or a passage from Joyce that they get from working on a car. Yet the intention of the New Criticism, particularly as one traces it in the critical essays of T. S. Eliot — the most influential critic in English of this century and the spiritual father of this movement in criticism — was just the opposite. For what Eliot emphasized, against the impressionistic critics before him who liked to dwell on their personal enjoyment of certain works, was the need to explain and to understand a poem in its own terms. For Eliot, criticism became an analysis of the poem in itself, the poem in the context of its immediate words; it meant conveying the necessity of those difficulties that were the greatest stumbling block to the reader. Like all true critics, Eliot's prime intention was to inspire enjoyment through greater understanding, and like all the great creator-critics in whose line he naturally follows — Ben Jonson, Dr. Johnson, Coleridge, Matthew Arnold — he was understandably a partisan of one literature and deeply opposed to another. But superb and extraordinarily effective as Eliot's early critical essays are — they created a new standard of taste — it was impossible even for Eliot, who as a critic functions on the highest level, brilliant shop-talk, not to give the impression that the great works of literature, which exist as created organic forms, become entirely accessible through the analysis of language. The result, as one can see in so many examples of the remarkable body of contemporary criticism, which is probably unrivaled for the passion and brilliance of its marginal comments on certain texts, is that the original emphasis on the purpose of the difficulty has been replaced by a passion for interpretation itself. When the sharp methods of the New Criticism are picked up by people who, unlike Eliot, know only the literature over which Eliot presides, they often miss the point of criticism and use it to establish their own ingenuity rather than to contribute to the understanding of literature.

The difference between Eliot and some of his routine followers is best established by the difference between his neo-Catholicism and their conventional liberalism. Eliot insisted on the necessary difficulty and complexity of modern literature because he thought that modern life, through debasement of culture and feebleness in belief, had so destroyed right standards that only work that symbolically conveyed the necessary complexity and forgotten profundity of human experience — like Dante's *The Divine Comedy* — could encompass and describe the anarchical flood of modern life. In 1923, writing in tribute to Joyce's *Ulysses,* he said:

> In using the myth, in manipulating a continuous parallel between contemporaneity and antiquity, Mr. Joyce is pursuing a method which others must use after him. . . . It is simply a way of controlling, of ordering, of giving a shape and significance to the immense panorama of futility and anarchy which is contemporary history. . . . Instead of narrative method, we may now use the mythical method. It is, I seriously believe, a step toward making the modern world possible for art. . . .

This pronouncement, at once so lofty and despairing, is a key document of the belief that only through difficulty and complexity can one represent — and by implication, reverse — the drift of modern life and the tragedy of disbelief. In Eliot's eyes, a work of literature has to be highly formal, concentrated, hard — in the same way that the Church, by hierarchy, dogma, and ceremony, saves man from the welter of mere subjective emotion. The conservative American critic Paul Elmer More could not understand why, despite this belief, Eliot's own poetry seemed to be, in the defiant fashion of the 1920s, so "chaotic" and disorderly. Poetry, replied Eliot, shows the world as it is: criticism, as it should be. And the world "as it is" — reflected not only in the actual content of Eliot's most famous poem, *The Waste Land* (1922), but in the deceptive chaos on the surface of the poem — represents in Eliot's mind (and in the minds of so many of his admirers) a contrast between the age of faith and the age of chaos in which we live. For Eliot "the immense panorama of futility and anarchy which is the modern world" is always to be compared with some other period — when art was not a religion but served religion. In the formal structure and ritualistic symbolism of *The Divine Comedy,* Eliot finds his favorite symbol of the order and complexity that he opposes to the present.

In one form or another, this despair of the present age is one of the staple themes of modern literature and art. This characteristic historical nostalgia is represented in the very plan of Flaubert's *Three Stories* (1877), which portrays man's degeneration in time from the world of paganism to the present age. And while the Homeric parallels in *Ulysses* do not signify devaluation of the present in favor of antiquity, there is in Joyce's great work, as in all the key works of twentieth-century literature, a profoundly felt complaint that human experience today is meaningless, that man has been deprived of fundamental values, that he has lost that sense of the miraculousness of his existence with which, historically, religion has always provided him.

In his horror of "the waste land" and "the hollow men" who live in it, Eliot comes to the very heart of modern literature as a criticism of life, and explains the power of this literature over the minds of people who have come to it reluctantly. For nothing is more central to contemporary experience, more obvious, than the increasing loss of religious faith—of belief in the providential, the sacred, the mysterious. In Eliot's *The Waste Land* quotations from classical and religious literature are put side by side with instances of modern chaos, so as to direct the reader's mind back toward the authority that he has lost, toward institutions. But however one may agree with Eliot as to the decline of religion in our period, Eliot's conception of tradition as synonymous with religion has had a sentimentalizing effect on the critical movement associated with his name. Before World War I, Eliot, along with Pound, helped to inaugurate experimental, reckless, sardonic modern poetry; after the war, he encouraged an unhistorical piety about the past, a haughty squeamishness about the present. In the writings of Eliot's more sedulous followers, there is a constant reiteration of modern "anarchy" and "heresy" that makes such defenders of modern poetry deny the actual strength and courage of literature and that portrays modern writers as if they were simply surrogates for the past. Eliot's notion of history as closed, his conception of order as necessarily aristocratic and hierarchical, minimizes the actual achievement of the modern movement. The revolutionary faith in personal consciousness from which the modern writer started is not merely an esthetic tool but a philosophical and religious achievement. Joyce significantly called himself, in Blake's phrase, "a priest of the eternal imagination." Proust, like Wordsworth and Blake before him, described the world of imagination as the only eternity to which man has access. D. H. Lawrence celebrated in sexual love man's ability to transcend his ordinary experience. Eliot's addiction to words like "heresy" and "orthodoxy," his churlish criticism of so bold and revolutionary a writer as Lawrence, contradict the complex personal experience that is expressed in his own poetry. When Eliot praises Joyce, who was even less of a believer than Lawrence was, one feels that he is mixing admiration of Joyce's genius with an American's envy of a traditional education. There is a cultural snobbery rather than a religious passion about Eliot's neo-Catholicism that reminds one of Henry James's complaint that America had no established church, no Oxford and Cambridge, no aristocracy. Expatriation can take place in time as well as in space, and Eliot seems to have accomplished both.

Yet there is a special irony in Eliot's nostalgia, for no student of twentieth-century literature can overlook the enormous role played in it by Americans like Eliot, Pound, Gertrude Stein, Ernest Hemingway. American writers are forced to deal with the chaotic modern world on its own terms, for they lack any tradition of ideas before the modern epoch began with the French and American Revolutions, and they are so different in origin that they naturally think in planetary terms — in terms of man as he is and can be, not as he might possibly have been in the twelfth century. This situation has been a constant stimulus to modern literature. For the American writer, like Ezra Pound of Idaho, tends naturally to feel that all traditions potentially belong to him, that all cultures fertilize each other into one. And just as the mélange of languages and traditions in Eliot's *The Waste Land* and Pound's *Cantos* are both as typically American in their feeling for the world scene as *Leaves of Grass* and *Moby-Dick*, so the very eagerness to build a "modern" tradition, so much associated with Ezra Pound, starts from Pound's concern with French and Provençal poetry in *The Spirit of Romance* (1910), and is seen in a whole series of works characteristically entitled *Instigations* (1920), *How to Read* (1931), *Make It New* (1934). Eliot's assumption that tradition is always behind us, something lost, contrasts strangely with the American passion for creating tradition, with Eliot's own creation of modern poetry as a tradition. Eliot said of Pound in 1946: "Pound did not create the poets: but he created a situation in which, for the first time, there was a 'modern movement in poetry' in which English and American poets collaborated, knew each other's works, and influenced each other." And in the same way, the American need to create, out of modern literature, the only real body of literature it has explains why Americans have been at the center of the modern movement, from the time that Gertrude Stein settled in Paris and gathered around her not merely Hemingway and Sherwood Anderson but Picasso and Braque. American expatriates like the painter Whistler, Stephen Crane, Henry James, Ezra Pound, show that the American, even when he goes abroad to learn, remains to instigate; that he marries his American importunity to the European tradition of art in such a way as to make a new kind of art.

This "new" literature in America is virtually a story in itself, for it is not merely the most remarkable body of writing that we have produced, but peculiarly an adaptation of the characteristically modern sensibility to the problems of modern man. But it is not actually a story in itself, and many Americans overlook the exciting historical dimension in the work of men like James, Eliot, Hemingway, Faulkner, because they overlook the extent to which the American concern with individual consciousness, with the lack of tradition, with the challenge from modern science, has seemed to European writers an unconscious prophecy of their own struggles. It is only when we see American literature against the background of European thought that we can understand why D. H. Lawrence thought the modern epoch began with Whitman; why Italian novelists like Cesare Pavese and Elio Vittorini translated and interpreted American literature as part of their struggle against Fascist dictatorship; why Hemingway became the sacred god of the new Italian concern with artistic "truth"; why Sartre was so carried away by the experimentalism of *U.S.A.* that he proclaimed John Dos Passos the greatest twentieth-century writer.

One of the essential elements in modern art has been its *élan,* the energy of challenge and not of "despair," as moralistic critics call it. The kind of creative wit and irreverent skill which one associates with the continuing energy of old men like Picasso and Stravinsky was long ago marked in the violence of H. L. Mencken, in the satire of Sinclair Lewis, in the dazzling originality of Faulkner, in the crushing experimentalism of Dos Passos. Such energy was one of the most interesting aspects of the modern movement. There is almost a special sanctity to rhythm in modern music. One of the reasons why there was such an immediate rupture between the old and the new can be seen in the virtual physical terror, the inability to respond without disturbance, to the charged-up beat of Stravinsky's *Rites of Spring,* to the confusing typography of Cummings's poems, to the almost physical assault on the eye made by Cubism, to the actual screams and bellowing of locomotives in the music of Arthur Honegger, of machines in that of Edgard Varèse. In a highly charged industrial civilization, with its emphasis on quick effects, on the rapid turnover of impressions, a civilization where life seems to proceed with intensified color, violence, quickness, as it so often does under the influence of the American atmosphere and American high spirits, art becomes synonymous with energy, with change, even with disturbance. And it is this that from the outset put Americans directly at the center of the "modern movement," and that, in unison with the increasing mechanization of American life, reversed the traditional thinness, academicism, and moralism of American art. Eliot said that "myth," or the sense of tradition, had made the modern world possible for art. It would probably be more true to say that only he who can assimilate the modern world — not perhaps on its own terms, but at least with an effort to discover what its terms actually are — can make art in the modern world. It is this *élan* of writers in the 1920s, which corresponds to the high spirits of so many Americans at the time, that helps to explain the extraordinary technical achievement behind Scott Fitzgerald's *The Great Gatsby* (1925) and Faulkner's *The Sound and the Fury* (1929), the rise of important new magazines like the *American Mercury, Time,* and the *New Yorker,* the social criticism behind Sinclair Lewis's *Babbitt* and Mencken's *Prejudices.*

The 1920s were everywhere the apogee of modern art. It was the last free period in Russia; the great period of experimental drama and painting in Germany; the time of the last authentic geniuses writing in English — Yeats, Lawrence, Joyce. But nowhere was this experimentalism so much at home with the times as in America, where for the first time we were getting a national literature, a literature that had been in the making from the 1880s on. For the first time there was modern drama in America as well as modern poetry, and even magazines now of mass circulation, like *Time,* characteristically took off from literary and "advanced" experiments in style, while the *New Yorker* became a byword for its satire and for a precision in style characteristic of the time when American writers prided themselves on being artists. The 1920s marked a true renaissance, with recognized cultural centers. Eliot, recalling his editorship of the *Criterion* in London, says that it belonged to a time when it represented literary authority, along with the *Nouvelle revue française* and the *Deutsche Rundschau.* It was a time when films were consciously an art, under Griffith, Pabst, Pudovkin, Eisenstein, Clair, Vidor; when there were great expressive artists of the silent screen — Chaplin, Garbo; a time when, starting from the prewar tradition of Picasso's sets for the Russian ballet under Diaghilev, Cubists and Expressionists still did the sets for Soviet productions of the classics. It was a time when the famous advance guard of modernism became more and more a cultural influence over the other public whom Mencken called the "booboisie," and when it seemed that the "intelligentsia" (a term borrowed from the traditions of the Russian Revolution) had become the advance guard of humanity itself.

« 5 »

The mid-1920s were the moment when typically modern writers and artists came into their kingdom. Then it seemed that the enormous preparations for freedom, challenge, spontaneity, individuality, which had been the essence of modernism ever since the eighteenth-century philosophers and poets had destroyed so much more than the old regime, were at last in the ascendancy. This was the moment not merely of success but of realization, when the moderns felt that at last it was possible to say fully what it meant to be modern, as they confronted the century on its own terms. This was the moment when certain names became great names: Hemingway, Joyce, Eliot, Picasso, Braque, Stravinsky, Bartok, Faulkner, Bertolt Brecht, Malraux, Yeats, Valéry, Gide, Céline, Colette; the moment when the last of Proust's thirteen volumes was finally published, completing the immense structure like a cathedral built over centuries. Now all the exciting "tendencies" and "trends" and "crusades" and "insurgencies" arose out of the manifestoes of Cubism, Dadaism, Vorticism, Futurism, and it was possible to see modern man at the apex of his freedom, confident of his integrity, sure that he had learned from the lessons of World War I — like

Picasso, a man beset by his own creativity, confronting into old age the infinitely expanding universe of skill and knowledge.

It is important to emphasize this pride because despite the "despair" in *The Waste Land* and the shivery warnings of dissolution sent down from Thomas Mann's *The Magic Mountain* (1924), it is a fact that the 1920s were a time of expansion in art as well as in society, and when the sense of freedom, the possibility of recklessness, the joy in open criticism, were matched by respect for the individual and by that general advance in the standard of living which in all periods is a necessity of artistic vitality. The very emphasis which was put on "style" — seen in the new magazines, in the acceptance of modern furniture and functional architecture, in the sense of economic power, in the growing feeling for luxury which was behind the esthetic posturing of writers ashamed of the realism that had preceded them — indicated how much artistic self-confidence depends on a general advance in society.

An essential reason for this modern *élan,* as one can see from the perpetual high spirits of Bernard Shaw, was the sense that the Victorian nineteenth century was falling to the standards of the new writers. Creative vitality in a group rests on attack — the Encyclopedists of the eighteenth century gave each other strength in attacking the superstitions of the old regime; the Romantics spoke together against the rationalism of the eighteenth century. Now writers like Shaw, Mencken, Gide, Colette, minor writers like Lytton Strachey in *Eminent Victorians,* proved the enormous effect of the long-standing battle against "moralism." One can even date the success of the new writers in America from the time when "Babbitt" became a term of opprobium. The nineteenth century fell over and over to the diatribes of Mencken and the laughter of Shaw; the genteel tradition was trampled underfoot, the old gods were done away with. The symbolic novel of the period, at least in America, was against the small town — *Main Street; Winesburg, Ohio; Moon-Calf* — and embraced the excitement of the big city — *Manhattan Transfer, The Great Gatsby.* The symbolic heroine was the "emancipated" woman; the symbolic crusade was against snoopers and vice-leaguers and book-censors. The common characteristic of the remarkable group of novelists who became famous in the 1920s — Dreiser, Anderson, Lewis, Hemingway, Willa Cather, Fitzgerald —

is that they were all from the Midwest, provincials seeking in the city a philosophy from which to attack the old values. The symbolic issue of the period was freedom.

But what we can see about the 1920s now is that the cause they fought for had long since triumphed and was on its way out. The effectiveness of a literary movement seems to be greatest when its *raison d'être* is past. The sense of triumph emerges only at the point when the movement is really over. It can be shown, in fact, that the real ascendancy of modern art lies in the exciting years before World War I. Jacques Barzun, in *The Energies of Art*, claims that by the end of the war, a quality of bitterness and self-pity, or hardness and insensitivity, had come into modern art — qualities which were not only falsely identified with modernism, but which actually diverted it from its original goals. Compare prewar and postwar works by the same man (Mencken, Gide); contrast those peculiarly pure writers who flourished before the war (Charles Péguy in France, Randolph Bourne in America) with the Dadaists and tough guys who came after it; think of the generation of poets who died in the war — from the group of "Whitmanesque" poets in Germany to British poets like Wilfred Owen and Isaac Rosenberg — and it becomes clear that the 1920s produced a particular hardness that is unmistakable in the fashionable poses of Hemingway's art, in the drift of Eliot's poetry away from satire and toward frenzied salvation-seeking, in the coarsening of Pound's verse and the paranoiac brutality of his political views. The decade was not an inauguration but a culmination. Writers and artists attacked the Victorian tradition as if it were still alive, but the crisis of modern art, perhaps even its eclipse, came at Verdun and Ypres, at Chemin des Dames and the Somme. In those terrible slaughters, the last idealism and political hopefulness of Europe disappeared, and from then on society was seen, even in periods of seeming health, to be impersonating health like a madman who has quieted down, but who may break out again at any time. In a famous short story, Hemingway insisted that all is *nada,* nothing. As early as 1921, in "The Second Coming," Yeats saw that

> Things fall apart; the centre cannot hold;
> Mere anarchy is loosed upon the world,

The blood-dimmed tide is loosed, and everywhere
The ceremony of innocence is drowned;
The best lack all conviction, while the worst
Are full of passionate intensity.

When Robert Graves offered the work of a young poet to Yeats for *The Oxford Book of Modern Verse,* Yeats declined it, saying: "Too simple, too sincere." The tone of hardness literally contracts; it does not expand or free, as one can see from the total career of Hemingway. Hardness has the unmistakable limitation of making the writer self-conscious, of confining him to the pose he first adopted. From now on, Eliot must always sound like a disapproving deacon; Hemingway may never desert the famous Hemingway style. It was once said of Victor Hugo — who was the most famous, probably the best, certainly the most uneven, French poet of his time — that he was a madman who thought he was Victor Hugo. This concern with one's own legend has become the staple of modern art, and museums are now erected to perpetuate it.

The "crisis" of modern art, perhaps even the "end" of modern art, came when it was made clear in the 1930s that the twentieth century had finally arrived in force — not just for writers and artists, but for everyone. In contrast to the eminent Victorians, the booboisie, the stuffed shirts, the genteel tradition — easy marks for a writer to attack, especially when the butt of the joke applauds — there now came the economic desperation of the 1930s, the hardening of Communism into Stalinism, of Nazism into the unspeakable slaughter of civilian populations on the basis of race. In 1914, when war was declared, the English Foreign Secretary Earl Grey, watching at nightfall the lamps being lighted on the Thames Embankment, remarked that "the lamps are going out all over Europe, and we shall not see them lit again in our lifetime." But only in 1929, 1933, 1939, did all men begin to see how dark it really was. Now was the time when so many writers of the 1920s died — either by their own hand, like Hart Crane, or, as with D. H. Lawrence, of long-standing illness brought to a crisis by the incongruity of his values in the period. Now Joyce, almost entirely blind, became the frenzied monologist and punner of *Finnegans Wake* where once he had spoken for all artists as young men. Now one felt the bitterness of the writers who had found themselves, in the 1920s, after so many early struggles for recognition, only to find themselves outside again — Willa Cather, Sinclair Lewis, Sherwood Anderson. The characteristic new writers of the 1930s are Auden, roaming over the gray debris of depression England, and Jean-Paul Sartre, whose *Nausea* (1938), one of the greatest books of our time, proclaims the broken connection between man and the world. In America the 1930s were a period of political literature, of "proletarian" literature, a literary period that was painful not only because so many bad books were written, but because so many writers were honestly misguided and did not realize that in giving themselves to a programmatic literature they were signing their death warrants as writers. Those who did not learn this in the Thirties or Forties learned it in the Fifties; but they all learned it, sooner or later.

The 1930s marked the end of the modern movement. One can tell this very easily: the essential ideals of freedom, spontaneity, individuality, were openly rejected by writers themselves. Whatever "modernism" may mean, it does not mean a fear of freedom. Yet as soon as this political episode ended among writers, at the end of World War II, one saw how completely the modern movement had become an institution. Now the Nobel prizes began to roll in — Lewis, O'Neill, Gide, Eliot, Faulkner, Hemingway. Now modern literature became the staple of literature in the universities, and the heresies of the first period became the academic clichés of the last. Modern literature and art now became not merely the subject of routine scholarship, the staple of mass taste, but had become its own tradition. The young writer no longer knows whether he is part of a continuing movement of modern literature or whether he is not justified, in view of the mummified modernity that surrounds him on every hand, in treating it as his enemy. The modern — modern literature, modern furniture, modern houses, modern taste, modern advertising — has become the enemy of the contemporary. Worse, modern as a routine description has become a mark of participation rather than of creation, and the vapidity of the term is shown in the thoughtlessness with which people assume that modern art can be accepted apart from its connection with modern politics, modern science, and modern people. In a notable description of some unusually humanistic war memorials in Europe, Lewis Mumford recently denounced the widespread belief that art is produced merely as a response to psychological stimuli, and noted that certain examples of modern art look as if our world had been recorded "in a decapitated brain, severed from heart and guts, from feeling and meaning."

Modern art as a fashion, a profession, a business has become so much its own justification for being that now that its histories are being written — and for the first time, they can be — one is not surprised to find art itself being interpreted wholly as a religion. The idea of literature itself as a sacrament is laughable — or pitiful; for it implies a subjective manipulation of materials which is akin to magic. But it is truer to say, as André Malraux does, that "One lives *in* art as if in a religion." Modern literature may have become an institution, a church, but for many people it is now simply a passion, and as modern life gets increasingly more organized and impersonal, literature may take its place simply as an odd human skill, as it appeared to Flaubert. What man, creative man, seeks above all else is a sense of his continuing creativeness, of possibility for the work of his hands in the universe. Like Ford Madox Ford, many a writer can now humbly describe himself as "an old man mad about writing." Literature as an activity can become a life in itself. In the course of things this cannot last forever, for literature can never be too "pure" an art, and whenever it seeks to become self-contained it loses much of its point. But at the moment we can see that "modern literature" has exhausted much of the strength that came from the attack on old institutions.

[1958]

II

Relevance of the American Past

Ishmael and Ahab

MOBY-DICK is not only a very big book; it is also a peculiarly full and rich one, and from the very opening it conveys a sense of abundance, of high creative power, that exhilarates and enlarges the imagination. This quality is felt immediately in the style, which is remarkably easy, natural and "American," yet always literary, and which swells in power until it takes on some of the roaring and uncontainable rhythms with which Melville audibly describes the sea. The best description of this style is Melville's own, when he speaks of the "bold and nervous lofty language" that Nantucket whaling captains learn straight from nature. We feel this abundance in heroic types like the Nantucketers themselves, many of whom are significantly named after Old Testament prophets and kings, for these, too, are mighty men, and the mightiest of them all, Captain Ahab, will challenge the very order of the creation itself. This is the very heart of the book—so much so that we come to feel that there is some shattering magnitude of theme before Melville as he writes, that as a writer he had been called to a heroic new destiny.

It is this constant sense of power that constitutes the book's appeal to us, that explains its hold on our attention. *Moby-Dick* is one of those books that try to bring in as much of life as a writer can get both hands on. Melville even tries to create an image of life itself as a ceaseless creation. The book is written with a personal force of style, a passionate learning, a steady insight into our forgotten connections with the primitive. It sweeps everything before it; it gives us the happiness that only great vigor inspires.

If we start by opening ourselves to this abundance and force, by welcoming not merely the story itself, but the manner in which it speaks to us, we shall recognize in this restlessness, this richness, this persistent atmosphere of magnitude, the essential image on which the book is founded. For *Moby-Dick* is not so much a book *about* Captain Ahab's quest for the whale as it is an experience *of* that quest. This is only to say, what we say of any true poem, that we cannot reduce its essential substance to a subject, that we should not intellectualize and summarize it, but that we should recognize that its very strength and beauty lie in the way it is conceived and written, in the qualities that flow from its being a unique entity.

In these terms, *Moby-Dick* seems to be far more of a poem than it is a novel, and, since it is a narrative, to be an epic — a long poem on a heroic theme, rather than the kind of realistic fiction that we know today. Of course Melville did not deliberately set out to write a formal epic; but half-consciously, he drew upon many of the traditional characteristics of the epic in order to realize the utterly original kind of novel *he* needed to write in his time—the spaciousness of theme and subject, the martial atmosphere, the association of these homely and savage materials with universal myths, the symbolic wanderings of the hero, the indispensable strength of such a hero in Captain Ahab. Yet beyond all this, what distinguishes *Moby-Dick* from modern prose fiction, what ties it up with the older, more formal kind of narrative that was once written in verse, is the fact that Melville is not interested in the meanness, the literal truthfulness, the representative slice of life, that we think of as the essence of modern realism. His book has the true poetic emphasis in that the whole story is constantly being meditated and unraveled through a single mind.

"Call me Ishmael," the book begins. This Ishmael is not only a character in the book; he is also the single voice, or rather the single mind, from whose endlessly turning spool of thought the whole story is unwound. It is Ishmael's contemplativeness, his *dreaming,* that articulates the wonder of the seas and the fabulousness of the whale and the terrors of the deep. All that can be meditated and summed up and hinted at, as the reflective essence of the story itself, is given us by Ishmael, who possesses nothing but man's specifically human gift, which is language. It is Ishmael who tries to sum up the whole creation in a single book and yet keeps at the center of it one American whaling voyage. It is Ishmael's gift for speculation that explains the terror we come to feel before the whiteness of the whale; Ishmael's mind that ranges with mad exuberance through a description of all the seas; Ishmael who piles up image after image of "the mightiest animated mass that has survived the flood." It is Ishmael who, in the wonderful chapter on the masthead, embodies for us man as a thinker, whose reveries transcend space and time as he stands watch high above the seas. And of course it is

Ishmael, both actually and as the symbol of man, who is the one survivor of the voyage. Yet utterly alone as he is at the end of the book, floating on the Pacific Ocean, he manages, buoyed up on a coffin that magically serves as his life-buoy, to give us the impression that life itself can be honestly confronted only in the loneliness of each human heart. Always it is this emphasis on Ishmael's personal vision, on the richness and ambiguity of all events as the skeptical, fervent, experience-scarred mind of Ishmael feels and thinks them, that gives us, from the beginning, the new kind of book that *Moby-Dick* is. It is a book which is neither a saga, though it deals in large natural forces, nor a *classical* epic, for we feel too strongly the individual who wrote it. It is a book that is at once primitive, fatalistic, and merciless, like the very oldest books, and yet peculiarly personal, like so many twentieth-century novels, in its significant emphasis on the subjective individual consciousness. The book grows out of a single word, "I," and expands until the soul's voyage of this "I" comes to include a great many things that are unseen and unsuspected by most of us. And this material is always tied to Ishmael, who is not merely a witness to the story — someone who happens to be on board the *Pequod* — but the living and germinating mind who grasps the world in the tentacles of his thought.

The power behind this "I" is poetical in the sense that everything comes to us through a constant intervention of language instead of being presented flatly. Melville does not wish, as so many contemporary writers do, to reproduce ordinary life and conventional speech. He seeks the marvelous and the fabulous aspects that life wears in secret. He exuberantly sees the world through language — things exist as his words for them — and much of the exceptional beauty of the book lies in the unusual incidence of passages that, in the most surprising contexts, are so piercing in their poetic intensity. But the most remarkable feat of language in the book is Melville's ability to make us see that man is not a blank slate passively open to events, but a mind that constantly seeks meaning in everything it encounters. In Melville the Protestant habit of moralizing and the transcendental passion for symbolizing all things as examples of "higher laws" combined to make a mind that instinctively brought an inner significance to each episode.

Everything in *Moby-Dick* is saturated in a mental atmosphere. Nothing happens for its own sake in this book, and in the midst of the chase, Ishmael can be seen meditating it, pulling things apart, drawing out its significant point.

But Ishmael is not just an intellectual observer; he is also very much in the story. He suffers; he is there. As his name indicates, he is an estranged and solitary man; his only friend is Queequeg, a despised heathen from the South Seas. Queequeg, a fellow "isolato" in the smug world of white middle-class Christians, is the only man who offers Ishmael friendship; thanks to Queequeg, "no longer my splintered heart and maddened hand were turned against the wolfish world. This soothing savage had redeemed it." Why does Ishmael feel so alone? There are background reasons, Melville's own: his father went bankrupt and then died in debt when Melville was still a boy. Melville-Ishmael went to sea — "And at first," he tells us, "this sort of thing is unpleasant enough. It touches one's sense of honor, particularly if you come of an old established family in the land." But there is a deeper, a more universal reason for Ishmael's apartness, and it is one that will strangely make him kin to his daemonic captain, Ahab. For the burden of his thought, the essential cause of his estrangement, is that he cannot come to any conclusion about anything. He feels at home with ships and sailors because for him, too, one journey ends only to begin another; "and a second ended, only begins a third and so on, for ever and for aye. Such is the endlessness, yea, the intolerableness of all earthly effort."

Ishmael is not merely an orphan; he is an exile, searching alone in the wilderness, with a black man for his only friend. He suffers from doubt and uncertainty far more than he does from homelessness. Indeed, this agony of disbelief *is* his homelessness. For him nothing is ever finally settled and decided; he is man, or as we like to think, modern man, cut off from the certainty that was once his inner world. Ishmael no longer has any sure formal belief. All is in doubt, all is in eternal flux, like the sea. And so condemned, like "all his race from Adam down," to wander the seas of thought, far from Paradise, he now searches endlessly to put the whole broken story together, to find a meaning, to ascertain — where but in the ceaselessness of human thought? — "the hidden cause we seek."

Ishmael does not perform any great actions, as Ahab does; he is the most insignificant member of the fo'c'sle and will get the smallest share of the take. But his inner world of thought is almost unbearably symbolic, for he must think, and think, and think, in order to prove to himself that there is a necessary connection between man and the world. He pictures his dilemma in everything he does on board the ship, but never so clearly as when he is shown looking at the sea, searching a meaning to existence from the inscrutable waters.

What Melville did through Ishmael, then, was to put man's distinctly modern feeling of "exile," of abandonment, directly at the center of his stage. For Ishmael there are no satisfactory conclusions to anything; no final philosophy is ever possible. All that man owns in this world, Ishmael would say, is his insatiable mind. This is why the book opens on a picture of the dreaming contemplativeness of mind itself: men tearing themselves loose from their jobs to stand "like silent sentinels all around the town . . . thousands of mortal men fixed in ocean reveries." Narcissus was bemused by that image which "we ourselves see in all rivers and oceans," and this, says Ishmael when he is most desperate, is all that man ever finds when he searches the waters — a reflection of himself. All is inconclusive, restless, and endless flow. And Melville's own style rises to its highest level not in the neo-Shakespearean speeches of Ahab, which are sometimes bombastic, but in those amazing prose flights on the whiteness of the whale and on the Pacific where Ishmael reproduces, in the rhythms of the prose itself, man's brooding interrogation of nature.

« 2 »

But Ishmael is a witness not only to his own thoughts, but also to the actions of Captain Ahab. The book is not only a great skin of language stretched to fit the world of man's philosophic wandering; it is also a world of moral tyranny and violent action, in which the principal actor is Ahab. With the entry of Ahab a harsh new rhythm enters the book, and from now on two rhythms — one reflective, the other forceful — alternate to show us the world in which man's thinking and man's doing each follows its own law. Ishmael's thought consciously extends itself to get behind the world of appearances; he wants to see and to understand everything. Ahab's drive is to *prove,* not to discover; the world that tortures Ishmael by its horrid vacancy has tempted Ahab into thinking that he can make it over. He seeks to dominate nature, to impose and to inflict his will on the outside world—whether it be the crew that must jump to his orders or the great white whale that is essentially indifferent to him. As Ishmael is all rumination, so Ahab is all will. Both are thinkers, the difference being that Ishmael thinks as a bystander, has identified his own state with man's utter unimportance in nature. Ahab, by contrast, actively seeks the whale in order to assert man's supremacy over what swims before him as "the monomaniac incarnation" of a superior power:

> If man will strike, strike through the mask! How can the prisoner reach outside except by thrusting through the wall? To me, the white whale is that wall, shoved near to me. Sometimes I think there's naught beyond. But 'tis enough. He tasks me; he heaps me; I see in him outrageous strength, with an inscrutable malice sinewing it. That inscrutable thing is chiefly what I hate; and be the white whale agent, or be the white whale principal, I will wreak that hate upon him. Talk not to me of blasphemy, man; I'd strike the sun if it insulted me. For could the sun do that, then could I do the other; since there is ever a sort of fair play herein, jealousy presiding over all creations. But not my master, man, is even that fair play. Who's over me? Truth hath no confines.

This is Ahab's quest—and Ahab's magnificence. For in this speech Ahab expresses, more forcibly than Ishmael ever could, something of the impenitent anger against the universe that all of us can feel. Ahab may be a mad sea captain, a tyrant of the quarter-deck who disturbs the crew's sleep as he stomps along on his ivory leg. But this Ahab does indeed speak for all men, who, as Ishmael confesses in the frightening meditation on the whiteness of the whale, suspect that "though in many of its aspects this visible world seems formed in love, the invisible spheres were formed in fright." So man, watching the sea heaving around him, sees it as a mad steed that has lost its rider, and looking at his own image in the water, is tortured by the thought that man himself may be an accident, of no more importance in this vast oceanic emptiness than one of Ahab's rare tears dropped into the Pacific.

To the degree that we feel this futility in the face of a blind impersonal nature that "heeds us not," and storm madly, like Ahab, against the dread that there's "naught beyond" — to this extent all men may recognize Ahab's bitterness, his unrelentingness, his inability to rest in that uncertainty which, Freud has told us, modern man must learn to endure. Ahab figures in a symbolic fable; he is acting out thoughts which we all share. But Ahab, even more, is a hero; we cannot insist enough on that. Melville believed in the heroic and he specifically wanted to cast his hero on American lines — someone noble by nature, not by birth, who would have "not the dignity of kings and robes, but that abounding dignity which has no robed investiture." Ahab sinned against man and God, and, like his namesake in the Old Testament, becomes a "wicked king." But Ahab is not just a fanatic who leads the whole crew to their destruction; he is a hero of thought who is trying, by terrible force, to reassert man's place in nature. And it is the struggle that Ahab incarnates that makes him so magnificent a *voice*, thundering in Shakespearean rhetoric, storming at the gates of the inhuman, silent world. Ahab is trying to give man, in one awful, final assertion that his will *does* mean something, a feeling of relatedness with his world.

Ahab's effort, then, is to reclaim something that man knows he has lost. Significantly, Ahab proves by the bitter struggle he has to wage that man is fighting in an unequal contest; by the end of the book Ahab abandons all his human ties and becomes a complete fanatic. But Melville has no doubt — nor should we! — that Ahab's quest is *humanly* understandable. And the quest itself supplies the book with its technical *raison d'être*. For it leads us through all the seas and around the whole world; it brings us past ships of every nation. Always it is Ahab's drive that makes up the *passion* of *Moby-Dick*, a passion that is revealed in the descriptive chapters on the whale, whale-fighting, whale-burning, on the whole gory and fascinating industrial process aboard ship that reduces the once proud whale to oil-brimming barrels in the hold. And this passion may be defined as a passion of longing, of hope, of striving: a passion that starts from the deepest loneliness that man can know. It is the great cry of man who feels himself exiled from his "birthright, the merry May-day gods of old," who looks for a new god "to enthrone . . . again in the now egotistical sky; in the now unhaunted hill." The cry is Ahab's — "Who's to doom, when the judge himself is dragged to the bar?"

Behind Ahab's cry is the fear that man's covenant with God has been broken, that there is no purpose to our existence. The *Pequod* is condemned by Ahab to sail up and down the world in search of — a symbol. But this search, mad as it seems to Starbuck the first mate, who is a Christian, nevertheless represents Ahab's real humanity. For the ancient covenant is never quite broken so long as man still thirsts for it. And because Ahab, as Melville intended him to, represents the aristocracy of intellect in our democracy, because he seeks to transcend the limitations that good conventional men like Starbuck, philistine materialists like Stubb, and unthinking fools like Flask want to impose on everybody else, Ahab speaks for the humanity that belongs to man's imaginative vision of himself.

Yet with all this, we must not forget that Ahab's quest takes place, unceasingly, in a very practical world of whaling, as part of the barbaric and yet highly necessary struggle by man to support himself physically in nature. It is this that gives the book its primitive vitality, its burning authenticity. For *Moby-Dick*, it must be emphasized, is not simply a symbolic fable; nor, as we have already seen, can it possibly be construed as simply a "sea story." It is the story of agonizing thought in the midst of brutal action, of thought that questions every action, that annuls it from within, as it were — but that cannot, in this harsh world, relieve man of the fighting, skinning, burning, the backbreaking row to the whale, the flying harpoons, the rope that can take you off "voicelessly as Turkish mutes bowstring their victims." *Moby-Dick* is a representation of the passionate mind speaking, for its metaphysical concerns, out of the very midst of life. So, after the first lowering, Queequeg is shown sitting all night in a submerged boat, holding up a lantern like an "imbecile candle in the heart of that almighty forlornness . . . the sign and symbol of a man without hope, hopelessly holding up hope in the midst of despair." Melville insists that our thinking is *not* swallowed up by practical concerns, that man constantly searches for a reality equal to his inner life of thought — and it is his ability to show this in the midst of a brutal, dirty whaling voyage that makes *Moby-Dick* such an astonishing book. Just as Ahab is a hero, so *Moby-Dick* itself is a heroic book. What concerns Melville is not merely the heroism that gets expressed in physical action, but the heroism of thought itself as it rises above its seeming insignificance and proclaims, in the very teeth of a seemingly hostile and malevolent creation, that man's voice *is* heard for something against the watery waste and the deep, that man's thought has an echo in the universe.

« 3 »

This is the quest. But what makes *Moby-Dick* so fascinating, and in a sense even uncanny, is that the issue is always in doubt, and remains so to the end. Melville was right when he wrote to Hawthorne: "I have written a wicked book, and feel as spotless as the lamb." And people who want to construe *Moby-Dick* into a condemnation of mad, bad Ahab will always miss what Melville meant when he wrote of his book: "It is not a piece of fine feminine Spitalfields silk — but it is of the horrible texture of a fabric that should be woven of ships' cables & hawsers. A Polar wind blows through it, & birds of prey hover over it." For in the struggle between man's effort to find meaning in nature and the indifference of nature itself, which simply eludes him (nature here signifies the whole external show and force of animate life in a world suddenly emptied of God, one where an "intangible malignity" has reigned from the beginning), Melville often portrays the struggle from the side of nature itself. He sees the whale's view of things far more than he does Ahab's: and Moby-Dick's milk-white body, the tailfeathers of the seabirds streaming from his back like pennons, are described with a rapture that is like the adoration of a god. Even in the most terrible scenes of the shark massacre, where the sharks bend around like bows to bite at their own entrails, or in the ceaseless motion of "my dear Pacific," the "Potters' fields of all four continents," one feels that Melville is transported by the naked reality of things, by the great unending flow of the creation itself, where the great shroud of the sea rolls over the doomed ship "as it rolled five thousand years ago." Indeed, one feels in the end that it is only the necessity to keep one person alive as a witness to the story that saves Ishmael from the general ruin and wreck. In Melville's final vision of the whole, it is not fair but it is entirely *just* that the whale should destroy the ship, that man should be caught up on the beast. It is just in a cosmic sense, not in the sense that the prophet (Father Mapple) predicts the punishment of man's disobedience in the telling of Jonah's story from the beginning, where the point made is the classic reprimand of God to man when He speaks out of the whirlwind. What Melville does is to speak for the whirlwind, for the watery waste, for the sharks.

It is this that gives *Moby-Dick* its awful and crushing power. It is a unique gift. Goethe said that he wanted, as a writer, to know what it is like to be a woman. But Melville sometimes makes you feel that he knows, as a writer, what it is like to be the eyes of the rock, the magnitude of the whale, the scalding sea, the dreams that lie buried in the Pacific. It is all, of course, seen through human eyes — yet there is in Melville a cold, final, ferocious hopelessness, a kind of ecstatic masochism, that delights in punishing man, in heaping coals on his head, in drowning him. You see it in the scene of the whale running through the herd with a cutting spade in his body, cutting down his own; in the sharks eating at their own entrails and voiding from them in the same convulsion; in the terrible picture of Pip the cabin boy jumping out of the boat in fright and left on the Pacific to go crazy; in Tashtego falling into the "honey head" of the whale; in the ropes that suddenly whir up from the spindles and carry you off; in the final awesome picture of the whale butting its head against the *Pequod*. In all these scenes there is an ecstasy in horror, the horror of nature in itself, nature "pure," without God or man: the void. It is symbolized by the whiteness of the whale, the whiteness that is not so much a color as the absence of color. "Is it that by its indefiniteness it shadows forth the heartless voids and immensities of the universe, and thus stabs us from behind with the thought of annihilation, when beholding the white depths of the milky way?" And it is this picture of existence, as one where man has only a peephole on the mystery itself, that constitutes the most remarkable achievement of Melville's genius. For as in the meditation on the whiteness of the whale, this becomes an uncanny attempt to come to grips with nature as it might be conceived with man entirely left out; or, what amounts to the same thing, with man losing his humanity and being exclusively responsible to primitive and racial memories, to the trackless fathomless nothing that has been from the beginning, to the very essence of a beginning that, in contradiction to all man's scriptures, had no divine history, no definite locus, but just *was* — with man slipped into the picture much later.

This view of reality, this ability to side with nature rather than with man, means an ability to love what has no animation, what is inhumanly still, what is not in search, as man himself is — a hero running against time and fighting against "reality." Here Melville puts, as it were, his ear to reality itself: to the rock rather than to the hero trying to get his sword out of the rock. He does it by constantly, and bitterly, and savagely, in fact, comparing man with the great thing he is trying to understand. Ahab may be a hero by trying to force himself on what is too much for him, but Melville has no doubt that man is puny and presumptuous and easily overwhelmed — in short, drowned — in the great storm of reality he tries to encompass.

This sense of scale lies behind the chapters on the natural history of the whale, and behind the constant impressing on our minds of the contrast between man and the whale — man getting into a small boat, man being overwhelmed by his own weapons. The greatest single metaphor in the book is that of bigness, and even when Melville laughs at himself for trying to hook this Leviathan with a pen — "Bring me a condor's quill! Bring me Vesuvius' crater for an inkstand!" — we know not merely that he feels exhilaration at attempting this mighty subject, but that he is also abashed, he feels grave; mighty waters are rolling around him. This compelling sense of magnitude, however, gets him to organize the book brilliantly, in a great flood of chapters — some of them very small, one or two only a paragraph long, in the descriptive method which is the great homage that he pays to his subject, and which so provides him with an inexhaustible delight in devoting himself to every conceivable detail about the whale. And, to go back to a theme mentioned earlier, it is this sense of a limitless subject that gives the style its peculiarly loping quality, as if it were constantly looking for connectives, since on the subject of the whale no single word or statement is enough. But these details tend, too, to heap up in such a staggering array as to combine into the awesomeness of a power against which Ahab's challenge is utterly vain, and against which his struggle to show his superiority over the ordinary processes of nature becomes blasphemous. The only thing left to man, Melville seems to tell us, is to take the span of this magnitude—to feel and to record the power of this mighty torrent, this burning fire.

And it is this, this poetic power, rather than any specifically human one, this power of transcription rather than of any alteration of life that will admit human beings into its tremendous scale, that makes up the greatness of the book — by giving us the measure of Melville's own relation to the nature that his hero so futilely attempts to master or defy. For though Melville often takes a grim and almost cruel pleasure in showing man tumbling over before the magnitude of the universe, and though much of the book is concerned, as in the sections on fighting and "cooking" the whale, with man's effort to get a grip on external nature, first through physical assault and then by scientific and industrial cunning, man finds his final relatedness to nature neither as a hero (Ahab) nor by heeding Father Mapple's old prophetic warning of man's proper subservience to God. Though all his attempted gains from nature fail him, and all goes down with the *Pequod* — all man's hopes of profit, of adjustment to orthodoxy (Starbuck), even of the wisdom that is in madness (Pip) — man, though forever alien to the world, an Ishmael, is somehow in tune with it, with its torrential rhythms, by dint of his art, by the directness with which his words grasp the world, by the splendor of his perceptions, by the lantern which he holds up "like a candle in the midst of the almighty forlornness." Man is not merely a waif in the world; he is an ear listening to the sea that almost drowns him; an imagination, a mind, that hears the sea in the shell, and darts behind all appearance to the beginning of things, and runs riot with the frightful force of the sea itself. There, in man's incredible and unresting mind, is the fantastic gift with which we enter into what is not our own, what is even against us — and for this, so amazingly, we can speak.

[1956]

Dry Light and Hard Expressions

"I LIKE," said Emerson, "dry light, and hard clouds, hard expressions, and hard manners." The writers who become our saints and sages, the wise men of our tribe, they who help us to live—there is only one way by which we can know them: their genius for compression. They are the ones who are always stripping life down to fundamentals and essentials, to aphorisms and parables and riddles, and if we ask what is holy about men whose life sayings often shock and hurt as much as they illuminate, the answer is that the final compression they get into their speech is a compression they have attained in their lives. The absolute in their writing is an absolute they have learned to live, and the sometimes overemphatic sharpness, the well-known intolerance by holy men, the cutting blow, the very quickness with which they sum up life and eternity in a sentence, is only the expression in words of the attempt to meet existence with the greatest possible directness.

This is what Thoreau meant when he said that he wanted to "drive life into a corner," when he appealed to his distracted countrymen: "Let us settle ourselves, and work and wedge our feet downward through the mud and slush of opinion, and prejudice, and tradition, and delusion, and appearance . . . till we come to a hard bottom and rocks in place, which we can call *reality*, and say, This is, and no mistake." The imagery — one might better say the music — with which he brings to an ecstatic end this second chapter of *Walden* is a whirl of variations on the single theme of the ultimate, the "*point d'appui* below freshet and frost and fire" — bedrock, facing a fact until it divides you through the heart and marrow like a sword, the sky whose bottom is pebbly with stars, the deep deep earth through which the intellect works like a cleaver. Thoreau, because he yearned to possess the infinite spaces suggested to him by his imagination, wanted to base this infiniteness on some image that would be immediately graspable, that would *look* so sharp and definite and accessible, in his telling of it, that he could lead you up to it, make you feel it, give it to you. Blake spoke of "the world in a grain of sand"; Thoreau's desire was to make you feel this in the ultimate sensation that man could possibly express of his connection with nature. If he could have rolled himself up in the world, have tasted it in every cell of his being, this and this alone would have made him feel that he was communicating his supreme privilege of ecstasy. And it is the attempt to mark this sensation of maximum contact that he tried to get into his prose — "wildness," the taste of a muskrat eaten raw, walking blind through dark woods at night, a swim in the infinite silence of Walden Pond. Fundamentally, Thoreau's best writing is an attempt to get up to the point where he can reduce human experience to communion with nature and this communion to images of total physical ecstasy.

But this same need of compression, of the absolute expression, of the ultimate in speech that will condense and contract your whole experience, can find easier forms. In Emerson, whom we tend these days to underestimate because of the priggishness that so often wars with his genius, the poet's need of condensation takes the form of epigram. There are epigrams in Thoreau, too, perhaps even more of them; but they are the steps up to his temple, the rehearsals of his style; they do not express the reaches of his ultimate feelings. In Emerson, on the other hand, epigrams, *aperçus*, bare notations which seem to cross his journal in a single motion from his eye to his hand, serve for that sidelong glance into things which expresses him far more characteristically than the ecstasies described in his first book, *Nature*. For Emerson's conception of himself was not as a solitary in nature but as an oracle, a clairvoyant, a seer; and his truest moments come when he speaks in slightly veiled disclosures from on high, when he exemplifies the quality that Thoreau missed in Carlyle — he retires "behind the truth he utters."

Emerson's compressiveness takes the form of intellectual wit, of the sentence that gives you not a description of external nature to be embraced, but a definition of things in which you can rest. He exemplifies the traditional role of the founder of new religions by providing his audience, his possible disciples, with a set of maxims which give spiritual tangibility to the otherwise nameless and indistinct blur of the outside world. Such maxims are definite names for spiritual things and so convince us of their reality; they lay down a pattern of stepping-stones across what would otherwise be the terror of an utterly alien world. Without man, there is utter silence; a true sentence cuts into this silence and gives man a habitation in the universe. "The maker of a sentence, like the other artist," Emerson wrote in 1834, "launches out into the infinite and builds a road into Chaos and Old Night, and is followed by those who hear him with something of wild, creative delight." Emerson's sentences are compressed because they are pronouncements; they show the way; they teach. He thought so habitually in "sayings" that he himself found "each sentence an infinitely repellent particle."

Emerson's professional task was to build up his scattered sentences into essays, but he naturally began with just those pronouncements that someone else would have thought it necessary to prove. He once noted of a new lecture "that it was a very good house, only the architect had unfortunately omitted the stairs." And the genius of Emerson is that he did not try to change himself, that his professional need to write essays and to deliver lectures did not pressure him out of his natural tendency to the orphic, the fragmentary, the epigram. By the 1870s, when his powers had begun to fail him, he allowed his daughter Ellen and James Elliot Cabot to put together new essays by "excerpting and compounding" from old manuscripts exactly as he had done for himself. He was not merely dependent upon such help but, in a very significant sense, indifferent to the final result.

« 2 »

Emerson's genius is in the sudden flash rather than in the suavely connected paragraph and page. He is a writer who is so natural a stylist that even in his masterpiece, the *Journals*, certain sentences come from the habit of writing well rather than from having anything to say. His good things, however, are always neat. "Love is the bright foreigner, the foreign self." "Dante's imagination is the nearest to hands and feet that we have seen." He will refer to Alcott as a "tedious archangel" and remark of the British that they remind him of old Josiah Quincy, "always blundering into some good thing." "Every new writer is only a new crater of an old volcano." "Life is in short cycles or periods; rapid rallies, as by a good night's sleep."

In that superb book, *English Traits,* he noted that "Loyalty is in the English a sub-religion. They wear the laws as ornaments," and went on to say that "The religion of England is part of good-breeding. When you see on the continent the well-dressed Englishman come into his ambassador's chapel and put his face for silent prayer into his smooth-brushed hat, you cannot help feeling how much national pride prays with him. . . . So far is he from attaching any meaning to the words, that he believes himself to have done almost the generous thing, and that it is very condescending in him to pray to God." He could be wonderfully sharp. "Their religion is a quotation; their church is a doll; and any examination is interdicted with screams of terror. In good company you expect them to laugh at the fanaticism of the vulgar; but they do not; they are the vulgar." "If Socrates were here, we could go and talk with him; but Longfellow, we cannot go and talk with; there is a palace, and servants, and a row of bottles of different coloured wines, and wine glasses, and fine coats."

The best examples of Emerson's compressiveness, his gnomic gift, lie in those sentences with which he surprised himself. Emerson's genius is so contentedly solitary (where Thoreau's is lonely) that one feels that for him the high point of his writing was the discovery of some aspect of nature (often human nature) which was an uncovered secret. Like his famous Aunt Mary, whom he called a sibyl, a Cassandra with a terrible gift of penetration, he had the clairvoyant's gift for letting life come to him. "A man finds out that there is somewhat in him that knows more than he does. Then he comes presently to the curious question, Who's who? Which of these two is really me? The one that knows more, or the one that knows less? The little fellow or the big fellow?" One feels about Emerson not merely that there was a private self concealed behind the public self, but that this private self was continually making discoveries that Emerson knew instantly how to seize.

In reading Thoreau's *Journals,* one senses always the heroism of a will tensing itself almost to the breaking point, a quest for details in nature that would distract Thoreau from his inwardness — details which he could assemble and fuse for that final encounter with nature in which he anticipated the consummation of his existence. "I come to my solitary woodland walk as the homesick go home." All of Thoreau is in that sentence. It is this everlasting preparedness, militancy, expectancy before nature, this perpetual gathering of arrowheads and meteorological data and Oriental scriptures, that makes Thoreau's lifework, the *Journals,* all one tension and that invests his frustration in the end with the truest quality of human tragedy — which does not make the effort to "drive life into a corner" any less heartbreaking. Sentence after sentence, gathered like the stones in David's sling, whitened and sharpened and polished — to be flung against a power too great to be conquered and too indefinite to be embraced! Emerson does not go forth to battle, he waits; and the communion with nature that he describes is not one which he has gone out to find but one that has revealed itself to him.

It is this that in a way makes Emerson a truer *observer* than Thoreau, though Emerson did not consciously look so much or so far — or so hard. Thoreau looked for the immanent connection; he saw in nature details that had been flung off from some larger whole that he still hoped to find; his most characteristic symbols are poignant, like the Indian arrowheads he was always finding under his feet in Concord, fragments of the vanished Indian past which he tried to reassemble in his notes. Thoreau is a true mystic: for him there is always a lost Eden, a divine background in nature. To this he can relate what he picks up on his walks, but of this he has lost something incommunicable, "a hound, a bay horse, and a turtle-dove." His description of the simplest objects in nature can be unbearably moving: one feels so keenly his own trembling at the veil that keeps the world from us. Who, after all, can possess the world, can put all nature into our hand? Thoreau's imagery has all the characteristically painful longing, the *Schmerz,* of the romantic mystic. But Emerson lights upon truths that delight in themselves, that reveal a hidden law. There is the well-known passage in his *Journals,* repeating his experience at the Jardin des Plantes in Paris:

The universe is a more amazing puzzle than ever, as you glance along this bewildering series of animated forms — the hazy butterflies, the carved shells, the birds, beasts, fishes, insects, snakes, and the upheaving principle of life everywhere so incipient, in the very rock aping organized forms. Not a form so grotesque, so savage, nor so beautiful but is an expression of some property inherent in man the observer — an occult relation between the very scorpions and man. I feel the centipede in me — cayman, carp, eagle, and fox. I am moved by strange sympathies; I say continually, "I will be a naturalist."

Emerson looks upon the universe as a witness, not as a lover. He waits for things to display themselves before him so that he can "yield to the law of their being." Without being in the least a scientist, he is often impressively disinterested and curious about phenomena. He complained that "Now many are thought not only unexplained but inexplicable; as language, sleep, madness, dreams, beasts, sex." Emerson is at his best not when he is announcing the Oversoul to the people or flattering his audience, but when he is idiosyncratic, spare and strange; in those moods of almost sleepy reflection and passive wonder one feels that he is entirely open to his unconscious, that he can get it to speak through him in the same way, to use his own image, as the tree puts itself forth through its leaves and branches. "The secret of the world is the tie between person and event. . . . The soul contains the event that shall befall it, for the event is only the actualization of its thoughts and what we pray to ourselves for is always granted." It is in this understanding that, as Thoreau says, the poet retires "behind the truth he utters," and then we feel that Emerson's writing arm somehow moves exactly to the pressure of the vision in his brain. Like Blake "taking down" the *Songs of Innocence*, he has only to dip his pen and write.

It is then that Emerson attains a greatness beyond that of the moral philosopher and national prophet. He can openly rejoice in the fact that he really has no disciples, and he shows himself not merely shrewd but uncomfortably penetrating. At his best, in his most private mood, his only aim is quiet understanding, to find the law which is spanned by the mind of that representative man whom he called "the poet." It is in these little bits of Emerson's *Journals* — scattered portraits, wayward reflections, fragments that are witty not only in the exactness of their expression but in the effect they have on the reader, for they disconcert and undercut — that we see the particular essence of a genius which, beginning as "self-trust," has made itself a kind of open channel by which truth can reach men, has converted itself wholly into an instrument of meditation and of style.

[1957]

Thoreau's Lost Journal

THE GREAT WORK OF Henry Thoreau's life — and of his art — is the *Journals*, published in fourteen volumes. There is no other work in American literature, perhaps no other writer's journal, which is quite like it. Although it is entirely a personal document in appearance, it is a formal literary work, often rewritten from rough field notes. It is not a "savings bank" for publishable essays, as Emerson called his own journal; even less is it an intimate confession, on the style of Baudelaire's famous challenge to writers to lay their "hearts bare." It is a highly stylized and endlessly deliberated work on the stark Romantic-Transcendentalist subject of man's solitary communion with the divinity of the world.

It can be compared, in style and intention, to other works of the same school — Whitman's "Song of Myself," Wordsworth's Immortality Ode, Emerson's early essays, the "mystical" sections of *Moby-Dick* which show us the world as seen directly by Ishmael the poet. But of course Thoreau's *Journals* contrast oddly with such works. For this greatest act of his life Thoreau perfected a particularly disciplined kind of prose and yet celebrates in his self-portrait the most mulishly solitary character in modern literature. The *Journals* are a wholly deliberate, plastic and imaginative work that became not a reading of life but Thoreau's only life. Without his ceasing to be an artist (except at the very end, when he faltered into

Consciousness in Concord: The Text of Thoreau's Hitherto "Lost Journal" (1840-1841). Notes and a commentary by Perry Miller. Boston: Houghton Mifflin Company.

imitating the scientist he had never wanted to be), his *Journals* became not only his art, but his mode of existence. He did not merely live for his book, as other great writers have; he lived nowhere else. The box he built of yellow pine to hold the thirty-eight manuscript notebooks was also to serve as his coffin.

It is Thoreau's psychological complexity that has so long kept people from recognizing the artistic grandeur of his *Journals*. Yet there is always the equal temptation: to forget just how peculiar Thoreau's literary lifework is and to read him as a pure visionary. Perry Miller has taken advantage of an unusual editorial opportunity to review the problem of the *Journals* in a more systematic and passionate way than, to my knowledge, has ever been done before. The occasion is the first publication of the so-called "Lost Journal" — which is simply the third notebook in a group of six composed during the earliest period of the *Journals*, but of which only five appeared in Volume One of the published journal itself. This "lost" notebook, which covers the period from July 30, 1840, to January 22, 1841, appears to have been mislaid by Harrison Blake, to whom Thoreau's sister Sophia had bequeathed the entire work in the famous pine box. It was Blake who first printed sections of the *Journals* under seasonal titles — a very misleading introduction to the inner mind of Henry Thoreau. The box passed through various hands and eventually went to the Morgan library, which in 1956 acquired the "Lost Journal" and for the first time in many years was able to fit the whole journal snugly into place.

The "Lost Journal" is a characteristic document of Thoreau's early journalizing, before he went to Walden and began to make deliberate literary use of his personal experience. It belongs to the period before Thoreau realized all that he could make of the journal as a form. As Mr. Miller says, it is really an anthology of his previous thoughts, and goes back to the period when Thoreau used the journal as a commonplace book rather than as the labor toward the full revelation of his consciousness that it eventually became. The greatest moments of the *Journals* — they record some unforgettable flights of the solitary mind — are not here. But Mr. Miller has seized the occasion for a thorough analysis of Thoreau's peculiar literary situation. If the book is more Miller than Thoreau, it is because there is something endlessly frustrating as well as fascinating in Thoreau's double use of the *Journals:* first as art, then as life.

The situation may be summed up this way. Thoreau, a Transcendentalist artist with unlimited faith in the symbolic resources and objective reach of his personal consciousness, conceived of his journal as a "song of myself" which, theoretically, could have had as much objective artistic validity in its daily "nature notes" as other works that have come out of the romantic cult of the imagination. It is not absurd to say that Thoreau's *Journals* have the same broad intention — to show the meeting of the inner and external worlds — that Proust shows in erecting his great symphonic novel on the foundation of introspective analysis. Thoreau's favorite myth — the imagination (or "soul") in the material world is like Apollo condemned to work as a shepherd for King Admetus — was especially dear to Proust, who in the form of a quotation from Emerson used it as the epigraph to his first book, *Pleasures and Days.*

Mr. Miller stresses the resemblance between Thoreau as the hero of his own book to Joyce's Stephen Dedalus. But whether one thinks in terms of Proust or Joyce, it is clear that like all the great twentieth-century writers whose concern with the stream-of-consciousness really starts from the romantic discovery of man's unconscious as a power of divination, Thoreau's whole literary faith is based on the mystic bonds between the private imagination and reality. Our generation is beginning to understand that Thoreau is not a "naturalist," and that the subject of his work is not the external scene, "nature," but the greater world of being with which the imagination claims affinities.

What makes Thoreau so different from the great modern Symbolist novelists is that he really had no subject but himself, and so had to strain for an "objectivity" that he could only simulate, not feel. Living in Concord with no real respect for anyone but himself, being a person with a shattering gift for holding his experience down to his image of what it should be, he let nothing grow wildly under his hand, allowed nothing to surprise him. He was always in control — in the *Journals* — and the life he held in such harsh control finally evaporated in his hands. He did not let the world flower under his benevolent gaze, as Whitman did — and Proust;

he kept it as *his*, all the time, until there was nothing to possess but the *Journals* which the world rather tends to see as the dead records of his vanished love.

If the essence of the romantic artist's faith in "consciousness" is that he thinks it puts him in touch with the Absolute, the tragedy of Henry Thoreau, as Mr. Miller succinctly names it, is that he tried to be the Absolute himself. The world which Proust was able to *discover* through his personal consciousness, Thoreau lost by trying to assimilate it entirely into his own. At the end of the *Journals*, as Thoreau himself seems to have acknowledged with dismay, he was forced to impersonate the deliberate and "scientific" observer of nature, to limit himself to the artificial "facts" and external shell of things he had always been able—in his rapturous and marvelous flights—to bypass before.

[1958]

Called Back

Emily Dickinson died in Amherst on May 15, 1886. A few days before, she had written her Norcross cousins, "Called back," and this phrase is on her stone in the Dickinson family plot.

Called back. Whatever the faith that this old-fashioned phrase may seem to express, it is more typical of Emily Dickinson's verbal economy than of her religion. No one who reads far into the 1775 poems that Thomas H. Johnson has edited with such scrupulousness and literary intelligence in *The Complete Poems of Emily Dickinson* (substantially the same text as the definitive three-volume edition Mr. Johnson prepared for the Harvard University Press in 1955, but without the variants for each poem) can miss the fact that Emily Dickinson was not sure of what being "called back" could mean. In poem after poem she expressed, in her odd blend of heartbreaking precision and girlish winsomeness, the basic experience, in the face

The Complete Poems of Emily Dickinson. Edited by Thomas H. Johnson. Boston: Little, Brown and Company.

of death, of our fear, our awe, our longing — and above all, of our human vulnerability, of the limit that is our portion. It is this sense of our actuality, this vision without certainty, this dwelling only on our possibility, that makes her poems so awesome and so witty, for she likes to catch things exactly, and implicitly expresses her delight in hitting the target.

> I cannot dance upon my Toes —
> No Man instructed me —
> But oftentimes, among my mind,
> A glee possesseth me. . . .

Until recently, however, it was exactly this quality of precision, bringing home the felt sensation, that in many instances her editors missed or blurred or omitted. The reason for this is a tragic-comic tale of genius in a provincial setting.

During her lifetime, Emily Dickinson had only seven poems published — all of them appeared anonymously and, as Mr. Johnson has said, almost surreptitiously. Each of them had in some way been changed and damaged by Victorian editors who distrusted her originality. Her only contact with the "literary world" had been the Boston critic Thomas Wentworth Higginson, to whom she had written in 1862 for guidance, and who advised her with a kindly obtuseness that did not make the seclusive Emily less lonely. After her death, in helping to edit the first volume of her poems (1890), he changed many lines in order to make them immediately acceptable. One mass of Emily Dickinson's poems, almost nine hundred of them, had been discovered by her sister Lavinia only after her death, and most of them, as Mr. Johnson explains in his introduction to the Harvard Press edition of the poems, were in different stages of composition and sewn together in little packets. No one in her immediate circle had guessed at Emily's productivity, and the discovery of a major poet by no means rejoiced everyone she had loved. When her sister Lavinia went for help to their brother Austin's wife Sue, who had been Emily's special friend, Sue sulkily sat on the poems until Lavinia went to the wife of an Amherst College astronomer, Mrs. Mildred Todd, who with Higginson's help put out a first selection of the poems in 1890.

Slowly, as Emily Dickinson's unexpectedly large reputation came home to Amherst, a contest over manuscripts began. The parties were Sue's daughter, Martha Dickinson Bianchi, who with Alfred Leete Hampson issued several editions of her aunt's poetry, and Mrs. Todd and *her* daughter, Millicent Todd Bingham. Eventually, Mrs. Bianchi's share was bought up and donated to Harvard, while the Todd-Bingham interests, so to speak, were transferred to Amherst College. Surely there is a new version of Henry James's *The Aspern Papers* in this tale. Even now, although Mr. Johnson was able to gather all the poems together for this great edition, rival claims persist. Yet aside from this purely human story, the real significance of the contest over the manuscripts lies in the amateurish and willful editing of the text. There is a well-known and very beautiful poem, number 712 in the present edition, that runs:

Because I could not stop for Death —
He kindly stopped for me —
The Carriage held but just Ourselves —
And Immortality.

We slowly drove — He knew no haste
And I had put away
My labor and my leisure too,
For His Civility —

We passed the School, where Children strove
At Recess — in the Ring —
We passed the Fields of Gazing Grain —
We passed the Setting Sun —

Or rather — He passed Us —
The Dews drew quivering and chill —
For only Gossamer, my Gown —
My Tippet — only Tulle —

We paused before a House that seemed
A Swelling of the Ground —
The Roof was scarcely visible —
The Cornice — in the Ground —

Since then — 'tis Centuries — and yet
Feels shorter than the Day

> I first surmised the Horses' Heads
> Were toward Eternity —

This poem was written about 1862. (Mr. Johnson has been the first to date many of the poems, and one of the significant features of his chronological arrangement is that it emphasizes how many of Emily Dickinson's poems, and especially her best, were written in the early 1860s, after the clergyman she had fallen in love with, Charles Wadsworth, had moved to San Francisco.) The poem was included in the first published selection of her poems under a title that the poet never gave to it, "The Chariot," and a fourth stanza was omitted! Where the poet had written, in the third stanza,

> We passed the School, where Children strove
> At Recess — in the Ring —

Higginson and Mrs. Todd replaced *strove* with *played;* for *At Recess — in the Ring* — they substituted *their lessons scarcely done.* In the penultimate stanza,

> The Roof was scarcely visible —
> The Cornice — in the Ground —

in the Ground became *but a mound,* and where in the last stanza Emily Dickinson had written

> Since then — 'tis Centuries — and yet

they replaced *and yet* with *but each.*

Look up the same poem in the so-called "Centenary Edition" that Martha Dickinson Bianchi and Alfred Leete Hampson put out in 1935. The fourth stanza is still missing; there are the same alterations in lines 9, 20, and 21, and, where the poet had written *where Children strove/At Recess—in the Ring,* the children now played *at wrestling in a ring.* And Mrs. Bianchi and Mr. Hampson nicely smoothed out the punctuation, replacing the poet's sometimes girlish but always meaningful dashes with proper commas and semicolons and periods.

I like Emily Dickinson's dashes. I am glad that Mr. Johnson has put them back. If that is the way she wrote, that is the way she wrote. The dashes have a light fierceness; they set the rhythm of her thinking. And in this great poem of Death's taking a lady out for a drive, the dashes help to create that "shudder of awe" that Goethe thought was man's only proper response to life and death. It is her ability to make us shudder that is Emily Dickinson's greatest achievement. No wonder that where some nineteenth-century American writers seem great, she is merely deep. "Deep" is not "great," for she does not have Whitman's scope, his ability to make us think of his poetry as the instrument of the world-process. On the other hand, greatness of a certain kind — greatness of subject, of vision, of voice — which we associate with Emerson and Whitman and Melville, has been so much more frequent than deepness that we rarely notice such a distinction. We do not even know that it can exist. The chief quality of our greatest writers is that each of them brings a wholly new world into being: each is the prophet of a new consciousness, virtually the teacher of a new religion. Their virtues are always rebelliousness, independence, self-sufficiency.

But the originality of a new religious teaching, though it can be electrifying in its power to change our minds, to make us see the world with new eyes, is not the only literary virtue. As literature, Whitman and Emerson and Thoreau do not have the texture constantly to engage and to surprise us, to uncover distinctions and to reveal new subtleties. Emily Dickinson does. She does not create a new world, as Whitman does; she gives us the range of this one.

Perhaps the quality that so fascinates me in her work is only the inherent quality of poetry itself, which with every word, stroke on stroke, establishes the poet's inner consciousness as our true world. It may be that in this country we have had all too little poetry (as opposed to declamation in the last century and fine word-painting in this), and so are constantly surprised by the precision of feeling, the depth of sound, that are found in so great a beginning as

> Because I could not stop for Death —
> He kindly stopped for me —
> The Carriage held but just Ourselves —
> And Immortality.

But surely the great quality of this poem, on the surface so painfully witty, so ironically demure, is that it remains enigmatic. The poem describes Death calling for a lady, and the journey they take, although described with touching brief glimpses of the world fast vanishing from her consciousness, remains mysterious and incommunicable. The horses' heads were toward Eternity; there is no going back. We can no longer see behind us, yet what Eternity itself is we cannot say.

To write of death with this wonder, this openness, this overwhelming communication of its *strangeness* — this is to show respect for the lords of life and death. This respect is what true poetry lives with, not with the armed fist of the perpetual rebel. But to know the limits is to engage subtlety and irony and humor; it is to write with a constant wariness of the gods. Emerson thought he had licked the problem of the gods by replacing worship with personal imagination. Thoreau, whose whole work is a mystic's quest for certainty, drove his entreaty into those overcharged single sentences that represent his artistic achievement. Whitman hoped that on occasion he might be mistaken for a god. Melville, who loved the myth of Prometheus, insisted on his antagonism to the gods. But all these are attitudes, whistlings in the dark, sharply in contrast with Emily Dickinson's provisional, ironic, catch-as-catch-can struggle with her own fears. She gave as her primary reason for writing poetry — "I had a terror — since September — I could tell to none — and so I sing, as the Boy does by the Burying Ground — because I am afraid." Perhaps she was thinking of the love she had never had, the pain of separation that can be like death, that is a death. So many of her poems are about death that the word, in her poems, finally becomes the symbol and the effect of all separation. In the great poem that I have been discussing, death is a journey out of the known world; it is a gradual separation from the light. Yet the tone of the poem on the surface is playful, even coy. The emotional charge of the poem, the mysterious sense of submission that it leaves us with, lies in the contrast between the whimsicality of language and the mystery of the destination even after the journey is over. There is even a particular achievement in identifying a Victorian lady's submission and weakness with the human condition!

We slowly drove — He knew no haste
And I had put away
My labor and my leisure too,
For His Civility —

With the next stanza (the third), the sense of the passage, of the slow separation from life that absorbed her in so many poems, is borne home to us in significant images of human struggle:

We passed the School, where Children strove
At Recess — in the Ring —

and of the ebbing world:

We passed the Fields of Gazing Grain —
We passed the Setting Sun —

The sense of increasing cold, the gradual passage toward death, the lady's finding herself inadequately dressed and armed against the hill of death — this reaches its unforgettable apogee in the revelation:

Since then — 'tis Centuries — and yet
Feels shorter than the Day
I first surmised the Horses' Heads
Were toward Eternity —

This last image catches first the drawn-out sense of intimation, and then the shock of irrevocability that is our strongest sense of death. When one thinks of how many human beings have tried to get around this fact, and how few have succeeded in expressing it, we have a sudden sense of the most that human beings can know and feel. We are "with it," as they say, all the way. We have a sense of the human soul stretched to the farthest, of valor encompassing the most that it can know.

[1960]

Good Old Howells

In his own lifetime (1837-1920), William Dean Howells was a great success. He belongs to the generation of Midwestern country boys who became industrial pioneers and millionaires, and in his own way he resembled the businessmen of the new generation and spoke for them. He was a self-taught Ohio boy who made his way up as a printer and reporter. A campaign biography of Lincoln made him American consul in Venice during the Civil War, and after the war he so quickly endeared himself to the Boston Brahmins that he became editor of the *Atlantic Monthly* and their petted symbol of the "good" Midwesterner, the faithful disciple of the genteel tradition.

Howells soon became restive in this role, and, in turning to the novel, he caught the historical moment when the Midwesterners of his own generation and background came into conflict with the pretentious culture of the Eastern seaboard. He became the most influential voice for "realism," and when he moved to New York in the 1880s, it was widely believed that he had taken the literary center of the country with him. He wrote with the undeviating industry of a librarian cataloguing books; he earned prodigious sums by his writing. He was the intimate friend of both Mark Twain and Henry James. He lived to be the first president of the American Academy of Arts and Letters—and a symbol to the 1920s of everything that a modern writer should *not* be.

This recoil was unfair, and for at least twenty years, starting in the 1930s, when politically minded critics began to defend Howells because of his brief flirtation with socialism in the 1880s and the Christian Socialist values in his novels of the period, there have been isolated attempts to revive interest in Howells. They have not succeeded. So far as I can see, Howells's novels mean even less to the general reader today than they did in the 1920s, when novel-

The Realist at War: The Mature Years of William Dean Howells, by Edwin H. Cady. Syracuse: Syracuse University Press.

ists like Sinclair Lewis took Howells seriously enough to attack him. Howells has come back only as a subject of academic research.

This biography (now concluded with the present volume) by Edwin H. Cady, though intelligent and interesting, is a perfect proof of how little Howells figures in literary thinking today. If it were a wholly biographical and evocative work, frankly nostalgic in the style of Van Wyck Brooks, one could at least enjoy such a book as a period piece. But this is a two-volume biography of a nineteenth-century literary eminence that symbolically carries no illustrations. Since Howells spent most of his eighty-three years writing books and editing magazines, his biography is essentially the history of his publications, and in this second volume Mr. Cady really does little more than go through Howells's literary opinions, year by year.

It is true that after 1885, when Howells more or less deserted Boston and in the "Editor's Study" column of *Harper's Monthly* became the American defender of "realism" on the French-Russian model, he broke, for the first time in years, with the established taste. And soon after, when the Haymarket Anarchists were hanged, Howells's defense of them brought the enmity of the respectable. But the "realism war," though a fascinating chapter in the emergence of writers like Stephen Crane and Frank Norris, whom Howells supported, cannot be studied, as Mr. Cady largely does, as a significant story in itself. By this time it is of no particular interest to know what Thomas Bailey Aldrich, H. C. Vedder and William Roscoe Thayer thought of Howells. What we would like to know is what it was about Howells (though he was generalissimo of the realists) that made it impossible for him to support Dreiser's *Sister Carrie* — a fact that Mr. Cady does not mention.

In attacking "romanticism," in speaking up for "realism," Howells was not only defending middle-class American experience against the old snobbish attachment to English literature, he was speaking, as he did all his life, for the emergent class of self-made businessmen who identified "romance" with the aristocratic culture in which they had no share. Now the problem of the American novelist, as Henry James pointed out with annoyance when Howells tried to enlist him in the "realism war," is just that "realism," though a vital social question at the end of the nineteenth century, did not answer to all his needs as an artist. Mr. Cady touches on this point when he notes that James fought alongside of Howells "up to the point where the integrity of his balanced insights seemed threatened."

It is just this "balanced insight" that one needs today in order to understand the limitations of Howells's own fiction. It has often been "romance" (not the Graustarkian kind that Howells hated, but the fantastic imagination that got into *Moby-Dick, Huckleberry Finn* and *The Wings of the Dove*) that has made the significant contribution to American fiction.

If one is not going to write a wholly old-fashioned and purely historical life of Howells, one should discuss his work with critical freedom. Mr. Cady writes with intelligence but not with critical freedom, as one can tell from his emotional complaint that there was "a monstrous legend of Howells current in 'modernist' circles of the Twenties and Thirties." He writes out of loyalty to Howells, but does not attempt to understand why, when so many critics have been writing about Howells with sympathy, it has still proved impossible to make out a real case for even Howells's "major" novels.

Every possible argument has been made out for Howells in our day. He had been admired for his political courage, his personal nobility, his devotion as a family man, his encouragement of younger writers. Hardly anyone has explained why his novels are so peculiarly thin and unsatisfying. The excited Freudian critics of the Twenties naturally thought that Howells was afraid of sex. No one seems personally to have been more afraid of sex than Henry James, who therefore was able to suggest its power far more convincingly than does Henry Miller.

Perhaps one explanation of Howells's almost self-induced smoothness is that he was such a steady producer, with such an immediate audience, that he could never break with anything for very long or allow himself to be disturbed. In his excellent recent book on the American novel, *The American Novel and Its Tradition*, Richard Chase goes to the heart of the matter when he complains that "the trouble with Howells . . . is that he never tried hard enough. There is a real laziness, as well as a prudishness, about his mind, and in his novels he was always making great refusals." It is this very self-saving quality, indeed, that helps to explain Howells's fantastic productivity—one might almost call it the ooze of his hundred books. It was so necessary for him to write easily, plentifully and publicly that he was rarely stopped by what he wrote.

The pity of Howells's smoothness is that he *was* so attractive and above all so intelligent a writer. Like his friend Mark Twain, he is a natural stylist—with a fresh, cool, easy style that makes him irritating precisely when he uses his virtuosity to gloss over difficult matters. There are few literary memoirs in the English language that are so beautiful as *My Mark Twain*, and there are many powerful scenes in his novels that make one angry at the fatal ease with which Howells drops them. Howells had got into the habit of success: success expressed not only as money, but as the instant understanding and approbation of his audience, his kind. He very rarely disappointed this audience, and when contact with it was lost, he quickly recovered it. The "realism war" did not last very long, for realism, like science and big business, was in the air. He was a good man and a great success.

[1958]

Stephen Crane's Scarlet Woman

ONE DAY in November, 1896, the twenty-five-year-old author of *The Red Badge of Courage* arrived in Jacksonville, Florida, and while waiting for a blockade-running ship to take him across to Cuba, then seething with revolt against the Spaniards, became extremely friendly with the proprietress of a high-class "sporting house." The Hotel de Dream (this sounds like the setting of a play by Tennessee Williams) was not exactly a brothel, and Cora Taylor, who was to live with Crane in England for the last three years of his life as Mrs. Stephen Crane, was certainly not anything like the nature of her business. She had been born in Boston of an extremely

Cora Crane, by Lillian Gilkes. Bloomington, Indiana: Indiana University Press.

good family, and technically at least she was still the wife of a well-known British colonial official whose father was a field marshal and had formerly been commander-in-chief in India. Cora was a cultivated, gifted, and well-bred woman who was soon to move in the company of Henry James, Joseph Conrad, H. G. Wells, and now lesser-known figures like Harold Frederic and Robert Barr. Crane had been her greatest literary admiration before she met him, and afterward they went together as correspondents to the Greek-Turkish War.

Stephen Crane, six years younger than Cora and infinitely more complicated in every respect, was to become the great passion of her life. And whether or not it was her dark past that appealed to the need of something "sinful" in his love affairs, there is no doubt that she was his only wife. Since the whole story of "Mrs. Stephen Crane" has been unwritten until now, Lillian Gilkes's full and sometimes breathlessly detailed biography, which draws on the collection of Crane papers recently acquired by Columbia, will be fascinating to anyone interested in the peculiar genius behind *The Red Badge of Courage* and "The Open Boat." This is the kind of exhaustive biography that really helps us to see people of another epoch — how they lived and what they thought about.

Yet the deeper interest of the book lies in the theme of illegitimate passion, of sexual daring — the revolutionary theme of so many novels of the end of the century. Publicly, at least, the Victorian repressions were all in force, and the underlying theme of writers like Crane, Norris, and Dreiser was the power of sex. This was exactly the period in which Freud was beginning to work up his first and perhaps most important book, *The Interpretation of Dreams*. The timid and thus infinitely suggestive treatment of sex that Henry James would soon get into novels like *The Ambassadors* and *The Golden Bowl* now marks the same revolt as Dreiser's *Sister Carrie* and Crane's obsessive concern with prostitutes in his early stories. Yet in a society still externally dominated by anxious middle-class prudery, the concern with sex was more challenging than social radicalism. The Socialists, already outside respectable society, had nothing to lose by threatening to overturn it; but there were writers of reputation who by dealing frankly with sex challenged the class that had established and now supported them.

This was true of Crane, who could not live with Cora in America; even in England, to which they went, George Gissing "reaped the social punishments meted out to those entering into a union outside wedlock"; H. G. Wells and Ford Madox Ford had their troubles. The American novelist and *Times* correspondent Harold Frederic, unable to get a divorce from his wife, lived openly with another woman and their children, and, after Frederic's death, many leading English writers put up a special fight to get his common-law wife recognized as his lawful heir. This was the golden age of "the line," the cocotte, the "fast" woman, the private room at fashionable restaurants — all of which, now translated from Colette's *Gigi* into words by Lerner and music by Loewe, seems as quaint to us as George Washington at his cherry tree. But many an innocent was helpfully made wicked by the self-righteous respectability of the times. When Cora first came to New York to live with an aunt, "nice" girls did not stay unchaperoned in New York, and the better-class boardinghouses "let in" no one without an introduction. Miss Gilkes has discovered that "In New York, in the 1880s, a woman could be arrested for appearing in public 'red in the face.' "

Judge now the effect that a woman of real individuality and unquestioned experience would have on Stephen Crane's timid relatives in Port Jervis, New York. As it happened, Crane and Cora could live in England — Crane always brought out the most amazing devotion and admiration in writers like James, Conrad, Wells, and Kipling; even the timid William Dean Howells always championed him. The really "advanced" and gifted people were all enthusiastic about Crane. It is significant that Cora herself appealed to many of these people as well. It is impossible to say how many of them knew about the Hotel de Dream, but it was also typical of the great company in which Crane moved that they admired her for herself as well as for her boundless devotion to Crane.

The exception was Henry James. Whether it was rumors of Cora's "dark past" or his usual snobbery, it is a fact that James seems to have been as covertly hostile to Cora as he was solicitously admiring of Crane himself. An American friend of Crane's reported that he "had to hear a great deal from some English friends about Mr. Henry James and his intense sufferings when he had to 'endure'

Mrs. Crane. Maybe! I do know that he came bowling over from Rye one day with a carriageload of people, all stuffed shirts, and announced that he had brought them to lunch. Mrs. Crane was mad as a hornet, but did not show it. She vanished into the kitchen and concocted a lot of extra lunch in a chafing dish." My own suspicion is that James, whose imagination was so much stronger than his experience — it had to be — could not stand so vital a woman. The more intensely repressed he felt, the more silky in his pomposity he became. Harold Frederic said flatly that James was an "effeminate old donkey who lives with a herd of other donkeys around him and insists on being treated as if he were the Pope." One of the incidental pleasures of reading so fully detailed an account of literary life sixty years ago is that we can see James's affectations minus the rosy hue that has been conferred on all of James's doings by our revival of his work. Even the actual rewards of reading James have been misrepresented as more significant than they really are. James never engages life at any really critical level; fundamentally, he is more concerned with the rich textures of life than with the shoals and abysses of human conflict. Despite his extraordinary gifts as a verbal artist, there is an essential heaviness of spirit to him, an inordinate pessimism, that speaks of complete sexual repression. The vitality that comes with personal hope was missing from James's later work, and the reason, I believe, was his inability to champion the instincts even as a symbol of social revolt against the middle classes who had made a cult of virtuousness.

Actually, many of the really good novelists of the period were concerned with the "primitive" instincts and the "lower" classes who were identified with these instincts. Crane was driven to seek out life on the lower East Side and on the Bowery. (He called the Bowery his old "university," and someone at Constance Garnett's thought he was referring to a school of fine arts.) His importance lies not only in those few works of his which completely come off, like "The Open Boat," but in his constantly seeking the primitive facts, the forbidden places, the dangerous people. Crane always got on badly with popular idols of the time like Richard Harding Davis, "the dandified idol of college youth," as Miss Gilkes calls him, "who deemed the author of *Maggie* and the Bowery tales a gifted but unwashed lunatic, a boor with suicidal proclivities and unfortunate leanings toward low associations." And as Crane himself said to an old friend, "Of course I am admittedly a savage. I have been known as docile from time to time but only under great social pressure."

Crane, worn out with trying to support by hackwork the immense establishment he and Cora kept up in England, died at twenty-eight of tuberculosis. Cora tried to finish some of his works herself, but unable to market them successfully or to get any money from Crane's relatives, went back to Jacksonville. Yes, and opened another house, the Court. In 1905 she married a man younger than herself, who eventually murdered another man in a jealous rage over her. She helped get him off, but he divorced her. She died in 1910, aged forty-five. A car had got stuck in the mud, and when she saw it, she rushed up to help pull it out. She died that day.

[1960]

A Leftover Transcendentalist: John Jay Chapman

THIS BOOK came out just as the Little Rock crisis began, and one morning, when the *New York Herald Tribune* reproduced on its editorial page the words that John Jay Chapman once spoke in Coatesville, Pennsylvania, after a lynching, there was a flare-up of the old pride and faith in many a soured American heart. For John Jay Chapman (1862–1933) was the last Emersonian, a man who tried to live by conscience as if it were an absolute, and, a year after a mob had burned a Negro to death under particularly horrifying circumstances, Chapman had gone down to Coatesville entirely on his own, and had held an individual prayer meeting there, exactly as Thoreau had once taken the Concord Town Hall in order to honor the memory of John Brown.

Chapman's great quality was always a gift for stirring up again

Selected Writings of John Jay Chapman, edited and with an introduction by Jacques Barzun. New York: Farrar, Straus and Cudahy.

the embers of our old faith. In a culture like ours, which possesses so few traditions in common that it must emphasize certain spiritual episodes in its past, a figure like Chapman, who on every side of him, up to his very name, incarnates continuity, serves with peculiar emotional force to remind us of the heroic period in our history, to revitalize the symbolic theme of our experience. And Chapman himself, like so many American literary critics, was himself so nostalgic, so imprisoned in memory by the epoch to which he thought he belonged, that he did his best work in magnificent essays on Garrison and Emerson — both included in this long-needed selection from Chapman's work.

Each of these essays — the first appeared as a book in 1913 — has a peculiar emotional vibrancy which reveals Chapman's passion and relief at being able to live again in his rightful period. In each, Chapman assumes the greatness of his subject as a matter of course, and though Garrison and Emerson are very different, Chapman manages to make the reader feel that they are part of the same movement of greatness in the American mind.

In reading these essays, one has the sense of being recharged and uplifted — not by mere partisanship of old causes, such as professional liberals give us when they invoke the past as a slogan, but through imaginative reinvolvement. Chapman prefaces the second edition of his book on Garrison by telling us of a historian who, while the Civil War was in progress, actually felt no interest in it, but who in 1895 became so absorbed and excited in writing a biography of Lincoln that "he lived it over again and could not sleep at night." Chapman had that gift of imaginative participation to an astonishing degree. But what is most astonishing about it — and peculiarly the mark of a critic rather than of a historian — is that he was excited by old ideas, fought them over again, saw them at work in his own life, wrote about them with a vehemence that makes the reader of these two extraordinary essays believe that Chapman wrote about Garrison and Emerson because he felt that he was engaged in exactly the same struggle.

But he was not. And it is this lack of actual historical sense, despite his strong identification of himself with the past, that makes Chapman so passionate and yet so baffling a figure. Chapman is "religious," a visionary, in the sense that he sees his own ideals as permanent and classic features of thought, cannot admit that the ideal may be present under another name, sees Emerson and Garrison struggling for the light against the commercial interests that, of course, particularly oppressed Chapman's own generation in the years between the Civil War and the First World War. Although Chapman's material is history, always history, he has actually little historical detachment, and this is why he excitedly relived Garrison's life instead of writing *about* him. Equally, the essay on Emerson, though magnificent in its moral exaltation, is really a portrait of the superior individual in the Industrial Age threatened by the mob; it does not come to grips with the first — and decisive — phase of Emerson's thought, his attempt to convert the religion of his fathers into a personal ritual. "If a soul be taken and crushed by democracy till it utter a cry, that cry will be Emerson." That cry was uttered by John Jay Chapman, not by Ralph Waldo Emerson. Emerson never cried out at all — at least not in public (and not very much, we may be sure, in private). Chapman *always* cried out. His tragedy, as everyone who has studied his career knows, is the tragedy of a man born out of his time (or who thought that he was, which can be the same thing), a man dominated by historical wistfulness and forced to posturings in his immediate circle, a man who kept fighting for causes that had long since been won because he was not able to define to himself the causes — partly personal, mostly circumstantial — that oppressed him in his own lifetime.

« 2 »

The proof of this is Chapman's telltale reliance on "passion" for its own sake, on "religion" as a self-conscious gesture, on vehement outbursts against "America" and the "modern" rather than against the comfortable clubmen among whom he lived and whom he always enjoyed, in his own complacent way, far more than he could admit. The causes that Chapman gave himself to in his own time were always incidental or incoherent. Exactly like Theodore Roosevelt (his one-time crony in civic reform movements) in his unconscious snobbery, his hectoring of the American people — he, too, hysterically insisted from 1914 on that America had to sacrifice its young men in the war, and when his son Victor died as an aviator with a French squadron, was able to write in the same letter that

. . . the consolatory feature of it is that the individual has so much power — a few insuppressible individuals change the reputation of a hundred millions. . . . The thing we need is depth of feeling, and this is religion.

Emerson has often been savagely criticized by traditionalists for having helped to destroy formal religion in America, but he would never have written anything so subjective and essentially incoherent as "the thing we need is depth of feeling, and this is religion."

A phrase like "depth of feeling," calling attention to one's own "spiritual" superiority in a period of great materialism, over and over again reveals Chapman's personal priggishness. He has the quality that one sees in Theodore Roosevelt's professional gusto and boyishness — the mark of a gifted individual who cannot or will not sacrifice the standards of his own particular clan and group and who dramatically converts his guilt into a theatrical exuberance and showmanship. Just as T.R. was always posing (and often just plain lying) in order to give policemen, soldiers, settlement children and other inferiors a touch of his showy "leadership," so Chapman was always the would-be saint, the spoiled priest of his preparatory school set, calling attention to himself as "religious" and "fiery" when he plainly felt peculiar and inert. Chapman's letters, as one reads them in Mark De Wolfe Howe's official biography, show a man who more and more was content to be the "wild man" of his clubby, chummy, smug little group. His utter hysteria about the First World War, like his later hysteria about Jews and Catholics, shows a man whose eye is not really on the ball, who devotes himself to causes but who is not really absorbed by any subject, who is constantly posing, "shocking" his little group, flitting from enthusiasm to enthusiasm.

In part this is the tragedy of a certain lack of *profession*. Admittedly, he was no more of an amateur than Emerson was, or than many American critics have been. They have all been commentators at large. But it is not his little plays and poems, his selective little translations of Dante, his presumption in writing a book on Lucian, that make him so irritatingly the pretentious country squire, the intellectual Boy Scout or T.R. of the period; it is his self-consciousness.

From Emerson to Mencken, we have always had a great tradition of the critic as iconoclast and reformer. But even Mencken, with his personal smugness, makes you feel that when he is lambasting the booboisie, he is really writing about *them,* not saving himself from them. And just as Emerson had this gift for raising his discourse above himself, so one feels about Chapman that he is always a little too conscious of being "mad Jack Chapman," the *enfant terrible* of his circle, the only man in it who *thought* it required great courage to speak out against President Eliot.

It is typical of Chapman's essential incoherency and complacency that when, in his old age, a friend urged him to "save" the Episcopal Church, he answered "there must be some things for which I do not agitate."

But, typically enough, it was middle-class Jews in Atlantic City that offended him, not the Sacco-Vanzetti case; it was Al Smith daring to run for the Presidency, not the smugness of Herbert Hoover, or the horrors of mass slaughter in the First World War. And the Chapman who hobnobbed with Nicholas Murray Butler at Fred Vanderbilt's party was the same man who could attack Whitman as a "tramp" and applaud Santayana only when the latter attacked German philosophy in the First World War; who was proud of being considered "mad" and "bad," but was simply the pet bulldog of his clan and, even more egregiously than Shaw, the pet entertainer of the group he was always pretending to defy, no danger to anybody. It was Chapman, ironically enough, who said of certain writers and painters of the Nineties that they were . . .

> . . . O my! all amateur. Neither John Sargent nor Whistler nor Henry James had the attitude of workaday artists toward their work. They were each doing a stunt. . . . And all these people gas and talk and attitudinize. As for Shaw, he's the caricature of a caricature — the monkey of the show.

But if these things are true of Sargent and Whistler and Henry James, what — O my! — should be said of John Jay Chapman, who never did a book that was a solid contribution to the subject, and who spent so much of his life evading any test of strength with his gifted contemporaries?

The truth is that John Jay Chapman is significant not for what he wrote but for what he was. He is the symbol of an ordeal —

the ordeal of the gifted and sensitive individual, almost crushed by an inimical setting, who no longer has a *subject* to turn to. Despite the many books that Chapman wrote, his life gives out an unmistakable suggestion of idleness and personal embarrassment. He knew how he wanted to live, not what he wanted to live for. When he writes that "All life is nothing but passion," he is of no interest. When he relives Garrison's life and flames out again, he is significant and moving because, in writing about Garrison, he dramatizes the plight of the individual conscience in his own time.

But unlike Garrison and Emerson, who actively disturbed the peace, who determined the history of this country, Chapman's importance is symbolic, circumstantial. What he wrote matters far less than what he represents in our modern history and the fact that he knew this himself explains not only his suffering, but — what I have not even touched on here — his extraordinary intelligence. In the last analysis, Chapman's bond with other great historical actors of this period — Roosevelt, William James, Shaw — is not his gift of "passion," but of intelligence. No one can read his work, as in this fine volume of selections, without realizing how much more Chapman could have given us, if he had not had to spend so much of his energy in saving himself.

[1957]

And the War Came

THIS YEAR we begin to play Civil War. On February 12, in Montgomery, Alabama, the bells "opened a week of pageantry commemorating the beginning of the Confederate nation and the Civil War that followed." In the State House of Representatives Chamber, where the Confederate convention met, legislators re-enacted the secession debates that took Alabama out of the Union "To make the celebration as realistic as possible," it was announced that "men would walk the streets wearing Confederate beards, top hats, and string ties. Their womenfolk have forsaken formfitting dresses for the ankle-length hoop skirts of Civil War days." In Atlanta *Gone*

With the Wind has been "screened again to kick off Georgia's centennial observation of the War Between the States."

A more somber note was struck in Charleston, South Carolina, where it was firmly announced that a Negro member of the New Jersey Civil War Centennial Commission, which had planned to attend the ceremonies marking the firing on Fort Sumter, would not be allowed to stay at the hotel with other members of her state group. Major General Ulysses S. Grant III, chairman of the National Centennial Commission, seemed puzzled by the disturbance over one Negro lady. When Allan Nevins, in his official capacity as adviser to the national commission, also protested, the general said to a reporter, "Who's Allan Nevins?"

In Virginia, opening *his* state's commemoration of the great event, Governor J. Lindsay Almond, Jr., drew a parallel between the present conflict over what he called states' rights and the "unhappy difficulties" of the nation on the eve of the Civil War. He lamented, "It has unfortunately been the course of our history that men have raised false issues which could influence the minds and stir the emotions instead of exercising constructive leadership in the effort to mold common opinion in support of that which is best for the nation and the world." And in a special series of articles called "The Needless War" for the *New York Herald Tribune*, Bruce Catton (the last survivor on either side) pointed out that the war need not have happened at all, and would not have happened if responsible leaders North and South had been less emotional. By 1861, says Mr. Catton, it could be seen "that the very cause of the dispute was itself dying and would, if men approached it reasonably, presently reduce itself to manageable size . . . The American Civil War . . . settled nothing that reasonable men of good will could not have settled if they had been willing to make the effort."

But the war did take place. As Lincoln said in his second inaugural, looking back to that anxious day in 1861 when, taking the oath for the first time, he had pleaded with the South to stave off the war: "All dreaded it, all sought to avert it. . . . Both parties deprecated war, but one of them would *make* war rather than let the nation survive, and the other would *accept* war rather than let it perish, and the war came." The war came, and to read about it now—in the superb history of *The Ordeal of the Union* by Nevins, in the chronicles of the antislavery movement, in the great debates in Congress, in the novels and poems of the time, in the memoirs of Grant, in the wartime diaries of Whitman, in the letters and articles of foreign observers on the battlefields, in the inflamed and exacerbated writings of abolitionists, slaveowners, ex-slaves, politicians, soldiers — is to realize at once the frigid emptiness of all this current play-acting, with its characteristic suggestion that the war would have been averted if only people had been sensible.

The inescapable fact is that if you look at the passionate writing that helped to bring the war about, that in turn came out of the war, and that, among Southerners at least, has never ceased to come out of the war, you can see why even the endless debates between American historians as to the causes of the war seem dry and inconclusive by contrast with the torment of principle, the convulsion of experience.

« 2 »

A civil war is terrible — so terrible that perhaps only an irrepressible conflict of interests and principles can explain it. It is as terrible as the murder of brother by brother described in the Old Testament, of mother by son in Greek tragedy. The very foundations of the human family are ripped asunder, and that is why such wars are never forgotten and perhaps never quite end. They show us a side of human nature that we can never forgive. When you read in *The Personal Memoirs of General Ulysses S. Grant* of Confederate raiders killing stragglers and then of being caught and lined up in the town square to be shot, the fact that these men all spoke the same language, were usually of the same stock, may even have come from the same towns in Kentucky, Maryland, and Missouri, gives these scenes the same quality of elemental bitterness that you recognize in the quarrels between the Greek chiefs in the *Iliad*. And equally, when Grant describes how, immediately after Lee had signed at Appomattox, members of his staff asked permission to go into the Confederate lines to greet old friends from West Point or the regular Army, the scene calls up images on a frieze of Trojans and Greeks going off the battlefield arm in arm.

But when the war itself broke out, nearer than such elemental feelings were the widespread anger and disgust over the danger to what had been until then the world's most advanced political experiment. There had been a prophecy of this by Jefferson in a letter of 1820, in which he said that the "momentous question [the Missouri Compromise], like a firebell in the night, awakened and filled me with terror." The passionate indignation that could be aroused by the steady weakening of national unity is heard in Lincoln's complaint that year by year the eighteenth-century spirit of free discussion was being narrowed. "Little by little, but steadily as man's march to the grave, we have been giving up the old for the new faith. Nearly eighty years ago we began by declaring that all men are created equal; but now from that beginning we have run down to the other declaration, that for some men to enslave others is a 'sacred right of self-government.' These principles cannot stand together."

Lincoln cited a Southern senator's statement that the Declaration of Independence was "a self-evident lie," and broke out: "Fellow-countrymen, Americans, South as well as North, shall we make no effort to arrest this? Already the liberal party throughout the world express the apprehension 'that the one retrograde institution in America is undermining the principles of progress, and fatally violating the noblest political system the world ever saw.' This is not the taunt of enemies, but the warning of friends. Is it quite safe to disregard it — to despise it? Is there no danger to liberty itself in discarding the earliest practice and first precept of our ancient faith?"

Earlier Lincoln had written to his friend Joshua Speed: "Our progress in degeneracy appears to me to be pretty rapid. As a nation we began by declaring that 'all men are created equal.' We now practically read it 'all men are created equal, except Negroes.' When the Know-Nothings get control, it will read 'all men are created equal, except Negroes and foreigners and Catholics.' When it comes to this I shall prefer emigrating to some country where they make no pretense of loving liberty — to Russia, for instance, where despotism can be taken pure, and without the base alloy of hypocrisy."

The peculiarly biting quality of this is the other side of Lincoln's gift for invoking "our ancient faith." In a country like the United States, ceremoniously founded on certain propositions of political theory, effective political utterances have naturally tended to invoke principle for purposes of common rhetoric. It was agreement upon a common basis of political aspiration, not the common experience of a "folk," that in one sense held the country together — this consensus was, indeed, the country's only real tradition. All political speeches had to attach themselves to '76, the Constitution, the Founding Fathers, the great and noble experiment in liberty and self-government that was the United States. Even the most extreme proslavery arguments, so reactionary in their views of human nature, appealed to the Constitution and to the enlightened political theory behind it. It is always this profound commitment to the Republic as his absolute political standard that gives Lincoln's writing its assurance.

As Allan Nevins says so tellingly in the volumes of his history that deal with *The Emergence of Lincoln*, Lincoln's mind was distinctly a "countryman's" mind — slow, deep, and careful. But the peculiar passion of Lincoln's greatest utterances stems from the belief, natural to his generation, that America was the greatest step forward that political man had yet taken. And since his own position, in regard to the Negro and slavery, was at once firm and moderate — slavery was to be kept out of the territories, but not molested in the Southern states — Lincoln's style itself expresses the patient hope for the future that was the essence of his position. In 1858, debating with Douglas, he made it clear: "I say in relation to the principle that all men are created equal, let it be as nearly reached as we can. If we cannot give freedom to every creature, let us do nothing that will impose slavery upon any other creature."

That is of a piece with the moral distinctness that runs through many of the great utterances on slavery before the Civil War. The extraordinary hold of the images and rhythms of the King James Bible, the constantly growing sense of crisis in the air, the peculiar assertiveness of strong-minded and highly articulate men, some of whom on the Northern side felt that they were battling for the Lord, not for the country that had betrayed "His poor," some of whom on the Southern side proved by the Bible that He had ordained the blacks forever to be hewers of wood and drawers of water for His elect — all this, symptomatic of the national excitement, gave an intensity to the great debates in Congress, in the newspapers, in the daily confrontation of Americans, that in our generation perhaps only a few Negroes and die-hard segregationists can understand.

One reason for this depth of feeling, on the Southern side, is suggested in a remark made by Kate Stone, a Southern woman who confessed after the war that she never regretted the freeing of the Negroes: "The great load of accountability was lifted." In a culture that took literally man's accountability to God, men might live with guilt but they could not deny it. They were creatures of passion who wanted to keep the Negro in his place so that they would know a higher place for themselves. The slaveowners used the Negro man in one way, and they were free to use the Negro woman in another. But however Southern ministers and politicians might explain slavery away, they had to work harder and harder at the job of explanation. They were accountable. And what they did not of themselves find to account for, the occasional atrocity at home and the unrelenting attack from the abolitionists pressed them to account for.

The high and moral style of the period came back to me in Russia, of all places, when I was looking over Tolstoy's study at Yasnaya Polyana. On the wall, big as life, was William Lloyd Garrison, and on the photograph of himself presented to his dear colleague, Leo Tolstoy, was the inscription in flowing hand, "Liberty for all, for each, for ever!" Think of Thoreau calling a meeting in Concord to commemorate the execution of John Brown and spitting out his bitterness at the American people: "You don't know your New Testament when you see it!" Only when you put together the constant pressure on the Southerner from his religion, his property, and his need to play the great lord can you begin to understand why Southern writers have always taken the opposite line from Thoreau's majestically simple rhetoric—why they have gone deeper, have been more subtle and complex in their rendering of human conduct than the abolitionist writers were. Hawthorne, the only great novelist that New England produced in its heyday, was a Democrat, a friend and biographer of the pro-Southern President Franklin Pierce, scornful of the extreme reformers and doctrinaires who surrounded him. Hawthorne died in 1864, and it has been said that he died of the war. He could not abide fanaticism of any kind, and when the qualities in American life that he had struggled against exploded into war, he collapsed first intellectually and then physically.

New England produced a kind of prophetic writer who thought of himself as the voice of the Lord. But the Southerners, some of them more detached about themselves, were wiser about human limitations. As that fine Southern historian C. Vann Woodward has said in his recent book, *The Burden of Southern History,* the South is the only section that has known the collective suffering and humiliation which most countries have experienced. In our own generation much the deepest kind of imaginative writing in this country has come from Southern writers. It is almost too easy for us to sympathize with the Lost Cause, to fancy the aristocratic party over what proslavery orators used to call the "mudsills" of the North. As millions know from *Gone With the Wind,* the South had all the romance and all the honor. As early as 1888, the carpetbagger writer Albion W. Tourgée admitted, "Not only is the epoch of the War the favorite field of American Fiction today, but the Confederate Soldier is the popular hero. Our literature has become not only Southern in type but distinctly Confederate in sympathy." Everybody today reproaches the abolitionists, everybody knows that John Brown had insanity in his family. In any event, if you want to write about the most dramatic event in American history, where else can you set it but where almost all the fighting took place, and who can your hero be but the man fighting for his home?

« 3 »

I still believe that Emerson and Thoreau, Garrison and Whittier, caught unforgettably the moral wrong of slavery. But it was Southern novelists and poets and diarists who came up against the complex human relationships of slavery. Inescapably the Civil War remains, so far as the war really was a tragedy and not a liberation, the Southerners' war. The worst things that could have happened happened to them. Look, for example, at the diary of Mary Boykin Chesnut, *A Diary from Dixie,* first published in 1905. Her husband, Senator James Chesnut of South Carolina, resigned his seat months before Lincoln took the oath in March; he joined the Confederate cabinet as Secretary of the Navy. South Carolina, which took the lead in secession, was a particular center of what used to be called "fire-eaters" — violently proslavery extremists eager for secession and war. The Chesnuts were big slaveowners. Yet Mrs. Chesnut, who from the beginning was in a central position to observe the highest councils of the Confederacy, made out of her diary a record which for its humor, detachment, patience, and dramatic interest is one of the most remarkable documents of the period. She is a diarist in the grand style, an observer of the most minute things; her writing has a candor about it that compels one to go on reading with the same fascination that one finds in great memoirs of Russian family life like Tolstoy's and Alexander Herzen's. She says of South Carolina's headlong secession from the Union: "South Carolina had been rampant for years. She was the torment of herself and everybody else. Nobody could live in this state unless he were a fire-eater. . . . South Carolinians had exasperated and heated themselves into a fever that only blood-letting could ever cure. It was the inevitable remedy. So I was a seceder." When her husband had taken office in the Confederate government, organized in Montgomery, Alabama, Mrs. Chesnut wrote with sly disparagement of the local inhabitants that when she discussed her recent experiences in Washington as a senator's wife, "These people — the natives, I mean — are astounded that I calmly affirm in all truth and candor that if there were awful things in society in Washington, I did not see or hear of them." She notes that her nephew has volunteered as a private, to be an example to his class, but that he conveniently has his "servant" (slave) with him, and she said to an Englishwoman as they were passing a slave auction, "If you can stand that, no other Southern thing need choke you."

There is a lightness of tone about Mrs. Chesnut's intimate records, a delighted interest in gossip, and a conscious artistry in the depiction of character that make particularly vivid the tragedy of the South. Just as we today cannot help noticing the contrast between the grand but often abstract principles announced by New England intellectuals and the concrete defiance, courage, and desperation of Southerners fighting on their home grounds, so Mrs. Chesnut's ingrained social sense, her ability to convey the concrete human style of the people she is talking about, above all her attention to the truth of any human experience apart from the cause in which it is enlisted, give certain passages in *A Diary from Dixie* the stamp of universal experience that we value most in literature. She says of a family named Middleton, "Their lives are washed away in a tide of blood. There is nothing to show they were ever on earth."

Southern writers, now as well as then, have insisted that the abolitionists and their sympathizers, concentrating on principle alone, were either hypocritical or fanatical, and in any case ignorant of what slavery was really like. The most striking thing about so many Americans just then, as we get a direct glimpse of them in their period, was their moral rigor, their direct knowledge of what the Lord had intended the relationship between white men and Negroes to be, forever. It is not easy to enter into the minds of people for whom the creation has a design which they alone are privileged to understand.

« 4 »

The cocksureness with which representatives of every opinion habitually spoke of the Lord's intentions finally aroused Lincoln, in 1862, to reply to a committee, representing religious denominations, that urged him to free the slaves immediately: "I hope it will not be irreverent for me to say that if it is probable that God would reveal His will to others on a point so connected with my duty, it might be supposed that He would reveal it directly to me; for, unless I am more deceived in myself than I often am, it is my earnest desire to know the will of Providence in this matter. These are not, however, the days of miracles, and I suppose it will be granted that I am not to expect a direct revelation. I must study the plain physical facts of the case, ascertain what is possible, and learn what appears to be wise and right."

Despite his habitual tentativeness and reticence in religious matters, even Lincoln's public utterances became increasingly more scriptural in tone as the killing went on. By the second inaugural, four years of war drove Lincoln to say that although neither side could claim that the Lord spoke through it alone, it was clear that "The Almighty has His own purposes. . . . If we shall suppose that American slavery is one of those offenses which, in the providence of God, must needs come, but which, having continued through His appointed time, He now wills to remove, and that He now gives to both North and South this terrible war as the woe due to those by whom the offense came, shall we discern therein any departure from those divine attributes which the believers in a living God always ascribe to Him? Fondly do we hope, fervently do we pray, that this mighty scourge of war may speedily pass away. Yet, if God wills that it continue until all the wealth piled by the bondsman's two hundred and fifty years of unrequited toil shall be sunk, and until every drop of blood drawn with the lash shall be paid by another drawn with the sword, as was said three thousand years ago, so still it must be said, 'The judgments of the Lord are true and righteous altogether.'"

For Lincoln, as Edmund Wilson has said, it was the American Union itself that became the sacred object of his religious mysticism. There is an unfailing moral exaltation in Lincoln's greatest utterances, riveting his arguments together like the linked verses of Biblical prophecy. The application of his Biblical metaphors and images to the very geography of America shows the ground of his feeling. "The Father of Waters again goes unvexed to the sea," he wrote to James R. Conkling, hailing the victory at Vicksburg that opened the Mississippi all the way down to the Gulf. And speaking of the part that so many sections of the country were playing in the great fight, he went on: "Thanks to all: for the great republic—for the principle it lives by and keeps alive—for man's vast future—thanks to all." In Lincoln's feeling "for the great republic" one sees the classical value of politics, loyalty to the commonwealth as the embodiment of general value above each sectional and class interest. Contrast this with the religious fundamentalism that justifies its special interests as God's providence and the Marxist belief that the state must represent one class or another. The historian David Donald, in an interesting recent article entitled "An Excess of Democracy: The American Civil War and the Social Process," argues that it was the pressure of so many self-proclaimed rights on the part of so many different elements of the population that helped to bring on the Civil War. Against what he calls "majoritarianism," Professor Donald cites Lincoln's appeal to the principles of the Declaration of Independence: "There are some rights upon which no majority, however large or however democratic, might infringe. Lincoln warned that the future of democratic government depended upon the willingness of its citizens to admit moral limits to their political powers. . . . Possibly in time this disorganized society might have evolved a genuinely conservative solution for its problems, but time ran against it." American society, as Professor Donald sees it, was so torn apart by competing interests that it had no resistance to strain.

Certainly nothing about the proslavery argument, as it hardened in the South in the 1850s, ending the comparatively tolerant discussion of slavery that had prevailed until then, now seems so presumptuous and so wrongheaded as the rationalization that what was good for the slaveowner had been fixed for all time by God. Alexander H. Stephens, who before the war had been one of the more moderate Southern spokesmen, announced as vice-president of the Confederacy that the new state rested "upon the great truth that the negro is not equal to the white man, that slavery — subordination to the superior race — is his natural and normal condition. This, our new government, is the first in the history of the world based upon this great physical, philosophical and moral truth." The peculiar irrationality of this insistence on the unchangeable nature of social relationships was to lead the Southern slaveowners to their destruction. Senator L. Q. C. Lamar of Mississippi confessed after the war that he had never entertained a doubt of the Southern system until he found out that slavery could not stand a war. As Lamar said, the fatal "mistake that was made by the Southern defenders of slavery was in regarding it as a permanent form of society instead of a process of emergence and transition from barbarism to freedom."

« 5 »

The rigid assurance that certain people alone knew what all human "destiny" was to be, the delusion that human experience could be fixed forever, was not, of course, limited to slaveowners. It was the mark of an age in which religion hardened in moral rigor as the direct sense of God's presence faded; without its original supernatural element, American Protestantism hardened into self-righteousness for its own sake. The obstinate belief in New England that America was the chosen land, and that here God's promise would be fully revealed again, turned the conflict over slavery into a holy war. With so much at stake in the vast new territories of the West, it was natural for Americans to believe that "man's vast future" lay in their hands. John Bown's favorite maxim was, "Without the shedding of blood there is no remission of sins," and it was of course for the Lord that at the Pottawatomie, in Kansas, Brown took five pro-Southern settlers out of their beds one night and murdered them. Even in his famous last speech to the Virginia court that condemned him for the raid on Harper's Ferry, Brown spoke of himself as having interfered "in behalf of His despised poor . . . Now if it is deemed necessary that I should forfeit my life for the furtherance of the ends of justice and mingle my blood further with the blood of my children and with the blood of millions in this slave country whose rights are disregarded by wicked, cruel, and unjust enactments — I submit; so let it be done!"

When Harriet Beecher Stowe showed her husband the single episode of Uncle Tom being beaten to death (she had conceived it during a communion service in church, in a kind of trance), he said: "Hattie, you must go on with it. You must make up a story with this for a climax. The Lord intends it so." In later life, after the extraordinary world-wide success of *Uncle Tom's Cabin,* she said many times, "The Lord himself wrote it. I was but an instrument in His hand." Yet the remarkable impression produced by *Uncle Tom's Cabin* was due in large part to the fact that until its publication in 1852, hardly anyone in the South had troubled to describe slavery in any detail. A Southern scholar, Professor Jay Hubbell, says that Southern writers were unable to meet the challenge of *Uncle Tom's Cabin* for this reason: "The South, content in the main to get its reading matter from the outside, now paid the penalty for its inability to convince the world that Mrs. Stowe's picture was a biased and distorted one."

As Lincoln is *supposed* to have said, Harriet Beecher Stowe was the little lady who started the great big war. One reason for her effectiveness is that the Southerners, though so much more social-minded and less doctrinaire, so much more fitted for literature, were in fact without much literature of their own. Southern plantation owners looked down on the native literature generally, and preferred to get their reading matter from England; they starved writers of their own like William Gilmore Simms, and when the fear of antislavery agitation finally turned the South into an authoritarian state, with vindictive penalties for anyone teaching Negroes to read and for the dissemination of forbidden literature, the hysterical crisis atmosphere it developed was as injurious to literature as a totalitarian atmosphere usually is. While Simms was being snubbed in Charleston for his lower-class origins, the fire-eater William Lowndes Yancey boasted that the South did not need literature: "Our poetry is our lives; our fiction will come when truth has ceased to satisfy us; and as for our history, we have made about all that has glorified the United States."

« 6 »

The Civil War was the greatest trauma that the American people had ever known. For more than a decade it had been gathering itself up, threatening to descend; yet even now, as one reads the exhaustive account of the coming of war in Nevins's *The Ordeal of the Union* and *The Emergence of Lincoln*, again following the bitter debates up and down the land, the violence in Kansas, the submission of three weak Presidents to the slave power, one has the curious sense that the outcome is still undecided, that the war may yet not take place.

When the war did begin with the firing on Sumter, and Whitman, staring incredulously at the headlines in the flaring light of a New York street, realized that the unthinkable had happened, a wave of horror and outraged patriotic emotion passed though the North. It was then that Whitman became the national poet that up to then he had merely claimed to be. In 1862, hearing that his brother George was wounded, Whitman went down into Virginia and saw the amputated legs and hands and arms on the tables, saw soldiers staggering back into Washington after battle to collapse in the streets. Now he was at last able to turn his songs of innocence into his book of experience. There is no better book on the Civil War than *Specimen Days*, Whitman's great diary of his observations and experiences as a volunteer nurse in the hospitals of Washington; his art here becomes a model of the rapid, casual brush stroke, the detached, consciously homely touch that was to characterize the new realistic literature that came out of the war. It is strange how little this great prose book of Whitman's is read, though in many respects it has the virtues of Whitman's poetry without the false touches. *Specimen Days* is a book that Whitman did not plan to write but that chose him: its subject took him by the throat, rushed him along, molded his style to perfection without giving him time to dawdle about style.

Out of his war experiences Whitman developed a new kind of impressionistic verse form whose very titles breathe the movement he described in these poems themselves — "A Sight in Camp in the Daybreak Gray and Dim," . . . "As Toilsome I Wander'd Virginia's Woods" — poems that preserve the freshness of Winslow Homer's classic pencil sketches done in the field. Whitman's own literary sketches, with their unforgettable ink-smudged description of Washington streets and hospitals, of Southern prisoners being marched up Pennsylvania Avenue, and of Union prisoners looking like concentration-camp victims as they came out of Andersonville, make up an incomparable document of the time.

Except for Whitman, none of the major American writers had any direct experience of the war. Henry James had incurred his mysterious back injury; Howells was in Venice as consul, and Henry Adams was secretary to his father, the ambassador at London. Mark Twain had the short and almost furtive experience as a volunteer in the Confederate militia that he later facetiously described in "The Private History of a Campaign That Failed." There are, of course, unforgettable passages on the war by Captain Oliver Wendell Holmes, Jr., who said that "In our youth our hearts were touched with fire. It was given us to learn at the outset that life is a profound and passionate thing."

Of the great American writers who lived through the war but did not participate in it, perhaps none has left a more touching record than Herman Melville, whose *Battle-Pieces and Aspects of the War* (1866), the poems of a great writer virtually retired from prose fiction, "originated in an impulse imparted by the fall of Richmond. . . . I have been tempted to withdraw or modify some of them, fearful lest in presenting, though but dramatically and by way of a poetic record, the passions and epithets of civil war, I might be contributing to a bitterness which every sensible American must wish at an end . . ."

One of Melville's least-known poems, describing the view from his rooftop over East Twenty-sixth Street, New York, during the terrible Draft Riots of 1863, brings home a despair of the democracy in which Whitman, at least in his published writings, never lost faith and which Lincoln recognized, in its promise for all men, as the root of war. Melville assailed as rats the rough street crowds who were burning and looting, and in the light of the flames rising over many streets in New York, he affirmed that stoic and classical distrust of human nature that is so familiar in his greatest writings. Yet Whitman, trudging through the hospitals with his little gifts of oranges and notepaper, felt that the war had somehow justified and vindicated the democratic dream, that the war had established forever the matchless reserves of courage and hope in the average man.

Slavery ended before the war did. Even in the Confederacy, Jefferson Davis recognized that slavery would have to be abolished, although, as Lincoln said in his second inaugural, neither side "anticipated that the *cause* of the conflict might cease with or even before the conflict itself should cease." Lincoln plainly named slavery as the cause of the conflict; he said that slavery was "the offense" through which the war had come. What other cause could there have been but slavery, the contradiction of democracy which made it impossible for other men to be free? In later times, as the heat of the war cooled down, it became easy for historians to argue that slavery was not the cause of the war, since most people, even in the North, had certainly not been against it. But if most people in the North were not against slavery, slavery was certainly against the freedom of most people in the North. There is a curious, statistical way of thinking today which claims that the cause of a conflict must be something that most people are consciously aware of and want to go to war for. But the deepest interests are often those which we are not entirely conscious of, issues we cannot escape.

The Negro was such an issue and he remains one. So long as he was a slave, no one else in America was really free. As soon as people even anticipated his freedom, they had to look further and anticipate his becoming a citizen like themselves. So Allan Nevins is right when he says, at the end of his conclusive review of the events leading up to the Civil War, that the war broke out over slavery *and* the future status of the Negro in America. Look around you.

[1961]

III

Old Boys, Mostly American

Dreiser: The Esthetic of Realism

THE NOVELS of Theodore Dreiser have survived sixty years of complaint against Dreiser. They have survived most of the novels published by the realists of Dreiser's own generation, and they have survived (this would not have seemed so easy a thing to do some years ago) almost all concern with Dreiser himself. They have even survived the epoch of rugged individualism and sexual squeamishness out of which they arose — both of which once seemed so inseparable from his novels that there are still many people who mistakenly believe that Dreiser's novels have lasted only as records of a vanished period.

But a new generation of readers — among them many college students who were born in the 1940s and so cannot remember the New Deal, much less a time when Americans were afraid that railroads might someday dominate the country — has been discovering that Dreiser is one of the few American novelists who have survived into the second half of the twentieth century. We now take it for granted that *Sister Carrie* and *An American Tragedy* stand with *Babbitt*; *The Great Gatsby*; *Winesburg, Ohio*; *The Sound and the Fury*. It is clear that Hemingway, though a far more delicate and accomplished artist than Dreiser, has never written a novel that has the objective power of Dreiser's best books. Dreiser has always stood high with his own. Faulkner has listed him as one of the four or five greatest contemporary novelists; Fitzgerald admired him deeply; even Allen Tate, who is not likely to admire Dreiser for his philosophy or his style, has listed Dreiser among the strongest talents in American fiction. Despite the storms over his books (*Sister Carrie* was kept back by its own publisher in 1900; *The "Genius"* was suppressed for a time) Dreiser has been steadily admired by novelists from Ford Madox Ford to Saul Bellow. Obviously Dreiser would not have survived at all, he would by now have been as dead a novelist as David Graham Phillips or Robert Herrick or Upton Sinclair, if it had not been for his genius. And now that the issues that raged around his books have changed, in some cases are even meaningless to a new generation, it is important to understand what Dreiser's "difficult beauty" consists in.

« 2 »

Dreiser is a particular example of the kind of mysterious strength, the strength with which a writer assimilates his environment, then recoils from it in order to tell a story, that makes the novelist's art possible. Although there were a good many possibilities in the novel that Dreiser never used and perhaps never understood, he grasped, in the symbol of his own drive for success and in the tragic careers of so many individuals in his own family, that the essence of narrative is the illusion of life, the suggestion of truth through the use of fact. However a novelist may create this illusion, it is indispensable. From his first novel, *Sister Carrie*, despite his *personal* commonness and proverbial lack of taste (we are told that Carrie "could scarcely toss her head gracefully" and that Hurtswood worked in "a truly swell saloon"), Dreiser was able to wheel into motion that enormous apparatus for suggestion and illusion that makes us lose ourselves in his books as if each were a profound and tragic experience of our own. The novel, as D. H. Lawrence said, is "the book of life." For more than two hundred years now it has been the only literary form able to suggest the ponderousness, the pressure and force, of modern industrial society. More significantly, it has been the only form, as we can see from novels that have externally so little in common as *Moby-Dick, The Brothers Karamazov, The Sound and the Fury*, that has been able to find objective symbols for that increasing alienation from himself which man has come to feel in a society that is insensitive to the individual and a universe that is wholly indifferent to him.

On both these issues Dreiser is immense. In the wholly commercial society of the early twentieth century, Dreiser caught the banality, the mechanical routine, the ignorance of any larger hopes, precisely because he was able to recognize the significance of his own experience. Dreiser was never a "realist" in the pseudo-objective style that has been developed by American muckraking, advertising and sociology. The facts dredged up by impersonal "research" are often dubious and quickly dated, whereas the sheer web of fact that Dreiser put together about clothes, house furnishings and finance fifty years ago retains its interest for us today. Dreiser was an artist who operated with the *facts* of a new era because he saw them as instruments of human destiny. He saw man, man naked as he essentially is, playing with skyscrapers, trains, stocks and bonds, the costumes that man wears in our time. Only an imagination which can see the circumstances of life as significant accidents, which can portray the vulnerability of the human person under the pressure of social fact, can really portray the limited but unmistakable area of determinism within which we operate. What makes Dreiser's novels so extraordinarily "real" is his ability to make us aware that the world was not always like this, that it is not entirely like this even now.

The sense for the hidden dimension with which a true imagination always sees the present fills Dreiser's first novels with unforgettable images of the rawness of Chicago on the eve of the twentieth century. A recurrent symbol in Dreiser's work is the prairie left on the outskirts of Chicago, where the few houses look like sentinels. This is the picture of Chicago in *Sister Carrie*, which opens with a young girl on a train coming into the city; this is the Chicago that is seen by the magnate Frank Cowperwood, the millionaire hero of *The Financier* (1912) and *The Titan* (1914), who, when he moves on to Chicago after his bankruptcy and imprisonment in Philadelphia, rises to the possibilities of the city with wonder and admiration. In *The "Genius,"* the dirty and tumultuous industrial scene around the Chicago River is the material which Eugene Witla discovers as a newspaper artist and which develops into his original and successful paintings of the modern city scene. This recurrent image of coming on the big city past lonely prairie houses has its most poignant expression in the second chapter of *Sister Carrie*, and expresses, in the innocence and awkwardness of its heroine, the experience of a whole generation. "The city had laid miles and miles of streets and sewers through regions where, perhaps, one solitary house stood out alone — a pioneer of the populous ways to be. There were regions open to the sweeping winds and rain, which were yet lighted throughout the night with long, blinking lines of gas-lamps, fluttering in the wind. Narrow board walks extended out, passing here a house, and there a store, at far intervals, eventually ending on the open prairie."

In such a passage we recognize that disproportion between man and his world which is one of the themes with which Dreiser is often able to create the sense of actuality. Only a writer who conceives of historical events in terms of personal sensation and emotion, who can describe the peculiar mercilessness of industrial society as an inarticulated experience in the human heart, can create for us a sense of the "times":

> Carrie looked about her, very much disturbed and quite sure that she did not want to work here. Aside from making her uncomfortable by sidelong glances, no one paid her the least attention. She waited until the whole department was aware of her presence. Then some word was sent around, and a foreman, in an apron and shirt sleeves, the latter rolled up to his shoulders, approached.
>
> "Do you want to see me?" he asked.
>
> "Do you need any help?" said Carrie, already learning directness of address.
>
> "Do you know how to stitch caps?" he returned.
>
> "No, sir," she replied.
>
> "Have you had any experience at this kind of work?" he inquired.
>
> She answered that she had not.
>
> "Well," said the foreman, scratching his ear meditatively, "we do need a stitcher. We like experienced help, though. We've hardly got time to break people in." He paused and looked away out of the window. "We might, though, put you at finishing," he concluded reflectively.
>
> "How much do you pay a week?" ventured Carrie, emboldened by a certain softness in the man's manner and his simplicity of address.
>
> "Three and a half," he answered.
>
> "Oh," she was about to exclaim, but she checked herself and allowed her thoughts to die without expression.
>
> "We're not exactly in need of anybody," he went on vaguely, looking her over as one would a package.

It is not Dreiser's laborious concern with external facts — the gas-lamps in the wind, the heaviness of clothes, the lights of the saloon in *Sister Carrie*, the brokerage business in *The Financier*, Chicago street-car franchises and big-city politics in *The Titan*, advertising and magazine publishing in *The "Genius"* — that creates this kind of "reality"; it is Dreiser's inability to take anything for granted: it is his usual sense of wonder at the dense, peopled, factual world itself. The great realists have always been those for whom the "real" world is always strange, who are fascinated by the commercial and industrial world because they know that this world is not *theirs*. For Dreiser the emotion of the provincial Carrie in the big city has become a powerful ingathering symbol of the interest and fascination of a society that, by reducing everyone in it to a feeling of complicity and powerlessness, makes *everyone* feel provincial. Only a writer like Theodore Dreiser, to whom success in the external world and some understanding of man's destiny were equal passions, could have created such unforgettable images of man's homelessness in both society and the universe at large as Dreiser did when he described Carrie rocking in her chair, or Cowperwood in prison looking up at the stars with a sense that he was no more strange to the world of infinite space than he felt himself to be to the conventional world of marriage and business. It has not always been noticed that it is precisely the imagination that sees modern society as a gigantic accident, as a paradigm of the infinite and indifferent universe, which creates, in the burning and vivid metaphors of Dreiser, Zola, Hardy, the feeling of truth about society. Without this necessary perspective, without some sense of wonder, or opposition, or fancy on the part of the realistic novelist, society gets so much taken for granted that it can no longer be fairly *seen;* and indeed this is exactly what has happened in many contemporary novels, where the concern with purely personal or sexual themes betrays a lack of perspective, of serious intention on the part of the novelist.

Dreiser's love of documentation, his naïve passion for "facts," recalls the poetic intent behind Whitman's "inventories" of modern city scenes. Dreiser attempts to create a sense of the material structure of modern life in much the same way that Whitman, in "Song of Myself," itemizes in quick detail the "blab of the pave, tires of carts, sluff of boot-soles, talk of the promenaders." As in Whitman, the external world is portrayed for its interest as *spectacle*, yet remains one to which man feels connected. Dreiser still writes in the spirit of the nineteenth-century discovery of evolution: nothing moves him so much as the realization that man has always been a part of nature. The concern with outward "reality" is one that contemporary novelists often reject in an age when the novel may seem as abstract as today's all-powerful science of physics. Dreiser was wholly under the influence of nineteenth-century biology and social philosophy. For him man is indissolubly part of the natural world itself: the order of nature reflects man's personal emotions in the same way that his fellow human beings, who belong to the same species as himself, reflect his longings and his weaknesses. Dreiser was able to portray modern society as an organism precisely because he recognized that although it did not always satisfy human aspirations, society itself was a natural growth: it expressed sexuality, greed, social ambition, in forms that are natural to man. In Dreiser's novels men like Drouet and Hurstwood, Frank Cowperwood and Eugene Witla can almost for the first time identify themselves with each other because they already identify themselves with plants and animals. And they make the identification in a way that conveys both the truth of the resemblance and the uncertainty about its purpose which plagues man's awareness of the natural process.

This sense of modern society as itself biological and evolutionary attains in Dreiser's novels a glow of romantic exaltation, a suggestion that everything in the universe is alive and seeking new shape. It is hard to think of other American novelists who have described this as powerfully as Dreiser does when he introduces Carrie to Chicago, Eugene Witla to New York, and Clyde Griffiths to Kansas City: the sense we carry away of infinite reverberations in society is the greatest achievement of *The Financier* and *The Titan.* The bias of Dreiser's fellow "naturalists," as we can see in Stephen Crane's masterpiece, "The Open Boat," and in Frank Norris's best book, *McTeague*, was in favor of the *reductio ad absurdum:* life must be portrayed in such strong terms as to seem positively hostile to man. Dreiser, who shares their philosophy, nevertheless identified the world with his own ambition and his compassion, and this is why one recognizes a maturity of involvement in Dreiser's work that is very different from the self-conscious stylization in Crane and the essentially patronizing and abstract manner of Norris. The truth is that for many writers, the philosophy of naturalism was a way of rationalizing their own indifference and apathy, their typically modern sense of alienation. For Dreiser, on the other hand, this "scientific" philosophy actually played the role that evolution had for romantic pantheists like Emerson and Whitman: naturalism provided a way of binding himself more firmly to the world.

Dreiser sees the modern scene much as did the tender realists of the "ash-can" school of painters who discovered the beauty of the big city; he is not one of the pseudo-Nietzschean naturalists, like Jack London or Frank Norris, who mixed their toughness with romance; nor is he in the least a crusader, like Upton Sinclair and many proletarian novelists of the 1930s, for whom a novel was a description of things to be eradicated. Dreiser's loving realism is directed toward an urban world that is always various and colorful. Even Frank Norris's *McTeague* ends in a scene of such melodramatic claptrap — the hero in Death Valley chained to the enemy he has just killed — that we can see that for Norris the height of feeling was to show the world as the ironic enemy of man's hopes, tricking him. Dreiser, on the contrary, writes as a contemplative, one who finds the significance of the external scene through his personal attachment to it.

« 3 »

The nearest analogy to Dreiser's "personal" realism is to be found in the painter Edward Hopper, who shares Dreiser's passion for transcendentalist writers, for images of trains and roads. Despite his similar choice of "ordinary" subjects, Hopper has written that his aim "has always been the most exact transcription possible of my most intimate impressions of nature." One critic has said that Hopper's pictures — a silent city street early on a Sunday morning, a Victorian house by a railroad track, an usherette musing in the corridor of a movie theater — are astonishingly poignant "as if they were familiar scenes solemnly witnessed for the very last time." One feels in the awkwardness, the dreaming *stillness* of Hopper's figures, the same struggle to express the ultimate confrontation of men and things that one does in Dreiser's reverent description of saloons, street-cars, trains, hotels, offices. The beauty of such realism, which contrasts with the photographic exactness of a Charles Sheeler, is inevitably allied to a certain pathos. Just as in *An American Tragedy* one feels about Clyde Griffiths's exultant discovery of hotel luxury the pitiful distance between the boy and the social world of tawdry goods that he is trying to win, so in Hopper's street scenes and lonely offices one can visualize the actual unrelatedness between men and the objects they use every day. It is one of the paradoxes of modern art that the more "external" and ordinary the object portrayed — a city street in Hopper, the complex record of a stock deal in Dreiser — the more personal is the emotion conveyed. The emotion consists in exactly this surprise of attachment to the world that so often dwarfs us. *An American Tragedy* begins unforgettably with a picture of a small missionary family in a big city, engulfed by the tall walls in its commercial heart; Sister Carrie is stupefied by the immensity of Chicago, and, when she asks for work at Speigelheim and Company, is looked over by the foreman "as one would a package"; even Cowperwood, magnetic and powerful as he is, is surrounded by "the endless shift of things," first in Philadelphia, then in Chicago. But it is the haunting feeling for objects that the hero of *The "Genius,"* a painter, conveys in his pictures of the Chicago River, the muddy industrial stream that significantly moves Witla to a "panegyric on its beauty and littleness, finding the former where few would have believed it to exist." Later in New York, Eugene does a picture of Greeley Square in a drizzling rain, catching "the exact texture of seeping water on gray stones in the glare of various electric lights. He had caught the values of various kinds of lights, those in cabs, those in cable cars, those in shop windows, those in the street lamp — relieving by them the black shadows of the crowd and of the sky." This might be a picture by Alfred Stieglitz. Despite the personal vulgarity and tinsel showiness in Dreiser's style, his fundamental vision of things is always the artist's.

Yet beyond this sensitivity to the once realized beauty of the modern city, Dreiser's greatest strength is as a dramatist of human relations. Although his narrative technique, especially in chronicle novels like *The Financier* and *The Titan,* often becomes mechanical, in alternating chapters describing Cowperwood's love affairs and business deals, Dreiser's curiously unconscious masterliness is emphasized by the way he virtually devours a subject. When Dreiser is bad, it is never because of the slowness or literalness of his technique; it is because of the imposition of a purely subjective emotion, as in parts of *The "Genius."* In Dreiser the writer was *always* wiser than the man. When his instinctive transformative powers fail him, when he imposes on the reader great blobs of incoherent personal emotion, one recognizes how silly the man Theodore Dreiser could be. An example is the tasteless endearments that Eugene Witla addresses to young Suzanne Dale. What made Dreiser powerful in *Sister Carrie* and *Jennie Gerhardt,* where he used the stories of his own sisters, was his ability to see his own family in historic and histrionic roles, exactly as if he had visualized them in dreams. In the Cowperwood novels, it was his candid self-identification with massive creatures of power, who represented the fulfillment of his own social yearnings to be, in twentieth-century terms, a hero. Even more, Cowperwood, of all Dreiser's many sensuous heroes, was able to convey best the humanity of Dreiser's own feeling for women, his exalted sense of their beauty—which Dreiser represented equally in Cowperwood's love of painting. In *The "Genius,"* however, Dreiser was writing too close to the bone of his marital troubles; the objective sympathy that had been available to him in describing his heroines, or in modeling Cowperwood on an American magnate of the period, Charles T. Yerkes, broke down because of his own notorious lack of humor. It is an interesting fact that one of the most powerful scenes in *The "Genius,"* the birth of Eugene Witla's child, seems to have had no parallel in Dreiser's life. On the other hand, Dreiser's maudlin descriptions of Eugene in love, even of Eugene's earlier breakdown and his odd success in advertising and publishing, *are* all based on Dreiser's life, and it is these scenes that are handled with that showiness of emotion which afflicted Driser's writing whenever he moved out of his natural orbit as a storyteller into too personal and confessional a tone.

It is this clumsiness in *The "Genius"* that explains why Dreiser's work is so often identified with pedestrian novelists of his own generation. Yet the theme of the book is significant, for Dreiser is always concerned with eroticism. Despite the many attacks on his books, this side of Dreiser's work is undervalued, for in his old-fashioned way Dreiser connects sex with money and social ambition. It is this connection that leads Clyde Griffiths to his death in *An American Tragedy,* as it is this that leads Hurstwood in *Sister Carrie* to rob his employer; one can see the connection even in Frank Cowperwood, who despite his immense personal authority, his fortune, his undeviating attraction to so many women, must himself go from woman to woman in a yearning for that "refinement," that ultimate "spell of beauty," which would represent a social victory higher than anything in Philadelphia or Chicago. The fact is that Dreiser is one of the most cogent novelists of sex we have had—so long as he sticks to the inescapable involvement of women, money and power, or can reveal a compassion for women that shows us such very different victims in Carrie, Jennie Gerhardt, and the utterly innocent Roberta Alden. In Dreiser compassion is as strong an emotion as lust. Compassion as a source of sexual emotion is so rarely expressed in contemporary novels that it is important to emphasize how different Dreiser is in this from the aggressive realists of our day. (John O'Hara in books like *A Rage to Live* imposes a masculine psychology on his women characters.) It is Dreiser's compassionate sense of what women themselves are likely to feel that explains why Carrie, who has seemed commonplace to many unsympathetic readers, and whose perverse success in life enraged old-fashioned moralists, figured for Dreiser himself as a true heroine of the modern world. "In your rocking-chair, by your window, shall you dream such happiness as you may never feel." Dreiser was able to portray not only the kind of woman who was the "prize," the "lure," for a man making his way up (Suzanne Dale in *The "Genius,"* Sondra Finchley in *An American Tragedy*), but he was able to show that a woman like Carrie could dazzle an ambitious man like Hurstwood and yet within herself remain a solitary and bewildered child still trying to understand the world that looked so inhuman when she first had come on it in Chicago.

« 4 »

The real objection that must be considered against Dreiser's work refers to more than his occasional vulgarity of style or to the naïveté with which he often furnishes a room. The force of the objection lies in the contrast between unassimilated actuality—the purely personal-historical portrait that Dreiser so often achieved—and what Henry James, who insisted on the novel as a wholly realized art form, called a "situation." James unfavorably compared fiction which gives us a "case" with fiction that presents a "situation," where the novelist can display so many connections with life at large that the form of the novel becomes a "reflection . . . to one's sense of life in general." Dreiser certainly does think of each of his novels as a "case." *Sister Carrie* is so rooted in reminiscent emotion, one critic has commented, that Dreiser wrote it as if he were taking down a vision; "it was something like translating the Golden Plates." *The Financier* and *The Titan* naturally became the case history of an individual in the setting of time which the hero helped to make. *The "Genius"* is again the portrait of a single man, and even *An American Tragedy,* though it is the one Dreiser title that might be taken to refer to more than an individual, is essentially the "history" of Clyde Griffiths. Henry James would not, in theory, have objected to Dreiser's material, or even to the style of a writer he might conceivably have accepted as "our American Balzac"—a type of which he saw the necessity, and from which he sadly excluded himself because of inadequate knowledge of American business. James's objection would have been that all of Dreiser's work, to use the titles of two books of Dreiser's stories, is either a gallery of men or a gallery of women. We feel the "case," the individual within the drama of history; the individual is surrounded by the actuality of experience, but we do not find the well-made novel that was James's ideal: one in which the plot and the subtlety of its development give us the sense that the situation is primary, and that everything which gives us pleasure in a novel—place, character, action—has been joined to bring about a singleness of effect.

Dreiser does not meet these specifications. When we read him, we are aware not only of the unevenness of style and intelligence that we get even in so strong a book as *Sister Carrie,* but we also discover that Dreiser's interest is in the individual within the immense struggle and pathos of historical circumstances. Sometimes, as in the Cowperwood novels, the individual has the strength to rise above these circumstances; usually, as in *An American Tragedy,* he falls entirely out of life. When we read Dreiser we are also aware of "extricable" meanings; we never forget the underlying pressure of life on him: there is always a sense of issues, of historical personages thinly disguised, of an actual murder trial and the newspaper reports of it, as in *An American Tragedy.* By the time we finish any Dreiser novel, the grit of actual life has got into the fine machinery of the novel, and we are left not with the worked-out "situation" but with case after case—Carrie, Hurstwood, Jennie Gerhardt, Frank Algernon Cowperwood, Eugene Witla, Clyde Griffiths, Roberta Alden. . . . In the end, the supposedly "pessimistic" novelist of determinism, of the ruthless social process, has really given us an extraordinarily large gallery of individuals who are symbolically divided from their society and who in one way or another evade its claim to full domination over them.

It is this essential solitariness that lingers in our imagination, and that gives us our conviction of Dreiser's lasting value. Undeniably, it is not the "situation" of art but the "case" of history itself, as it afflicts the individual, that is the ruling image in Dreiser. In fact, we cannot help admiring Dreiser for exactly those insights that James suggested were fundamental to the novel, when he said early in his career that the novelist succeeds to the "sacred office" of the historian. We think of Dreiser's work as a series of indelible episodes in the moral history of twentieth-century man; we cannot help being aware of an interest outside of the novelistic "situation" itself. But more than this, we are aware that we feel this historical interest because, when we read Dreiser, we are directed to it by his art. In the classic way of art, the issue, the moment, the historical drama, all have been fused to give us an image of the human person that has outlasted the issues themselves. Without the "case," we would by now have little sense of the times themselves; these individuals are by now out of time precisely because they have been caught so well in time. May it be, then, that the real objection we feel to the "case" technique is that Dreiser makes us feel the solitude of the individual even in society, the individual ultimately undetermined by "forces," outside the net of facts? May it be that in Dreiser we see the human soul, though almost crushed by circumstances, nevertheless irreconcilably free of them, its own freedom made clear in the light of inarticulate longing?

The truth is that Dreiser's books belong to a period of literature in which the individual is still large, epochal, heroic — not crushed. What gives his characters stature is not what *they* accomplish in history (only Cowperwood has creative force, but his actions are morally dubious) but what one may call their innocence: they can never become nonentities, for as provincials in the city they have too much to think about. More and more the contemporary novel is stocked with individuals who have nothing to think about except themselves, and who in their dullness justify the mechanical psychology with which they are conceived. They are engulfed, they have been taken over, they hardly exist. Dreiser's individuals are *large* because they still have an enormous capacity for suffering — and for realizing their suffering. In their defenselessness they recapture the reality of the human person. They are so alone that we watch with awe what is happening to them. We are entranced, because we are watching a social process that in Dreiser's novels, despite what he *says,* is not yet finished, that may turn out another way. We watch with admiration because we know that despite Dreiser's philosophy, Dreiser's novels prove that history does not simply ride over man but is in some sense an expression of him. In creating history, in suffering it, man becomes vivid; there, however we may change, is the unmistakable light of reality itself.

[1959]

The Mystery of Gertrude Stein

YEARS AGO in Italy, I met Gertrude Stein's brother Leo, a vividly eccentric man as interesting for his many crotchets as he was on the subject of his sister. She had died the year before, but he still talked about her with lively resentment. Leo Stein was fascinating to be with, one long day in Settignano and Florence, for he had known many of the painters and poets who created "modern" art in the great years just before the First World War, and he was flavorsomely himself — honest, cranky, neurotic, gossipy, and above all ruminative. To meet him was to be given instant access to everything he was thinking at the moment. He not only shared his meditations with you; he made you feel like a psychoanalyst and brain surgeon invited to poke at his mental insides. He was such an original that you couldn't help wondering what it was that had held him back so long, that had kept him at seventy-five so bitterly jealous of his famous sister.

Afterwards, when I turned to some of Leo Stein's critical essays,

The Third Rose, by John Malcolm Brinnin. Boston: Little, Brown and Company. An Atlantic Monthly Press book.

I discovered that it was almost impossible to read him. A desperate juvenile conceit shone out of everything he said, and I remembered his hints that privately he had hit upon many of the most influential insights in contemporary psychology and esthetics, but that he had lacked the concentration — or narrowness of interest, as he allowed you to infer — that had permitted others to make their fame out of such discoveries. The trouble with Leo Stein, I discovered, was that although, in the course of his long self-analysis, many fleeting glimpses of higher things than himself had crossed his mind, he did not know how to work up these ideas, for they were too much attached to himself. Like everyone who is really outside of things, he could function only on the single plane of logicality. He was like Robinson Crusoe stolidly piling one piece of driftwood on another to make a habitation; he thought that he could reason himself into self-confidence, into greatness — in any field. And operating in the same way, he reasoned himself into the belief that not only was he stupendously intelligent, and so could have been a great painter, a great philosopher, a great scholar, but also that other people (like sister Gertrude) were just dumb.

Now sister Gertrude was anything but dumb, and unlike her brother Leo she did not (at least not with strangers) show so many cracks in her armor. She achieved for herself the fame of mental independence, of leadership in the world of art and intellect, that Leo Stein always dreamed of. He must have realized that but for her he would have been overlooked. Yet his real bitterness — that someone as endlessly analytical as himself should have succeeded in one field where he failed in all — was surely misplaced. For if anything is clear about Gertrude Stein's work today, it is that in the great mass of her work she, like her brother, is unreadable; that her work is now a curiosity, and has no part in our thinking. Mr. Brinnin's book is the best proof of this, for though he has written a book on Gertrude Stein, I cannot see that he gets any more out of her work than most people do. He is engaging and informative on the external social facts of a life lived so much in the creative stream of twentieth-century literature and art, and he is perceptive and deft in his handling of Gertrude Stein's complex personal character. But whenever Mr. Brinnin comes up against her work, it seems to me that he dodges a fundamental problem in connection with it —

whether there is something there that people can read and use; whether the work truly *exists* or not.

« 2 »

In writing about Gertrude Stein it is possible to overlook the possible final significance of her work even when one seems to be writing about the work itself. She figured importantly (and often just self-importantly) in the best writing of the 1920s, and right now can symbolize our nostalgia for past greatness. Mr. Brinnin writes, "Beyond the luster that poets continue to give this literary age, the excitement of books written thirty, forty and fifty years ago are, sad to say, still the only excitements." Say "Gertrude Stein" to a literary intellectual, and he automatically thinks of Hemingway and Picasso. He may keep thinking of Hemingway and Picasso even when he *reads* a little of Gertrude Stein — so fervently has the record of her associations and teachings impressed itself upon everybody, which is what she tried to do by deliberate lucidity in *The Autobiography of Alice B. Toklas* and *Everybody's Autobiography.* And it is perfectly possible to analyze Gertrude Stein's intentions as a writer, to trace the history of her work, without ever coming to grips with the actuality or lack of it in her work. Since she was one of the first to buy Picasso and among the first to appreciate Cézanne, and, as everybody now knows, tried to reproduce in writing certain values of postimpressionist painting, it is possible to discuss her vision, her mode, her intention, as if certain famous pictures themselves gave reality to her work. Mr. Brinnin explains that Gertrude Stein composed her most famous book, *Three Lives,* beneath Cézanne's portrait of his wife — a picture in which the subject is seated in a red chair and wearing a blue dress. Mr. Brinnin, describing her intention, explains that "by a ceaseless flow of half-articulated thoughts, worn phrases of speech and homely inflections from domestic life, she would match Cézanne's iterations of the qualities of light."

Now Mr. Brinnin does not deny that her work is often unsatisfactory. He clearly communicates his exasperation with those lesser works, like *Brewsie and Willie,* that convey her enthusiasm at having been taken up by so many G.I.'s who sought her out in France. Throughout the book he is careful to distinguish between her abstract intentions and actual achievements, and his account of her limitations is certainly correct. As he says, "Perhaps never in all the long association of poets and painters in the same creative climate has a writer attempted with such unabashed literalness to adopt methods springing from the theory and practice of painting. . . . The only course open to literature that would emulate painting was that of contemplating its own structure and image." My objection to his book is not that he overrates her work but that I cannot see a motivating reason for his own book. To write about Gertrude Stein without justifying her work is, at this stage, simply to recall her fashionable doings. Mr. Brinnin manages not only to say all the right things about her work but to hold it at a distance, to make us feel that the work is not pressing, of secondary importance.

One can deliberately understress a writer's work in a biography; it is easy to imagine a romantic biography of F. Scott Fitzgerald that does not discuss his work at all. But the importance of Fitzgerald's work would always be in our minds, would alone justify a biography at all. What, without the same mental weight given to her work, justifies a biography of Gertrude Stein? What is the real interest behind it? Partly, no doubt, it is the record of her associations in Paris before and after the First World War. Familiar as much of this material is, Mr. Brinnin makes a fluent social chronicle out of 27, rue de Fleurus, when Picasso came to call, and Matisse and Hemingway and Fitzgerald and Glenway Wescott and Sherwood Anderson and Virgil Thomson and Thornton Wilder. There is still something glorious and incomparably free about that early period — above all, about the years before the First World War, when modernism had not yet lost its connection with revolutionary thinking in all social and ethical fields, had not yet taken on the desperation of the late 1920s, was a long way from the safe investment in established taste that it has become today.

Yet by now the record of Gertrude Stein's influence on so many famous writers is not only familiar but mysterious. Consider how much she is supposed to have done for others, and how little she ultimately achieved for herself! I would suggest that one reason for her influence is the fact that these writers were usually men, and that despite her spectacular outward lack of female charm, it was as a woman with a deep rudimentary common sense that she influenced so many male writers. Whatever the sterilities and the self-infatuations in her work, she was a woman of extraordinary insight. She understood men who were writers, she understood fellow minds. Her influence was enormous because writers could pick up extraordinary suggestions from her thinking. She studied the world, from her mind as its center, with an intensity that literally made her a stream of consciousness, and writers could find particles of thought anywhere in this stream. Because of her quickness and her social sense, she was able to size up people quickly, and many of her verbal judgments on people — carefully repeated in her more popular books — are unforgettable. She said of a well-known novelist who has been "promising" all his life — "He has a certain syrup, but does not pour."

But if Gertrude Stein herself has become finally unreadable, it is because she did not think in terms of books at all but in orphic sayings, sentences, rhythmic paragraphs that brought home the sound of herself thinking to herself. She was fascinated by ideas, the outlines of things, the possibilities inherent in all subjects, the hidden voice of the individual beneath his social personality. Unlike so many writers today, who see their opportunity only in the generally accepted, she was utterly fearless and tried everything; there was nothing she ever found in her own mind that seemed alien to literature. If courage were the same as creativity, Gertrude Stein would have been Homer. But creativity is a matter of achieving whole works, not of ideas for books or brilliant passages in books. Gertrude Stein could make a Hemingway or Anderson or Fitzgerald — at times even a Picasso — glow with ideas. But when she sat down to write, she let the stream of all her thoughts flow as if a book were only a receptacle of her mind. One came to suspect that her wisdom was more in the realm of theory than of actuality.

Gertrude Stein's genius for suggestion actually stays more with poets than it does with novelists. Poetry, by its very character, deals with a world of essences that can be intimated but not always communicated, and the critical writing of poets is always essentially philosophical. It is noteworthy that Mr. Brinnin, a poet himself, thinks that the only luster today in literature comes from poets, and that in writing about Gertrude Stein's work he communicates more enthusiasm for her intentions—which are pure literary ideas—than for her books, which are usually dead novels. Gertrude Stein may have tried to inject into the novel as a form some of the power that poetry always exerts on the unconscious. So did Joyce and Proust. But both these writers were able to carry through epic works. Even *Finnegans Wake,* though often termed a failure except as "poetry," exists as a shape, is connected from the first word to the last, in the way that Gertrude Stein's works never were.

Both Gertrude and Leo Stein were remarkable people. They were remarkable because they visualized for themselves a power that most people never dream of: they saw themselves as conquerors through thought, through pure thought. Leo Stein hoped, by coming to the root of his difficult personality, to unlock his hidden genius as a psychologist and esthetician; Gertrude Stein dreamed of finding the formula that would put all other modern writers behind her. She thought she had found it, and she went on writing with the imperturbable smile on the face of a Buddha; she trusted in her thoughts as if she were Moses tuned in to the Almighty. But the trouble with these pure thinkers in art, criticism, and psychology is that the mind is always an instrument, not its own clear-cut subject matter. No one, not even a Freud, has ever been really sure just what pure mind is; Freud had too much respect for the truth to think that he had found a realm absolutely detachable from everything else. Gertrude Stein's error was not that she thought of herself as a "genius"—who can say what that is?—but that she identified this genius with pure intellect. She even defined a genius as a representative of the human mind, partly because he understands, without submitting to, the force of human nature. Artists, she thought, are slaves to human nature, are bound by resemblances, subject to sorrow, disappointment, and tears. But "the human mind writes what it is . . . the human mind . . . consists only in writing down what is written and therefore it has no relation to human nature." There is the root of the conceit that unheedingly drove her work into a corner. Gertrude Stein had a very good mind. But it was not as good as she thought it was, or else she would not have assumed that literature can be written about nothing but the mind itself.

[1960]

Lady Chatterley in America

RECENTLY Grove Press of New York sent me a copy of *Lady Chatterley's Lover,* the unexpurgated text of Lawrence's third and final version, with an introduction by Mark Schorer and a preface by Archibald MacLeish; on the jacket were admiring testimonies to the book's nobility and lovingness from Jacques Barzun and Edmund Wilson. I hadn't looked at Lawrence's book or thought of it particularly since 1956, when I had bought a copy of the unexpurgated edition in a Stockholm department store, and I was pleased that a young American publisher devoted to twentieth-century literature had had the imagination and the courage to bring out the book in this country for the first time.

I had an errand to do, and was not able to turn to the book immediately. I live in a vaguely middle-class neighborhood of New York, though, in the fashion of middle-class neighborhoods in New York, it is getting slightly "beat," and so I was irritated not more than usually when a group of mingled white and Negro young men, wearing earrings, very tight narrow trousers, with hair greased back into ducktails, swished past.

At the corner newsstand, where I stopped to pick up my afternoon paper, I could hardly see the papers for the sex magazine covers. There were at least a dozen females in languishing poses, so hugely uddered and yet so coyly draped that I marveled at the enormous effort it must take to play peekaboo with curtains, aprons, and blouses. While remembering a friend of mine who writes "serious" stories for one of these magazines and who sent me one, to the inexpressible delight of my eleven-year-old son, who hadn't thought he could decently get to see so much, I noticed that there are now as many homosexual smut magazines as there are heterosexual ones; the number of heavily muscled young men, occasionally arrayed against a Grecian background with hands on their waists, made me wonder what my dour newspaper vender thinks of it all.

But I didn't ask him; I was too busy thinking of some of the contemporary novels I had looked at that week. One was about necrophilia, another on sodomy between priests, a third on incest. Although I had discharged my ideas on the subject in a review of John O'Hara's *From the Terrace,* I was still angry about the misuse of his social talent on idolatrous descriptions of sexual intercourse. However, thinking of some equally talented but much younger writers, I had to admit that in his old-fashioned way O'Hara was still romantic about sex; like Scott Fitzgerald, he thought of it as an upper-class prerogative! By contrast, I recalled Norman Mailer, whom I had seen on television some weeks before explaining, in a discussion with Dorothy Parker and Truman Capote, that the aim of life should be "personal growth," that he admired Fidel Castro for looking "beat," and that it was important to be "good" in bed.

Well, I thought to myself, Lady Chatterley *is* out of date. Wasn't it Kinsey who managed to amass statistics on the number of ejaculations certain men have a week, and to sell this stuff to the public as scientific information? I remembered my students — the Smith sophomore who, in a discussion of Hemingway's characters, tossed her young head contemptuously and announced in a shrill piping voice that they were "afraid of sex." At Amherst, I had discovered, eighteen-year-olds would discuss the homosexuality of Whitman or Hart Crane as soberly and clinically as psychiatrists at a convention.

In England, during the war, I had heard of an American bureaucrat still old-fashioned enough to turn his wife's picture to the wall whenever he brought a girl back for the night; but, standing on Broadway and Eighty-sixth Street on a beautiful April day, I remembered how much my friends and I in college had loved Lawrence, I recalled Blake's insistence,

> What is it men in women do require?
> The lineaments of Gratified Desire.
> What is it women do in men require?
> The lineaments of Gratified Desire,

and I felt unbearably nostalgic, middle-aged, passé. O Lord, I thought to myself, is there no room for old-fashioned rebels who still love Lawrence and Whitman and William Blake and Sigmund Freud? Have the yahoos taken over here, as everywhere: the beatniks with their infernal smirks of frankness, the chorus girls who just adore *Lolita* — it's so cute — the sexologists?

I recalled the *New York Times Book Review* some weeks before, when I had seen ads for half a dozen manuals on "how to achieve sexual competence," and, thinking of the ex-leftist fanatics turned superanalyst wise guys, of all the sniggers, the sex manuals, the dirty magazines, the self-infatuated homosexuals, the incest, the necrophilia, the call girls and their businessmen, I not only felt *démodé*, but glad of it. To hell with sexual "competence" and hurray for the lineaments of gratified desire, for Whitman's "the sweet hell within." Down with competence and up with passion!

Is there anybody, I wondered, hurrying back to my first edition of *Lady Chatterley's Lover*, is there *anybody* in America who could still think of this book as immoral, who could miss Lawrence's romantic-religious, antinomian, ecstatic faith that sex is holy? Is there some police chief in Boston or Sioux City, some postal official in Washington, who, though he may know little enough of Lawrence's seriousness as an artist, may know even less of the actual effect of such books on the mind and think it dangerous? Undoubtedly, I had to admit. Just as the beatniks at one extreme personify the ridiculous ideal of sensation for its own sake, of freedom for the sake of sensation, so there is something about the legal or judicial or clerical mind which assumes that one person can be corrupted by one book — while overlooking the growing development in our culture toward a sexual permissiveness hard to tell from personal desperation, the desperation of juvenile delinquents for whom sex means the thrill of violence. And what would these custodians fix on in this book but certain four-letter words which — while they represent exasperated failure for the unquiet desperation that masses of men feel, lodged together in armies, prisons, ships — represented to D. H. Lawrence, born in 1885 and brought up in the Congregationalist Church, his wistful and hoped-for symbols of a new loving frankness between men and women? Despite the external smut — or rather, because of it and the divisions which it symbolizes in ourselves — there is something about the American mind that is quick to identify what it is afraid of or just ignorant of as "immoral."

Some years ago there came to America a mildly touching Italian film about a weak-minded peasant girl who was seduced by a stranger whom she thought of as "Saint Joseph." The protest line in front of the New York theater carried placards; one of them, never to be forgotten, read: "We give Europe our wealth and they reward us with filth." Was it possible that the same people could identify Lawrence's "daring," his Derbyshire-miner's-son horror of English gentility, with filth — only because he had used certain words, because he believed that "the holiness of the heart's affections" (Keats's phrase) could be realized in sexual intercourse? That *this* would at last be the path of freedom, of sacredness, of a new communion which would give men and women their only refuge from the hated abstractions and constant meddling of modern industrial society? The usual objection to the book, in more genteel times, had been conventional responses to Lawrence's romantic defiance, his cult of love. Was it possible that in our increasingly closed-up world there would now be a serious political objection to human beings who pursued sexual love too strenuously for its own sake? The crime of hero and heroine in Orwell's *1984* was literally that they ignored the state, devoted themselves entirely to each other. So the real crime of Lady Chatterley and her gamekeeper, in 1959, could be that they were not sufficiently "adjusted to the group," that they ignored their "social responsibility," that in devoting themselves wholeheartedly to the act of passion, they were making a contemptuous and unforgettable comment on the triviality and fanaticism of their times.

This "crime" is one of the few lessons of love in contemporary fiction; nowadays a man and a woman meeting to make love make a political criticism which is far more trenchant than the old radicalism. The contempt for ideology that can be expressed by passion, I discovered, is the real sense of *Lady Chatterley's Lover* in 1959. Yet how ironic this could be, the unintended fruitfulness of Lawrence's intelligent genius, since the whole purpose of Lawrence's tract-novel is to establish sexual love as a revolutionary weapon *against* our industrial society! Thus far have we traveled in the West, all of us, in the thirty years since Lawrence finished the final version of his book. Before the hardening pattern of our society set in for good with World War II, men still hoped to change our society, not to escape it. Lawrence is in the great tradition of English and American literary radicals, with Emerson and Thoreau and Whitman as surely as with Blake and the young Wordsworth and Shelley, in his belief that "the holiness of the heart's affections" can revolutionize society, can transform "the mills of Satan," the hated cities, the industrial reek and blackness which Lawrence saw as the enemy of the free human spirit.

« 2 »

This call to the higher powers as revolutionary instrument is indeed the great purpose of *Lady Chatterley's Lover*. It is a novel in praise of love, of physical love's exaltations, that symbolizes the union of the old yeoman stock, personified by Mellors, the gamekeeper, with the best of the English liberal intellectual class. Lady Chatterley was originally Constance Reid, daughter of a Scottish painter and herself a Fabian, and her passion for Mellors is a protest against the incapable and despotic upper classes, in the person of her husband Sir Clifford, who comes back from the war paralyzed from the waist down. Not only is he unable to give his wife a child, but he becomes increasingly selfish, querulous, "proper," as his paralysis comes to include, as a natural part of his experience, the meanness and helplessness of the old English upper classes. For Lawrence's most subtle and penetrating perception (Mark Schorer remarks in his introduction), "the knowledge that social and psychological conflicts are identical, is so firmly integrated in the structure of his book that it is almost foolhardy to speak of his having two themes when in fact he had one vision."

Lawrence is still in the great tradition of the English and American Romantic poets, those Protestant radicals for whom the "living intuitive faculty," the wild and irrepressible call of the spirit, made church authority unnecessary; they automatically interpreted all experience by that belief in the ideal unity of man's faculties which is typical of the religious imagination. Lawrence's novel was an effort to give religious value to relations between the sexes; so the sympathy born of sexual happiness would work itself into every part of life, would militate against the purely external relationships, the increasing deadness, of industrial society.

It is because Lawrence's supreme subject is love, not sex, that he is, in the Romantic tradition, political. His argument, like those of all religious reformers, is personalistic; nothing in the image of society avails against it, for it absorbs and grows on everything like itself. The external side of life in our time is too fierce, heavy, hard; when Lady Chatterley motors through town, the darkness of the industrial Midlands has crept into everything: "the brick dwellings are black with dust, the black slate roofs glisten their sharp edges, the mud is black with coal-dust." Yet life, in its vulnerability, like the newborn chick which the gamekeeper showed his lady — "there it stood, on its impossible little stalks of legs, its atom of balancing life trembling through its almost weightless feet into Connie's hands" — is the only measure of the value that one must preserve; above all, that one can respect. Mellors, who looks so much like Lawrence in his last racked years, fragile and dead-white of body, also represents the physical fragility of man in the present era; he gives himself wholly to passion, but he is also sorely hurt by life and often grumbles at how little passion can do against all those "mental states" absorbed from punishing labor, from the increasing lack of contact with his fellow men, from the habit of separateness and the ease of vice.

Yet Mellors accepts the risks of passion, the beautiful and terrifying involvement to the depths that comes with carnal knowledge, as opposed to the mythomania, the acting out of fantasies, that goes with casual amours and prostitution and smut: "It's life. There's no keeping clear. And if you do keep clear you might almost as well die." He knows, above the harried tenderness that is the message of the novel (and Lawrence's first title for it was *Tenderness*), that an even worse time is coming, that society will never get away from its compulsive outlet in war.

Reading the book in 1959, I recognize the political moral of tenderness, present to Lawrence's mind in 1928, as an alternative still present to us. With all the despondency Lawrence felt in his last illness, he still believed that honest human realization of man's physical needs, a resolute struggle against the spite and hatred that he identified with the purely mental life, could make people freer and more loving in a society visibly corrupted by suspicion and distrust. Yet at the same time every new development in Western industrial society, every ebbing away of the strength and sweetness of the old country life, was proving too much for the individual. The note of quiescence, the drooping away at the end of *Lady Chatterley's Lover* as the lovers, temporarily separated, await their divorces and the birth of their child — this is the natural intermittency of passion. But the long letter from Mellors on which the book closes also brings home to us, as much in Lawrence's novel does, the final insufficiency of a language too strained for the feelings. Lawrence once wrote that "We have no language for the feelings, because our feelings do not even exist for us." That is the measure of his original effort, his stand for integral human nature. Yet it is also true that the increasing sense of love as escape, from the all-enveloping society and passionless conformism, gives *Lady Chatterley's Lover* that slightly hysterical edge which results from too determined an effort to capture the feelings.

Lawrence wrote always with passionate urgency; he succeeded in giving his style the quickness of life, the immediacy of breath, the aroused physical rhythm of passion itself. But the more his fatal illness pressed on him, the more he tried to evoke in language those states of feeling, of sexual arousement and ecstasy, which are more successfully revealed by indirection and compression. It is folly to think that words, even D. H. Lawrence's words, can ever get to the heart of passion. The language of mystics is often unbearable in the tension, the verbal effort to tear through the external surface; if words could even begin to suggest the Divine Presence, the mystic would not have to work so hard at language.

Lawrence's rushing, swift, extraordinarily keen language for sensations often creates a splendid reality in language, the reality of a poem, which is parallel to the love-making ecstasy it seeks to describe and actually conceals from us. The more one studies art, the more one recognizes that it is not an imitation of life, that it never comes close to actual human experience, but is an independent creation, an addition to nature rather than a description of it. Language so passionate and breathless as Lawrence's ultimately describes the ecstasy of art, not of passion. To the ultimate of passion — fortunately! — there is no bridge in the language of mental consciousness.

Lawrence is not pornographic, as snoopers and censors and moralists would charge; in one sense he is not even "real." The excitement of the best scenes in *Lady Chatterley's Lover*, and these are not always the love scenes, lies in the beauty with which life is praised. Lawrence is so naturally religious about experience, his motivating purpose is so naturally the Protestant's exultant identification of his single consciousness with life itself, that behind the flowing freedom and ease of his prose is the stirring of language itself, the individual's embrace of life as he extends his private feelings to external nature. It is an ironic and beautiful fact that the very excess of religious spirit that led Lawrence to identify sex with the Holy Ghost exposed him to the hostility of moralists who believe that sex should be kept in its place. Of course Lawrence made too much of sex, as he made too much of life; we do not have the same keen sense of value. In an age when most writers lack that overwhelming responsibility for the whole human community which Lawrence had, it is Lawrence's overinsistence, his inability to think of sex as partial or furtive, that is likely to produce the characteristic response today that he is naïve rather than dirty.

In this sense, *Lady Chatterley's Lover is* out of date, for Lawrence's last great effort to establish love as a counteravailing power in our society offers us a conception of the novel, as of the sacred symbol of love-making, that is too much for the diminished individual, too lyrical, too unabashed, too free. The external niceness that we have come to value ever since Henry James put the seal of "form" on the contemporary novel militates against Lawrence. So does our belief in psychology as determinism, since to us love is helpless and compulsive. So does the sheer lack in America of that rural mystery, the old English wood in which the lovers make love. Lawrence's exultant, almost unbearably sensitive descriptions of the countryside can mean little to Americans, for whom the neighborhood of love must be the bathroom and the bedroom, both the last word in sophisticated privacy.

Lawrence's descriptions of the naked lovers gamboling in the rain, his ability to describe a woman's sensations and a man's body with feminine sureness — all this belongs to another world. *Lady Chatterley's Lover* brings back memories of a time when men still believed in establishing freedom as their destiny on earth, when sex was the major symbol of the imprisoned energies of man, for when *that* castle was razed, life would break open and flow free.

[1959]

The Youngest Man Who Ever Was

IMAGINE that you have just entered college, that you were born in 1941 or 1942, and that you have never or just barely heard of Ezra Pound, an elderly American poet who now lives in Italy. The textbook assigned to you in freshman composition is the present collection of documents — "The Case Of Ezra Pound: Pro And Con Selections Intended to Be Used as Controlled Source Material for the Freshman English Course." It is a remarkable collection; there is nothing like it anywhere else, for here you can read even the citation of his alma mater, Hamilton College, when it gave Pound an honorary degree. Included are newspaper and magazine stories on the case, the official medical report of 1945 by psychiatrists at St. Elizabeth's Hospital in Washington declaring Pound "insane and mentally unfit for trial," a reminiscence by a former editor of *Poetry* magazine on listening to Pound's broadcasts in England while waiting for D-Day, a remarkable memoir by a soldier who was one of Pound's guards when he was kept in a special wire cage in disciplinary barracks near Pisa, the statement of the judges who awarded Pound the Bollingen Award for the best book of poetry published in 1948, a sampling of the literary controversy, observations of Pound in the mental hospital, documents and statements on Pound's eventual release last year and return to Italy.

Now, students, when you have read the documents in the case you will of course write a paper, and in the back of this excellently arranged and thoughtful book you will find "Topics for Research Exercises." The editors explain that "All the topics below can be developed in 300-1000 words from the documents in this volume, but students should be encouraged to extend their investigations with the resources of the library." By all means extend your investi-

A *Casebook of Ezra Pound*, edited by William Van O'Connor and Edward Stone. New York: Thomas Y. Crowell Company.

gations! Still, only a few of you freshmen will actually extend them, and it is only these rare ones who will be puzzled or made unhappy by the case of Pound; the more you look into it, the more puzzled you will be.*

All other students, being clever enough to get into college anyway, will recognize this book as another aberration of the middle-aged professors who have unbelievable and inaccessible memories of the revolutionary 1930s and apocalyptic 1940s. Being sensible boys and girls, you will read the documents in the case as if you understood them, and on the basis of this one book you will write your little research papers, report your own opinions pro and con as if you knew all about the case, and drop Pound just in time to become sophomores.

History, someone said, is written by the survivors, but it has to be arranged so that freshmen can come to grips with it. In an "American problems" course I once taught, apple-cheeked youngsters, after listening to a few outside lectures on transcendentalism and after reading one pamphlet made up of highly selected passages on and about Emerson and Thoreau, had to write a paper defending or attacking the actual course of opinion that these writers followed. Of course most students had no real opinion, just as they had no direct knowledge; but I remember with admiration how well they impersonated understanding.

So the case of Ezra Pound, poet and madman, the author of some of the most beautiful lyrics in twentieth-century English poetry, who celebrated Nazi massacres as "fresh meat on the Russian steppes," becomes a research topic for kids who were just getting born when Pound was broadcasting his useless, idiotic, unintelligible, and often obscene messages to the great democracy "held captive" by Franklin D. Roosevelt. It is not a fault that these kids were born in 1941 or 1942, or that these days in America it is often unfashionable for young

* Ezra Pound could be a beautiful poet, in dribs and drabs of isolated lyric pieces. His real gift is for pastiche. He has imitated the Greeks, the Chinese, and finally his own youth. But he has always been obsessed; for a number of years he was clearly insane, and what makes him puzzling — if you really look into him — is his manic oscillation between savagery and tenderness, between real insight and phony scholarship. Any man of good will *must* be divided about Pound. For myself, surrounded as I am by inexpungible memories of the millions of dead, I cannot think of the purely literary case made out for Pound without horror.

people to have a normal share in the memories of older people. Young people have learned that the 1930s were seditious and the 1940s a mistake, and they have conveniently developed amnesia about dangerous times. (But it is amazing how quickly their *feelings* can be stirred on issues, like the New Deal, on which they are supposed to have no data.) Nor can we criticize Messrs. Stone and O'Connor for drawing up so useful a collection of documents — on the contrary! But it is worthwhile to remember, while a few of us are still around to oppose the truth to the "facts," that these documents cannot convey the anguish and folly of the "Pound case" to freshmen. And oddly enough, for all the students who will be mystified by Pound the dogged Bohemian and official traitor, there will be many more, missing the real shame and horror of the case, who will be delighted with his example of manic courage, his jazzy directness, his frenetic style.

To many young people Pound could re-emerge as an aged hipster and clown, a man who all his life has defied conventional authority and been agin the government. I once discovered in a Southern college that from the hospital Pound kept up a constant correspondence with the literary set. His notes, always referring to himself as "Ez," written in his well-known telegraphic style, full of obscene puns and heavy attacks on their teachers and the ruling literary scholars of the day, delighted these students. What a change! They were excited by his sauciness, his freshness, his profane and nervous style. From one point of view, "Ez" was someone who had never grown respectable, who had kept all his life the perpetual air of defiance that is so necessary to young people. Both as a poet and teacher, Pound has always, on principle, been against everything in sight. It is interesting to note that the famous beard which in the early 1900s got him fired from his teaching jobs for being "too Latin Quarter," the beard which at one time seemed the very flag of the *avant-garde,* has in our time become the symbol of pseudo-orphic jazz musicians and the beatniks.

Pound was the youngest young man who ever was; Nathaniel Weyl reports that shortly after Ehrlich discovered the "magic bullet" — 606 — Pound wanted to take his old friend William Carlos Williams with him to the North Coast of Africa. "He thought there were enough syphilitic chieftains there so that they could both make a fortune and retire within a year to write poetry. Nothing came of the scheme." Even at sixty, when he gave himself up to the American authorities in 1945 and was kept in the disciplinary barracks near Pisa, he made a particular appeal to young soldiers. They recognized him as a fellow victim of the brass, and a regular fellow. Probably the most interesting single document in the *Casebook* is the account by a highly literate soldier, Robert Allen, of Pound's early captivity. Pound himself said later: ". . . They thought I was a dangerous wild man and were scared of me. I had a guard night and day and when they built a cage out of iron mats from airplane runways and put me in the cage for the merriment of all, they posted a guard outside. Soldiers used to come up to the cage and look at me. Some of them brought me food. Old Ez was a prize exhibit."

Allen himself quite obviously shared the admiration of Pound's courage, openness, daring, that he reports among the troops. He writes: "Pound, always spoken of as 'Ezra,' became sort of a hero among the trainees when word was spread that he had 'made a dummy of the psychiatrist'—that he had turned questions around so that even the psychiatrist became confused. In the end, the unofficial opinion of the psychiatrist was that Ezra Pound was sane, although perhaps 'a little exotic,' as one of my friends put it." The trainees marching by or working in the area considered Pound with awe, "taking the reinforced cage as evidence that he was a particularly tough customer." Another guard in the disciplinary training center remembers that Pound was so much admired that one young prisoner risked his chance for clemency by making a rough table for him.

« 2 »

Even the usual literary case for Pound, the claim that Pound's *Cantos* (an epic poem saturated in history) can be treated as "pure poetry," always implied that Pound's personality, his political and social opinions, were too violent and uncontrolled to be judged. Professor Ray West, whose unimportant personal record of the Pound controversy is characteristic of the anxious sophistication that has replaced scholarship among literary professors, says nervously that "No one that I know considers Pound correct in his thinking."

John Berryman, in a *Partisan Review* essay on Pound's poetry — an essay cited but not reproduced in this book — romantically compared Pound to Sir Roger Casement. Dwight Macdonald, who as a journalist has always been uncontaminated by any conventional opinion, even if it makes sense, went into ecstasies over the Bollingen Award because it showed what a free country we are compared with the Russians.

Time and again the feeling for Pound was that of young people or middle-aged people still young who, with typical heartlessness or lack of imagination, thought that Pound's most disgusting statements were simply not serious. Just as the art-worship of our time is a symptom of perpetual youth, for we excuse any daub as self-expression, so some of the sympathy for Pound came, very naturally and understandably, from people who want art to be "pure," to control it, to keep it for a world removed from real human suffering, belief, entanglement. Professor West, lamenting Pound's most unfortunate anti-Semitism, said that "I should prefer to have the anti-Semitism of our age (and who will deny that it exists?) written from a point of view contrary to Pound's, just as I should have preferred it if Eliot had not joined the Church, if Huxley had not been converted to mysticism, if André Malraux had not become a De-Gaullist, if Breton had not become a communist, and if William Faulkner had not so bitterly resented the Civil Rights bill."

In short, Professor West doesn't like writers to think of anything but writing. His students, however, may see things a little more mischievously; they may welcome in Pound exactly those qualities which older poets like Yeats and Robert Frost have always deprecated. Though it was Frost, in gratitude for Pound's early help, who finally got Pound off (and Pound snarled that Frost had waited long enough to do it), Frost's disapproval of Pound is no secret. Yeats, whom Pound also befriended, nevertheless described Pound's cantos as ". . . nervous obsession, nightmare, stammering confusion; he is an economist, poet, politician, raging at malignants with inexplicable characters and motives, grotesque figures out of a child's book of beasts."

Young people find just this exciting. The more inexplicable the world becomes to them, the more they feel it necessary to lash out at wrongdoers, and since they can't locate the culprits any more, they find admirable the exasperation, the undirectable nervous force that became more and more characteristic of Pound's personality. T. S. Eliot remembers that even in Pound's early days "he seemed always to be a temporary squatter," he had "a kind of resistance against growing into any environment." In a world that seems to be hardening into collective mankind, it is ironic, amusing, and terrible to think that Pound — the poet as permanent revolution, the literary rebel incarnate, the Pound whose manic screeches and ugliest writings have always been particularly shocking because of the peculiar tenderness of his best work — might become the very type of the hipsters' hero. *Any* cause will do for some people nowadays, so long as it is "agin" something still left to be "aginst." Some of the most bizarre material in the Ezra Pound casebook deals with the maniacs and fanatics who hung around him when he was in the mental pokey. Among his visitors was "David R. Wang, a member of the Dartmouth class of 1955, distinguished as being the only Chinese poet of record who devotes himself to the cause of white supremacy. Since graduation, the *Dartmouth* reports, Wang has been touring the Ivy League colleges with the purpose of setting up White Citizens' Councils on the campuses. He has characterized Secretary of State Dulles as a 'wishy-washy Socialist.'"

Crazy, Man! Crazy!

[1959]

Sinclair Lewis: Hail and Farewell

GRACE HEGGER LEWIS was Sinclair Lewis's first wife. They met in 1912, they married in 1914, and by 1925, the point at which this memoir ends, they were tacitly separated. Since this is the period of Lewis's emergence as an important novelist and of his best work — *Main Street, Babbitt, Arrowsmith* — the book has a distinct value. It shows Lewis as a modest, harassed, highly romantic and conven-

With Love from Gracie: Sinclair Lewis: 1912-1925, by Grace Hegger Lewis. New York: Harcourt, Brace and Company.

tionally ambitious young man who was still a wage slave in publishers' offices, wrote his early novels at night and on commuters' trains, and who thought he had reached the heights by getting into the *Saturday Evening Post*. Then, in 1920, the utterly unexpected smash success of *Main Street* transformed the lives of this young couple beyond their wildest dreams — or rather, exactly according to the specifications of their dreams.

They were free, they were in the big money, they moved in the company of other celebrities. Lewis was not only a famous novelist but a national figure. But the personal effect of his success, as Mrs. Lewis describes it, was a tragedy. Lewis's really creative period did not outlast the Twenties, and his increasing irritability and despairing restlessness made a havoc of his personal life. He was to die in Italy, very much alone, in 1951.

No man — especially a practicing writer — is perhaps ever entirely a hero to his ex-spouse. With all the tenderness, humor and solidarity which the first Mrs. Lewis has brought to this account of their early struggles together, there is an unmistakable bitterness behind the story. This makes us see the personal failings of Sinclair Lewis rather more sharply than perhaps we have a right to see someone who, after all, must be judged by his work and not by what Mrs. Lewis presents here as indifference to their son and compulsion to be noticed and admired.

Yet with all this, it is obvious to anyone who reads this book how much of Lewis's personality — his mimicry, his nervous restlessness, his peculiar blend of sentimentality and sharp-eared malice — went straight into his novels. Even more, you can see that a great part of Sinclair Lewis's tragedy, the very symbol of it, is the fact that he could never distinguish between his life and his work. As has happened so often with American writers, each new book had not only to give him a very good living and to make or keep him famous; it had to be on everyone's lips, it had to be admired by everyone, and all the time.

Only in this way, it seems, could Lewis feel that he had arrived, that he had justified his ambition as a writer. But if a novel "failed," if it did not increase his success, then he had failed not only as a writer but as a human being. Other writers would look down on him; Somerset Maugham or Arnold Bennett or John Galsworthy (how Minnesota felt that the English still had the last word!) might not invite him to meet — Hugh Walpole.

Even when he was at the top of his fame, Lewis could feel: "Everyone at table seemed to be enjoying the spectacle of being superior to funny me." Later, when he was publishing some very bad books, he would lash out at critics with incredible bitterness and violence — "What other job is there where an unqualified, ignorant, talentless sonofabitch is allowed to tear your work in shreds — and be paid for it?"

Lewis's inability to detach himself from his work — to think of a novel as something that had to stand or fall entirely on its own terms — often comes through to us in this book because Mrs. Lewis shares these views. One sees it in the competitiveness with which she describes other American writers of the 1920s. Speaking of Scott Fitzgerald, she says: "Most Americans at that time lived more like Sinclair Lewis characters; there was more substance to life than Fitzgerald's glossy version." This is carrying the identification of art with life beyond the point at which it is possible to tell whether the author is praising Sinclair Lewis or Americans of the Twenties. In another passage, she boasts that "Lewis was no disciple, as Hemingway was, of Sherwood Anderson and Gertrude Stein." Does the fact that one is a "disciple" — of an art which, unlike Lewis's, has to be *learned* — make the slightest difference if, like Hemingway, one preserves his originality?

Sometimes this identification of art with life becomes naïve, as when Mrs. Lewis, comparing *Main Street* with *Madame Bovary*, notes that "Flaubert was coldly, clinically objective; Lewis was warm in his sympathy or hotly angry in his condemnation of his characters and the village where they dwelt. . . . He was more than approving of what Carol Kennicott was trying to do to better Gopher Prairie, whereas Emma Bovary only wanted to better life for herself."

Yet naïve as Mrs. Lewis is on the comparative merits of *Madame Bovary* and *Main Street*, the fact remains that what Carol Kennicott wanted for Gopher Prairie, Sinclair Lewis wanted for his books. They were to "better life." In great part, this new life represented the dream of a whole generation for freedom. Lewis had a distinct and admirable belief in literature as an instrument of popular education, in the sense that Voltaire and Dickens and H. G. Wells understood it. In some early notes for *Main Street* he wrote of his heroine: "Her desire for beauty in prairie towns was but one tiny aspect of a world-wide demand [for] alteration of all our modes of being and doing business; it was one with [the] universal and growing desire to chuck out pompous priests and all manner of kings, noblemen, leaders of society, and their paid or unpaid valets."

In addition, literature had to be a way of making money and making oneself famous; the writer in America had to be, all at once and all at the same time, an artist, a celebrity and a businessman. And it was this identification of himself with the compulsive side of American business, as everyone knows who has read his insistently commercial letters to his publishers (*From Main Street to Stockholm*), that helps to explain Lewis's personal misery. He was constantly trying to settle the problem of personal happiness and of artistic creation at one blow.

His books had to bring in money, a lot of money; by 1925, Lewis was expecting $100,000 a year, and he lived at a rate which makes it clear that he had to write best sellers each year. He had to be crazily generous, wildly open-handed; his compulsion to travel, to uproot and move and fly, was obviously a deep necessity — and one that is made clear in the nervous rhythms of his writing. And yet, the tragedy was not that he had to make money — for he was not a hack — but that he could believe in his own novels only if they "succeeded." His whole life was determined and changed by *Main Street*. But later, much later, when the critics would not always applaud, when Arnold Bennett said something to indicate that he thought Lewis uneducated; when, with all Lewis's pride in his effect on American thinking, it was clear that someone or other thought less well of him than of Fitzgerald or Hemingway, then — oh, tragedy of American tragedies for the writer — it was not only his work that had failed, but his life itself.

Against this, as he grew older, Lewis could muster only the nervous restlessness of his impressions, the excited rhythm of his life back and forth between America and Europe, the sensation of constant uprooting — all these things that can give a writer the "feel" of creativity, apart from the actual books he writes.

The tragedy of Sinclair Lewis's last years is not that he wrote many bad books but that he felt that his life itself had "failed"—putting his best work in doubt. And when we look back at the early and charming young Lewis described in this memoir, the Lewis who wrote pale romantic verse to his girl that he called "Tennyson-and-water," we can see that the pain of his last years is that life seemed to send him back to the time when he wrote his novels on trains, when success meant the *Saturday Evening Post*, when he was still a nobody. And yet—cannot one say that this "failure" is something that Lewis should not have felt? That he exaggerated its pain by his craving for success—and so was never able to detach himself for a minute from the very different responsibilities of the novelist and the American dream? But let us also remember that Lewis's best work comes out of his closeness to American experience. As so often happens both in life and in art, he made his "failure" out of just those qualities that had made him the writer he was.

[1956]

John P. Marquand and the American Failure

THE HERO of John P. Marquand's new novel, *Women and Thomas Harrow*, is an American playwright and director of fifty-four who is unhappy with his third wife, unsure of his ability to turn out a new Broadway hit, and who lives in a fabulously costly old mansion in the small New England town where he grew up. He is charming and bright, a gentleman as well as a wit; he is as respectful of the traditions of the little old New England home town (once a famous seaport) as he is of the hard professionalism of the theater, and he would be as much at home in that town as he is in New York were it not for his uncomfortable sense of irony about his life, his mocking awareness of every situation as one which he might have written and directed himself.

Women and Thomas Harrow, by John P. Marquand. Boston: Little, Brown and Company.

It is the unforgotten bite of poverty and comparative social inferiority in his youth that helps to explain his sudden undoing. Ever since his unexpected first success in the 1920s with a sardonic play about a war hero's return, which enabled him to marry a local girl whose father was a failure, Tom Harrow's regular success in the theater has driven him to spread himself more and more recklessly. His first wife, Rhoda, who is obsessed with a desire for security, finally left him for real money when he was whooping it up in North Africa during the war; characteristically, he gave her an excessively generous settlement. His second wife, a hard, ambitious actress, still gets lavish alimony from him; his third, a duller woman than the first two, an unsuccessful actress who is getting stouter than she would like, feels imprisoned in the house which her husband keeps up only out of piety to the traditions that surrounded his youth. All these handsome gestures, these symbolic excesses and improvidences, led Tom to risk his investments with a costume musical comedy which failed. With his capital gone, his wife turns on him; his first wife, who had discovered that life with big money can be dull, offers to return both his original settlement on her, and herself. In a fit of despair, Tom barely saves himself from going over a cliff in his big new car and realizes that from now on he must go it alone.

Summarizing the story makes Tom Harrow sound more of a money writer than he is. The point about him is not that he is venal, but that he is used to success; not corrupt, and the very opposite of cheap, he is a writer with a definite public who has always written with professional self-respect and skill. The trouble with him is not that he is a grasping *individual*, like the self-betraying hero who used to figure in American novels about the vanity of success, but that, one of many Americans who have done their best and enjoyed the profits, he has been betrayed by life itself — by the mediocrity of the society in which he lives. Thomas Harrow reminds us of many Americans today. He suffers not from a lack of honor — the old-fashioned explanation of misery in a highly competitive society — but from a lack of differentiation in both his character and the America he lives with. It is no longer a tragedy of character that such heroes act out, but a world depressed by its own lack of expectation. Tom Harrow has done his best, but the America in which he lives has become increasingly inflationary and socially pretentious, and the disappointment and disgust that sensitive Americans feel about our failure as a civilization unsettle him.

Everything Thomas Harrow has to look at is either, like his beautiful old house, too distant from contemporary experience to be meaningful or, like the overlarge and overcolored automobile in which he finally tries to die, an example of the submissiveness and vulgarity that the "juke-box civilization" of mid-twentieth-century America has come to. The house, built by local shipwrights, represents for Tom "a revolt and a craving for luxury which its builder had never known," while his present wife, Emily, is by his own admission perhaps not so shallow as she seems when she complains that he has absurdly sacrificed a comfortable bathroom to keep an old prayer closet. Tom Harrow has collected three-pronged forks, rat-tail spoons, pistol-handled knives, Crown Derby china, George the Second candlesticks, Chippendale tables, but recognizes that "he had in reality been travelling rapidly all his life over a shoddy road, decorated meretriciously . . . with plastic refreshment booths and overnight motels . . . places of temporary respite for temporary indulgence, but no more." When he walks down the main street of the dear old town and passes the church where he was first married, he reads that the next sermon topic is "How happy are you inside?"; and when he steps into the beautiful and simple church, the Reverend Ernest W. Godfrey greets Tom as a fellow professional, describes the church as a psychological filling station for troubled souls, and reveals that he's been in "this game long enough to know that every single one of us has his own problem and his own method of motivation as well as his particular means of adjustment, and his own particular subconscious mind."

« 2 »

Thomas Harrow lives in the American world we all have to live in these days. When he reflects, in the dark night of his soul (the bank is calling in the stocks he put up as collateral), that "national life was approaching an average that expressed itself in gastronomical and in spiritual mediocrity, and he had always hated mediocrity. . . . They would all soon be engulfed in the wave of the commonplace," we agree that the essence of Tom Harrow's relation to women has been his concern with old-fashioned standards of aristocratic ease, gaiety, personal honor, which his wives have been too frightened or too hard to respect. These women symbolize the increasing spiritual imperfection, the anxious and external greediness, which to many observers has made the American woman seem unnatural. Tom Harrow, the parfit gentil knight, lavishes enormous marriage settlements on wives who have run off with millionaires and thinks wistfully of his old Aunt Edith, who, like so many New England women of her generation, never married but "was able to understand nearly everything from the basis of almost no appreciable experience." Rhoda, his first wife, his true wife (in his old-fashioned way Tom Harrow reflects that no matter how many times you married, you truly married only once), was constantly worried because change made her feel insecure. Rhoda used to say: "Do you have a feeling that everything is beginning to move so fast that we'll have to run to keep up with it? . . . I like things so I know where they'll be tomorrow."

But isn't this Tom Harrow's feeling as well? Rhoda's fear of change took the form of greed; Emily's, of dread that she would be left alone; Tom's takes the form of cultural piety to beautiful old houses in old seaports like Newburyport — where John P. Marquand and the heroes of so many of his novels grew up. The ruling and obsessive image in all of Marquand's novels is that of traveling the American road to the point of no return, to the hour when there is so little time. In this book the conception of life as loss has become the dramatic image of a successful and attractive American trying to kill himself in the chromium, long-finned, grotesquely colored car which incarnates all the showiness that he loathes. It is perhaps not the "shoddy" American road that troubles Tom Harrow so much as it is the mechanical defeat of life itself; it is not our great and confused America of the Eisenhower age, with its weapons that reach to the stars and its people — many of whom look as if all wisdom had been squeezed out of them by the strain of American life — that comes into play so much as it is the fact that people get old, and that when they get old enough, they die.

What bothers John P. Marquand, as it bothers Thomas Harrow, is the suspicion that as people get older in America, they do not get wiser; they just reminisce. No matter how much one may admire

Marquand's social skill, his wit, his sense of tact, above all his cool honesty, one knows that a Marquand novel will sag into flashback as surely as a Shakespearean hero will spout blank verse. What is wrong with so much reminiscence — which in this case, despite all Marquand's charm and wit, makes a sad, soft, rather self-indulgent book out of *Women and Thomas Harrow* — is the fact that, among other faults, Marquand no longer bothers to find a very convincing or dramatically interesting frame for these flights into the past. The evening the Harrows are giving a dinner party, Tom tells Emily that they are busted; she denounces him; he gets thoroughly soaked on Martinis, champagne, brandy, Scotch; then, sitting up most of the night in an alcoholic haze of self-reference, he goes over the failure of his life. Technically, this makes a hole in the book only because there is so much formal separation between Tom Harrow in the present and the Tom Harrow he is remembering that we cannot believe very much in the strength of a character who is largely shown on the shady side of his life. The flashback is usually the structural center of a Marquand novel, but in previous books the past was shown as inaccessible — not, as it is symbolically in this book, unrelated. The symbol is that of the unconnection in Tom Harrow's own mind between past and present America; the American failure is always the inability to find the past or to learn from it: sure breeding ground for nostalgia.

The looseness with which the flashback is handled in *Women and Thomas Harrow* is significant. It is typical of all those novels in which Marquand presents too uncritically characters who represent his professional experience — the writer in *Wickford Point,* the play doctor in *So Little Time* — or the social exclusions of his own early life in Newburyport and at Harvard, as in *Point of No Return* and *Sincerely, Willis Wayde.* Marquand's best book is still *The Late George Apley,* for he functions superbly as a satirist of the genteel tradition. Every social novelist has an evident conception of himself in relation to his subject. Marquand's role is that of the background observer, the man from the public schools of Newburyport who is relatively the outsider, who can observe upper-crust Boston with a critical sharpness that at the same time reveals his sympathy for a class he was of but not in. What makes *The Late George Apley* so good is the fact that Marquand himself, setting the scenes and pulling the strings, is evident everywhere and visible nowhere; he knows where he stands and his control is perfect. Even in *H. M. Pulham, Esquire,* one can see that, apart from the jokes at the expense of the booster in the Harvard class of 1915, Marquand is no longer distant enough from Pulham to sustain the satire, for in age Pulham could be a son to Apley, and thus he is not only Marquand's contemporary and a man who has shared in the same historic experiences, but the symbol of a vanishing social order.

Marquand's dilemma, even in a relatively satiric and external book about an upper-class man like Pulham, is that he cherishes Pulham's gentlemanly values far too much for him to stay in the background as a satirist. Instead of feeling free to describe the values of Pulham with the old detachment, Marquand has gone through the same helplessness before the defeat of the past, before the gradual extinction of our old American world, which he once satirized in the helplessness of Apley. And the more he has been forced to write from a point of view too reminiscent of naked experience, the more Marquand has softened and saddened, to the point where all satiric edge eventually disappears from *Women and Thomas Harrow.* And we are made uncomfortably aware, in what are intended to be the dramatic crises of the book, that there is an excessively personal tone to Marquand's reflections on the hazards and self-deceptions of a writer who has relied too long on his own professional facility.

One of the recurrent themes in the book is the hero's inability to connect life and the theater, in which he has worked so successfully. He not only sees every situation with a detachment that cuts him off from immediate human emotion, but when he goes to work in the old coachhouse he has converted into an office (he keeps the driveway heavily coated with gravel so that Emily in her high heels will not be able to walk down and disturb him), he cannot rid himself of the suspicion that his long habit of easy success has made him a mechanical contriver of situations and effects. Without in the least consciously sacrificing his integrity, he does feel that he has lost his freshness; and this complaint is likely to strike the reader as significant in view of the manifest lack of vital dramatic energy in Marquand's new novel, in which an increasing impatience and despair have gone hand in hand with the now ungovernable nostalgia.

« 3 »

I admire Marquand very much, for in a society like our own, which is always in danger of being overinterpreted, the social novelist, the novelist of manners—Marquand, Cozzens, O'Hara, and Edith Wharton and Ellen Glasgow before them—nails life down by writing about a particular social class from a definite point of view, and Marquand has done this with steady ease and skill. America has been more of a society, even a class society, than the long tradition of solitude in our literature reveals to outsiders, and Marquand's kidding of the Transcendentalist tradition in *Wickford Point* and his outburst against Melville, "the great god of literature in America," in this new book reflect the impatience of the practiced social observer with the theoreticians and visionaries who have always stood for American literature.

But the social novelist in America has his problem. He writes about a society which does not want to be a society, one in which individuals distrust the very idea of society, in which social distinctions are considered immoral or irrelevant, as they are by solitary voyagers, like Ishmael, to whom the world is a metaphysical problem. Since the social novelist, by the very nature and accessibility of his material, is likely to be prolific and fluent, he must not exploit the fluency of his manner to describe a purely personal crisis. We do not want a novel by Jane Austen to resemble *Wuthering Heights,* or John O'Hara to lose his temper when describing the country club set in *Appointment in Samarra.* We want to see the relationships of people who are divided by class; we want to see human beings rise above class but not be unconvincingly free of class. When George Apley has to give up his Irish girl, we are touched, for we recognize the human need to defy convention—and the durability of convention itself. But George Apley (1866-1934) still had conventions to submit to, and perhaps it is only a novelist of New England, born in 1892, who can still be so much aware of them. Only in New England or the South, in the day just before our day, were there conventions enough to produce social novels: novels whose essence is that society exists independently and exerts power over those who live in it.

What has happened to Marquand's novels is perhaps due to the fact that the local traditions which have always represented class in this country have increasingly disappeared under the pressures of a technological society. The novelist of manners, like Marquand (or Cozzens or O'Hara), who has always depended on a tradition stable enough to include the satirist himself, now finds himself angrily crying out against the absence of values themselves. In *By Love Possessed* we saw just how angry James Gould Cozzens could get, for it is a novel whose real drive is unlimited and profane bitterness at the degradation of the republic. And in *Women and Thomas Harrow* we can see just how melancholy and nerveless Marquand can get when he is concerned with the same problem of a middle-aged American, now of the old school, who recognizes that he is fighting not for freedom *from* convention, as George Apley did, but *for* conventions — standards of belief and behavior — that will allow him to function as a human being again in a world where beliefs are shared.

The basic human experience is our consciousness of mortality. Everyone dies, and sooner or later everyone's life takes shape from that limitation. That is why Proust named his great book a quest of time gone; he recognized that only what is immaterial can remain: still in life, the human mind can transcend its imminent extinction to deliver us from time. Mortality is a theme that a sixty-five-year-old novelist is naturally concerned with, and the fifty-four-year-old hero of this book is immediately concerned with it. And how does Mr. Marquand handle this fundamental problem of our necessary deliverance from time? Tom Harrow does not believe in it; he does not believe in the imagination — which is all we have — because his very facility as a writer has made him suspect the imagination. "The late Dr. Albert Einstein, or others vaguely in the Einstein category, had advanced the theory that time, being immaterial, was indestructible — and perhaps it was. . . . Yet, granted that the past was indestructible, exactly where was it now? Was it in good order, in keeping with theories of relativity? He did not believe it was. The past in his experience was in a tangled mess like ticker tape." The intellectual poverty of this, I firmly believe, accounts for the description of the past in Mr. Marquand's flashbacks as a mess of ticker tape. There is only one place where the past ever makes sense — inside the creative human mind. To forget this under the pressure of the ever-increasing American complaint — that life is not what it was — is to show up cruelly our lack of connection with ourselves. The social novelist in America pays for his lack of ideas when he is left without the social traditions on which he has depended so long for his sustenance as a man and for his achievement as an artist.

[1958]

William Faulkner: The Stillness of Light in August

Light in August begins unforgettably with a pregnant young woman from Alabama sitting beside a road in Mississippi, her feet in a ditch, her shoes in her hand, watching a wagon that is mounting the hill toward her with a noise that carries for a half-mile "across the hot still pinewiney silence of the August afternoon." She has been on the road for a month, riding in a long succession of farm wagons or walking the hot dusty roads with her shoes in her hand, trying to get to Jefferson. There, she firmly expects, she will find her lover working in a planing mill and ready to marry her, and there — that is the big city — she will put her shoes on at last.

This opening chapter, so dry and loving in its pastoral humor, centering on the picture of Lena and her precious burden being carried in one wagon or another, by one farmer after another, to her hoped-for destination in a husband, ends sharply on the outskirts of Jefferson, from which she can see smoke going up from a burning house. It is the house of Joanna Burden, who has just been murdered by Joe Christmas. And the images that have been crowding us with the dust and the heat of the unending road — with Lena continually amazed at how far a body can go, the serenity of the deserted young woman whose face is "calm as a stone, but not hard," the "sharp and brittle crack and clatter" of the "wagon's weathered and ungreased wood and metal," the identical and anonymous wagons, the mules plodding in a steady and unflagging hypnosis, the drowsy heat of the afternoon; with Lena's faded blue dress, her palm leaf fan, her small cloth bundle in which she carries thirty-five cents in nickels and dimes; with the shoes that she takes off and carries in her hand as soon as she feels the dust of the road beneath her feet — all provide us with that foundation in the local and the provincial, the earth and the road which man must travel on it, against which are set images of fire and murder, of aimless wandering and of flight, embodied in the figure who soon enters the book and dominates it in his remorseless gray anonymity. Joe Christmas does not even have a name of his own, only a mocking label stuck on him at the orphanage where he was deposited one Christmas Eve. "Joe Christmas" is worse than any real name could be, for it indicates not only that he has no background, no roots, no name of his own, but that he is regarded as a *tabula rasa*, a blank sheet of paper on which anyone can write out an identity for him and make him believe it.

It is the contrast of Lena Grove and Joe Christmas, of the country girl and the American wanderer, who is a stranger even to himself, the ultimate personification in modern loneliness, that frames the book — literally so, since Lena Grove begins and ends it, while Joe Christmas's agony and crucifixion are enacted as within a circle round which he runs in an effort to catch up with himself. When he finds that he cannot run out of this circle and stands still at last in order to die, the book comes back to Lena Grove and ends on her ritualistic procession up the road with her baby and Byron Bunch — Faulkner's version of the Holy Family. By the time we have finished *Light in August*, we have come to feel that the real greatness of Faulkner in this book (and indeed of his extraordinary compassion) lies in the amazing depth which he brings to this contrast of which American writers are so fond, particularly in Southern writing, between the natural and the urban, between Lena Grove's simplicity and the forces personified by Joe Christmas's walking all smooth city pavements with the same isolation and indifference, eating at the coldly smooth wooden counter, and murder. Faulkner even leads up to a strange and tortured fantasy of Joe Christmas as Lena Grove's still-unnamed son. There is virtually an annunciation to Lena, in the moving last phase of the book when Lena, delivered of her child just as Joe Christmas is running for his life, hears Mrs. Hines, Christmas's grandmother, calling the baby "Joey" — he who is a "nigger" murderer, and whom Lena has never seen. The reader comes to this with a shock, only because of Faulkner's reckless, desperate eagerness to wrest all the possible implications from his material, to think it out interminably, since there is no end to all one's possible meditations round and round the human cycle. One of the conflicts of which the book is made — between life and anti-life, between the spirit of birth and the murderous abstractions and obsessions which drive most of the characters — is in Faulkner himself, in his attempt to will his painful material into a kind of harmony that it does not really possess.

But in any event, it is Lena who opens the book, Lena's world, Lena's patience, that set the ideal behind the book — that world of the permanent and the natural which Joe Christmas seeks all his life without knowing that he does, and, seeking it, will run full tilt into the ground. "Light in August" is itself a country saying: Light as a mare or a cow is light after delivery.* And it is this world of Lena Grove from Doane's Mill — the tiny hamlet which was too small for any post-office list; yet even Lena, living in the backwoods, had not seen it until her parents died — with the sound of the wagon wheel taking her away from it, that remains in the book not merely a world that Faulkner celebrates but a mythic source of strength. As indeed it is. For it is this intense sense of itself, it is this superb registering of country sights and sounds as the stillness is broken by the creaking and lumbering wagon coming up the hill, that is the secret of Southern writing. In his attachment to the irretrievable, in his obstinate feeling for the earth, the good Southern writer makes so much writing in America seem as shallow as if it had been composed by a young instructor in English sitting in his study surrounded by manuals on the great novels. Albert Camus, talking appreciatively about Southern novelists, once remarked to a friend of mine that what he liked about their books was "the dust and the heat." And to the man from North Africa, with his memories of that blazing world described in *Noces*, that world into which Paris can never enter, Faulkner's sense of local color must be especially moving. But after all, it is this sense of place that is the great thing about all American writing. It is the "mossy scabs of the worm fence, heap'd stones, elder, mullein and poke-weed" in "Song of Myself"; the land-

* Faulkner now denies this, and claims that the title just came to him because he liked the phrase. [1961.]

scape that in *Walden* seems always to be reflected in water; the strong native sense of the here and now that is the basis of Emerson's esthetic; the edge of the world seen from Hemingway's Michigan woods; "reading the river" in *Life on the Mississippi* and *Huckleberry Finn;* the "snow, the real snow" seen only beyond Chicago that Scott Fitzgerald described so rapturously in his memories of Midwesterners in Eastern colleges going home for Christmas. And if we ask what is so remarkable about that sense of place, which is, after all, essential to imaginative writing, the answer is that we Americans are in fact just the opposite of the homogeneous mass we are always trying to be, and that what distinguishes American writing is exactly the fact that we are strange to each other and that each writer describes his own world to strangers living in the same land with himself.

Now of all parts of the United States the South is certainly the strangest to the others; it is, in fact — or used to be — a separate nation. And almost all the good Southern writers have this sense of local color to an extreme, for to the same degree that the South is what it is because of its rural background, its "backwardness," its isolation, its comparatively homogeneous white population, to this same extent does the American need to value and venerate one's own region or place as the only escape from American bigness, American smoothness, American abstractness, American slogans, the juggernaut of American progress, find (at least it used to find) its deepest expression in the South. Even poverty, which in America certainly is a disgrace, becomes in Southern writing a sign of the natural man (Huckleberry Finn) or the earth-mother (Lena Grove). And, as so often happens in Southern writing — for the sensitive Southerners are likely to feel that they are lost in the modern industrial world and, in mourning their traditional homeland, to see the immediate world around them as damned — Faulkner's pictures of the impersonal modern world, the opposite of Lena's sacred grove, are lurid. As Lena is all fertility, the others are all barrenness. Destruction, fire, obsession, inhumanity, anonymity, the "friction-smooth" wooden counter at which Joe Christmas eats, the hard cold eyes of Bobbie the prostitute and Mame the madam and Max the pimp: set these against the images of locality, the farmers in their faded and patched but clean overalls, and of time, the wagon along the road and the "heelgnawed porch" of the country store around which the farmers sit. As soon as we get to Jefferson, we catch the typical dialectic of life and anti-life, the contrast of birth and destruction on which the book is founded, in the fact that the slow patient rhythms of Lena, the wagon, the road, are immediately followed by the whine of the saw in the planing mill, the reiteration of *smooth*. The world is narrowing down to the contest between the good Christian laborer, Byron Bunch, the very essence of the common ordinary good man, and those, like Lena's seducer, who have either taken on a name which is not their own, "Brown," a name too conventional even to be *his* name, or who, like Joe Christmas, have no name to begin with.

« 2 »

This contrast is familiar enough in Southern opinion, and one can find the same horror of miscegenation, of uprooting, of the city man's anonymity, in any expression of Southern agrarianism. But Faulkner does not stop at the abstraction of the alien: he carries it on, he carries it out, to astonishing lengths. And it is this intensity of conception that makes the portrait of Joe Christmas compelling rather than believable, makes him a source of wonder, of horror, yet above all of pity, rather than of pleasure in the creation of a real human being. For Joe Christmas remains, as he is born, an abstraction; from the moment he appears, "there was something definitely rootless about him, as though no town nor city was his, no street, no walls, no square of earth his home." He comes to work in the only clothes he has, a serge suit and a white shirt; and Byron Bunch, watching him, knows that Joe Christmas "carried his knowledge with him always as though it were a banner, with a quality ruthless, lonely, and almost proud." So from the moment Joe Christmas appears, he is seen as what others say about him, he is only a thought in other people's minds. More than this, he is looked at always from a distance, as if he were not quite human, which in many ways he is not.

We see Joe Christmas from a distance, and this distance is the actual space between him and his fellows. It is also the distance between the name "Joe Christmas," which is clownish, and the actual suffering of someone who has to live up to the nonhumanity of his name, to the obsession (founded on hearsay, not on actual evidence) that his father had "some" Negro blood in him. Joe Christmas, then, is really "Man" trying to discover the particular kind of man he is. He is an abstraction created by the racist mania of his grandfather, a former preacher whose tormented life is spent insisting that Negroes are guilty in the eyes of God and must serve white men. When his daughter ran away with a "Mexican" circus hand, Doc Hines not merely killed the man, and, after his daughter died in childbirth on Christmas Eve, left the baby on the steps of an orphanage, but later took a job as a janitor in the orphanage in order to make sure that his "nigger" grandson would never be allowed to contaminate anyone. This obsessiveness about race goes hand in hand with a Calvinist obsession of the elect and of the hopeless sinfulness of others, an obsession which is found both in Joe Christmas's rigidly doctrinaire foster-father, Calvin MacEachern, and in Joe's future mistress, Joanna Burden, a descendant of New Hampshire Puritans who remains in the South though she is the sworn enemy of its ways. All these obsessions about purity and guilt are, Faulkner indicates, the remnants of an inhuman religion that has added bigotry and arrogance to the curse of slavery. They are the symbols of a church that has lost its spiritual function, and that has been deserted by the Reverend Gail Hightower, who spends his days in endless reveries of the South's irretrievable glory. The obsessions are all summed up in the fate of Joe Christmas, who is trying to become *someone*, a human being, to find the integrity that is so ripely present in Lena Grove. Lena does not have to try; her symbol is the wheel on the road. Joe Christmas's is flight: flight on the same road, but flight toward himself, which he cannot reach, and away from hatred of himself, which he cannot escape. Only his pursuers catch up with him, to murder and to castrate him.

Joe Christmas is an abstraction seeking to become a human being. In the race-mad South, many a Negro — and Mexican, and Jew — is turned into an abstraction. But this man is *born* an abstraction and is seeking to become a person. He is an orphan, brought up in a foundling home, who in earliest childhood is watched by his own grandfather as if he were a caged beast. He is then bribed by the dietitian, whom he has heard making love with the intern, as if he knew enough to betray her. He is adopted by a farmer who renames him, lectures him, starves him, beats him for not memorizing the catechism. He is robbed and beaten by the pimp of the prostitute with whom he has fallen in love. He is constantly treated by his Negrophile mistress, Joanna Burden, as if his own personality were of no account, and is beseeched in her sexual transports as "Negro." And finally, after being starved, betrayed, flogged, beaten, pursued by bloodhounds, he is castrated. The essential picture behind Joe Christmas is that of his grandfather carrying him to the orphanage and then from it in a savage parody of loving care. Joe Christmas is nothing but the man things are done to, the man who has no free will of his own, who is constantly seeking a moment of rest ("When have I ever eaten in peace?") and who looks for an identity by deliberately provoking responses that will let him be *someone*, if only as a white man among Negroes, or as someone calling himself a Negro in an effort to shock the white prostitute he has just slept with. His passivity, his ability to lend himself to situations and to people who will "carry" him for a while, is immense and pitiful.

Joe Christmas is the most solitary character in American fiction, the most extreme phase conceivable of American loneliness. He is never seen full face, but always as a silhouette, a dark shadow haunting others, a shadow upon the road he constantly runs — a foreshadowing of his crucifixion, which, so terrible and concentrated is his suffering, already haunts the lives of others like a black shadow. For, almost *because* he does not look it, he becomes the "Negro," or the thought of, the obsession with, Negroes in the minds of those who, looking at Joe Christmas, can think of nothing else. And Joanna Burden, whose abolitionist grandfather was murdered in the South, whose whole life has been an obstinate carrying-on, deep inside Mississippi, of her family's coldly abstract espousal of Negroes, shows us how much of an abstraction Joe Christmas is when she makes love crying to him "Negro! Negro!" Whether the "Negro" represents the white man's guilt or the white man's fear, he is always a thought in the white's mind — and in the South, an obsession. So Joanna Burden, who befriends him, and Doc Hines, who hates him, come to see in him the cause of guilt that is finally the image of guilt. "I thought," Joanna says to her lover,

. . . of all the children coming forever and ever into the world, white, with the black shadow already falling upon them before they draw breath. And I seemed to see the black shadow in the shape of a cross. And it seemed like the white babies were struggling, even before they drew breath, to escape from the shadow that was not only upon them but beneath them, too, flung out like their arms were flung out, as if they were nailed to the cross.

And she quotes her father: "In order to rise, you must raise the shadow with you. But you can never lift it to your level. I see that now, which I did not see until I came down here. But escape it you cannot. The curse of the black race is God's curse. But the curse of the white race is the black man who will be forever God's chosen own because He once cursed Him." The grounds of this obsession, then, can be a compassion for the Negro that is as profound as hatred, and equally removed from brotherhood. This compassion seems to me the essence of Faulkner's approach to Joe Christmas, and the triumph of the book is Faulkner's ability to keep his leading character a shadow, and yet to make us feel all his suffering. Compare Joe Christmas with the types of the Northerner, the city man, the "stranger" in Southern writing, to say nothing of the Negro, and you realize that where so many neo-orthodox Southern literary critics are hysterically fearful of the "stranger," Faulkner, by a tremendous and moving act of imagination, has found in Joe Christmas the incarnation of "man" — that is, of modern man, reduced entirely to his unsupported and inexplicable human feelings. There are no gods in Faulkner's world; there are only men — some are entirely subject to circumstances, some protest against them, some are even moved to change them. The hero of *A Fable* is of the last; Joe Christmas is of the first. He is human to us because of the experience he undergoes, but his passivity is so great that he is finally a body castrated, a mere corpse on a dissection table — or someone whose body has been turned into the host, material for a ritual, so that his last agony will earn him the respect he never earned while he was alive. He is not, like the Christ of *A Fable,* a man who gives new meaning to life; like Benjy in *The Sound and the Fury,* he is an incarnation of human suffering, unable to speak — except in the tremendous action near the end of the book when he stops running from his pursuers and waits for them, and attains, in this first moment of selfhood, the martyrdom that ends it.

« 3 »

We see Joe Christmas always from a distance. This distance from ourselves to him seems to me the key to the book, for it explains why Joe exists for us principally as a man who is described, not seen. He is so far away that we cannot see him; he is reported to us. And this distance is filled with the stillness of a continuous meditation. *Light in August* tells a story of violence, but the book itself is curiously soundless, for it is full of people thinking to themselves about events past. As soon as Lena Grove arrives in Jefferson, at the end of the first chapter, the story of Joe Christmas comes to us through flashbacks, through talk by the other men at the planing mill, through a whole chapter of summary biography, through rumors and gossip by the townspeople, and at the very end, when Joe Christmas's whole story is put together for us, by Gavin Stevens's telling a stranger about the grandparents. Almost everything we learn about Joe Christmas comes to us in the form of hearsay, accusation, the tortured memories of others; even his death is told as an incident in the life of his murderer, Percy Grimm. All these reports about the stranger sufficiently suggest his alienation. But in themselves they also create that stillness, that depth of meditation into which all the characters are plunged.

This meditation begins in Joe Christmas himself, who in his distance from other men is constantly trying to think himself back to life, and who, without knowing exactly how his ordeal began — and certainly not why — finds himself like a caged animal going over and over the same ground. We hear him talking to himself, and we follow his slow and puzzled efforts to understand the effect of his actions upon others. We see him as a child in the orphanage, eating the toothpaste, frightening the dietitian out of her wits because he is staring straight at her, trying to understand what she is accusing him of. We watch him walking the path between his cabin and Joanna Burden's house for his meals, thinking out everything he finds between the four walls of her kitchen. Finally we watch him running, and thinking deliriously in his flight, until, in that magnificent and piercing scene near the end of his flight, he falls asleep as he runs. The pressure of thought, the torture of thought, is overwhelming—and useless, since Joe Christmas does not know who he is, and so cannot locate the first cause of his misery. But still he thinks, he broods, he watches, he waits. And it is this brooding silence in him, fixed in attention over he does not know what, that explains why he is so often described in the book as looking like a man in prayer—even like a "monk." There is a strange and disturbing stillness about him that eases him, more swiftly than most men, into the stillness of nonbeing.

The stillness of the book has, of course, an immense reverberation within it. Describing Doc Hines, Faulkner notes about him "a quality of outworn violence like a scent, an odor," and the actual violence of Joe Christmas is always felt about him even when he sits rigidly still at counters like a man in prayer. When Joe's back history is run off in the rapid newsreel style of Dos Passos, one feels not only his personal insignificance, but the just-leashed violence of American life of which Joe is, in his way, completely the creature:

> He stepped from the dark porch, into the moonlight, and with his bloody head and his empty stomach hot, savage, and courageous with whiskey, he entered the street which was to run for fifteen years.
>
> The whiskey died away in time and was renewed and died again, but the street ran on. From that night the thousand streets ran as one street, with imperceptible corners and changes of scene, broken by intervals of begged and stolen rides, on trains and trucks, and on country wagons with he at twenty and twentyfive and thirty sitting on the seat with his still, hard face and the clothes (even when soiled and worn) of a city man and the driver of the wagon not knowing who or what the passenger was and not daring to ask.

Yet it is a stillness of thought that generally pervades the book, in the form of enormous meditations by which Faulkner tries to lift his material into place. The stillness is interrupted by shooting, burning, beating, the barking of bloodhounds and Percy Grimm's mutilation of Joe Christmas, which interrupt like the sound which nails must make when they are driven into wood through human flesh. Yet, just behind this obvious figure of the Roman soldier torturing Christ, there is a pastoral world. As Irving Howe has noted, the arrangement of the book "resembles an early Renaissance painting—in the foreground a bleeding martyr, far to the rear a scene of bucolic peacefulness, with women quietly working in the fields." Despite its violence, *Light in August* is one of the few American novels that remind one of the humanized and tranquil landscape in European novels. Its stillness is rooted in the peaceful and timeless world which Lena Grove personifies and in which she has her being. It is the stillness of the personal darkness inside which Joe Christmas lives. But this stillness is also the sickly, after-dark silence of the Reverend Gail Hightower sitting in his study, with his stale clothes and stale thoughts, going over and over the tragedy of his life, his grandfather's "glorious" death, his wife's desertion and suicide — and finally and typically summing it all up into a stale round of human illusion and defeat. Faulkner wishes us to understand that Hightower finally cuts the Gordian knot of his thoughts when he delivers Lena's baby and is finally struck down by Percy Grimm as he stands between him and Joe Christmas. But Hightower, whether brooding out upon the street from behind the study window, or sitting behind the green lamp in his parlor when he receives Byron Bunch, his only visitor, enlarges the stillness, increases its weight, by personifying what is immediately present in the book and throughout Faulkner's novels — the Southern effort to explain, to justify, and through some consummation in violent physical action even to lighten, the burden of this obsession with the past.

Hightower, by general consent, is one of the failures of the book: he is too vague, too drooping, too formless, in a word too much the creature of defeat and of obsession, to compel our interest or our belief. But this is so partly because Hightower is both a surrogate figure for Faulkner's meditations and a kind of scapegoat on whom Faulkner can discharge his exasperation with Southern nostalgia and the endless searching in the labyrinths of the past for the explanation of the Southern defeat and of the hold it keeps on the descendants of the Confederate aristocracy. Hightower is a failure because Faulkner both uses and parodies him. Because of the absurdly literal symbolism of his name, his constant watchful position behind the green lamp, his useless reveries, he is never on the same scale as the other characters, who are equally obsessed by the past, but who function on the plane of some positive action. Hightower not only lives by his thoughts; he has no life but his thoughts. We miss in him the lifelike element of violence (the only possible end to characters so entirely formed of reverie) that we find in Joanna Burden's degeneration, in Joe Christmas's hatred, in Percy Grimm's fanaticism, in Doc Hines's mania. Hightower, acting in various sections of the book as a foreground observer, brings to them not merely a stillness but a deadness which intervenes between us and the other characters. This shapeless, ghostly body of thought has its symbolic place in the mind of Hightower. For just as his life is over, and he has no function but to brood, so Faulkner has signified in Hightower that wholly retrospective, watchful concern, not with the past but with their bondage to the past, that seems to me the essence of what Faulkner's characters are always thinking about.

Joe Christmas, Joanna Burden, Gail Hightower — each of these is the prisoner of his own history, and is trying to come to terms with this servitude in his own mind. That none of them can ever lift himself out of the circumstances that enclose him, Faulkner sees as the condition of man. Man is engulfed in events that are always too much for him. Hightower, listening to Byron Bunch make plans for Lena's confinement, thinks: "It is because so much happens. Too much happens. That's it. Man performs, engenders, so much more than he can or should have to bear. That's how he finds out that he can bear anything. That's it. That's what is so terrible. That he can bear anything, anything." Endurance, as we know, is the key word in Faulkner's system of values. At least this was so up to *A Fable*. There, Faulkner himself has told us, the highest value is represented not by the young Jewish pilot officer who said, "This is terrible. I refuse to accept it, even if I must refuse life to do so"; not by the old French quartermaster general who said, "This is terrible, but we can weep and bear it"; but by the English battalion runner who said, "This is terrible, I'm going to do something about it." *Light in August* does not arrive at this step. Man never thinks of changing the world; it is all he can do to get a grip on it, to understand some part of what has happened to him and to endure all of it. Any release that occurs is a purely individual one, as when Hightower finally frees himself, in the one profoundly unselfish act of his life, by delivering Lena's baby. In the freshness of the early morning, after Lena has given birth, Hightower feels that he is in touch with the earth again — the symbol throughout the book of rightness, authenticity, peace. But the earth is not his life, as it is

Lena Grove's. Man's highest aim in this book is to meet his destiny without everlasting self-concern. Yet this profoundly tragic cast to *Light in August*, so much like a Hardy novel in the implacable pattern that unrolls against a country background and in the inarticulate stillness of its leading characters, is matched by Faulkner's ironic awareness that man, even in his endless brooding over the event, can never stop, that the event is nothing compared with the speculation that follows and in a sense replaces it. One of the most revealing phrases in Faulkner's rhetoric is "Not that"—it is not peace, not an end, that his people ever want. The violence may be "outworn," but it is the human passion. He describes his chorus, the townspeople, scurrying around Joanna Burden's house after her murder, looking "for someone to crucify":

> But there wasn't anybody. She had lived such a quiet life, attended so to her own affairs, that she bequeathed to the town in which she had been born and lived and died a foreigner, an outlander, a kind of heritage of astonishment and outrage, for which, even though she had supplied them at last with an emotional barbecue, a Roman holiday almost, they would never forgive her and let her be dead in peace and quiet. Not that. Peace is not that often. So they moiled and clotted, believing that the flames, the blood, the body that had died three years ago and had just now begun to live again, cried out for vengeance, not believing that the rapt infury of the flames and the immobility of the body were both affirmations of an attained bourne beyond the hurt and harm of man. Not that.

We can never let the event go, for that would mean an end to the human history that is lived in retrospection. Just as Faulkner's language is full of words, like "avatar" and "outrage," which are really private symbols left over from his unceasing meditation, and just as his style is formed from the fierce inner pressure of problems which give no solution, so the actual texture of *Light in August* suggests, in the tension and repetition of certain verbal motifs, that man can never quite say what the event originally meant, or what he is to think of it now. Language never quite comes up to the meaning of events. To adapt Faulkner's phrase, it is not that, or that. The townspeople exist in *Light in August*, as in so many Faulkner novels, to ask questions whose very function is to deny the possibility of an answer. Faulkner's grim sarcastic asides show that he views language as in some basic sense unavailing. The astounding repetition of certain key phrases and verbal rhythms in his work signifies his return back and back on the question.

Call the event history, call it the Fall: man is forever engaged in meditating, not the past itself, for that would bring knowledge, but man's guilt, for that may bring freedom. Guilt, not history, is the nightmare from which all of Faulkner's deepest characters are trying to escape. The guilt arises from man's endless complicity in his own history, as when the innocent, gravely staring child that Joe Christmas was, ate her toothpaste and listened to the dietitian making love. Hightower is guilty because his sickly, foolish nostalgia for his grandfather's one day of glory made him unavailable to his own wife, who committed suicide; Joanna Burden feels so guilty that she has remained an alien in the Southern town in which she was born, accepting her isolation as the price of her identification both with her abolitionist forebears, who were shot down in the South, and with the Negroes, on whom a curse must have been laid. Even Doc Hines and Percy Grimm murder in order to "clean" life of the stain that Negroes have put on it, for as the Negroes were cursed by God, so they have cursed life, and the maniac "saviors" of Southern racial purity have to save their hallowed country from contagion. But just as no one of them can really distinguish the hate they feel for others from self-accusation, so no one can say with whom guilt began, where the ultimate human crime was committed. The paths which lead back to the human past are endless through the human brain, and sitting at his study window after he has gained new self-respect by delivering Lena's baby and by standing up to Percy Grimm, the dying Hightower still ruminates, goes over and over the past, as "the final copper light of afternoon fades" and "the world hangs in a green suspension in color and texture like through colored glass." The everlasting reverie begins again, but now the wheel of life that brought Lena Grove to Jefferson begins to slow down, runs into sand, "the axle, the vehicle, the power which propels it not yet aware." These memories are endless, and the style in which they are described is overcolored in a way that shows how static action often becomes in Faulkner's work, how much it serves as the raw material for reflection, which is why he can lavish so many Joycean compound words on objects which do not seem to move of their own accord, but to be rallying points in Faulkner's tortured concern with guilt.

Guilt is endless; in the labyrinths of the mind, there is turning but no deliverance. Like T. S. Eliot, Faulkner is a favorite today because he takes his stand on human guilt; this is the side of ourselves that we can recognize and, curiously, stand by; for in this alone, as we feel, is the possibility of our freedom. When men feel so wretchedly small before their own past, they must be guilty. So runs the legend. This is the argument behind Faulkner's novels: of the God who made Yoknapatawpha County. In the beginning, life was free and good and natural; but something inexplicable, a curse, was put on it. Perhaps the curse is nothing more than man's effort to get the better of events that are "too much for us"; the evil lies in arrogance. Doc Hines hears God addressing him personally, ordering him to act for Him. Calvin MacEachern, Joe Christmas's adopted father, starves and beats him because he cannot memorize portions of the catechism on order. "He asked that the child's stubborn heart be softened and that the sin of disobedience be forgiven him also, through the advocacy of the man whom he had flouted and disobeyed, requesting that Almighty be as magnanimous as himself, and by and through and because of conscious grace." Even Joanna Burden tries to play God to her Negro charges. *Light in August* is one of the sharpest criticisms of Calvinism ever written, but unlike so many Southern writers on Puritanism, Faulkner knows that the same religion is found in Doc Hines and Joanna Burden. The guilt that is the mainstay of their faith is embodied in the assumption of excessive authority by fathers, lawgivers, teachers, ministers. Everyone wants to play God to the orphan Joe Christmas. In Faulkner's eyes, life is an ironic and tragic affair that is beyond human rule and misrule; but Calvinists like Doc Hines and Calvin MacEachern, or the children of Calvinists like Joanna Burden, even murdering simon-pure "patriots" like Percy Grimm, take life in their hands, they dominate, and they murder. Joe Christmas is their favorite charge; he is the man "things are done to." His final ignominy comes when his mistress, Joanna Burden, regarding him in her new phase as a Negro charge to be "brought up," tells him that she wants him to go to school so that he can become a lawyer. And it is at this point that he breaks. It is this point that has always been the signature of the everlasting victim. Other men are the lawgivers; the law is passed out to him, through him, inflicted on him. And so finally he murders and dies, a pure victim, shot, castrated, treated like a thing. It is the final ignominy. But in the very unattainability of his suffering, in its inexpressibility, is the key to his healing power over others. For where life exists so much in the relation of master to man, of the elect to the sinner, the only possible consummation man can ever reach, for Joe Christmas as for Uncle Tom, is in the final consistency of his suffering, in a fate so extreme that it becomes a single human word which men can read. This is what Faulkner means in that exalted passage after Joe Christmas's immolation:

> . . . when they saw what Grimm was doing one of the men gave a choked cry and stumbled back into the wall and began to vomit. Then Grimm too sprang back, flinging behind him the bloody butcher knife. "Now you'll let white women alone, even in hell," he said. But the man on the floor had not moved. He just lay there, with his eyes open and empty of everything save consciousness, and with something, a shadow, about his mouth. For a long moment he looked up at them with peaceful and unfathomable and unbearable eyes. Then his face, body, all, seemed to collapse, to fall in upon itself, and from out the slashed garments about his hips and loins the pent black blood seemed to rush like a released breath. It seemed to rush out of his pale body like the rush of sparks from a rising rocket; upon that black blast the man seemed to rise soaring into their memories forever and ever. They are not to lose it, in whatever peaceful valleys, beside whatever placid and reassuring streams of old age, in the mirroring faces of whatever children they will contemplate old disasters and newer hopes. It will be there, musing, quiet, steadfast, not fading and not particularly threatful, but of itself alone serene, of itself alone triumphant.

Joe Christmas has attained the stillness that will finally allow us to see him. Of sufferings alone is he made, and in this sense, and in this sense alone, is he a figure whose condition is so total that he reminds us of Christ in the sense of Christ's integrality. That tortured and would-be Christian philosopher, Simone Weil, understood this when she found in *malheur*, affliction, that it could become so much in itself that she felt riven to the universe by bonds of pain. The archvictim may not be a "martyr," as students of modern totalitarianism have noticed, but there is a kind of suffering in our time which is so extreme that it becomes an integral *fact* of the human condition. Father Zossima bowed down to Dmitri Karamazov because of all the affliction he would undergo. So marvelous is Faulkner's compassion, he can visualize in the man who was nothing but a victim the shadow thrown from the Cross of Christ, who was nothing, as it were, but Himself. Men are men because events are always "too much" for them; Joe Christmas became one with his life in that extreme moment when even he had no longer to search out the past. The figure on the Cross is the most tremendous interventive symbol in history; the castrated man on the floor has only one free power in his life — to stop running at last and to face his murderer. Faulkner intends no parody; he is moved by the likeness of totality to totality. But neither is he a Christian. There is no redemption; there is not even in *A Fable* — but there man has the courage to redeem circumstances by denying their fatality. In *Light in August* the past is not merely exigent; it is even malicious, the spirit of pure bad luck, a godlike force that confronts man at every turn with everything he has been, and so seems to mock and to oppose him. This is called "The Player": Lena's seducer, "Brown," still running away from her at the last, sends a Negro boy to the sheriff for the reward money he has earned in informing on Joe Christmas, but knows despairingly that he will never see the money.

"He wont do it. He cant do it. I know he cant find him, cant get it, bring it back." He called no names, thought no names. It seemed to him now that they were all just shapes like chessmen — the negro, the sheriff, the money, all — unpredictable and without reason moved here and there by an Opponent who could read his moves before he made them and who created spontaneous rules which he and not the Opponent, must follow.

This is the Opponent that Joe Christmas decides finally not to elude again, the "Player" who moves Percy Grimm unerringly from position to position:

He was beside the ditch now. He stopped, motionless in midstride. Above the blunt, cold rake of the automatic his face had that serene, unearthly luminousness of angels in church windows. He was moving again almost before he had stopped, with that lean, swift, blind obedience to whatever Player moved him on the Board. He ran to the ditch.

All things are fated; man is in any place because the Player moved him there. Our past sets up the positions into which we fall. This is why Joe Christmas's grandmother, Mrs. Hines, utters the most significant lines in the book when, at the end, she pitifully cries out:

> "I am not saying that he never did what they say he did. Ought not to suffer for it like he made them that loved and lost suffer. But if folks could maybe just let him for one day. Like it hadn't happened yet. Like the world never had anything against him yet. Then it could be like he had just went on a trip and grew man grown and come back. If it could be like that for just one day."

And it is in these terms that we come to understand why Joe Christmas, in running away from a past that he cannot escape, seems constantly to be looking back as he runs. Not only is no one free of his past; he even has, at the most critical moments, the sense not of moving at all, but of being silently lifted from position to position. It is because of this curious effect of immobility in Faulkner's characters as they run (as if they were held up in the air by wires) that Faulkner can lavish such idle poetic largesse upon them, can see in a Percy Grimm that "serene, unearthly luminousness of angels in church windows," and at various points throughout the book emphasize Joe Christmas's rigid likeness to a man in prayer. Even the countrymen in overalls move at one point "with almost the air of monks in a cloister." The reason is that all these characters are lost in contemplation as they are moved here and there by the Player. There is no free action for anyone: everyone is carried, as Lena Grove was carried to Jefferson in a whole succession of farm wagons, by the fate that was and so shall be.

« 4 »

Faulkner's world is grim — a world in which the past exerts an irresistible force, but against which there is no supernatural sanction, no redeeming belief. He believes in original sin, but not in divine love, and he is endlessly bemused by the human effort to read fate or to avoid it. The highest reach of his belief is the effort to become "a saint without God" (Albert Camus), but this is a point not yet tried for in *Light in August*. Correspondingly, there is great power in his work, but little color, and *Light in August*, for all its brilliance, somehow wears the lackluster look of the year in which it was published, 1932. It is a grim book, and the countryside described in it already has the pinched, rotted look that one sees in so many depression novels about the South. The greatest fault of the book is its overschematic, intellectualized cast. Although Faulkner himself has lived more like Joe Christmas than like the Sartorises, he is socially far from the world of Joe Christmas and Lena Grove, and there are telltale signs in the novel that it is written *down* — for Faulkner, too much from his head down, and about people whom he tends to generalize and to overpraise, as if he saw them only as symbols rather than as entirely complex beings. And it is a simple fact that the opening of *Light in August* is so beautiful that nothing else quite comes up to it.

On the other hand, it is one of Faulkner's greatest books, and although it does not have the blazing directness of *The Sound and the Fury* (a book written more directly out of Faulkner's own experience), it has much of the creative audacity which is Faulkner's highest ideal in art. With this book, published in 1932, Faulkner completed a period of extraordinary fertility. He was only thirty-five; since 1929, he had published, in rapid order, *Sartoris, The Sound and the Fury, As I Lay Dying, Sanctuary,* and *Light in August*. It was a period of tremendous creative power. When he was recently in Japan, Faulkner said of this time: "I think there's a period in a writer's life when he, well, simply for lack of any other word, is fertile and he just produces. Later on, his blood slows, his bones get a little more brittle, his muscles get a little stiff, he gets perhaps other interests, but I think there's one time in his life when he writes at the top of his talent plus his speed, too. Later the speed slows; the talent doesn't necessarily have to fade at the same time. But there's a time in his life, one matchless time, when they are matched completely. The speed, and the power and the talent, they're all there and then he is . . . 'hot.' "

Light in August comes out of that "one matchless time." The only possible objection one can have to the book is the number of implications which Faulkner tries to bring out of his material — for just as the characters' own lives are "set" for them to mull over, so Faulkner constantly mulls over them, wringing a poetry that has grandeur but also an intensity of contemplation that is sometimes more furious in expression than meaningful in content. If we see Faulkner's narrative method as essentially recollective, in the form of individual meditation over past events, we can recognize the advantage he has over most "naturalistic" writers and we understand why Faulkner refers to himself as a "poet." For what makes the portrait of Joe Christmas so astonishing is the energy of imagination lavished upon it, the consistency of texture that derives from the poet's sense that he has not only to *show*, in the modern realistic sense, but to *say* — that is, to tell a story which follows from his contemplation of the world, and which preserves, in the nobility of its style and in the serene independence of its technique, the human victory over circumstances.

It is this that makes us hear Faulkner's own voice throughout the book, that allows him to pull off the tremendous feat of making us believe in a character who in many ways is not a human being at all — but struggling to become one. And this, after all, is the great problem of the novelist today. Joe Christmas is an incarnation not only of the "race problem" in America, but of the condition of man. More and more, not merely the American novel, but all serious contemporary novels, are concerned with men who are not real enough to themselves to be seriously in conflict with other men. Their conflicts, as we say, are "internal"; for they are seeking to become *someone.* Joe Christmas lives a life that is not only solitary but detached. He lives in society physically, but actually he is concerned only with the process of self-discovery, or of self-naming, even of self-legalization. This is a fate which, as we know, can be as arduous and deadly as that of the classic heroes. But in Joe Christmas's case, there is no conflict from positions of strength, no engagement between man and man — only the search of the "stranger," *l'étranger*, to become man.

[1957]

William Faulkner: More Snopeses

In the country of William Faulkner's imagination — Yoknapatawpha County — the Snopes clan plays a role that is by now wholly symbolic. The Snopeses are not like the Compsons, the McCaslins, the Sartorises, the De Spains (and the Faulkners), who were the ruling class of this highly stratified society — and with whom Faulkner so naturally identifies that his greatest works, like *The Sound and the Fury* and *The Bear*, come out of his anguished sense of decline. They are not like the Negroes, whom Faulkner also knows intimately, and from whom he has often drawn his noblest and most significant characters. The Snopeses, at least in origin, are poor whites, "peasants," with a genius for trade, for sharp dealing. They are rapacious and grotesque-looking, impassive, inhuman and unbeatable. By applying an extreme shrewdness and an unsleeping eye to every situation in life that can possibly be turned into cash, they always come out on top. In Faulkner's eyes, they are the great symbol of what has happened to the old order in the South. They are the fixers, the termites, the outsiders, the Neanderthal men of the new age who, by cunning alone, with an utter lack of tradition and culture, have stolen in from their corner in Mississippi, Frenchman's Bend — see *The Hamlet* (1940) — and, taking every possible advantage, are now winning over the "town," Jefferson, where they prepare the way for the final downfall of Faulkner's own class.

Symbolically, the principal Snopes, Flem, is impotent; symbolically, he wears, every day of his life, a nastily impersonal little metallic black bow tie. Symbolically, Snopeses are named I. O., Eck, Mink, and name their children Vardaman and Bilbo, after the more extreme racist Mississippi Senators. Other children pop up as Montgomery Ward Snopes, Wallstreet Panic Snopes, Admiral Dewey Snopes. Symbolically, the Snopeses now own the hotel; and Flem, the most ignorant of men, appears as superintendent of the municipal power plant — his wife is the mistress of Mayor De Spain.

The Town, by William Faulkner. New York: Random House.

Faulkner even makes a pun on the strongest element in Flem's nature by having him steal the brass safety valves off the boilers. Symbolically again, Flem soon becomes vice president of the old Sartoris bank of which his wife's lover, the Mayor, is president.

When one Snopes goes to France in 1917, he not only spends his time behind the lines running a soldiers' canteen but turns it into a brothel; when he returns home, he rents a store and makes money projecting dirty postcards on an illuminated screen. One Snopes deliberately tempts kids to raid his watermelon patch so that he can shoot at them. And I have forgotten to add that I. O. Snopes hired a man to tie up his mules on a railroad track so that he could collect indemnity from the railroad company after the train killed them, and that when the man himself also got killed, this Snopes thought that, as the man's employer, he deserved a share of the widow's life insurance.

The Snopeses certainly are a symbol, and they are so inhuman in their effrontery, coldness and greed that they seem to do nothing all their lives but to work up some still more outlandish swindle. Episode after episode, each one weirder and more fantastic than the other, with Faulkner constantly outguessing the reader as to what possibly can come next from the unbelievable and innumerable tribe of Snopes. When he runs temporarily out of episodes, he just brings in more Snopeses. At the end of the book, one is not surprised to find a whole new generation of Snopeses, the products of an alliance between Byron Snopes and a "Jicarilla Apache squaw in Old Mexico" — all of whom carry knives, never use words at all, and are portrayed simply as wild prairie dogs with very sharp teeth.

Wildly extreme and insanely grotesque as many of these Snopes antics are, they do not make up comic episodes any more; they are synthetic jokes. The truth of the matter is that Faulkner does not believe the Snopeses are human enough to be taken seriously, and by now the "symbolic" pattern that you are supposed to see in the very name of Snopes has become a weak rubber stamp. I don't even believe that Faulkner sees the Snopeses as a causative agent in the decline of the old order; "Snopes" has become just a trade-mark, like the crazy family names in comic strips. The two Snopes brats who trick their grandfather back into the watermelon patch are simply the Katzenjammer kids.

The book is a string of anecdotes, some of which are worked up from old short stories, and it is dramatically so loose that it is plain that Faulkner himself has tired of the Yoknapatawpha saga. He does something here that he never did in any book before — he coyly serves up whole summaries of the saga to link this book with the others. In the past, he would offer such material not as "information" to the reader, but as the compulsive repetition of certain themes. And everybody out of his old books comes on stage in this one, as in the grand finale of a revue. It is a striking example of the loose, improvised, sometimes gagman quality of the book that the county attorney, Gavin Stevens, who figures so importantly in other Faulkner novels, here becomes a completely silly character, is constantly out of focus, and at times sounds more like a parody of Quentin Compson, the romantic intellectual in *The Sound and the Fury,* than like the sage, wise conscience of the old order that he was in other books.

And yet — tired, drummed-up, boring, often merely frivolous as *The Town* is — you can never forget that it comes from one of the most astounding literary imaginations in the modern world. As so often happens with a Faulkner book, one is conscious of Faulkner's own voice, of his unflaggingly passionate mind, above all, of his intense and brooding grief, as the most lifelike element in the book. The truth is not merely that *The Town* is a bad novel by a great writer, but also that Faulkner has less and less interest in writing what are called "novels" at all. It is significant that, despite his enormous influence on intellectuals, he means very little to many practicing novelists, and that professional storytellers often look upon him as a very queer duck indeed. Nor is it an accident that, of all the noteworthy American novelists of our time, the one most admired by Faulkner should be the self-centered Thomas Wolfe, who took the most "chances," or that Faulkner should constantly describe himself by the old-fashioned and generic name of "poet."

A better word for it would be soliloquizer. Just as one hears, louder and firmer than anyone else's, Faulkner's own voice, and with it those highly abstract words like "impervious" and "outrage" and "intractable" that flood into this book as regularly as the waves of the sea, so the episodes, the anecdotes, the jokes, even the characters, figure in *The Town* never as themselves but as devices to make points with. They are the dots and dashes, the punctuation marks, in his private unending soliloquy on the past. He is a man possessed, possessed not so much with his characters and incidents as with what they symbolize in his vision of things.

When he knows these characters well, or when he feels profound compassion for them, then he is magnificent; when he is concerned only with the symbol, his talk is abrasive and hysterical. And just as he can describe things only as a function of his own brooding meditation, so, in this book, the story is told by a succession of witnesses for whom everything is an illustration, a symbol, an example. He even needs two foreground observers, Gavin Stevens and the itinerant sewing-machine agent, V. K. Ratliff, to keep reporting to each other on the Snopeses, to keep outguessing each other on what Snopeses will do next, in order to retain the interminable brooding that is the very essence of Faulkner's mind and of the grief that fills it.

The grief is not over what the Snopeses have *done*. It is over a Southerner's constantly unavailing effort to make sense of history, to come to terms with the unexplained failure of the past. The Snopeses do not mean to Faulkner what they do to certain genteel Southerners who think of the past as "ruined" by a discernible lower-class enemy. Faulkner is not sentimental about the old order, and he shows, in this book, how the De Spains, the Stevenses, the Mallisons, the "old" families, have been only too eager to accommodate the Snopeses. But if the Snopeses do not figure in his mind as the devil in Southern history, they do indeed figure as the grotesque, the subhuman men, which his impatient, angry, irritable mind lights on as the generic illustration of what the South has come to.

One of the really compelling anecdotes in the book tells of the time that Flem Snopes had a whole house of furniture moved in on the promise that it would be fit for the "vice president of a bank." Flem didn't know anything about furniture, but the dealer understood him perfectly and shipped a whole house of furniture suitable to a vice president. It is no wonder that the Snopeses remind one of the freaks in comic strips: they have the same indistinguishable grotesqueness, the same horrible reality of modern men. They are symbols all right, not of a class but of a condition.

And the less Faulkner is able to understand this condition, the more he piles up the grotesqueness. He is talking to himself, trying to reason it all out. This is why, even when incidents are dragged out of old books, the characters renamed and the jokes refurbished, one feels, despite Faulkner's relaxed weariness with so old a tale, the immense, the still unspent, the inextinguishable power of his brooding concern. I am not saying that this power is enough to change *The Town* into a good novel. I am saying that it is a book with Faulkner's stamp and brand and fire all over it. One can be irritated with it, but not indifferent.

[1957]

William Faulkner: The Short Stories

FAULKNER'S short stories are not of the kind that has made the *New Yorker* famous; they are not even the stories of a writer who often writes stories; many of them are not really "short stories" as that peculiarly contemporary branch of literature has been invented, patented, and mechanically imitated in the United States — tight, deft, wholly dramatic and polished fables of social life that present symbols rather than characters whose uniqueness is the prime concern of the writer. So little is Faulkner a short story writer, in fact, that several of these stories — and by no means the best! — were written for the slicks: something that could never be done by the kind of short story writer who specializes in the art of the miniature, and for whom each short work has to be perfect.

Faulkner has often turned to the short story in order to relax. There is a hammy and grandiloquent side to his imagination — as well as to his rhetoric — a kind of sodden and mischievous looseness of manner that easily spills into his stories. It reminds me of W. C. Fields presiding over a banquet. One side of Faulkner's literary manner is that of the temperamental impresario presiding over his created world — a manner that recalls the gigantic confidence of Dickens and Balzac working away at their great blocks of

Collected Stories of William Faulkner. New York: Random House.

marble. The fact that there is no other American novelist today who suggests such impressions to the reader is an instance of the power and breadth of Faulkner's imaginative world. Faulkner has an abiding sense that the whole human race can be fitted into his own native spot of Mississippi earth, no larger "than a postage stamp." The characters in these stories range from Indians on the old Mississippi frontier, who had *their* Negro slaves, down to Mid-westerners who have been transplanted from their frontier into houses, in Southern California, backed "into a barren foothill combed and curried into a cypress-and-marble cemetery dramatic as a stage set and topped by an electric sign in red bulbs which, in the San Fernando valley fog, glared in broad sourceless ruby as though just beyond the crest lay not heaven but hell."

As such fiercely inimical phrases suggest, Faulkner pays out steady moral judgment on all that has unfolded in his *comédie humaine* of American life. Moving from the Indian swamps to Hollywood (past the South before and after the war, the clash of the poor Snopeses with the haughty De Spains and Sartorises, the young aviators in the Royal Flying Corps, traveling air circuses in the 1920s), the reader has a constant sense, in Faulkner's work, not of "America" but of world history on this soil, from the time when "New Orleans was a European city." A whole procession of races, clans, tribes, and classes moves through these stories, and you sense that you are reading not from story to story, from "gem" to "gem," as they say of collections by Katherine Anne Porter or J. D. Salinger or Hemingway (these are really virtuosi of the short story and perhaps exclusively of the story), but from anecdote to anecdote fallen from the novels that are themselves recurrent stories of what has happened on this "postage stamp" of land in Mississippi.

Of course there are stories in this collection, like "A Rose for Emily," that are famous anthology pieces — stories that show all too clearly how airily Faulkner can reproduce the manipulation of the reader's emotions that is the real aim of the commercial short story. "A Rose for Emily" is the story of the old maid who fell in love with a Northerner but resisted being jilted once too often; only after her death, when the curious townspeople were able to enter her house at last, did they discover that she had kept her dead lover in the bed where she had killed him after their last embrace. But even in "A

Rose for Emily," the intended Gothic touch of horror counts less with Faulkner than the human drama of the Southern gentlewoman unable to understand how much the world has changed around her. And in a far greater story, "That Evening Sun," in which the characters are the Compson children from Faulkner's great novel, *The Sound and the Fury,* the emotion of the Negro servant, Nancy, who is pregnant by another man and lives in terror of being killed by her husband, is built up with such skill and communicates so well the bewilderment and anxiety of the children themselves (Quentin, the oldest, is the narrator) that the terror of the woman becomes the atmospheric center of the story, communicating itself to the children as the first absolute fact they must learn to recognize.

"That Evening Sun" begins with a description of "old" Jefferson in the days when Negro laundresses still walked about carrying baskets of wash on their heads, and were able to stoop under fences without dropping their load. And the use of this opening comes back to us when young Quentin describes Nancy telling a story to him and the children — ". . . like she was living somewhere else, waiting somewhere else. She was outside the cabin. Her voice was inside and the shape of her, the Nancy that could stoop under a barbed wire fence with a bundle of clothes balanced on her head as though without weight, like a balloon, was there."

This concern with emotion as a fact in itself, virtually an absolute, that stands apart from history and survives it — this is nowhere more pronounced than in "Red Leaves," probably the high point of this collection. An Indian chief has died, and his Negro slave, knowing that by custom the dog, the horse, and the body servant of a chief must be buried with him, runs off to the swamp. Faulkner indulges in a certain amount of mischievous humor, Southern white man's humor, at the expense of Negro slaves. With his marvelous sense of costume, he describes an old Indian, barefoot, in a long linen frock coat and a beaver hat, busily complaining that "This world is going to the dogs. It is being ruined by white men. We got along fine for years and years, before the white men foisted their Negroes upon us. In the old days the old men sat in the shade and ate stewed deer's flesh and corn and smoked tobacco and talked of honor and grave affairs; now what are we to do? Even the old wear themselves into the grave taking care of them that like sweating." And the torpid, tubby Indians go after the runaway with a kind of sadness — they are vaguely sorry for him, but sorrier that he cannot understand and accept fully the ritual that obliges him to be buried with his master, thus putting Indians to exertions that are undignified and useless. These Indians are philosophical-minded, yet they are so detached in their fatalism (the world moves as it must and men must die) that they can insist on their ritual without, as it were, having to respect it. The Negro slave, by contrast, is portrayed as *misunderstanding* his proper function as a man; he seems to find satisfaction in the exertion of flight itself (as does Joe Christmas in *Light in August*). When he gets panicky, he identifies himself with the animals in the woods, and all in all is shown operating on a level that causes the Indians to shake their heads. Yet as in his great novel, *Light in August,* Faulkner rises above these reflections on the race his own class so long held in servitude; the story ends on a concentrated image of the slave, begging for water before his end and unable to swallow it. On capturing the slave, who had nowhere to run but back home again, this Indian had said, "Come. You ran well. Do not be ashamed." Now he simply says, in a final, not unkindly order — "Come." It is a marvelous story, and not the least for the sense of fatality in human affairs that unites the Negro and Indian at last; this sense of what *must be* is always the deepest element in Faulkner's imaginative sense of things.

Perhaps it is this quality that interests me in a story, "Beyond," that is admittedly slight and even a bit forced in emotion. But Faulkner, portraying a dead father who in a brief interlude of consciousness after death has been searching for his son, who died at ten, has the man say, ". . . anyway, there is a certain integral consistency which, whether it be right or wrong, a man must cherish because it alone will ever permit him to die." At times, as in the story "The Tall Men," this classical understanding in Faulkner, his insistence on the supremacy of character over everything, tends to get propagandized. In this story an old Southern law officer says to a stranger: "Yes, sir. A man gets around and he sees a heap; a heap of folks in a heap of situations. The trouble is, we done got into the habit of confusing the situations with the folks." And Faulkner practically smirks as the old fellow says it. Still, the fact remains: it *is* "folks," not "situations," that make up the real life of fiction. "Situations" make short stories, but "folks" make life. Faulkner is interested in "folks." No wonder that his interest sometimes gets too big for the mold to which stories are fitted.

[1961]

Graham Greene and the Age of Absurdity

IN 1943 I saw a draftee, in a long line of men waiting in their underwear for an Army physical, reading Graham Greene's *The Confidential Agent.* It was a perfect book for the occasion, since it is possible to ignore almost anything while reading it; and since it deals with a much-troubled Loyalist agent in England during the Spanish Civil War, it was still highly suitable to the times. Graham Greene's "entertainments," as he now calls books like *The Confidential Agent* and *The Ministry of Fear,* to distinguish them from his later "serious" novels, reflected perfectly the pervasive anxiety of the Hitler-Mussolini age. In these thrillers the average man, the muddled and anxious man who usually appears in Greene's fiction as if he had stepped in a grimy mackintosh out of a London tube station, personified everyone's feeling of dread before the inhuman monsters of Nazism-Fascism. At the same time, the Greene hero personified that acute and enigmatic sense of guilt, usually arising from some surprising passion in his personal life, which so often made one irrationally feel that Hitler-Mussolini expressed the dark side of *everyone's* nature.

The sense of guilt is the essential theme of all Greene's fiction. It explains the chase after the hero in his "entertainments," and as the aftermath of adultery it results in the inner struggle on the brink of damnation that is the stuff of supposedly more "serious" books like *The Heart of the Matter* and *The End of the Affair.* The protagonists in both the entertainments and the novels are essentially decent and haunted human beings who are led into sins of violence and despair by the unexpectedness of some human attachment. They are fools, martyrs and clowns of love, and through their

Our Man in Havana, by Graham Greene. New York: Viking.

love we see parallel lines — love for a human person, love of the divine law — that cannot meet in time. In the nightmare world of the 1930s and 1940s, a man had good reason to connect his personal guilt with the even now incredible sadism of Hitler. When governments can turn civilized society into a literal hell on earth, it is hard for the average man, with his conventional share of original sin, not to feel that the world has been turned, in a bad dream, into the ministry of fear.

The Hitler period marked the high point of Greene's entertainments and concealed, because of its psychological pressure, the essentially hysterical personal emotions that Greene was able to whip up. He was able to find dramatic symbols for states of anxiety and dread because of his concern with plot, a neglected element in contemporary fiction. The Hitler age made for melodrama, the spy chase. In his later "serious" novels, Greene betrayed the subjectivity of his thinking by trying to make plots out of the complex moral dialectic of sin itself — the non-Catholic reader of *The Heart of the Matter* and *The End of the Affair* is embarrassed as well as baffled to find himself being invited to take points of doctrine as if they were universally accepted dramatic actions. As George Orwell complained, Greene, "by trying to clothe theological speculations in flesh and blood," produces psychological absurdities. Nevertheless, the plight of husbands and wives who fall passionately in love with people they are not married to furnishes in Greene's "serious" books the same authentic sense of imminent damnation that Hitler and Mussolini did in his scary "entertainments."

With *Our Man in Havana,* which is advertised as a new entertainment, we can see that the Khrushchev-Dulles age lends itself not to dread but to farce. Our plight is now so universal and at the same time so unreal that the age of anxiety has turned into the age of absurdity. The Greene hero has not changed. He is still defeated, sad, and the clown of love: an Englishman who sells vacuum cleaners in Havana, he was deserted by his wife and left with a young daughter to bring up. Like all true Greene protagonists, he feels guilty because *he* was deserted. That is the characteristic bit of adult psychology that one always finds in a Greene novel.

But otherwise, what a change is this! The engrossing nightmare thrillers of the 1930s and 1940s have turned giggly and empty. Formerly, a man became a spy for a cause he did not *quite* believe in because he was trapped by his own guilt, his sense of his human inadequacy. But now, Mr. Wormold (Worm-mold? — the average man and his destiny couldn't be more explicitly conveyed) accepts an invitation from the British secret service in order to accumulate a dowry for his pretty daughter. Our anti-hero is recruited in the men's room; the code book is Lamb's *Tales from Shakespeare* (the director for the Caribbean couldn't find duplicate copies of anything else except *Uncle Tom's Cabin*). Mr. Wormold industriously goes to work, collecting wages and expenses from London for wholly fictitious agents and for reports largely rewritten from the Latin-American section of *Time* and information bulletins put out by the Cuban government. In a rare moment of inspiration, Mr. Wormold thinks up and draws the plans of a superbomb that reminds his chief in London of a vacuum cleaner, but of course he cannot get away with it. This is not because London doubts him but because rival spies also take him seriously. This leads to murder, a chase, and to the final clinch between Mr. Wormold and the assistant sent out from London — a lady who left her husband because he was permanently in conference at UNESCO. When she discovers the deception Mr. Wormold has practiced on the British government, she realizes that he is priceless. "Do you think that I would ever have left Peter if once — just once — he'd made a fool of UNESCO? But UNESCO was sacred. Cultural conferences were sacred. He never laughed."

You are all expected to laugh with *Our Man in Havana*. But Mr. Greene still has strong feelings. The wicked police chief in Havana, who carried a cigarette case made of human flesh, "squeezed out a smile. It seemed to come from the wrong place, like toothpaste when the tube splits." The preposterous secret-service chief in London wears a black monocle over a glass eye. The eye itself is "pale blue and unconvincing; it might have come out of a doll which said 'Mama.'" These feelings are directly expressed in his lady's tribute to Mr. Wormold. "I don't care a damn about men who are loyal to the people who pay them. . . . There are many countries in our blood . . . but only one person. Would the world be in the mess it is if we were loyal to love and not to countries?" This is significant doctrine, but to use it against material — the cold war — that is portrayed as essentially meaningless can be dangerous. Mr. Greene has never believed that anything but love is significant. Once the times concealed this from him — from us — by lending him something really terrible to write about. In the age of terror, melodrama made sense. In the age of absurdity, a farce like this is just petty. It hardly exists.

[1958]

The Great American Bore

JOHN O'HARA's latest novel, *From the Terrace,* is almost nine hundred pages long, costs almost seven dollars, and is such a mercilessly repetitive and meaninglessly detailed documentary of upper-middle-class life in the first half of the American Century that it was sold to the movies long before publication and will undoubtedly become a best seller. It is the kind of book that Hollywood producers can pick and choose from without ever troubling with the author's point of view; and for the same reason it will be read by a great many people who derive cultural prestige by buying a "big" book. Also, it has more scenes directly describing sexual intercourse than any other recent "big" American novel, and some of the details are even more flavorsome and unexpected than the descriptions of sex in Mr. O'Hara's own A *Rage to Live,* James Gould Cozzens's *By Love Possessed,* James Jones's *From Here to Eternity,* and Vladimir Nabokov's *Lolita.*

From the Terrace is a book that makes no great demand on anyone's mental faculties, for the narrative (which even has footnotes!) is so loose and so full of extraneous information that one can nod over dozens of pages without losing the thread. There is no plot, no dramatic unity of any kind to enforce suspense or even tension. The book is simply the biography of a Pennsylvania steel manufacturer's son, Alfred Eaton, who becomes an investment banker and an Assistant Secretary of the Navy in 1943. He could be James V. Forrestal or Robert Lovett or any comparable figure of his period; one derives the same pleasure from the story of Alfred

From the Terrace, by John O'Hara. New York: Random House.

Eaton that one gets from any solidly documented biography—except that biographies deal with people who are real to begin with, which this character is not, and that in biographies there is usually no occasion to itemize every sex experience a man may have in some sixty years of living.

Why are such books called novels? *From the Terrace* has no story except in the external sense, no dramatic situation apart from the historical circumstances, which everyone already knows. There are several minor characters who appear only as names, and there are others—no less minor in their effect though they often reappear in the book—for whose conduct there is not the slightest explanation. The book is simply a large piece of American history in our time, ripped out of the reference books, and it is only because Mr. O'Hara is relentless in his determination to get on paper everything he knows—or can find out—about the upper middle class in this country that the book exists at all.

Mr. O'Hara's mimetic talent for fiction, which is considerable, has never been accompanied by a point of view that is anything but surly. So long as he wrote in his early novels as a social sorehead from the wrong side of the tracks in Pottsville, Pennsylvania, his fiction still had wit and organization. But for some time now Mr. O'Hara has been as vain and oracular as any Broadway celebrity in "21," and with the disappearance from his fiction of any real point of view, his books have become overgrown and meaningless in the vanity of their documentation, to the point where someone whose talent was always for the ironic social fact, for the thrust and bite of the short story, no longer knows how to keep a book under control. He pointlessly brings in characters from his other books; he even coyly refers to himself, in a way that makes us realize that he has substituted his own creative vanity for an imagined subject. But he can do this because the form of the "big" novel, the "great American novel," is one that Americans identify with their history.

The "great American novel" is a form which Americans respect, not only because it seems equal to the "grandeur" and size of the country and the universal implications of its history, but because in some way its looseness, its broodingness, its very size seem about to yield up the secret, *the* essential truth of American life. Its repute rests on the idea that one book, necessarily a very big book, can deliver up the mystic substance of American life. The "great American novel" is not only *Giant* and *Ice Palace, Main Street* and *Of Time and the River*; it is also *Moby-Dick* and even *Leaves of Grass*. Probably because of the overwhelming historical self-consciousness of a new country, the need to provide some central and lasting interpretation of American experience, the American has always believed that there is peculiar authority about one book, one *great* American book.

As the country grew in power and the success of American history came to seem the great romance of the nineteenth century, the natural literary interest in reporting the westward expansion was equated in the minds of many Western Americans with the belief that their region and experience had replaced in authority the arrogant New England tendency to speak for the country. Faith in the "big" novel is identifiable with the cult of the frontier, when the Westerner came to think of himself as the symbolic American; and big books about the West seemed to come near the "heart" of America, exactly as Franklin's autobiography had in the eighteenth century given a human face and will to the necessary American myth of that era. Indeed, books like Franklin's autobiography, the saga of the self-made man, correspond to the myth that American history must emphasize one hero and one theme in exactly the same way that, in *Moby-Dick,* Melville celebrated American whaling men as the prototype of all modern know-how. By now the "voice" of American history, the essence of what Americans like to call the "mainstream," the broad popular tradition, had become the common man, and the significant literary test of the "great" American book had become not only that it be a novel (which in a sense even Whitman had tried to write) but that it be "rich," "lusty," "truly American" — descriptions which fit Melville and Whitman and Faulkner as easily as they do Edna Ferber and Frank Yerby, and which indeed explain why anyone sensitive to American literature has never, at least not until recently, sneered at this "main" tradition, for it has included our highest flights of literary imagination as well as our standard potboilers.

The "great American novel," then, has never in itself been a bad tradition; it has been simply a tradition. Its weakness lies in the steady identification of this loose form with its subject matter; the writer who is interested in documentation for its own sake, who has no real sense of the tragedy — perhaps of the final incommunicability — of human experience will be tempted to make out of the "great American novel" what, in the age of journalism, radio, television, is simply unnecessary. What has turned the "great American novel" into the great American bore is the fact that most of its practitioners simply have no point of view. *An American Tragedy* has all the faults of the genre, plus a few that only Theodore Dreiser could have invented; but it is an extraordinary novel because the masses of fact on which it rests, and the enormous spread of the story with all the repetitions which Dreiser allows himself, stem from a deep and painful sense of the social process as it afflicts the innocent. In the same way *Look Homeward, Angel,* though far less good a book, transcends the inevitable American limitation of form by the way it sets up a poetry of pathos — Wolfe's sense of personal doom reiterated in the image of a locked door — against the bitterness of a real family situation.

But the increasing documentation of our mechanical age has gone hand in hand with the evaporation of any true motive for this activity, and it is for this reason that the early novels of Sinclair Lewis, which also rest entirely on the worship of facts, are so superior to those of a writer like O'Hara, who has the same desire for finicky accuracy of speech, but who invariably stresses tricks of speech like the unexpected emphasis on certain syllables rather than the devastating banality, the fatal ordinariness and meaninglessness which one can hear in the speech of people who are always trying to sell or impress each other. There was sense in documentation when "the big change," as Frederick Lewis Allen called it, made it imperative and fascinating for Americans to describe the technological revolution in American life. But the great period in American fiction that coincided with this change was possible because so many "provincial" Midwesterners like Scott Fitzgerald and Sinclair Lewis, Sherwood Anderson and Willa Cather, could still be startled by a transformation that is no longer news to us, one in which we have permanently hardened as a result of the Second World War.

« 2 »

The American novelist finds it increasingly difficult to react with any sense of shock or recognition to society, and for this reason even gifted writers tend to collapse after one big strong book, floating home on a tide of overwhelming personal emotion, or — once the personal connection with material is lost — helping themselves out with the external facts. The "great American novel" had already become the great American bore in the big blowsy novels of the Second World War that were written out of journalistic encounters rather than real experience — compare a strong and harsh book like *From Here to Eternity* with Irwin Shaw's *The Young Lions*. The farther away Americans actually got from the war, in the maze of the table of organization, the more they plumped for stereotypes; the pathos of the "common man" was seen in duplicate, along with the wealth of showy and unmeaning technical information that was now disgorged in "novels" about the Air Force, parachute troops, the Signal Corps, and even the OWI. More and more in recent years, with the evident collapse of any real sense of fiction, the "big" American novels have come to read alike. The absence of a point of view has led to the indecent size of these books, until, as if this were a disease where the body swells as the mind disappears, we have these tumescent, nine-hundred-page novels which read as if they had been composed mechanically, on electric typewriters, to be read by people who come alive only when the books turn, as they always do, to raw sex.

The increasing tendency of American writers to tell us everything about each sexual encounter springs from the same naïve belief that a novel exists in order to disgorge information; the naïveté, the utterly vulgar naïveté, lies in the belief that sex is a wholly physical activity which can be described in the same terms that we might use to describe a fight or a dance. The late Dr. Kinsey sincerely believed that statistics on the number of ejaculations men have a week tells us something about sex in America. He was no less naïve, however, than John O'Hara, who can never describe an encounter between lovers without telling us what each partner wore, how much each disrobed, what happened where, and exactly how long it took. Sex, as everyone who has read O'Hara's other novels knows, is a subject whose external — and therefore standard — manifestations have unbelievable interest for him; it is not unfair to suggest that the emotional resonance is so powerful because sex still seems evil and even outrageous to him. In his recent novels it is always the female of the species who is rapacious, who despises love as "sentimental" in favor of raw sex. Mr. O'Hara goes to great trouble in this book to note exactly what debutantes might have worn at a Long Island dance in 1921, and he even lists in a footnote the subjects necessary for entrance to the Princeton class of 1915. But he will not bother to get the psychology of individuals down right, and if his women characters often sound suspiciously like Broadway males at Toots Shor's, even when they are supposed to be Southern ladies, it is because the real uselessness of this kind of novel, either as literature or as social reportage, is that it is based on general types, not on individuals at all.

The persistent weakness of all American sociological thinking is that it is precise and statistical to an extreme without ever clearly defining the object of its interest. Much of this sort of writing rests on social envy, on the outsider's feeling that he can nail something down by being entirely factual; it is based, like so many stories in *Time*, on adoration of the American as success. What O'Hara, too, is concerned with is not the true novelist's question — *Who* is this human being? — but the typical American competitive question — *How* did he get this way? Just as the story of a celebrity in *Time* finds it necessary to first-name or nickname the subject in order to bring him down to our level, so the reportorial "big" novel functions by denying the humanity of the hero, which is inevitably what happens when you begin with the type and have to work up to the individual. O'Hara certainly does want to work forward; he is a writer who is obstinate rather than crude, and no one can miss the enormous effort he has put out in an attempt to make us realize the individual "psychology" of Alfred Eaton. (The formula for this: his father preferred a younger brother to Alfred, and Alfred slowly takes on the coldness and inner weakness of his father. But this is not made clear until the end, and is explicitly stated rather than dramatically visible.) But an artist does not try to reach an individual by way of a type: one realizes the type in the individual.

O'Hara is so full of his hard-won knowledge as a social observer that he simply runs off the track half of the time trying to pin down the exact emphasis of speech, the actual food eaten, the courses taken at Princeton. He cannot describe the sex life of a married couple without psychologizing crudely in terms that have only the most general application; hence these pearls of wisdom: "What had happened to her was that she unconsciously abandoned the public virginity and, again unconsciously, began to function as a woman." He describes the difficult relationship between the two brothers in terms that sound as if he had been reading Dr. Spock: "If William slapped Alfred or otherwise punished him, the difference in age was always mentioned while William himself was being punished; and each time that that occurred the age separation contributed to a strengthening of the separation that was already there because of, among other considerations, the two distinct personalities." This is from a novel!

O'Hara's knowingness belongs to the television era, the celebrity-on-the-quiz show, the age of Gunther. But in his case, as always, the unforgivingness of the lower-class man deprived of access to the prep school and to Princeton has been rendered not only pedantic but meaningless by his admiration for everything in this class, from the Racquet Club tie and bar to the line of roll-top desks that the partners occupy at a famous private bank.

Nine hundred pages! Nine hundred pages of characters who appear for a paragraph and are forgotten; nine hundred pages of rapacious females who talk about sex like college sophomores discovering that "sex is nothing but sensation anyway." Nine hundred pages of detail about rich men's stables, what workmen ate for lunch in a Pennsylvania steel mill in 1900, of careful notations about lemon phosphates and who was mad at whom and who slept with whom, and what people ate at a prep-school lunch in the 1920s ("Excellent potato salad, excellent baked ham, excellent summer sausage . . . choice of milk, tea, or coffee"). Nine hundred pages — to tell us that in the early 1920s it was still called "the Martini cocktail," not a Martini, and that in this same period collegians at a dance would tuck their black ties under their collars, that "almost every young man thus attired wore a gold watch chain from which depended a collegiate charm, and the majority parted their hair in the middle."

What is all this information for? Why does O'Hara pour it on so? The answer is that "intensity" and "sincerity" — the cardinal American virtues when you are trying to sell something — take, when it comes to novels, the form of massive blockbusters, of stampeding you with information. It is true, as Mr. O'Hara has said in a recent interview, that the first half of this century was the most exciting time in the world's history. But what exactly do we learn of this period from his novel that we did not know before? We never know exactly why one leading character in the book turns homosexual, or why a big Texas oil man, after being sentimentally and almost fulsomely admired for his kindness to the hero, is shown up as a monster. But we are deluged, suffocated, drowned in facts, facts, facts, until the American need to have news of ourselves finally turns into the same obscene narcissism as the mirror on the bedroom ceiling and the same meaningless technical efficiency as the great American science of duplicating and spreading and illustrating information.

The dream of the "great American novel" — that in it we would find the ultimate figure in the carpet, the secret theme of American life — has turned in books like these into a mechanical intensity of accumulation, and it is about time that someone pointed out that the great sex thrill for which so many people turn to these books has finally, as in American psychology generally, become a department of human activity as humdrum as the parent-teachers' association. In such books the collapse of the novel as a form, of plot as a device for bringing out the unexpected drama of life, of character as a response to a situation, has made for a final irony. Where once the "great American novel" sought to uncover the essence of American life, there must, by now, be a book of this kind for each period, class, race, and stratum in American life. In this accumulation of brute fact, novelists like John O'Hara have finally succeeded in making America seem as unremarkable as themselves.

[1958]

IV
Famous Since the War

A Brilliant Boy from the Midlands

THERE were — there are — many countries that far more actively practice inequality than does England; surely there is none in which people *care* so much about keeping up the external form of it. Poor but brilliant boys can advance very fast and very high in England; the cabinet, the upper civil service, Oxford and Cambridge — all ranks are open to the deserving, all are full of exceptional men whose fathers were crofters, clerks, insurance agents. Yet there is not one of them, in my experience, who has not been permanently branded by self-consciousness, who has not had to become intellectually sharper, more competitive and wary, than is always natural to the development of genuine gifts.

This situation is really serious in literature, which has always been close to the central sources of power. The "lower-class" writer who is not a genius like Dickens or D. H. Lawrence, the writer who can no longer operate within a revolutionary framework as did H. G. Wells, is handicapped by the traditional connection between literature and society. The English writer finds himself in a period when the revolutionary *élan* is gone, when no young radical from the provinces can identify himself with the scientific utopianism of Wells's time, when the Labor party is dispirited and "angry" young novelists announce publicly that they are bored with it. It is difficult for such writers to put themselves forward. In the past the great energy of writers like Dickens and Lawrence and Wells was that they represented the revolutionary new impulse that would make England over in their image. Dickens accomplished this by his effect on social reform and Lawrence by his moral influence on the intelligentsia. But in our time, when England has become not only a declining power but when its radicals can no longer muster the challenge to power, the rising writer must find a new myth, some ruling idea to connect with.

This is the social situation behind the novels of C. P. Snow. Snow's situation in contemporary fiction often appears more unusual than it really is: he was trained as a physicist, did research in crystallography, and during the war was in an important government post as a director of scientific personnel. Because of this background, Snow has often written about science with more intimate and exact knowledge than literary men can usually muster. But as a critic he has unfortunately tended to attack the "novel of sensibility"—so often identified with Virginia Woolf and Bloomsbury—as if his scientific background itself had given him some healthier and saner perspective, one that could assist the literary imagination, so hard-pressed by science in our time, to become more usefully concerned with "reality." This suggestion that writers would do better if they knew more about science seems to me misleading. Snow's animus against the "novel of sensibility," the highly formal art novel, is surely based on the exclusiveness, both social and esthetic, of the Bloomsbury school even more than it is on any special insights Snow may have derived from science. It is part of the age-old quarrel in English literature between H. G. Wells and Henry James, between the school of experience and a wholly esthetic coterie. There is an irreducible gap between the intellectual elite of Bloomsbury and self-made writers from the Midlands like C. P. Snow; between a social experience like Virginia Woolf's, so comfortable that it permitted a life wholly devoted to art, and one like C. P. Snow's, whose novels tell over and over of the struggles of poor boys for careers.

Snow's frequent invocation of science does not convince me that the literary imagination can somehow broaden itself, become more balanced and wise, by learning science. It is simply his way, as a novelist, of connecting himself with the new rulers: the scientists themselves. Snow, born in 1905, arrived too late to believe in science as Utopia, a faith that failed even Wells in the last years of his life. But unlike young novelists whom he tends to connect with himself, writers who tend to be sunk in the minutiae of provincial and domestic life, "kitchen" novelists, Snow *is* old enough to have grown up believing in the ascendancy of poor boys to power, in the great career as a real subject, and this seems to me the essential concern behind his novels.

« 2 »

There are no contemporary novels quite like the *Strangers and Brothers* cycle; one reason is that they are not altogether novels. Snow, in opposing his work to the formal esthetic of Woolf and Joyce, has also saved himself from artistic risks and demands in which he is not interested. Snow's work is entirely personal in spirit and theme; it is as essentially private a form as any work so deeply autobiographical and historical must be. These seven novels are the record of a man's career, and the different volumes often depend on the reader's own historical experience and sympathy, on his awareness of other details in the series, in a way that makes the reading of Snow's books an emotional experience rather than the experience of an objective work of art. These novels are unusual, but they do not, as some of Snow's admirers often glibly suggest, offer a new technique to the English novel. No books so loosely personal in form can give a pattern to other novelists. Snow's achievement is a tragic conception of life, founded on the contrast between the will with which a gifted boy makes his way up in England and the accidents of life that determine his actual fate.

One of the most striking things about Snow's novels is that they are remarkably intelligent and exceedingly melancholy. They have none of the careless hearty vigor, the animal force, that one associates with English writers of the "people." They are so obviously the products of a man who has had to think long and hard that one of the real pleasures in reading Snow is actually the way in which he draws the reader into this gentle activity of reason. Characters in Snow's work are not so much presented as interpreted; the narrator and central figure in the series, Lewis Eliot, spins everything out of his reflections and memories. The method of reminiscence permits Snow the greatest possible freedom as a novelist. He can refer to incidents in preceding books, or point ahead to others; he can refer passingly to a story, like the unhappy marriage of Lewis Eliot himself, which he has begun in one novel, *Time of Hope,* and will conclude several years later in *Homecoming.* The frame is always Lewis Eliot's own career inside contemporary English history, politics, business, and university life. Again and again, as in an autobiography, Snow will refer to a date, 1938 or 1940, so that the reader will fill out the sketchy picture for himself, and he often refers to activities not seen on stage, activities that are merely named, in a way that would have horrified a novelist like Conrad, who said that above all the novelist must make the reader *see*. There are many details, scenes, characters in Snow's work that he does not bother to make us see; and what we do see is filtered through the interpretative wariness of Lewis Eliot's mind, who has learned from childhood to examine, to dissect, to understand quickly, to size up.

This wariness seems to me basic to the psychology of Snow's novels; it fascinates me because it is so obviously an English social habit that has been made full use of in creating character. Lewis Eliot makes his way up in the English world, from a poor family and a clerk's job; he becomes a barrister, an adviser to a powerful industrialist, a Fellow at Cambridge, and, during the war, one of the administrators of the secret atom-bomb project. As he recounts the various episodes in his life, he interprets people around him constantly in terms of their powers and possibilities, on how much they measure up to. The emphasis on the will, starting from Lewis Eliot's own will to escape the provinces, is as significant as Eliot's emphasis on brains. In the English fashion, the highest places are open — but only to the highest possible concentration of ability, energy, devotion. To an American, used to the waste, self-indulgence, and the salesmanship that are so rife in a country that is only beginning to recognize the need for trained intellectuals, there is an unusual fascination in Snow's constant concern with the competitive English elite and with his own powers for sizing up character.

It is no wonder that C. P. Snow was chosen to administer scientific personnel and that he was recently knighted for this work; he has an awareness of people such as only a poor and gifted boy who has had to depend for everything on his intellectual resources can develop; it reminds me of the sharp, rousing, malicious, but uncomfortably objective conversation of English scholars gossiping in commons rooms about each other. The field is open, the race is to the best; every possible trait of energy, decision, confidence, counts in the final sum. This is a society of ambitious people who have learned to sharpen their wits on each other. Snow is able to tell us things about poor law clerks in small towns (*Strangers and Brothers*), Cambridge dons (*The Light and the Dark* and *The Masters*), lawyers and industrialists and even provincial clergymen (*Time of Hope*), rich English Jews (*The Conscience of the Rich*), and atomic scientists (*The New Men*) that make us realize how fascinating, how stimulating to a novelist's powers, can be a society full of intellectuals on the make, delicately balancing off against each other native gifts, racial background, physical strength, energy, stubbornness, originality. No wonder, I often think when I read Snow, that the English did so many primary studies in genius, in character, in race; no wonder that they have so blunt and realistic a conception of power and are so brutally frank to each other about different races. They size up men as coldly as a trainer examining horseflesh, yet their public manner is always careful, starched, externally "correct" — and this, too, is strength.

It is this theme that makes Snow's novels always absorbing. The interest of characters who appear always from this competitive point of view is immense: lawyers like George Passant, Herbert Getliffe, and Eliot himself; physicists like Francis Getliffe and Nightingale, doctors like Charles March; scholars like Roy Calvert and the old master, Winslow. Even aristocrats like Lord Boscastle in *The Light and the Dark* try consciously, in the interests of their own superiority, to beat down the middle-class traits surrounding them. These are people who are always vying with each other, who are quick to note the slightest gaucherie, to count on the subtlest weakness. Yet what redeems this world from hardness, what keeps it from the viciousness and even murderousness that one associates with similar themes in French fiction, is the fact that this competition is for prizes all can agree on. The national idea is so strong that the code of the gentleman operates with equal force on those who must approach it from the outside. There is a sense of professional excellence, of scholarly truth, which, when it is lacking, works against the aspirant as severely as if he were found stealing. In Snow's recently reissued first novel, *The Search*, the physicist-hero gives up science altogether when he realizes that his sense of truth is not as compelling as his ambition for power. It is characteristic of the *esprit de corps* that is built into this competitiveness in England that the hero judges himself, and finally excludes himself from science, as sharply as if he were one scientist sitting in judgment on another.

The only force in Snow's novels that works against this emphasis on personal ambition is the sometimes tragic mystery of personality, which often unmakes the career that the will has made. The pervasive melancholy of Snow's work comes from his constant sense of the trickiness of the human heart, the perverseness and indisposability of human character, which binds us to people we should not love, to actions that are destructive of everything we value. The *Strangers and Brothers* series is actually a succession of tragic individuals — George Passant the reckless optimist, Roy Calvert the brilliant Orientalist who is a manic-depressive, Jago the candidate in *The Masters* who is defeated because his wife seems to others unfit to occupy the master's lodge, Martin Eliot in *The New Men,* old March in *The Conscience of the Rich*. The chief symbol of this recurrent defeat is Lewis Eliot himself, who marries an unstable woman, Sheila Knight, and cares for her so desperately that he is prevented from reaching the highest place in his profession. It is typical of Snow's instant use of explanation in presenting character, and of the humanity and sadness of his explanation, that Lewis's attachment to Sheila is explained as a passion for "waifs," for victims, that allows him to keep his privacy. At the end of *Homecoming,* when Lewis finally decides to marry a woman who is much better for him, he consciously affirms that he can now give himself fully to a woman, that he can drop the "spectator" position, the watchful, marginal strategy that has always been behind his passion for helping others.

But the real significance of this "spectator" position lies in the fact that it permits Snow — through Lewis Eliot — to spin novels richly and continuously out of his reserve of private meditation. Although Snow has often written about the novel as if he had a healthier and broader interest in society than "sensibility" novelists like Virginia Woolf, although some of his more enthusiastic admirers have often suggested that Snow has invented a new form, the truth is that the "spectator" position which Eliot feels has protected him from involvement is actually the strategic position which has permitted Snow to write so many interesting novels at a time when many writers are in despair about the novel as a form. Despite Snow's strictures against excessive personal sensibility in fiction, his own work depends on such sensibility; and what James called the "foreground observer," the leading character who unites all strands of a story in his central consciousness, is fundamental to Snow's work. All the virtues and all the faults of Snow's writing stem from the elastic control made possible by the foreground observer, the hero as thinker. It gives him the range, the sense of social scene, that is the great strength of the books, the fascination of society that returns us to the living stream of the novel. On the other hand, it also means the mechanical scenes of reverie, the half-sentimental night walks in all of Snow's novels which are so nerveless and weak, scenes which make us feel that Snow, in his reliance on analytical intelligence, has gone as far with character as explanation as he can go, and that he is merely catching his breath. There is a slackness of artistic rhythm in Snow's books, a marked decline of intensity, that makes us realize that in depending upon his remarkable intelligence and the external history of England since 1925, he has worked out the urgent emotions that took the brilliant boy to London. He has not yet assimilated fully into his scheme the persistent theme of social inequality that has become more and more a burden on the imagination of England. At a wedding party of two aristocrats in *Homecoming,* Lewis Eliot, looking around him, thinks:

> When I had first met them both, it had seemed to us all self-evident that society was loosening and that soon most people would be indifferent to class. We had turned out wrong. In our forties we had to recognise that English society had become more rigid, not less, since our youth. Its forms were crystallizing under our eyes into an elaborate and codified Byzantinism, decent enough, tolerable to live in, but not blown through by the winds of scepticism or individual protest or sense of outrage which were our native air. And these forms were not only too cut-and-dried for us: they would have seemed altogether too rigid for nineteenth-century Englishmen . . . quite little things had, under our eyes, got fixed, and except for catastrophes, fixed for good.

[1959]

The Southern "City of the Soul"

FAULKNER once wrote that "For every Southern boy fourteen years old, not once but whenever he wants it, there is the instant when it's still not two o'clock on that July afternoon in 1863, the brigades are in position behind the rail fence, the guns are laid and ready in the woods . . . and it's all in the balance, it hasn't happened yet." But after he has passed fourteen, a Southern boy who is unusually sensitive and intelligent and lives in an age like ours may find it impossible to dream back to that moment when it was all revocable. The legacy of the war has become all too real, and the contrast with what Southern hotheads once hoped for it can be torturing. No wonder that, like Faulkner's greatest characters, so many honest and intelligent contemporary Southern writers seem to be engaged in a wrathful quarrel with themselves — as if, with their moving sense of responsibility, they were both the past and the present, both the South that they love and the North that as intellectuals they find it easier to live in. No longer is it possible for *them* to pretend that "it's all in the balance, it hasn't happened yet." For Southern writers with this painful attachment to the past, all too much has happened, and the attempt to be morally equal to the present can be wearing. Sometimes the only way out of the circle of defeat, disillusionment, and guilt is a certain mordancy about human nature in general, an impatient cry that one should not have expected too much of people anyway.

An active sense of disillusionment, an insistence that human nature is flawed, endlessly paradoxical, and in a very real sense untrustworthy, recurs rather insistently in Robert Penn Warren's novels and poems and essays. Both in the character and in the political philosophy of Willie Stark, governor of a state very much like Louisiana, it became the theme and furnished the plot of Warren's best-known work, *All the King's Men;* even the title, *Brother to Dragons,* of Warren's book in verse about the sickening butchery of

The Legacy of the Civil War: Meditations on the Centennial, by Robert Penn Warren. New York: Random House.

a slave by a Virginian related to Thomas Jefferson told of his quarrel with Jefferson's eighteenth-century "illusions" about human nature. To judge from the recurring scene in Warren's novels of lovers guiltily expecting to be discovered, his harsh concern with guilt seems to be psychological as well as historical — and in fact Warren's more recent novels have replaced with "Freudian" explanations what in his first and perhaps best novel, *Night Rider*, was presented in theological terms.

But whatever changes of philosophical emphasis Warren has made over the years — in this new book he conveys his own belief as "pragmatism" — the theme of his work always comes to me as a complaint against human nature. So much do I hear it as a complaint rather than as a positive point of view that I associate it with some cherished innocence that has been destroyed. Just as Warren has written one of his most famous poems directly about original sin, so all his work seems to deal with the Fall of Man. And if in reading Warren's books I have come to be more and more wary of his handling of this theme, it is because of the nostalgia that it conveys, the strident impatient language with which it is expressed, the abstract use to which it is put. To complain in every book that man is a brother to dragons, that "it's human to be split up," that human nature is full of "bitter paradoxes" — this, though not for me to disprove in our baleful times, seems to me not the attitude of an imaginative artist. My objection is that Warren tends to make rhetoric of his philosophy, as in Governor Willie Stark's well-known saying, so much admired by American undergraduates, that "Man is conceived in sin and born in corruption and he passeth from the stink of the didie to the stench of the shroud." Whatever human nature may or may not be, Warren tends more and more merely to *say* these things about it, often in bombastic language. The effect of these hotly charged statements is curiously to make him sound sentimental about his own theories and impatient in applying them to his analysis of events.

« 2 »

In a sense all of Warren's work could be called *The Legacy of the Civil War*. This little book has the honesty and intelligence and nervous force one expects of Warren's writing. But I must confess that I am baffled by the enthusiastic reviews it has been receiving from distinguished historians. Can it be that there is now so little to say about the Civil War that this very slight essay, thoughtful and unexceptionable as it is, seems of importance because it has been written by Robert Penn Warren? I will admit that I turned to it myself because of my interest in Warren, but despite his verve as a writer, I cannot see that it contributes anything new to the subject. So far as the Civil War itself is concerned, I wonder that Warren can take up so cursorily a subject that requires more detailed handling. After all, this "legacy" is nothing less than the emergence of the modern United States.

Yet Warren can take on the subject because it is this legacy that he has had to face all his life. By now he tends to state it with abrupt positiveness. The truth is that despite Warren's enormous production of fiction and poetry and his influence on the teaching of literature, his habit is to sum things up rather than to portray them for their human interest. And since he is also a powerful and impulsive rhetorician, with a great tendency to use words for the pleasure he himself gets out of using them rather than because they are the most suitable words, his writing is often impatient in tone. Readers of *All the King's Men* will remember how much Warren hung on the expression "the Great Twitch" to denote modern deterministic philosophies (and on Willie Stark's litany about sin, corruption, and the didie). In this book he likes to call the Abolitionists "Higher-Law Men," as if that phrase took care of them all, and he writes, "The philosophy of the Southern apologists did, however, offer space in its finely wrought interstices," that ". . . we should seek to end the obscene gratifications of history . . ." And he speaks of "charismatic arithmetic." This language seems to me abstract, curiously excessive, and hurried. Yet this tendency to write in emotional shorthand can also put him right on the mark, as when he notes of the Abolitionists that they thought they had "a treasury of virtue" and that Southerners have used the war as "the Great Alibi." "By the Great Alibi the South explains, condones, and transmutes everything. By a simple reference to the 'War,' any Southern female could, not too long ago, put on the glass slipper and be whisked away to the ball. . . . By the Great

Alibi the Southerner makes his Big Medicine. He turns defeat into victory, defects into virtues."

Warren's main point, of course, is that the war showed that North and South were more alike than they had thought. As he says of the argument over slavery between the extremists on both sides, "If in the North the critic had repudiated society, in the South society repudiated the critic." For every Southern failing, he has a Northern one to match it; for every glorious achievement on the Northern side, he can cite one equally glorious among the Confederates. The war did away with the inhuman abstractions of the Abolitionists as well as with the inhuman fantasies of unlimited power held by the slaveowners. The North was not for the Negro but for the Union; the South was full of people who felt more loyalty to the Union than they were able to avow. Human nature was the same on both sides, and the final outcome was to produce on both sides a society in which people would not demand the impossible of themselves.

Warren's impartiality of analysis, I must say, interests me more for what it reveals about a Southern writer arguing with himself than for what it reveals about the war. He quotes an unreconstructed Southerner who prayed "to feel different, but so far I can't help it." Warren says that "Even if the Southerner prays to feel different, he may still feel that to change his attitude would be treachery — to that City of the Soul which the historical Confederacy became, to blood spilled in hopeless valor, to the dead fathers, and even to the self. He is trapped in history." The last phrase (it recurs in Warren's writing, like the words "obscene" and "vicious" he applies to experience) conveys a good deal of anguish to me. The war is of course analyzed by Warren as the great school of experience in our history. But even when he shows the lessons it brought, you feel that it figures for him as the event which more than any in our history symbolizes the loss of innocence. He notes that Washington and Jefferson can never interest us now as do Lincoln, Lee, and Stonewall Jackson; the latter we see as "caught in dark inner conflicts." And in an eloquent yet tremulous passage, Warren comes closest to revealing the nature of his own attachment to the subject when he says: "A civil war is, we may say, the prototype of all war, for in the persons of fellow citizens who happen to be the enemy we meet again, with the old ambivalence of love and hate and with all the old guilts, the blood brothers of our childhood. In a civil war — especially in one . . . when the nation shares deep and significant convictions and is not a mere handbasket of factions huddled arbitrarily together by historical happenso — all the self-divisions of conflicts within individuals become a series of mirrors in which the plight of the country is reflected, and the self-division of the country a great mirror in which the individual may see imaged his own deep conflicts, not only the conflicts of political loyalties, but those more profoundly personal."

What is new in Warren's book is his use of the term "pragmatism," which he seems to have taken on not only as a corrective of the abstractions and fanaticisms that prevailed before the war but as a personal philosophy that accepts our split-up, contradictory human nature and that views life as a matter of endless experiment. What Warren means by pragmatism, I would guess, is the symbol it furnishes of the American mind's usual opposition to dogma and fanaticism and the excessively theoretical. Perhaps it simply means to be skeptical. But can an imaginative artist really proclaim himself a pragmatist in this purely critical and even negative sense of the term? Can pragmatism — not as a philosophy in law or economics, such as came out of the Civil War — serve a novelist applying its lessons negatively to human nature? In reading these references to "pragmatism" as an outcome of the war, I automatically nodded agreement; but in Warren's sudden enthusiasm for the term, I saw what it is about his novels and poems that so often bothers me.

The truth is that no matter what philosophy of life a novelist may claim, no matter how astringent or realistic or "pragmatic" he may set himself up to be, literature itself consists in saying "Yes" to life — not just to the "open" life that Warren praises, but to the life in every man, whether he is an Abolitionist or a slaveholder. Warren shows us the lessons that Americans learned from the Civil War, that we can learn still; one reads these pages in full agreement. But should *theories* of human nature interest a novelist this much? Don't all these "pragmatic" lessons show up our own superficially questioning attitude toward life as shallow and smug?

Whatever it may be in general, life, perhaps for the artist alone, is life in particular, the life that in some deep sense never can disillusion or dismay.

Nelson Algren on the Wild Side

It is difficult to take *A Walk on the Wild Side* seriously. To begin with, it is essentially a personal memoir of New Orleans in the depression era that begins as a kind of novel, but it never follows through as an objective narrative. It has genuine moments of interest only when Nelson Algren tells us in his own voice what the unbelievable year of 1932 was like, as seen by an unemployed newspaperman who was fascinated by low life in the French Quarter. But even worse than Mr. Algren's amiable confusion about what kind of book he is trying to write is the fact that his text is so full of meretricious, overcolored writing, so utterly charged up and jazzed up, that it gives at least one reader the definite impression that Mr. Algren is not even trying to describe anything accurately, for the whole thing has a boozily artificial and contrived quality that makes me think of it as a fantasy.

Although Mr. Algren writes here about extremely violent characters and situations — prostitutes, pimps, hobos, sex maniacs, thieves — I don't think his book has anything real about it whatever. His talent seems to me essentially that of a surrealist. It is not low life he is interested in but freaks; not tough people but grotesques; not the poor but the abnormal. "The Wild Side" is not a place in any city, not a state of mind, so much as it is the exaggeration of reality that fantasy delights in. Mr. Algren likes, above all else, to let himself go in fancy, exuberance, tumid writing; nothing he actually describes in this book interests him so much as the extravagance of his own feeling.

That is why the most violent things and situations occur without the reader feeling anything. What *can* a reader feel when nothing is ever worked out to a meaningful conclusion and Mr. Algren beats

A Walk on the Wild Side, by Nelson Algren. New York: Farrar, Straus and Cudahy.

the drums with prose that takes us "past broken men and breaking ones; wingies, dingies, zanies and lopsided kukes . . . ulcerous panhandlers, lame and cancerous, tubercular pencil peddlers, staggering lushes"? This kind of self-consciously "significant" writing is typical of his book. We read that "the light lay pasted like a second-hand shroud against a guilt-stained wall."

The thin thread of story that holds Mr. Algren's book together concerns a Southern yokel named Dove Linkhorn (joke on Lincoln), the all-time American sucker, who, needless to say, comes through a hundred adventures by making a fool of others. Yet this isn't what the book is about; for the point that Mr. Algren wants to make about Dove, and everybody else in the book, is that these are "lost" people. "Lostness" means lonely, lost love. If we ask why most of the book ends up in the red-light district of New Orleans, it is because the brothel is, in Mr. Algren's opinion, the place to which all the lost repair — to be taken in by others as lost as themselves. But even this puerile sentimentality becomes an excuse for endless descriptions of sexual hilarity, fantasy and debasement. Yet oddly enough this topic, though usually calculated not to miss, seems meaningless here.

The reason, I suspect, is that although Mr. Algren tells us he is writing about "lost" people, people who, he says, "develop into greater human beings than those who have never been lost in their whole lives," he does not feel much interest in them as human beings, and so can summon up for them, at most, only a vague literary pity. It is impossible to feel that he really cares about these people, that he is interested in them, that these are human beings he has observed. What I object to most in this book is the plainly contrived quality of this pretended feeling about characters whom Mr. Algren writes about not because they are "lost," but because they are freaks.

It can be said, I think, that the characters in that harrowing and grimly honest book, *The Man with the Golden Arm*, were also freaks of a kind, and that this was the secret of Mr. Algren's attraction to them. But although that book was equally sentimental and editorial in style, it was about something real: the life and death of a man. And it was written out of such a genuine belief in determinism that any reader could feel life mercilessly crowding down on Frankie Machine. The book made sense, it hurt like a blow, because Mr. Algren saw his lost and damned characters as victims of a system. He showed us how all parts of this system, from the politicians crowding the police at election time down to the smallest crooks, worked on and against each other to make up the iron meanness of Chicago. This new book shows, all too clearly, that Mr. Algren's usual material no longer points an accusing finger at anything or anybody. It is just "picturesque."

[1956]

Good-by to James Agee

JAMES AGEE, who died in 1955, was a writer who gave all of himself, and often it was himself literally that he gave, to every medium that he worked in — poetry, fiction, reportage, criticism, movies, television. He was not only one of the most gifted writers in the United States, but such a natural as a writer that he found a creative opportunity in every place where drearier people pitied themselves for potboiling.

He was the only writer on *Time* who could reduce a managing editor to humility; the only critic who could ever conceivably write about movies for the *Nation* with love; the only documentary reporter for *Fortune* who could make a wholly original book (*Let Us Now Praise Famous Men*) out of an assignment to cover sharecroppers. He wrote two of the best and funniest movies of recent years, *The African Queen* and *The Bride Comes to Yellow Sky*. He wrote the commentary for that tender movie about a little Negro boy, *The Quiet One*. He did a series on Lincoln, for Omnibus, that has been called the most beautiful writing ever done for television; and John Huston thought that Agee was the best screen writer "we have."

In themselves, such distinctions can be meaningless, since not even the serious writers who work for movies or television always take them seriously. But Agee was a writer who actually did better

A Death in the Family, by James Agee. New York: McDowell, Obolensky.

in popular and journalistic media — where certain objective technical requirements gave him a chance to create something out of his immense tenderness and his high sense of comedy — than when he let himself go in purely speculative lyricism. He was a natural literary craftsman, not a literary intellectual, and it was only *avant-garde* associations that ever misled him. His most beautiful poems — like the title poem of his first book, *Permit Me Voyage* — are those which are most traditional in form.

Like so many Southern writers (he came from Knoxville, Tennessee), he had such an immense capacity for feeling and such easy access to the rhetoric of English poetry that when not taken in hand by his medium, he could oppress the reader with merely beautiful words. His almost ecstatic feeling for music itself led him to seek unexpected dimensions in prose, and extraordinarily like Thoreau in this, he tried, in *Let Us Now Praise Famous Men,* to convey his feeling for the American land in highly charged rhythms that would stick close to the facts. Still, it is easy to overrate *Let Us Now Praise Famous Men,* for so many other books of the 1930s now seem unbelievable. Agee wrote of the sharecroppers with such love and rage that it is impossible to read the book without sharing his suffering. But despite its overpowering beauty of language and its immense personal nobility, the book is a turbulent preparation for a work of art that was not achieved.

Agee published in 1951 a short novel, *The Morning Watch,* and at his death he left a virtually complete manuscript which has now been published under Agee's own title, *A Death in the Family.* To anyone who knows how introspective and self-accusing Agee's less successful work could be, both these books show a disciplined control of his narrative material which, if anything, went too far. In both, Agee worked from his earliest memories in order to show the impact on a child of what was plainly a major factor in Agee's own life — the death of his father in the early Twenties.

A Death in the Family is worked out with the most immense care and slowness, showing the effect of the father's death upon a family in Knoxville — on the mother, Mary; on the six-year-old Rufus and his sister Catherine; and on the circle of the mother's close relatives. There are several scenes in it that are really hair-raising — especially one where the family, sitting together, concertedly feel the spirit of the dead father coming into the room; and one where little Rufus, too young to realize the immensity of his loss, argues with the kids on the block that he now has a special distinction.

Yet what makes the book so significant is actually not the dramatic qualities of a novel, but a universe of feeling, of infinitely aching feeling, which is built up so thoroughly, with meticulous truth to the agony of bereavement, that we finally have the sense of a wholly tangible sorrow, a materialization of human grief. The book is remarkable as a literary performance because, although obviously written from within — almost as if in obedience to a hallucination — it tries entirely to describe it as an objective situation. The little boy is an unconscious participant in what will hit him only later; unlike his older self in *The Morning Watch*, here he is not old enough to be aware or "interesting."

The trouble with the book as a novel, however, is that although Agee wrote with an almost unbearable effort at objectivity, one feels from the writing that this effort was made to externalize a private grief, not because he thought of the characters in the book as outside himself. The personality of the dead father actually comes through better than any of the living, for he is the single fact outside them to which they all respond as one.

To speak of faults in a book by James Agee is to point up the absurdity of literary comparisons. Agee's book cannot be judged as another novel-of-the-week; it is an utterly individual and original book, and it is the work of a writer whose power with English words can make you gasp. A brother-in-law, looking at the dead man, feels that he is looking down "upon a horned, bruised anvil; and laid his hand flat against the cold, wheemed iron; and it was as if its forehead gave his hand the stunning shadow of every blow it had ever received." The sense of the father in this book, of both the place he filled in life and of the emptiness created by his death, is one of the most deeply worked out expressions of human feeling that I have ever read. And to think of Jim Agee, with his bad heart, writing with such fierce truth so soon before his own death is to marvel, all over again, how literally it is himself that a writer will give to his task.

[1957]

Lawrence Durrell's Rosy-finger'd Egypt

I HAVE NEVER been to Alexandria, but having read *Justine* and *Balthazar* and now *Mountolive* — the first three novels in Mr. Durrell's tetralogy — I plan never to be disenchanted by an experience of the real thing. No place on earth could be so dense with literary atmosphere and poetic suggestion as Mr. Durrell's Alexandria. In the first volume, *Justine*, there are innumerable loving touches to bring home to us "the white city . . . whose pearly skies are broken in spring only by the white stalks of the minarets and the flocks of pigeons turning in clouds of silver and amethyst"; in the second, *Balthazar*, even the foreign warships in the harbor "turned in their inky reflections — the forest of masts and rigging in the Commercial Port swayed softly among the mirror-images of the water"; in *Mountolive*, "suddenly the sky line was sliced in half by a new flight, rising more slowly and dividing earth from air in a pink travelling wound; like the heart of a pomegranate staring through its skin. Then, turning from pink to scarlet, flushed back into white and fell to the lake level like a shower of snow to melt as it touched the water — 'Flamingo,' they both cried and laughed, and the darkness snapped upon them, extinguishing the visible world."

Lawrence Durrell writes prose like a man seeking the maximum sensuous enjoyment from each word. It is a poet's failing — when he writes prose. Some years ago, when Randall Jarrell published a novel, he is supposed to have exclaimed, "I didn't know it was this easy!" It isn't, and even so gifted and intelligent a poet as Mr. Durrell, when he writes novels, never gets near enough to life to know what he has left out. The English ambassador to Egypt, David Mountolive, who in youth had been the lover of an Egyptian Christian, Leila, discovers that her son, Nessim, has been sending arms to the Jewish underground in Palestine. Nessim has anticipated the rise of Arab nationalism and believes that with the

Mountolive, by Lawrence Durrell. New York: Dutton.

decline of Anglo-French imperialism, only a Jewish Palestine will be able to protect the non-Moslems in the Near East. Mountolive is deeply troubled. "Once in bed he entered a narrow maze of shallow and unrefreshing dreams in which he floundered all night long — images of the great network of lakes with their swarming fish and clouds of wild birds, where once more the youthful figures of himself and Leila moved, spirited by the soft concussion of oars in water, to the punctuation of a single soft finger drum across a violet night-scape. . . ."

"Soft concussion" is just the phrase for my experience of Mr. Durrell's novels. There are no sharp edges, no painful passions, no real losses, no hurts. People hop in and out of beds as if sex did nothing but induce gentle reflections on life; ancient Englishmen in the Egyptian police force become transvestites and are beaten to death by English sailors; homosexual dwarfs have hatpins thrust through their brains and are discovered at the end of a ball under a mound of coats on a bed; Leila's other son, Narouz, kills a hostile employee with a bull whip and goes hunting with his brother carrying the victim's head in his hunting bag; the suave and handsome ambassador is beaten and robbed by a crowd of child prostitutes. But everything is reduced to a vaguely diffused sensuousness of word and sensations; even the honest pangs of sex are muffled in the jasmine warmth and flowers of Alexandria, in words that represent the poet's effort to reach that absolute which is inherent in language itself. What is wrong with this in a novel is that it does not carry anything forward; it does not even help to create an atmosphere from which an action can follow. It is writing that exists merely to call attention to Mr. Durrell's exceptional literary sensibility, and that it does — to such a point that reading the novels is as cozy an experience as one can have these days. You know that Mr. Durrell will jog pleasantly along, more in touch with his own delightful imagination than with any of the notorious stinks, festers, sores, and dungheaps of Egypt.

« 2 »

This coziness makes a particular appeal to the kind of literary imagination that wants the exotic brought down to its own size. Mr. Durrell is a classical scholar, a man enraptured with all the ancient and poetic associations of the city, and the appeal his novels make just now is entirely understandable, even if he is writing a travelogue of Alexandria in Technicolor. Above everything else, Mr. Durrell has a way of suggesting that our grip on the external world is now so uncertain that all truth simply becomes relative to the observer. This indeed is the theme of his novels. "Fact is unstable by its very nature. Narouz once said to me that he loved the desert because there 'the wind blew out one's footsteps like candle-flames.' So it seems to me does reality. How then can we hunt for the truth?" Or as Balthazar puts it in the second novel: "Truth is what most contradicts itself in time." And in the third, after the novelist Pursewarden has committed suicide in contrition for his failure, as a British intelligence agent, to discover Nessim's plot to arm the Jews in Palestine — "Truth naked and unashamed. This is a splendid phrase. But we always see her as she seems, never as she is. Each man has his own interpretation."

This elegant skepticism is by now a familiar conception in the novel, and for at least fifty years the most interesting intelligence devoted to the novel has attacked the old conception of "reality" as something which the novelist had only to copy. But as Mr. Durrell explains in the preface to *Balthazar,* he has modeled his novels not on the Proust-Joyce method of prolonging the individual's experience of time but on the space-time continuum of relativity. The first three novels show the "three sides of space" and are "deployed spatially, not linked in a serial form. They interlap, interweave, in a purely spatial relation. Time is stayed. The fourth part alone will represent time and be a true sequel. The subject-object relation is so important to relativity that I have tried to turn the novel through both subjective and objective modes."

Unfortunately, I do not know what this means, and in his practice of fiction Mr. Durrell seems to me more adept at creating a prose-poetry about Alexandria than he is in making clear to us the kind of new vision he is trying to incorporate into his novels. To me he is a lyric writer with a highly fragmented intelligence, an innocent delight in Egyptian upper-class society, and a profound capacity for sensuous enjoyment. His mind is more independent, more genuinely reflective, than that of many contemporary novelists; but I am thoroughly convinced, after reading these three novels, that when his characters describe truth as unstable, they are really speaking, not wisdom, but for Mr. Durrell's own uncertain sense of reality. Again and again the reader of the novels suspects this, for he cannot help noting that when Mr. Durrell so sharply separates space from time he is attempting something which in the representation of actual human experience is impossible, since we do not think of space apart from time. It is to the point, too, that whereas Mr. Durrell told us that *Mountolive* would be "a straight naturalistic novel in which the narrator of *Justine* and *Balthazar* becomes an object, i.e., a character," this character, Darley, hardly appears in *Mountolive!* And Nessim's running of arms to Palestine, the situation on which *Mountolive* turns, one which is supposed to explain at last the peculiar relations between Nessim and his wife, Justine, is as improbable, artificial, and unserious a literary device as it is a political situation.

When I say "unserious," I do not mean frivolous but literary; the literary can be the enemy of literature. Mr. Durrell seems to me fundamentally a writer concerned with pleasing his own imagination, not with making deeper contact with the world through his imagination, as Proust and Joyce did. As Henry Thoreau, the Romantic incarnate, put it, "I went far enough to please my imagination." Mr. Durrell, who like Kipling was born in India, who is saturated in the warmth and freedom of Mediterranean culture, who has written with such beauty of Cyprus as well as of Egypt, seems to me the latest example of that blind adoration of the East that has been the staple of so many distinguished British writers from Kipling and Doughty to T. E. Lawrence. He has redeemed with his own sensibility the pains of imperialism, has sweetened the gall and wormwood of the East with the "perfumed sails" and "love-sick winds" of Shakespeare's Egypt. Alexandria, its very name from the great conqueror himself, its evocation of *Antony and Cleopatra,* its mingling of so many races and nations, gives a sensitive civil servant like Mr. Durrell a chance to relish the sweetness of the primitive and the corrupt, to eat his fill of the honeyed air, without ever getting any closer to the actualities of real political life and real Near Eastern dirt than he ever needs to. This saturation in atmosphere, this adoration of the primitive, is the British way of escaping the puritanism and responsibility of the national life and at the same time, by paying tribute to the victims of British power, of trying to make up for the actual guilt in which even a poet like Mr. Durrell, simply by being *there*, has shared. The enchantment of these ex-official travelers with the East is one of the great chapters in British literature, and no one can read Mr. Durrell's novels without sharing in the sensuous pleasures of Alexandria. But I cannot take these novels seriously; the greatest impression they leave on me is what a good time Mr. Durrell had in writing them.

[1959]

The Posthumous Life of Dylan Thomas

DYLAN THOMAS's posthumous life began before he died. Before he died, before he lay for days in a coma in St. Vincent's Hospital, New York, while the literati, literary hostesses, patrons, and others milled around the hospital — one lady even came into his room and stared at him for half an hour while he lay trussed up in an oxygen tent, with tubes is his mouth and nose — anyone up and down the broad literary-academic acreage of this country who heard him read, or watched him drink, could have said to himself (more usually herself): "That man is great, that man is disturbing, nothing so exciting has happened to me since I passed my Ph.D. orals, I am going to remember this; he will soon be dead."

He will soon be dead. The legend of the poet-dying-young is based not merely on the opposition between poetic idealism and a materialistic society documented by Chatterton, Keats, Shelley, Hart Crane, but on the romantic faith that true poetry is of a shattering intensity that destroys the poet even as it brings out of him, in letters of fire, the poetry itself. And the expectation is superstitious. What is peculiarly dear to us, what really transports and charms us, what brings new life to us from the hero, the poet, the great man — this, by an automatic human discount, is vulnerable and frail. But beyond these general considerations was the overwhelming single consideration of Dylan Thomas, who not only seemed more gifted, more eloquent, more joyous than any other poet of his generation, but was peculiarly available to all and everyone, so utterly without pose and literary pomp — he was always ragging his own poetry and, as he beerily filled out, the little barrel figure he made — that, alive, he was already "Dylan" to every casual pubmate and literary pick-me-up, with the impending appeal, winsome and rakish, of a Frank Sinatra.

It was this combination of genius and plainness, of force and sweetness, that made so many people write him off from the living before he was dead. He had an old-fashioned "big" gift that made people identify him with the "big" tragedies of old-fashioned poets. Just as many people in England and America who had no contact with advanced poetry read him with a puzzled but obstinate sense that he was important, while foreigners in Germany and Sweden, puzzling out his poems, would say with a sigh, "*This* is a poet," so they knew, they all knew, that he would "die soon." For beyond everything else — beyond the fact that he was endlessly available, that he conducted his life in public, so that everyone knew whom he loved and whom he drank with and how he had turned over a table full of food and drink at Sweet Thing College — lay the overwhelming fact that he was so obviously not in control of his life and did not pretend to be. Perhaps no one is in control any more and it is only in America that people still pretend to be. But the ruling fiction in government and philosophy and education, and even among writers, is that we must all know exactly where we are going and how to get there. As *Time* once noted admiringly about a suburban housewife, "she had life by the tail."

It was just the other way with Dylan Thomas. And it was because in an age full of supremely careful people searching for the "security" of personal happiness Dylan lived without sense, without a bank account, without an analyst, that he provoked the most tremendous astonishment and affection from people who had understandably forgotten what an enormous personal force can lie behind poetry. But he also aroused a certain fear, a fear for him and just as strong a fear of him, of all he could do to people's arrangements and engagements, and this often took the form of wishing "justice" to be done to him. He was so *outrageous*, as a student once complained, that in certain quarters his death aroused moral approval. And this belief in punishment, in righteous wrath against the outrager, was something that Dylan himself felt. When he first got the d.t.'s near the end of his life, he said that he had seen "the gates of hell." With his background in the shabby-genteel and the Nonconformist Welsh conscience, with his all-too-schoolteachery father and profoundly influential mother (to whom he paid dutiful daily visits at home), he not only felt at the end that he was in hell but that he deserved to be.

Of course he felt this — nobody brought up in our Hebraic-Anglo-Saxon-Puritan tradition ever sins carelessly, is ever totally apart from the sense of "sin." But the essential fact remains that Dylan Thomas didn't yield to that peculiarly American and modern folly of imagining that one can morally ensure one's destiny. As a poet and as a very canny observer in several countries, he felt that life in the twentieth century is peculiarly chaotic and measureless, full of desperate private rebellions and self-blame in a society which less and less gives most people any ideal to be faithful to. He felt that metaphysically we have no knowledge and no certainty — he said that his poems had been written "in praise of God by a man who doesn't believe in God" — and that only "the force that through the green fuse drives the flower," the life process from love to death, is real.

And since he lived what he believed, or rather what he didn't believe, it was quite clear — oh, terribly clear long before his death! — that Dylan Thomas was wonderful but extreme, and that he would die soon. It was not merely that he behaved badly, that he turned over the plate of canapés at one place and addressed ribald remarks to the pretty young dean of women at another. What made him outrageous to some — and exactly as challenging to others — was that he had, in the provocative sense, no hope.

He had no hope. I don't pretend to know exactly why this was, and it's too easy to say, as so many have, that he drank in order to recover the first excitement of his lyrical gift. I think that fundamentally his lack of hope came from the lack of ideas suitable to the boldness of his temperament and vocation. He had no philosophy or belief that could express for him, that could work for him, that could even explain the burden of love and terror before the natural world that is the subject of all his poetry. He was almost the pure type of the romantic artist in our world, determined to write only "happy" poems that would show life as joy. But he was unable or unwilling to bridge the gap between the splendor of his solitary conception and the deadness of the world without the poet's light on it. All of Thomas's poetry shows the profound romantic need to intensify existence, to make it all come alive as it is in personal consciousness. But where so many great poets — Blake, Wordsworth, Keats, even Whitman — have recognized that their task is not to lose their new vision to the commonplace world but to explain and to unite it to human existence, Thomas felt absurd and histrionic, acted like a man who in his heart thought himself a fake.

He was too humble. It is a strange thing to remember of anyone whose gift was so personal and sweeping, but he regarded his own gift as slightly absurd; he sheltered it, wouldn't have his poems discussed, because he couldn't admit that poetry *is* thought, and that what he said in his poems many of his contemporaries really believed and were most deeply grateful to a poet for saying again. He was left with his fantastic linguistic gift as if it were something to read from, to entertain with, but not, in the artistic sense, to practice as a criticism of life.

But then, how could he have felt this in our age? The great Romantic manifestoes were charters of human liberation by poets who identified themselves with new classes and revolutionary new ideas in society. In the gray drab British welfare state, Dylan Thomas felt like a "spiv," a juvenile delinquent. Being an utterly accessible and friendly and idle-feeling man, he couldn't help seeing himself as a faintly comic version of that universally respected legend, "The Poet." The public entertainer in him exploited the miseries of that humble bloke, that rumpled and tired Welshman, Dylan Thomas, who had no trouble enjoying his gift but who sometimes looked on it as something that had oddly been given *him* — he couldn't say just why! About other poets he could be utterly conventional in his admiration; his BBC talks on poets of Welsh background are banal. He even read the poetry of others with steadier power than he did his own. But if he was more reserved with people and perceptive about them than anyone watching him would have guessed, he was, about himself, without hope in the sense that he had nothing with which to explain and to justify the utter naturalness and human application of his poetry.

He believed in himself as a poet, there is no question about that; what he didn't believe in was what it was peculiarly the task of someone with *his* genius to believe in: that his poetry gave us truth about life and was a judgment on all of us, not just on himself. When people say that he drank in order to recapture the old ecstasy, his first excitement, they forget that his problem was not merely to recover this ecstasy, which understandably flagged, but to believe in it. Only this would have shown that he was in fact as great as others knew he was.

But guessing at his vulnerability, people foresaw his early death; and observing his abandon, they mistook his hopelessness for confusion. Obviously no poet of such fierce perception can tidily put his life away when he is not writing. The poet lives the truth he has to write, and when he is not writing he may live it in a chaos of unorganized sensations, of an excitement throwing itself upon life, that can bound back and destroy him. And Dylan Thomas's lack of "hope," in the specific sense in which I have tried to state it, should not obscure the central fact that as a poet he was the very opposite of the anxious salvation-seekers who are so dear to contemporary poetry. The tremendous vogue of Thomas's poetry stems from the fact that after the era of would-be "hard," pseudo-Christian verse of T. S. Eliot's followers and the self-conscious ironies of Auden, Thomas brought back to poetry the resonance of feeling, the connection with nature, love, and death which is the peculiar power of poetry and which Rilke defined as "the past that breaks out in our hearts."

The deepest side of such poetry—and of such an attitude to poetry—is not merely that it rests on images which are to be accepted literally in their unmediated force, but that it represents an attitude toward life itself which is the opposite of control, complacency, and deliberation. In Thomas's poetry, life speaks *through* us:

> The force that drives the water through the rocks
> Drives my red blood;

man is an instrument of the energy that is divine; he is not, to use the American idiom, "structuring" life to make all things neatly realizable and containable. Ours is an irreverent culture. In the work of Thomas — and of Thomas's beloved Whitman — life, in the final vision, attains not a definite character but the quality of a worshiped and awesome natural force. It becomes a great fire, beyond man's ability to put it out, but to which he is glad, at most, to get near, still nearer, so as to be able to get down in words a breath of this radiant flame.

« 2 »

Obviously, then, Dylan Thomas represented for many Americans a rare touch of greatness, a relief from the ever-pressing success story. He embodied, without a word said to this effect outside his poetry, the pure romantic vision that is still admired in America underneath the automatic responses of our culture. No matter how fussily detailed and self-conscious our lives become, there is in our fundamental classlessness and our physical restlessness freedom from the frigid respectability that can be so depressing a feature of middle-class life in Britain. And Dylan was so friendly, in this respect so much like an American, so easy to call by his first name! He encountered a welcome here which made him feel as if he were free-floating in a sky made up of unlimited parties, girls, and liquor, and in the heady, inflated, overprosperous, overstimulated atmosphere of America since the war, this must have made him, with his peculiarly heightened capacities for life, feel that he had been sent spinning out of the damp, dark wrappings of seaside life in Wales and hackwork in London. The more uncontrolled he felt about life, the more he fell upon American parties, American excitement, American adulation, as if everything came from a rich, infatuated, always indulgent mistress. He drank here not like an alcoholic who enjoys his liquor, but like a fat boy gobbling down chocolate bars who can't believe that they make him fat. Inevitably, his death here made it seem to many glumly envious and depressed Britons at home as if Dylan Thomas had died of America as well as in America, and as soon as the news of his death at thirty-nine reached London, the word went out from his old literary pals that "America killed Dylan Thomas."

In a sense it was true. Just as many Americans die of the American way of life, of the American pace, of American traffic, so Dylan

Thomas's end was certainly speeded by that unlimited supply of hard liquor without which nobody dares entertain any more, and which is not only more difficult to obtain in Britian, on British incomes, but which became to Dylan what poetry might have been if, in his own rueful words, he hadn't been flying over America "like a damp, ranting bird."

But it is also true that since the war a great many Britishers haven't needed to find in Dylan Thomas's death a reason for being exasperated with America: they already have so many. Any American who follows the British literary and highbrow press becomes hardened to the bitter and sometimes hysterical jealousy of this country — particularly from Marxists who can't bear to admit how much, in different fashions, Russia and the gray British welfare state have let them down — but it is ironic that Dylan Thomas's death should be blamed entirely on America. Like so many Romantic writers, he felt a natural affinity with this country, while in Britain, being utterly outside the "Establishment," he was regarded with a certain loving contempt by some of the snobs who so righteously gnashed their teeth after his death. Nevertheless, Thomas's death was a terrible loss to his own people, to his own kind, and it is really because the mediocrity of literature today is less cleverly concealed in Britian than it is in this country that the death hit so hard.

« 3 »

The posthumous life of Dylan Thomas as a legend and a symbol — the last Romantic poet in a conformist society, the Welsh lyric singer corrupted by the American fleshpots — became really intense when the personal rivalries between those who had loved Dylan came out into the open. Now that he was dead, many people felt an enrichment of their lives through their retrospective share in him. The fact is that Dylan Thomas was a peculiarly lovable as well as magnetically gifted person, that he inspired a great many gifted people with the sense of an unusual radiance in their lives. And just as the many elegies after his death addressed him with an intimacy that is inconceivable in relation to any other famous poet of our time, so the extraordinary agitation he inspired lives on after him in the fascinated reportage of every detail of his life by people who obviously preferred Dylan drunk to anyone sober.

John Malcolm Brinnin's *Dylan Thomas in America** was, of course, the principal tool in shaping the posthumous legend of Dylan Thomas. And it is a mark of Thomas's fantastic vitality in death that a great many people who don't read his poetry, but who very properly see his life as a symbol of it, have found in Brinnin's book the documented record of what they regard as the very poetry of excess. They love this excess because it gives them a touch of the old romantic heedlessness and abandon, the price of which they do not have to pay, and which, as they read in Brinnin the account of Thomas's terrible last days, makes them shudder at an end so violently consistent with his life.

It is no accident that in our period the unconscious protest of so many young people against an overregulated but vacuous society is embodied in the admiration of recklessness which one sees in the cult of the young movie actor James Dean, who died speeding; and that among a great many of the young intellectuals there is a similar cult of "Dylan," whose extraordinary records are fancied by the same people who admire the new jazz and hot rods. In colleges all over the country, listening to Dylan's voice as, "crooning" his poems, he still tries to catch his breath between lines, young people get from him the same suggestion of pure feeling that they get from good jazz. The California poet, Kenneth Rexroth, has linked as heroes of "the beat generation" "two great dead juvenile delinquents — the great saxophonist Charlie Parker, and Dylan," and insists that "if the word deliberate means anything, both of them certainly destroyed themselves. . . .

"Both of them," Rexroth has written, "were overcome by the horror of the world in which they found themselves, because at last they could no longer overcome that world with the weapon of a purely lyrical art. . . . Both of them did communicate one central theme: Against the ruin of the world, there is only one defense — the creative act. . . . Dylan Thomas's verse had to find endurance in a world of burning cities and burning Jews. He was able to find meaning in his art as long as it was the answer to air raids and

* *Dylan Thomas in America*, by John Malcolm Brinnin. Boston: Little, Brown and Company. An Atlantic Monthly Press book.

gas ovens. As the world began to take on the guise of an immense air raid or gas oven, I believe his art became meaningless to him." And in a violent but moving elegy to Thomas, "Thou Shalt Not Kill," Rexroth attributes the poet's death to the superficiality of his contemporaries:

> Who killed the bright-headed bird?
> You did, you son of a bitch.
> You drowned him in your cocktail brain.
> He fell down and died in your synthetic heart.

The bitterness in these lines is by no means unusual. All over the country, often in isolated places, there are people, more especially young people, who look on Thomas as a rebel against mass society and a victim of the organization man. It is in America, at the antennae of the modern age, where the full force of technological culture is felt, that the cult of Dylan Thomas has reached its peak — documented, too often, from the remorseless day-by-day record of Thomas the drunk and the wastrel which Brinnin put down with so much fervor and unconscious resentment against the elusiveness of this magnetic figure. So closely do people feel related to Thomas that there are endless arguments still about Brinnin's book, for people tend to identify with Thomas to the point where they resent its itemization of his "lapses." When Brinnin admitted that he could not really account for Thomas's more extreme behavior, he meant that he did not want to and was punishing him for being so unmanageable. But to the "ardents," Thomas's life in itself, not in relation to them, has a heroic significance quite the opposite of the continuous disintegration that Brinnin leaves us with.

« 4 »

It was in protest against this impression that Dylan's widow, Caitlin Thomas, offered a brief foreword to Brinnin's book. And now that her own memoir, *Leftover Life to Kill*, has finally been written, a most important word from the most intimate source of all has been said.* In his posthumous life Dylan Thomas really speaks now, through his widow. Caitlin Thomas's book is not the "answer"

* *Leftover Life to Kill*, by Caitlin Thomas. Boston: Little, Brown and Company. An Atlantic Monthly Press book.

to Brinnin — the mere justification of her husband — that had been expected. It is better than that. It is an amazing duplication of Thomas's own strength and recklessness and abandon by a woman who obviously was the only person with a spirit equal to his and who consequently fought him and hated him and loved him to the point where their conflicting intensities almost killed each other. I don't like the self-pity in the title and a would-be pathos, at the end as at the beginning; but the self-pity is utterly shown up and exploded by the fierce emotional charge of the book and a style which, once she gets control of it, gives one the same pleasant Celtic resonance from her careening Irish sentences that one gets from his tipsy Welsh ones.

The people who will be shocked by Caitlin Thomas's book would be shocked by Dylan Thomas if he were alive. A posthumous life is easy to take, for us who deal with it as symbol; Caitlin Thomas is so much alive that her book, which is as much about herself as about Dylan, never explains Dylan's directness and eloquence so much as when, with amusing honesty and perfect tenderness, she recounts her life on the Isle of Elba with a young Italian miner, surrounded by the hostile respectable.

There is about her, as about Dylan, a perfect genius for trouble. She is a born rebel who in today's situation doesn't know what to rebel against. She has her husband's instinct for extreme and desperate situations. But reading the account of her dismal life in Wales after Dylan's death, and of her flight to Elba with her five-year-old son, I could not help feeling that, given her temperament, she behaved with exemplary courage and humanity. What makes the book so remarkable is that, time and again, whether she is writing about Dylan, or herself, or her children, one hears the boisterous Thomas lilt, the authentic note, the lyrical cry from the heart that gives his style its force. And most unexpected and revealing, she makes it clear that in her, as in Dylan, is the fatal mixture, with her powerful temperament, of that intellectual frailty, that excessive availability and need to be loved, which so many pettier types have known how to protect themselves from.

The tragedy of Caitlin Thomas is not what she says it is — not entirely a matter of the tempestuous life with a genius as erratic as herself or of the subsequent loss which, frightful as it is, has obviously given her back to herself. The tragedy is in the excessive vulnerability, the constant readiness to be hit in the face, which, in a person with her insurrectionary heart, cripples her at the very moment that she can rise to her full strength. She tells us that she had a passion for solitary dancing à la Isadora Duncan, where she could feel the "flowing"; but "as soon as I spotted the 'glance' of an audience, I was finished: the brain on the alert, all suspicion again, put the pincers on, and the capricious flow stopped abruptly. . . .

"That was one reason, now I come to think of it, why Dylan found it so annoying: it is the direct opposite of words. . . . It may be one of the substances that poetry is made of; that words are formed from; but its elemental — right back, through the encumbering ages, to the creation, the planets, the dinosaurs; the skeletons and protoplasm — force is, above any other point of supremacy, *wordless*. . . ."

Actually, her sense of what art means to her — this elemental force, right back through the encumbering ages — is exactly what makes her husband's poetry so vivid. In her, as in him, there is this same exciting and disturbing combination of force without hope — without a meaning she can assign to her experience that would relieve her from emotional suffering. Her rule of life, she says, is "always be ready to clasp the impending disasters," and I believe her. So that despite the essential modesty that seems to me the key to the tragedy of Dylan Thomas and the long-delayed emergence of his wife, it is this elemental force for which one remains grateful in reading her book. It is so much rarer than a "defense" of Dylan Thomas — who needs none.

[1957]

Bernard Malamud: The Magic and the Dread

THE STORIES of Bernard Malamud are a striking example of the opportunities — and hazards — that are faced these days by "minority" writers who have rejected special pleading in favor of modern

The Magic Barrel, by Bernard Malamud. New York: Farrar, Straus and Cudahy.

art. Writers like Ralph Ellison and James Baldwin are no longer tempted to sing the chain-gang blues once favored by Negro writers in this country; originals like Saul Bellow, Daniel Fuchs, and Bernard Malamud are not likely to retrace the kind of sentimental or aggressive pathos that has afflicted so many recorders of Jewish experience in this country, from Fannie Hurst to Michael Gold — a style that has found its last haven in the Hollywood of Irwin Shaw and other nostalgic readers of *PM*.

The newer writers (who seem "new" not because they are young but because it has taken them so long to climb out of the depression and war and to discover themselves as individuals) have turned their backs on what James Baldwin has jeeringly called "everybody's protest novel" — Uncle Tom, the Negro or the Jewish Christ dead of American capitalism, the saintly victim. But agile and really gifted as these new writers are, they have been just as unwilling or unable as Jewish and Negro writers always have been to let their experience alone, to describe it as something that may be valued for its own sake. It is here that one sees the peculiar nemesis of writers who feel that they can fit themselves to American life only by trying to give universal meaning to each piece of their experience.

The patron saint of these writers is always Dostoevsky — the supreme example of the novelist whose characters must always search for meaning, who cannot for a moment allow life to exist without scrutinizing intervention. But where Dostoevsky had equal ability to embody the emptiness and sloth of nineteenth-century Russia, these new American writers itch with symbolism. They have been exposed so continually to modern literature and modern art that they find it hard to find their way back to what Herbert Gold has called the lesson of Balzac's "stupidity." Although these writers have produced a peculiarly penetrating kind of fiction, haunting as well as haunted, there is a certain overeagerness in them all to stand and deliver, to be freed of certain painful experiences through the ritualistic catharsis of modern symbolism. The Jewish or Negro writer, far from being mired in his personal pathos as of yore, is now so aware that his experience is "universal" that he tends to escape out of his particular experience itself, to end up in the great American sky of abstractions.

Of all these new writers, Bernard Malamud seems to me the most unnecessarily tempted by symbolism. For he is the most compassionate, the most concerned and involved of them all, and whenever I turn back to the best scenes in his fine novel, *The Assistant*, or to the little masterpiece about a rabbinical student in search of a wife who went to a marriage broker (the title story of this collection), I get something of the same deep satisfaction that I do from the great realistic masters of Yiddish literature.

Malamud's world has its own haunting archetypes: the desperate and sickly storekeeper, the refugee who turns up in Rome or New York to accuse his fellow Jews of heartlessness, the lonely student with ovoid eyes in staring search of love, the American intellectual abroad who finds it impossible to escape his Jewish past. The scene is always the down-at-heels grocery, the winter street, the irreversible hardness of the modern city. Malamud has caught as one the guttural toughness of big-city speech and the classic bitterness of Jewish dialogue. The remarkable story "Take Pity" contains the typical situation of all his work — a great love condemned to ineffectuality. A man who has committed suicide so that he can leave all his property to a widow who always refused to accept him during his lifetime sits in the other world telling a "census-taker" (his name is Davidov) how the woman's husband died. "Broke in him something. . . ." "Broke what?" "Broke what breaks. He was talking to me how bitter was his life, and he touched me on my sleeve to say something else, but the next minute his face got small and he fell down dead, the wife screaming, the little girls crying that it made in my heart pain. I am myself a sick man and when I saw him laying on the floor, I said to myself, 'Rosen, say goodbye, this guy is finished.' So I said it."

This is the talk of people who are not merely on edge but who really live on the edge. Their tense expressiveness is one of the cultural symbols of the Jews, in art as in religion; just as the great Rabbi Hillel could be challenged to give the whole meaning of the Law while standing on one foot, so there is a Doomsday terseness to Jewish speech — as if the book of life were about to close shut with a bang. Malamud has caught this quality with an intimacy of understanding that is utterly remarkable. But in their terseness, his characters fundamentally express despair rather than any spiritual refusal of the great world. His world is all too much an inner world — one in which the city streets, the houses, the stores, seem, along with the people who broodingly stand about like skeletons, some with flesh, always just about to fold up, to disappear into the sky. People talk to each other disbelievingly, as if each felt that the other was about to disappear, as if the world under their feet were itself unreal. People flit in and out of each other's lives like bad dreams.

It is a curious, almost uncanny transformation of the old Jewish mysticism, where earth is so close to heaven — or to hell — that the supernatural and the trivial jostle each other. From the historic standpoint of Jewish theology, of the seemingly incredible Jewish experience itself, everything is entirely real. Life is always strange and God always moves in unpredictable ways. In Malamud's stories everything real becomes unreal; we are under the sign not of theology but of surrealism. Sometimes this is unbearably effective; but when the symbols become too explicit, as in "The Lady of the Lake" or "Angel Levine," Malamud's own tone is undecided between the mysterious and the silly. In "The Mourners," an old man, suffering for the guilt of having deserted his family years back, is about to be evicted; the landlord is driven half mad trying to get the dirty old man out of the tenement. The old man begins mourning for him, the landlord, as dead — he is spiritually dead — and the landlord, staring in unbelief, is engulfed in the sudden upsurge of his own shame and becomes a mourner too. The symbolism here is not only explicit, it is positively allegorical. And indeed, Malamud explains, in his Hawthornesque touches, why Hawthorne and symbolist novelists like Kafka so often read alike.

But Malamud is at his best in those stories which depend not on surprise but on the moment of ungovernable human feeling. In "The Loan," an old friend turns up in a baker's shop to ask for a loan — to pay for a headstone for his wife's grave. The baker's wife, his *second* wife, steadfastly refuses to countenance the loan, and at the end of the story the two friends, each bereft in his own way, "pressed mouths together and parted forever." In the title story, Malamud's usual attempt to escape "realism" is brilliantly, triumphantly justified. It is the marriage broker's own daughter whom the rabbinical student falls in love with, from a photograph, and at the end of the story the ambiguities of life and death are so close that one has the sense of being caught in a dream. Life is never very solid for these Jews, these people "who live on air"; they are always on the verge of saying good-by and departing for the other world.

« 2 »

The otherworldly feeling in the great Jewish writers of the past was supported by a conviction that earth and heaven are connected. Malamud captures the strangeness of Jewish experience brilliantly, but he relies on compassion, not on the covenant. He is so concerned with the dread, the flimsiness of the human material in our age, that he has to outwit his own possible sentimentality. This, as I see it, is why he so often turns to symbolic endings, goes through his material so quickly. The result is that while this book seems to me masterful and indescribably haunting, it is surprising to note, when one closes it, how many of the people fade indistinguishably into each other. What remains in the reader's mind is not a world, *the* world, but the spectral Jew in his beggarly clothes — always ready to take flight.

It is an extraordinary fact that although the great Yiddish writers in Czarist Russia could not call the country their own, they gave the earth of Russia, the old village, a solid reality, as if it were all the world they had left to cherish, like the Jewish graveyard that is lovingly kept up even when the houses decay. Malamud, the closest in wit and depth of feeling to the great Yiddish writers, nevertheless falls into the same abstractness that is the bane of so many new writers in America. Unlike those who are abstract because they have only their cleverness to write from, Malamud is abstract out of despair: despair of the world itself, which can no longer be represented.

In this one sees the curious danger of the American writer who has been influenced by Kakfa, Joyce, Eliot, *et al.* Life in America changes so quickly, and people are so quick to change into each other, that the everlasting thinness and abstractness of American writing, which comes from our lack of "society," of a solid core of leaders, manners, tradition, is likely to be intensified by our new writers, who have a society but don't believe in it enough to describe it — to deal with it not merely as it is but as something that *is.*

One of the things we now long for in contemporary literature is escape from the tyranny of symbolic "meaning." We want to return to life not as a figure in the carpet but as life in its beautiful and inexpressible materiality—life as the gift that it actually is rather than as the "material" that we try to remake.

Malamud provokes these reflections because he is so gifted. There seems to me no writer of his background who comes so close to the bone of human feeling, who makes one feel so keenly the enigmatic quality of life. The only thing I miss in his work is a feeling for the value of life, for the body of this world—for that which cannot be explained because it is too precious to turn into symbols.

[1958]

The Alone Generation

THE OTHER DAY A prominent American publisher advertised a book of stories by a Continental writer who died some time ago: "These stories, never before published in English, could only have been written by a great writer who flourished before World War II. They are stamped by that unobtrusive assurance, perfect sympathy with their subjects, and resonant tone which have become, it would seem, lost secrets in almost all the fiction of the immediate present." Not very encouraging, what? Yet I must admit that while I see a host of brilliantly talented writers all around me, I don't often get a very profound satisfaction out of the novels they write.

I am tired of reading for compassion instead of pleasure. In novel after novel, I am presented with people who are so soft, so wheedling, so importunate, that the actions in which they are involved are too indecisive to be interesting or to develop those implications which are the life-blood of narrative. The age of "psychological man," of the herd of aloners, has finally proved the truth of Tocqueville's observation that in modern times the average man is absorbed in a very puny object, himself, to the point of satiety. The whole interest of the reader seems to be summoned toward "understanding" and tolerance of the leading characters. We get an imaginative universe limited to the self and its detractors. The old-fashioned novel of sensitive souls, say Somerset Maugham's *Of Human Bondage* or even Sinclair Lewis's *Main Street,* showed a vulnerable hero or heroine battling it out (*a*) for principles which he identified with himself and (*b*) against social enemies who were honestly opposed to the protagonist's demand of unlimited freedom. Now we get novels in which society is merely a backdrop to the aloneness of the hero. People are not shown in actions that would at least get us to see the conditions of their personal struggle. Carson McCullers's beautiful first novel, *The Heart Is a Lonely Hunter,* characterized a stagnant society in the silent relationship between two mutes; in her third novel, *The Member of the Wedding,* the adolescent loneliness of Frankie fills up the scene, becomes the undramatic interest of the book, to the point where the reader feels not that he is witnessing a drama but that he is being asked to respond to a situation.

American society is remarkable for the degree of loneliness (not solitude) in which the individual can find himself. In our mass age, the individual's lack of privacy, his unlimited demand for self-satisfaction, his primary concern with his own health and well-being, have actually thrown him back on himself more than before. Our culture is stupefyingly without support from tradition, and has become both secular and progressive in its articulation of every discontent and ambition; the individual now questions himself constantly because his own progress — measured in terms of the social norms — is his fundamental interest. The kind of person who in the nineteenth-century novel was a "character" now regards himself in twentieth-century novels as a problem; the novel becomes not a series of actions which he initiates because of *who* he is, but a series of disclosures, as at a psychoanalyst's, designed to afford him the knowledge that may heal him. It is astonishing how many novels concerned with homosexuality, on the order of Truman Capote's *Other Voices, Other Rooms,* are apologies for abnormality, designed to make us sympathize with the twig as it is bent the wrong way.

I would suspect that it is the intention of extracting "understanding" that accounts for the extraordinary number of children and adolescents in American fiction; at least in the imaginative society of fiction they can always be objects of concern. Even in a good writer like Capote, the movement of the book comes to a standstill in the grinding machinery of sensibility. As in James Baldwin's *Giovanni's Room,* sympathetic justice is always accorded homosexuals. No Vautrin as in Balzac, no Charlus as in Proust, no honest homosexual villains! The immediate result is the immobilization of narrative, the fashionable mistiness of prose; first the hero is cherished to the point of suffocation, then the style. *Other Voices, Other Rooms* is a brilliant effort of will, but it is unmoving rather than slow, retrospective rather than searching. In the past, the movement of fiction was more energetic than life; now fiction becomes vaguer, dimmer, an "exercise" in "craft."

« 2 »

This demand on our compassion is not limited to the quivering novels of sensibility by overconscious stylists; it is the very essence of the deliberately churned-up novels of the Beat Generation. I mention Jack Kerouac here only because his novels, in which he has increasingly developed the trick of impersonating spontaneity by bombarding the reader with a mass of deliberately confused impressions, depend on a naked and unashamed plea for "love," understanding, fellowship, and are read and enjoyed only because this pleading so answers to our psychological interest in fiction that we indulge Kerouac without knowing why. Nothing human is now alien to us; after all, the fellow's problem could be our problem! It is ridiculous that novels can now be sent off as quickly as they are written and published immediately afterwards in order to satisfy the hopped-up taste of people who, when they open a novel, want to feel that they are not missing a thing. The sluttishness of a society whose mass ideal seems to be unlimited consumption of all possible goods and services is the reason for the "success" of writers whose literary strategy is to paint America as an unlimited supply of sex, travel, liquor — and lonely yearners. The individual who is concerned entirely with his aloneness will inevitably try to invade society, "the other" in his universe, by writing stormily, angrily, lashing the reader with a froth of words. But we are at fault in allowing the addict quality of such books to stand for "intensity" in fiction. More and more we judge novels by their emotional authenticity, not their creative achievement; we read them as the individual testifying for himself in a confused and troubling time. But the testimony is so self-concerned that we equate this glibness of feeling with recklessness of style. And here I come to another complaint, the increasing slovenliness, carelessness, and plain cowardice of style in fiction today.

We were wrong when we thought that the ghost of Henry James had put his too, too careful hand on our young 'uns. It is true that some of the new professor-novelists, Benjamin DeMott in *The Body's Cage* or Monroe Engel in *The Visions of Nicholas Solon,* like Capote himself in his first book and his stories, can remind us of the rage of style in the fiction of the Forties. So talented a writer as Jean Stafford has of late years often seemed to bury herself in fine phrases. It is a rare professor-novelist, Robie Macauley in *The Disguises of Love,* who can escape the ostentatious carefulness, the jogging of the reader: *Please don't lose sight of my arm as I put together this beautiful edifice of words.* But actually, the increasing fussiness of our social ideals and the plain boredom of a period in which writers so often feel incapable of imagining decisive roles for their characters have led to the opposite quality. John Wain recently wrote:

"At the moment, the literary mind of the West seems to be swamped in one of its periodic waves of what George Orwell once called 'sluttish antinomianism,' which he defined as 'lying in bed drinking Pernod.'"

What we get now is not the style of pretended fineness — the *New Yorker* ladies with every tuck in place — but the imitation of anger, the leer of the desperado. You can't fool us with your genteel learning, we're young American men who have been around and who have a punch! So I read in an article on fiction, by Herbert Gold, that something-or-other is like kissing a girl with spinach on her teeth. Wow, bang, and slam. Kerouac and whoever it is who follows *him* are "wild" in the hope of getting out of themselves, in finding some person, thing, or cause to latch onto. Gold is slovenly in the hope of sounding "cool"; he is understandably alarmed by the softness that threatens young novelists in so self-pitying an age as this. In England the young men are angry because still made to feel inferior; in America, young novelists get angry because they hope to sound belligerent and positive, *alive,* against the doldrums of the Eisenhower age.

One root of their difficulty is the irresistible example of Saul Bellow's *The Adventures of Augie March.* Anyone who has read his first two novels, *Dangling Man* and *The Victim,* knows that Bellow began with an almost excessive nobility of style, that the open and comically pretentious style in which Augie talks is a *tour de force.* Bellow has always been fascinated by characters who, in the deep Existentialist sense, are conscious of being *de trop,* excessive of themselves and their society, insatiable in their demands on life. All his representative men, in the phrase of Henderson the rain king, cry, "*I want! I want!*" This excess of human possibility over social goals, of the problem, man, over his intended satisfactions, led to a prose in *Augie* which is rapturously, not whiningly, faithful to all the signs and opportunities of experience. "If you've seen a winter London open thundering mouth in its awful last minutes of river light or have come with cold clanks from the Alps into Torino in December white steam then you've known like greatness of place." In *Augie,* Bellow attained a rosy deliverance from the grip of his past, he discovered himself equal to the excitement of the American experience, he shook himself all over and let himself go. "I am an American, Chicago born — Chicago, that somber city — and go at things as I have taught myself, free-style, and will make the record in my own way. . . ."

But just as no poet should attempt free verse who has not performed in traditional forms and meters, so no novelist should identify toughness with "free-style":

> He brought his hand with the horny nail of his index finger in a wide circle, swinging an invisible lassoo, looping their belly-eyed gaze and taking it at his eye. They were caught first at the spongy wart on his nose and then in his eyes, working it for themselves now like the flies caught wriggling in sticky-paper. That wart made a stiff flop when he tossed his head in beckon and hitch toward the pungent foot-darkened sawdust at the door of Grack's Zoo, a gobble of cajolery up from his throat and the swollen Adam's apple.

This is from Gold's most admired book, *The Man Who Was Not With It,* and makes me think of what was once scrawled on a student paper at Harvard by ancient Dean Briggs: "Falsely robust." I think I understand where such worked-up militancy of phrase comes from: from the novelist's honest need, in the spirit of Henry James, to have language do the work of characterization. There is so much for a novelist to put together before he can invite people into the world of his imagination; there are so many things to say about human beings who, in the absence of public beliefs, appear arbitrary to themselves and to everyone else. The novelist feels he has to work ten times harder than he used to, falls into despair, and tries to ram it all home. Things aren't as clear as they used to be, and there's no kidding ourselves that they are. The true novelist wants only to set the stage, to get people going, to tell his story, but as Augie March says, "You do all you can to humanize and familiarize the world, and suddenly it becomes stranger than ever." The sense of that strangeness is vivid despite the murky powers of contemporary novelists; no wonder, having to make language work all the time for them, that they often escape into an assumed violence and negligence of tone.

Sometimes the language of violence fits. Ralph Ellison's *Invisible Man* is a series of episodes, but the screaming crescendo on which the book opens — the hero in his Harlem cellar, all the stolen lights ablaze, collaring the reader and forcing him to notice and to hear — is an unforgettably powerful expression, at the extreme of racial experience, of the absurdity, the feeling of millions that the world is always just out of their reach. I don't care for novelists who ignore what H. G. Wells himself called the "queerness" that has come into contemporary life since the bomb. The ways of escape from this queerness are legion, but let me name some who don't try to escape it. Paul Bowles doesn't, although his values are so skittery that he sometimes seems to escape from horror into a Fitzpatrick travelogue. The American writer is so likely to see more of the world, and to experience it more openly, that, like Hemingway at the end of *Death in the Afternoon*, he always wants to get in after the bell all the sensuous travel notes he hadn't been able to fit into his book. Bowles tends to fall into this sophisticated romanticism; sometimes he reports North Africa and Asia instead of setting his imagination in them. On the other hand, the landscape in *The Sheltering Sky* itself represents the inhumanity of people who can no longer communicate with one another, the coldness of a world that now seems to put man out. What minimizes the symbolic values in *The Sheltering Sky* and deprives us of the "resonance" we used to get in fiction is the aloneness of people who are concerned entirely with the search for their own sexual satisfaction. The slightly depressing atmosphere of anxiety that hangs over Bowles's novel is characteristic of the effort to find an identity for oneself wholly in sexual terms. Norman Mailer, a writer with so much more native power than Bowles, with so much more ability to confront American life directly than he seems to acknowledge, has created in *The Deer Park* the same essential atmosphere of paralysis, of the numbness that results when people feel themselves to be lost in the pursuit of compulsions.

Mailer's novels, at least for me, personify the dilemma of novelists who are deeply concerned with history but dangerously oversimplify it; if they seem consumed by their interest in sex it is because they are always seeking some solution for "the times." In many ways Mailer seems to me the most forceful and oddly objective novelist of his age, objective in the sense that he is most capable of imagining objects to which a reader can give himself. You see this, despite the obvious debts to older writers, in *The Naked and the Dead* and in the satire behind the wonderful exchanges between the producer and his son-in-law in *The Deer Park*. Yet Mailer's interest in the external world has dwindled to the point where the theme of sexual power and delight — which Mailer feels to be a lost secret in contemporary life — has become a labyrinthine world in itself. Mailer now seems bent on becoming the American Marquis de Sade, where once he seemed to be another Dos Passos. Yet the energy, the often unconscious yet meticulous wit, above all the eerie and totally unexpected power of concrete visualization are curious because Mailer is able to make more of a world out of his obsessions than other writers are able to make out of the given materials of our common social world.

Here I come to the heart of my complaint. I complain of the dimness, the shadowiness, the flatness, the paltriness, in so many reputable novelists. I confess that I have never been able to get very much from Wright Morris, though he is admired by influential judges. In reading Morris's *The Field of Vision*, I thought of

George Santayana's complaint that contemporary poets often give the reader the mere suggestion of a poem and expect him to finish the poem for them. Morris's many symbols, his showy intentions, his pointed and hinted significances, seem to me a distinct example of the literary novel which professors like to teach and would like to write: solemnly meaningful in every intention, but without the breath or extension of life.

There are many writers, like J. D. Salinger, who lack strength, but who are subtle and interesting. He identifies himself too fussily with the spiritual aches and pains of his characters; in some of his recent stories, notably "Zooey" and "Seymour: An Introduction," he has overextended his line, thinned it out, in an effort to get the fullest possible significance out of his material. Salinger's work is a perfect example of the lean reserves of the American writer who is reduced to "personality," even to the "mystery of personality," instead of the drama of our social existence. It is the waveriness, the effort at control, that trouble me in Salinger; the professional hand is there, the ability to create an imaginative world, plus almost too much awareness of what he can and can't do. Only, it *is* thin, and peculiarly heartbreaking at times; Salinger identifies the effort he puts out with the vaguely spiritual "quest" on which his characters are engaged, which reminds me of Kierkegaard's saying that we have become "pitiful," like the lace-makers whose work is so flimsy. The delicate balances in Salinger's work, the anxious striving, inevitably result in beautiful work that is rather too obviously touching, and put together on a frame presented to it by the *New Yorker*.

But I must admit that the great majority of stories I read in magazines seem only stitchings and joinings and colorings of some original model. No wonder that in so much contemporary fiction we are excited by the intention and tolerate the achievement. We are so hungry for something new in fiction that the intention, marked early in the handling of a story, will often please us as if it were the dramatic emotion accomplished by the story; the intuition of hidden significance that usually waits for us at the end of a Salinger story is both a reward to the reader and the self-cherished significance of the story to the writer himself.

Salinger's characters are incomparably larger and more human than those of John Cheever, but Cheever has a gift for being more detached and at the same time more open to what *is* — to the ever-present danger and the half-felt queerness of contemporary existence. It is a pity in a way — I am thinking here of Cheever's stories, not his novel — that contemporary American fiction must derive so much of its strength from the perishable value of social information. James Jones wrote a really extraordinary novel in *From Here to Eternity,* and ever since, like so many Americans who wrote extraordinary first novels directly out of experience, he has had the look of someone trying to invent things that once were conferred on him. So Cheever, in the *New Yorker* style, sometimes takes such easy refuge in the details of gardens, baby-sitters, parks, dinners, apartment houses, clothes, that he goes to the opposite extreme of the beat writers (who present the sheer emptiness of life when human beings are not attached to a particular environment): he falls into mechanical habits of documentation, becomes a slyer John O'Hara. It is as if he were trying to get back to the social reportage and satire that worked in our fiction so long as the people writing these stories, like Sinclair Lewis or Scott Fitzgerald, knew what values they could oppose to the "rich." As one can see from O'Hara's novels, which get more pointless as they get bigger and sexier, it is impossible to remain an old-fashioned "realist" unless you can portray a class or an individual opposed to the dominant majority. (James Gould Cozzens was able to do exactly this in *Guard of Honor* but not in *By Love Possessed,* which is more of an aggrieved complaint against the destruction of values.) O'Hara's *Appointment in Samarra* was an exciting book because it involved the real conflict of classes in America; *From the Terrace* suggests that the transformation of our society has proceeded beyond the power of a commonplace mind to describe it deeply. For depth of description demands that the writer identify himself with a social force to which he can give symbolic significance, that he can discern a pattern in history, that he not only can plot his way through it but can recognize himself to be a figure in it.

This social intelligence is now lacking to our novelists — except to those brilliant Southern writers, like William Styron and Flannery O'Connor, who can find the present meaningful because they find the past so. But other Southern writers run the risk of being as confused as anyone else once they get off that safe subject, the betrayal of the past, which has been Faulkner's great theme. The bigger, richer, and more anxious the country becomes, the more writers in the traditional mode, like O'Hara, or writers who are now formidably "hip," like Mailer, find themselves trying to find in sex as individual appetite the drama of society in which they can see themselves as partisans and judges. This lack of breadth and extent and dimension I have been complaining of: what is it but the uncertainty of these writers about their connection with that part of reality which other novelists include in their work simply because they are always aware of it — not because they have strained to know it? What many writers feel today is that reality is not much more than what *they* say it is. This is a happy discovery only for genius. For most writers today, the moral order is created, step by step, only through the clarifications achieved by art and, step by step, they refuse to trust beyond the compass of the created work. There has probably never been a time when the social nature of the novel was so much at odds with the felt lack of order in the world about us. In the absence of what used to be *given,* the novelist must create a wholly imaginary world — or else he must have the courage, in an age when personal willfulness rules in every sphere, to say that we are *not* alone, that the individual does not have to invent human values but only to rediscover them. The novel as a form will always demand a common-sense respect for life and interest in society.

« 3 »

Whatever my complaints, I never despair of the novel. As someone said, it is more than a form, it is a literature. I hope never to overlook the positive heroism of those writers who believe in the novel and in the open representation of experience that is its passion and delight — who refuse to believe that there can be an alternative to it for an age like ours. And it does seem to me that the tangibility, the felt reverberations of life that one finds in a writer like Bernard Malamud, spring from his belief that any imaginative "world," no matter how local or strange, *is* the world, and that for the imaginative writer values must be considered truths, not subjective fancies. It is really a kind of faith that accounts for Malamud's "perfect sympathy" with *his* characters in *The Assistant* and *The Magic Barrel.* Though it is difficult for the alone to sympathize with each other, it is a fact that fiction can elicit and prove the world we share, that it can display the unforeseen possibilities of the human — even when everything seems dead set against it.

[1959]

The World of Saul Bellow

In Saul Bellow's *Seize the Day* (1956) there is a scene in which the panicky middle-aged hero and a quack psychiatrist have lunch in a Broadway cafeteria. ". . . Dr. Tamkin came along with a tray piled with plates and cups. He had Yankee pot roast, purple cabbage, potatoes, a big slice of watermelon, and two cups of coffee." Mr. Brendan Gill of the *New Yorker*, in reviewing this book, warmly saluted Bellow's talent, acknowledged his pre-eminence among the younger American novelists, but shuddering at the sentence above, expressed his earnest hope that Bellow would drop such writing — which, I suppose, seemed a dull and gritty naturalistic catalogue.

I know that there are many people to whom Bellow's novels seem the familiar material of American naturalism, and who even think of him as a tough, aggressive writer. But I do not understand them. To me Bellow's world is far from being identical with the mass big-city America he writes about. It is distinctively a world of his own — in style, in speculative intelligence, in the anguish of its feeling and the conscious buffoonery of its wit. It as little resembles even the European tradition of the novel Bellow would like to follow as it does those young American novelists who have lately found in him the kind of strength they would like to capture. Bellow, even for a writer, is so much his own man that the various cultural labels that come with him — the Chicagoan, the Jew, the one-time anthropologist — figure more as themes in his work than they explain *him*. One of the key themes in his fiction, however, is the attempt of his protagonists to get a grip on existence, to understand not themselves (they know that this is impossible) but the infinitely elusive universe in which, as human creatures, they find themselves.

Yet at the same time Bellow is very much a novelist of the known, familiar surfaces. From the Chicago winters and boardinghouse blues of his first novel, *Dangling Man* (1944), to his latest, which begins with Henderson on his Hudson Valley farm, feeding his pigs, stripped to the waist like a convict, breaking stones with a sledge-hammer, Bellow has caught, particularly in the New York City scenes of *The Victim* (1947) and the unforgettable "grandeur of place" that informs *The Adventures of Augie March* (1953), the heaviness, the violence and the energy of American life. But Bellow describes the clammy big-city world as Hardy described Wessex fields, as the unconnected spectator of man's hopes; he never writes about these separate and cruel forces with the half-nostalgic feeling of earlier realists like Dreiser, or with the infatuation of "tough" sentimental reporters of the big city like Nelson Algren. There is no class for which Bellow has the proletarian novelist's political sympathy. The external world, for Bellow, is always the covering, not the home, of a spirit not so much disaffected as unattachable. He is a novelist who in this sense reminds one of "metaphysical" American novelists like Melville, for he identifies man's quest with the range of the mind itself. Even when he describes a sinister mountebank dismally carrying pot roast and purple cabbage to a cafeteria table, Bellow sees in him multiple aspects of the human condition.

What makes Bellow's work so unusual, and in its very sense of the extreme often so comic, is the fact that his characters are all burdened by a speculative quest, a need to understand their particular destiny within the general problem of human destiny. This compulsion, even when it is unconscious, as is the case of Asa Leventhal in *The Victim* or Tommy Wilhelm in *Seize the Day,* or mocked in himself as it is by Augie March, is the motivating energy of his heroes. And in his latest novel, *Henderson the Rain King,* the cry "I want! I want!" forces the hero to desert his family for Africa.

« 2 »

The problem of destiny is the need to accept one's whole fate as a human being, to recognize the "axial lines" of life, as Augie March puts it. But to know whether the axial lines that we see, or think that we see, are what fate *had* to draw, is not merely the theme of Bellow's fiction, it is the overriding passion of his characters. And it is this extraordinary prominence of speculation in Bellow's novels that gives him his unusual, his involuntarily provocative, place in American fiction.

For the fact is that we do not like our novelists to be too intelligent; we like them to be tough, hard, external, concerned with "facts." And if the facts of life in a novel concern speculation about destiny as much as they concern money or sex or business or family? Then we say that the authors are not novelists but intellectuals. We will easily admit intelligence as manner, in the now-classic style of Henry James, but not life and death and destiny as passionate subjects in themselves.

Now, Bellow is anything but a "philosophic" novelist in the German style of mock-profundity. He is, like Augie March himself, Chicago-raised ("Chicago, that somber city") and the sharp, questioning, exultantly self-educated mind of the immigrant's son is on every page. But a novelist is defined not only by his mind, his style, his address; he is defined as well by his ruling subject, the idea of drama that is his obsession, by that point of view which is not only the content of his work but also its truly driving and unconscious side. Bellow's novels offer the deepest commentary I know on the social utopianism of a generation which always presumed that it could pacify life, that it could control and guide it to an innocuous social end, but which is painfully learning, as in *Augie March* and the end of *Seize the Day*, to celebrate life, to praise in it the divine strength which disposes of man's proposals.

It is this problem, first of representing all that a man intends and plans, and then of getting him not merely to recognize the countervailing strength of life but to humble himself before it, that is the real situation in all Bellow's novels. In *Dangling Man* young Joseph, caught in a legal tie-up with his draft board, unable to join the Army and unable to continue a normal life, calls himself "that creature of plans. He had asked himself a question I still would like answered, 'How should a good man live; what ought he to do?' Hence the plans. Unfortunately, most of them were foolish."

Yet Joseph's response is not one of cynical sophistication, for it is not the defeat of plans that concerns Bellow. It is the fact that in obedience to the external sophistication of society, one makes plans in accordance with conventional standards. Actually one's real plans, to discover all one's potential freedom as a human being, must yield with a kind of furtive reverence to the ultimate power which one can only call God. In all of Bellow's work man's realization of his illusions, of his greedy expectation, so deepens that Henderson asks, "Does truth come in blows?" He has learned to receive it on his body and in his face, to wrestle with it and to be humiliated by it; he has learned, as the profounder Jewish spirits have learned, that God is not easy, but must be fought with, as Jacob wrestled with the angel.

Man proposes and God disposes. Americans in particular propose a very great deal, but life always catches up with them — at least with the protagonists of Saul Bellow. But the way of Job, of ultimate tragedy and the high manner, is not the way of a novelist from Chicago. The other way, the Augie March way, is the longing to embrace in life itself, in its most commonplace texture, the actual miracle of existence, the great gift itself, conferred and confirmed and to be praised in every breath, richer than any man's words for it. Augie March praises life by learning to say *no* to men. In his elusiveness, he is faithful not to men and their schemes and plans for him — but to existence made manifest in himself. The plans of Augie's contemporaries — and it is to the point that the novel was originally entitled *Life among the Machiavellians* — betray not merely egotism but petty vision. They want, they want . . . to make the world like themselves. But as Augie says, "You do all you can to humanize and familiarize the world, and suddenly it becomes stranger than ever." To know strangeness is to recognize that fate itself is character. Or as Augie puts it in one of those monologues that bring home the sulphurous world of self-made intellectuals from Chicago: "I have a feeling about the axial lines of life, with respect to which you must be straight or else your existence is merely clownery, hiding tragedy. I must have had a feeling since I was a kid about these axial lines which made me want to have my existence on them, and so I have said 'no' like a stubborn fellow to all my persuaders, just on the obstinacy of my memory of these lines, never entirely clear. . . . Lately I have felt these thrilling lines again. When striving stops, there they are as a gift."

For Augie this wisdom resulted in an attachment to life itself, at every turn and in every breath of his monologue to the reader. The beauty and exhilaration of this novel showed that Bellow could turn the sense of destiny, his respect for what Henderson would call "blows," into comedy. Bellow's sense of comedy is always a human being's diffidence before the superior forces of life, a Chaplinesque sense of himself as the accidental and paltry vessel on which life has been conferred. Privately, Bellow has always had this humor to a surpassing degree. I've never known any writer who has more clearly both a sense of his destiny as a writer and a humorous self-deprecation before his fate. Some time ago, when a Fuller Brush man at his door who had got nowhere with him finally demanded, "Won't you even take it as a gift?" Bellow is supposed to have replied, "I've been given the gift of life, and it's more than I know what to do with."

From the ex-radical dangling man to the man who sees in himself the comic hero of destiny is a short step; the amazing relaxation of Bellow's work, from the anxious soberness of style in *Dangling Man* and the tight nightmare plot of *The Victim* to the rapturous ease of *Augie March*, has finally reached its climax in the open buffoonery and philosophical shenanigans of *Henderson the Rain King*.

Henderson is a work that does not really please me. Yet it is typical of Bellow's growing power as a novelist that he can now create a comic hero who is openly and jeeringly his own predicament, who feels the pang of the human situation in his six feet four, his 230 pounds, his millions, his pig farm, his two wives, his bad teeth. In Bellow's earlier novels the leading protagonists were gray, urban and dim, specters, *Luftmenschen,* who did not altogether convince me that they could put up much of a fight. They were almost too easily put upon. Even Augie, *picaro* and adventurer that he is, is too much a thought in Bellow's own mind to impress us with the weight that he can put into his plans to outwit life. But Henderson is from the beginning built to the size of the titans, the wrestlers-with-God, as the Russians used to describe the type. He is an American eccentric, a gentleman farmer, a war hero, a desperately unavailing husband and father, built to scale.

I gave up fishing and sat on the beach shooting stones at bottles. So that people might say, "Do you see that great big fellow with the enormous nose and the mustache? Well, his great-grandfather was Secretary of State, and his father was the famous scholar Willard Henderson who wrote that book on the Albigensians, a friend of William James and Henry Adams." Didn't they say this? You bet they did. . . . In the dining room I was putting bourbon in my morning coffee from a big flask and on the beach I was smashing bottles. The guests complained to the manager about the broken glass . . . me they weren't willing to confront.

I came, a great weight, a huge shadow on those stairs, with my face full of country color and booze, and yellow pigskin gloves on my hands, and a ceaseless voice in my heart that said, *I want, I want, I want,* oh *I want — !*

With this one, then, the possible testing of himself against life offers new possibilities. The extraordinary freedom of style that Bellow learned with Augie has resulted here in an intimate connection of temper and thought, an ease and gaiety that gives the key scenes in the book with Dahfu the native king, a new sense of the laughter that Bellow can bring to intellect.

It is the kind of book that no one else could have written, and which is so much in the necessary line of his development that Henderson naturally takes his place alongside those other agonists, those constant strivers, who make up the significant gallery of Bellow's heroes.

My quarrel with the book has to do with my feeling, suggested to me even in so good a work of its kind as *Seize the Day,* that these Jacobs give up to life a little too eloquently, that they do not struggle enough with the angel before crying out in reverence and submission, "I will not let thee go, except thou bless me." In *Seize the Day* Tommy Wilhelm, after making a mess of things all day long and in every way, realized only by intercepting a funeral that there was something more than himself to weep for, that he could weep only in weeping for another. I was troubled by the excessive awareness of the submission, by the lack of someone big enough to fight with life. In *Henderson,* scene after scene is brilliantly inventive, but the spaces in between do not sufficiently convey the weight that the antagonists bring to the struggle. This Africa is still too clearly a further station along the way for the anxious pilgrim through life. The typical Bellow hero must travel not to struggle with the angel but in search of an angel or demon or God to submit to.

But the beauty of the last scene, when the hero, on his way home, steps off his plane at Newfoundland to run over the fields with a child — "I guess I felt it was my turn now to move, and so went running — leaping, leaping, pounding, and tingling over the pure white lining of the gray Arctic silence" — catches perfectly that sense of man in the middle of things, a joyous consciousness in accidental space, that gives us the abiding vision of Saul Bellow's novels.

[1959]

Gravity and Grace: The Stories of J. F. Powers

SOME YEARS ago Mr. J. F. Powers startled us with a book of stories called *Prince of Darkness.* They came out of the dry and vast plains of Middle Western boredom, and they were mostly about life in Catholic rectories. Remembering what James Joyce had said about his own first book, *Dubliners,* that he had tried for a style of "scrupulous meanness," I thought that Mr. Powers had managed with almost the same saturated plainness to draw just the opposite conclusions. Joyce showed his people in a limbo of cultured hopelessness, people who were moving from faith into the secular bleakness of the modern city. Mr. Powers showed in the Church the ferocious process of "Americanization," of "normalization," the world of utter mediocrity in which everybody's daily life is lived. And it made no difference. The spirit triumphed every time — but so quietly and unexpectedly that the effect was one of humor rather than zeal. "Grace," to use the formula of Simone Weil, won over the law of "gravity" that keeps *everybody* with his feet too much on the ground.

What made these stories so remarkable was maturity. American fiction is always striking an attitude or being "psychological" or just reporting the violence of some unusual experience. Mr. Powers's work was about a *world;* it constantly yielded literary vanity to the truth and depth of this world. He was subtle, funny, precise, and always unexpected. The book seemed to come out of a longer background than most young American writers of fiction ever own.

And now here is a new book, stories again, for Mr. Powers thinks

The Presence of Grace, by J. F. Powers. New York: Doubleday and Company.

in stories. He is a miniaturist, a close thinker, close as a chess player at times. When you take on a Powers story, you find yourself working hard from line to line, and constantly being outguessed. Nevertheless, the point is usually the same: the world falls at the feet of the spirit; the smart sophisticated young curate somehow gets his comeuppance, while the deaf impossible old coot he is trying to replace as pastor not only retains his post, but stands supreme in his dignity at the end, representing a truth, a charity, that makes him beautiful. Indeed, the usual situation in Powers is not even a struggle on equal terms between the world and the spirit; it is, more usually, the vain struggle of the ambitious young curate to make his place in the church through "realism," salesmanship. And in his constant defeat, we are expected, I suppose, to see that the wisdom of the Church is deeper than even it knows.

In story after story the space in which we move is one of "gravity," but the victory that is won is one of grace. Gravity not only holds us down to earth; it is the fatal ordinariness of life that brings everybody down, even priests. The humor is that ordinary American materialism can operate as a *means* to ends that are implicit in the faith. The point that he always makes so quietly is that clerical housekeeping gets as muddled as any other. The coffee, apparently, is a particular horror, and there is an obsessive amount of bread-pudding. Itchy; everything needs painting; the vow of chastity includes the usual absent-minded American overeating. Everybody's life in the morning, especially, is one of gravity, and these priests are no exception. The atmosphere Mr. Powers creates is exemplary in its suggestion of dyspepsia, overfeeding, and competitiveness. And grace? The point about grace is that it is always mysterious. Its presence is a gift. In the title story, there is even a complicated pun on the word, for the lady named Grace is a gossipmonger, a horrid Pharisee who has broken with her best friend, a middle-aged lady who has taken in an eligible widower for a boarder. The presence of grace nevertheless makes itself felt — or rather, the intimation of it is felt as possible — when Grace's gang of ladies are stopped by an old priest who in all other respects appears incompetent.

I admire Mr. Powers very much — story after story is worked out to the finest possible point; this is work that manages, by fusing intelligence and compassion, to come out as humor. There is real love in his heart, but he knows that the *heart* does not write short stories, and that the beauty of grace can appear only against the background of the horrid daily element, which is gravity. Gravity and grace are the *only* possible elements in which a true imagination can work. The one stands for "reality"; the other for ideal beauty. Most American writers don't even know that they are necessary to each other. Their world has no background, nothing by which to judge the pitifulness of our daily actions.

But may I, very softly, complain? Mr. Powers has fallen into a rut, he now works too much by formula, and the deplorable cuteness into which he sometimes falls is there because he knows too well in advance what his material "means," so that we find him looking for situations with which to "handle" his material. Two stories here are told by cats; one would have been enough. Mr. Powers offers us so "shrewd" an outcome, in story after story, that by now it is clear not only that he is writing about life in the Church, but that he is dramatizing the Church itself, constantly pointing to the unpretentious means by which it wins its true ends. There were several times when I definitely saw Bing Crosby and Barry Fitzgerald in this collection as the lovable priests. Like any other fictional "world," Mr. Powers's scenes from clerical life have become, from too close exploitation, rather obviously picturesque.

But I must not close without saying again what an original Mr. Powers is, and what a true writer he seems on the immature American scene.

[1956]

In Praise of Robert Lowell

ROBERT LOWELL's poetic style has been marked by a peculiar force, one that might well have been called violence but for its learning, bookishness, and nostalgia for traditional order. In the book that made him famous, *Lord Weary's Castle,* he wrote with the precision of passion, he cut his phrases as fine as Braille; but between the

Life Studies: New Poems and an Autobiographical Fragment, by Robert Lowell. New York: Farrar, Straus and Cudahy.

elegantly turned tumult of style and the invocation of Catholic glory and order, he was saved not only from violence but also from confronting his own past too directly, from getting too close to rude experience. The formal beauty of his style was extraordinary. Yet shaken as I was by *Lord Weary's Castle*, I felt that Lowell had not only learned (or intuited) a style from reading many books, but that this same rapid and mountainous eloquence had kept him chaste before life, had saved him from some more necessary and desperate encounter with himself. There was something clingingly literary about the tone of these strong poems, as there was about his going to prison during the war as a Catholic conscientious objector. He seemed to be more intense about life than intimate with it.

Life Studies is a remarkable book precisely because Lowell has had the wit — or is this simply the virtue of his imagination? — to face his past and to strip his style without sacrificing its native elegance. It is the book of an absolutely first-rate talent; and, what is so rare, it is a *book,* not an arrangement of poems. It includes a prose autobiography, "91 Revere Street," that presents all the personal themes developed in the poems, and in itself is the vividest example that I have seen in years of how witty, light, seemingly negligent, and always controlled the prose of a really gifted poet can be.

Robert Lowell is a . . . Lowell, and comes out of the heart of Lowell country — Beacon Hill. His memoir, though acerb and wise and tender, has above all that extraordinary subtlety of upper-class commentary on itself (something you don't find in so good a book as *The Late George Apley*) that is possible to Americans who don't really know anyone beyond themselves but who have the gift of experiencing and expressing their own situation to the depths. It is this that made Henry Adams, with all his pretentiousness, such a marvelous autobiographer; Robert Lowell has only, poker-faced, to write "In 1924 people still lived in cities" for us to know exactly where we are. The Lowells bought 91 Revere Street ("looking out on an unbuttoned part of Beacon Hill . . .") because the poet's mother wanted to get her husband out of the Navy, and a civilian address was the opening wedge, since the commander of the Boston Navy Yard disapproved of his officers' living in town. "My mother felt a horrified giddiness about the adventure of our address. She once said, 'We are barely perched on the outer rim of the hub of decency.'"

The portraits of Lowell's parents are superb in their ease and suggestiveness. The mother "was hysterical even in her calm, but like a patient and forbearing strategist, she tried to pretend her neutrality." The father, a kindly and dim naval engineer, seems always to have been under attack by forces more articulate than himself. "By the time he graduated from Annapolis, he had a high sense of abstract form, which he beclouded with his humor. He had reached, perhaps, his final mental possibilities. He was deep — not with profundity, but with the dumb depth of one who trusted in statistics and was dubious of personal experience." The hand of conventional expectation in Boston was heavy on Brahmin boys enrolled at birth in St. Mark's. "We were darkly imperiled, like some annual bevy of Athenian youths destined for the Minotaur. And to judge from my father, men between the ages of six and sixty did nothing but meet new challenges, take on heavier responsibilities, and lose all freedom to explode."

« 2 »

The poems open with a meditation on Rome in 1950 that catches the nervous sense of other people's grandeur that the American is likely to feel in Europe — and that also catches the poet's romantic disillusionment and Boston self-enclosure:

> There the skirt-mad Mussolini unfurled
> the eagle of Caesar. He was one of us
> only, pure prose. I envy the conspicuous
> waste of our grandparents on their
>   grand tours —
> long-haired Victorian sages accepted
>   the universe,
> while breezing on their trust funds
>   through the world.

The regret that Mussolini was "one of us/only, pure prose" seems to me a revealing expression of that overliterary inflation which Lowell learned from Ezra Pound along with Pound's dash and speed. But the conscious wit of the poem is remarkable, far more controlled and poised than such set pieces in Pound's *Cantos*. Just as Pound so often reminds one of Browning, so Lowell seems, through Pound, to have gone straight back to Browning.

It is 1950, the year of the dogma of the Assumption, and Lowell catches the excitement and density of the Roman crowds, the memory of the dead idol:

> The Duce's lynched, bare, booted skull still spoke.
> God herded his people to the *coup de grâce* —
> the costumed Switzers sloped their pikes to push,
> O Pius, through the monstrous human crush.

It is this vividness, the energy and texture of each image, that is Lowell's distinct achievement. He specializes in place, in eloquent vertigo, in stylizing the communion with self that is the essence of dramatic monologue, and I can't think of any poet of his generation who has polished the dramatic sense, rare enough, to such acuteness. One of his favorite words is *jack-hammer*, and there is a similar intimation of strength in all his language, like the lash of the sea images in his earlier book, that comes through even in isolated bits. Marie de Medici speaks after the assassination of her husband, Henri IV:

> And so I press my lover's palm to mine;
> I am his vintage, and his living vine
> entangles me, and oozes mortal wine
> moment to moment.

The poem on Eisenhower's first inauguration reproduces the leaping style of Hart Crane:

> The snow had buried Stuyvesant.
> The subways drummed the vaults.
>   I heard
> the El's green girders charge on Third,
> Manhattan's truss of adamant,
> that groaned in ermine, slummed
>   on want . . .

but ends with a steely passage that Crane could never have held up:

> Look, the fixed stars, all just alike
> as lack-land atoms, split apart,

and the Republic summons Ike,
the mausoleum in her heart.

But beautiful as these opening poems are — the soliloquy of Hart Crane, the address to Santayana in the Protestant Cemetery in Rome, and others — my greatest pleasure in this book is in the "life studies" proper. Here Lowell has achieved the nakedness toward which all good poets yearn — freedom from the suffocating traditions of fine style that in our day have again overcome poetry. When I first saw these intensely personal, brilliantly candid poems about mental breakdown and marital dolor, I was not able to imagine how natural the whole group of them would look in a book. Any good writer will learn to trust his inner impressions, but in a relatively minor poem like "Memories of West Street and Lepke," it is the cross-stitch and variation of line that gives Lowell's "new" simplicity its exhilaration. As a conscientious objector in jail, Lowell saw the "T-shirted back" of Lepke, the Czar of Murder, Inc.

there piling towels on a rack,
or dawdling off to his little segregated cell full
of things forbidden the common man:
a portable radio, a dresser, two toy American
flags tied together with a ribbon of Easter palm.
Flabby, bald, lobotomized,
he drifted in a sheepish calm,
where no agonizing reappraisal
jarred his concentration on the electric chair —
hanging like an oasis in his air
of lost connections . . .

The vividness, picture after picture, is striking. Lowell describes his father, who, leaving the Navy, drifted from job to job, and every time he lost a job bought a better car:

but his best friend was his little black *Chevie*,
garaged like a sacrificial steer
with gilded hooves,
yet sensationally sober . . .

Lowell's mother died in Italy, and he relates how the body was taken home for burial in the States. "Mother travelled first-class in the hold;/her *Risorgimento* black and gold casket/ . . . In the grandiloquent lettering on Mother's coffin/*Lowell* had been misspelled LOVEL./The corpse was wrapped like *panetone* in Italian tinfoil." Even a poem about life in a mental hospital has this typical wit, the ease and neutral tone with which Lowell speaks of "These victorious figures of bravado ossified young." But the poem ends, unforgettably, on the lines "We are all old timers,/each of us holds a locked razor."

In these poems twentieth-century poetry comes back to its great tradition as plain speech; comes back, in Pasternak's phrase, "to its sister, life."

[1959]

J. D. Salinger: "Everybody's Favorite"

THE PUBLICATION of his two well-known stories from the *New Yorker* in book form, *Franny and Zooey*, brings home the fact that for one reason or another J. D. Salinger now figures in American writing as a special case. After all, there are not many writers who could bring out a book composed of two stories — both of which have already been read and argued over and analyzed to death by that enormous public of sophisticated people which radiates from the *New Yorker* to every English department in the land. Yet Salinger's fascination for this public is so great that although he has refused this book to every book club, it may yet sell as if it were being pushed by book clubs. Since 1953, when *The Catcher in the Rye* was reprinted as a paperback, it has become the favorite American novel on the required or suggested reading lists of American colleges and secondary schools, and it has sold well over a million and a half copies. Yet no less unusual is the fact that the *New Yorker* — which if it did not originate certainly brought to perfection the kind of tight, allusive, ironic story with which Salinger's earlier stories (reprinted in *Nine Stories*, 1953) felt so much at home — published in

Franny and Zooey, by J. D. Salinger. Boston: Little, Brown and Company.

"Zooey" (41,130 words) the longest story it had ever published, and a story for which the *New Yorker* obviously felt personal affection and some particular intellectual sympathy.

In one form or another, as a fellow novelist commented unlovingly, Salinger is "everybody's favorite." He is certainly a favorite of the *New Yorker*, which in 1959 published another long story around the Glass family called "Seymour: An Introduction" (almost 30,000 words), and thus gave the impression of stretching and remaking itself to Salinger's latest stories, each of which has been appearing, like a visit from outer space, at two-year intervals. But above all is he a favorite with that audience of students, student intellectuals, instructors, and generally literary, sensitive and sophisticated young people who respond to him with a consciousness that he speaks for them and virtually *to* them, in a language that is peculiarly "honest" and their own, with a vision of things that captures their most secret judgments of the world. The only thing that Salinger does not do for this audience is to meet with them. Holden Caulfield said in *The Catcher in the Rye* that "What really knocks me out is a book that, when you're all done reading it, you wish the author that wrote it was a terrific friend of yours and you could call him up on the phone whenever you felt like it." It is well for him that all the people in this country who now regard J. D. Salinger as a "terrific friend" do not call him up and reach him.

A fundamental reason for Salinger's appeal (like that of Hemingway in the short stories that made *him* famous) is that he has exciting professional mastery of a peculiarly charged and dramatic medium — the American short story. At a time when so much American fiction has been discursive in tone, careless in language, lacking in edge and force — when else would it have been possible for crudities like the beat novelists to be taken seriously? — Salinger has done an honest and stimulating professional job in a medium which, when it is expertly handled, projects emotion like a cry from the stage and in form can be as intense as a lyric poem. A short story which is not handled with necessary concentration and wit is like a play which does not engage its audience; a story does not exist unless it hits its mark with terrific impact. It is a constant projection of meanings at an audience, and it is a performance minutely made up of the only possible language, as a poem is. In America, at least, where on the whole the best stories are the most professional stories and so are published in the most famous magazines, "second-rate" stories belong in the same limbo with unsuccessful musical comedies; unless you hit the bull's-eye, you don't score.

This does not mean that the best-known stories are first-rate pieces of literature any more than that so many triumphant musical comedies are additions to the world's drama; it means only that the story has communicated itself with entire vividness to its editor and its audience. The profundity that may exist in a short story by Chekhov or Tolstoy also depends upon the author's immediate success in conveying his purpose. Even in the medieval "tale" which Tolstoy in his greatest stories seems to recapture in tone and spirit, the final comment on human existence follows from the deliberate artlessness of tone that the author has managed to capture like a speech in a play.

« 2 »

What makes Salinger's stories particularly exciting is his intense, his almost compulsive, need to fill in each inch of his canvas, each moment of his scene. Many great novels owe their grandeur to a leisurely sense of suggestion, to the imitation of life as a boundless road or flowing river — to the very relaxation of that intensity which Poe thought was the esthetic perfection of a póem or a story. But whatever the professional superficiality of the short story in American hands, which have molded and polished it so as to reach, dazzle and on occasion deceive the reader, a writer like Salinger, by working so hard to keep his tiny scene alive, keeps everything humming.

Someday there will be learned theses on *The Use of the Ashtray in J. D. Salinger's Stories*; no other writer has made so much of Americans' lighting up, reaching for the ashtray, setting up the ashtray with one hand while with the other they reach for a ringing telephone. Ours is a society complicated with many appliances, and Salinger always tells you what his characters are doing with each of their hands. In one long stretch of "Zooey" he describes that young man sitting in a bathtub, reading a long letter from his brother and smoking; he manages to describe every exertion made and every sensation felt in that bathtub by the young man whose knees made "dry islands." Then the young man's mother comes into the bathroom; he draws the shower curtains around the tub, she rearranges the medicine cabinet, and while they talk (in full) everything they do is described. Everything, that is, within Salinger's purpose in getting at such detail — which is not the loose, shuffling catalogue of the old-fashioned naturalists who had the illusion of reproducing the whole world, but the tension of a dramatist or theater director making a fuss about a character walking just so.

For Salinger, the expert performer and director (brother Buddy Glass, who is supposed to be narrating "Zooey," speaks of "directing" it and calls the story itself a "prose home movie"), gesture is the essence of the medium. A short story does not offer room enough for the development of character; it can present only character itself — by gesture. And Salinger is remarkable, I would say he is almost frenetically proficient, in getting us, at the opening of "Franny," to *see* college boys waiting on a train platform to greet their dates arriving for a big football weekend. They rush out to the train, "most of them giving the impression of having at least three lighted cigarettes in each hand." He knows exactly how Franny Glass would be greeted by Lane Coutell — "It was a station-platform kiss — spontaneous enough to begin with, but rather inhibited in the follow-through, and with something of a forehead-bumping aspect."

And even better is his description of the boy at a good restaurant taking a first sip of his martini and then looking "around the room with an almost palpable sense of well-being at finding himself (he must have been sure no one could dispute) in the right place with an unimpeachably right-looking girl." Salinger knows how to prepare us with this gesture for the later insensitivity of a boy who is exactly one of those elaborately up-to-date and anxiously sophisticated people whom Franny Glass, pure in heart, must learn to tolerate and even to love in what she regards as an unbearably shallow culture.

But apart from this, which is the theme of *Franny and Zooey*, the gesture itself is recognized by the reader not only as a compliment to himself but as a sign that Salinger is working all the time — not merely working to get the reader to see, but working to make his scene itself hum with life and creative observation. I don't know how much this appearance of intensity on the part of Salinger himself, of constant as well as full coverage, is due to *New Yorker* editorial nudging, since its famous alertness to repetitions of words and vagueness of diction tends to give an external look of freshness and movement to prose. Salinger not only works very hard indeed over each story, but he obviously writes to and for some particular editorial mind he identifies with the *New Yorker*—look up the stories he used to write for the *Saturday Evening Post* and *Cosmopolitan*, and you will see that, just as married people get to look alike by reproducing each other's facial expressions, so a story by Salinger and a passage of commentary in the *New Yorker* now tend to resemble each other.

But whatever the enormous influence of any magazine on those who write regularly for it, Salinger's emphasis of certain words and syllables in American speech and his own compulsiveness in bearing down hard on certain details (almost as if he wanted to make the furniture, like the gestures of certain people, tell *everything* about the people who use them) do give his stories the intensity of observation that is fundamental to his success. Lane Coutell, sitting in that restaurant with Franny and talking about a college paper on Flaubert he is horribly well satisfied with, says: ". . . I think the emphasis I put on *why* he was so neurotically attached to the *mot juste* wasn't too bad. I mean in the light of what we know today. Not just psychoanalysis and all that crap, but certainly to a certain extent. You know what I mean. I'm no Freudian man or anything like that, but certain things you can't just pass over as capital-F Freudian and let them go at that. I mean to a certain extent I think I was perfectly justified to point out that none of the really good boys—Tolstoy, Dostoevski, *Shake*speare, for Chrissake—were such goddam word-squeezers. They just *wrote*. Know what I mean?" What strikes me about this mimicry is not merely that it is so clever, but that it is also so relentless. In everything that this sophisticated ass Lane Coutell says, one recognizes that he is and will be *wrong*. Salinger disapproves of him in the deepest possible way—he is a spiritual enemy.

Of course it is a vision of things that lies behind Salinger's expert manner. There is always one behind every manner. The language of fiction, whatever it may accomplish as representation, ultimately conveys an author's intimation of things, makes us hear (not in a statement but in the ensemble of his realized efforts) his quintessential commentary on the nature of existence. However, the more deliberate the language of the writer, as it must be in a short story, the more the writer must convey his judgment of things in one highlighted dramatic action, as is done on the stage.

At the end of "Franny," the young girl collapses in the ladies' room of the restaurant where she has been lunching with her cool boy friend. This conveys her spiritual desperation in his company, for Lane typifies a society where "Everything everybody does is so — I don't know — not *wrong*, or even mean, or even stupid necessarily. But just so tiny and meaningless and — sad-making." Her brother Zooey (Zachary Glass), at the end of the long second story, calls her up from another telephone number in the same apartment and somehow reaches to the heart of her problem and gives her peace by reminding her that the "Fat Lady" they used to picture somnolently listening to them when they were quiz kids on the radio — the ugly, lazy, even disgusting-looking "Fat Lady" who more and more typifies unattractive and selfish humanity in our day — can be loved after all, for she, too, is Jesus Christ.

« 3 »

In each story, the climax bears a burden of meaning that it would not have to bear in a novel; besides being stagy, the stories are related in a way that connects both of them into a single chronicle. This, to quote the title of a little religious pamphlet often mentioned in it, might be called "The Way of a Pilgrim." Both Franny and Zooey Glass are, indeed, pilgrims seeking their way in a society typified by the "Fat Lady" and even by Lane Coutell's meaningless patter of sophistication. No wonder Franny cries out to her unhearing escort: "I'm sick of just liking people. I wish to God I could meet somebody I could respect. . . ."

The Glasses (mother Irish, father Jewish) are ex-vaudevillians whose children were all, as infant prodigies, performers on a radio quiz program called "It's a Wise Child." Now, though engaged in normally sophisticated enterprises (Franny goes to a fashionable woman's college, Zooey is a television actor, Buddy a college instructor), they have retained their intellectual precocity (and indeed their precocious charm) and have translated, as it were, their awareness of themselves as special beings into a conviction that they alone can do justice to their search for the true way.

The eldest and most brilliant of the children, Seymour, shot himself in 1948 while on his honeymoon in Florida — this was the climax of Salinger's perhaps most famous story, "A Perfect Day for Bananafish." And it is from Seymour's old room in the Glass apartment that Zooey calls up his sister Franny — on a phone that is normally never used, that is still listed in the name of Seymour Glass, and that has been kept up by Buddy (who does not want a phone in his own country retreat) and by Zooey in order to perpetuate Seymour's name and to symbolize his continuing influence on them as a teacher and guide. It is from reading over again, in Seymour's old room, various religious sayings from the world's literature that Seymour had copied out on a piece of beaverboard nailed to the back of a door that Zooey is inspired to make the phone call to Franny that ends with the revelation that the horrible Fat Lady is really Jesus Christ.

This final episode, both in the cuteness of its invention and in the cuteness of speech so often attributed to Seymour, who is regarded in his own family as a kind of *guru* or sage, helps us to understand Salinger's wide popularity. I am sorry to have to use the word "cute" in respect to Salinger, but there is absolutely no other word that for me so accurately typifies the self-conscious charm and prankishness of his own writing and his extraordinary cherishing of his favorite Glass characters.

Holden Caulfield is also cute in *The Catcher in the Rye,* cute in his little-boy suffering for his dead brother Allie and cute in his longing for his sister, "Old Phoebe." But we expect that boys of that age may be cute — that is, consciously appealing and consciously clever. To be these things is almost their only resource in a world where parents and schoolmasters have all the power and the experience. Cuteness, for an adolescent, is to turn the normal self-pity of children, which arises from their relative weakness, into a relative advantage vis-à-vis the adult world. It becomes a "role" boys can play in the absence of other advantages, and *The Catcher in the Rye* is so full of Holden's cute speech and cute innocence and cute lovingness for his own family that one must be an absolute monster not to like it.

And on a higher level, but with the same conscious winsomeness, the same conscious mournfulness and intellectual loneliness and lovingness (though not for his wife), Seymour Glass is cute when he sits on the beach with a little girl telling her a parable of "banana fish"—ordinary-looking fish when "they swim into a hole where there's a lot of bananas," but "after that, they're so fat they can't get out of the hole again. . . . They die." His wife, meanwhile, busy in their room on the long-distance phone to her mother in New York, makes it abundantly clear, in the hilariously accurate cadences and substance of her conversation, why her husband finds it more natural to talk to a four-year-old girl on the beach than to her. Among other things, Seymour expects not to be understood outside the Glass family. But agonizing as this situation is, the brilliantly entertaining texture of "A Perfect Day for Bananafish" depends on Seymour Glass's conscious cleverness as well as on his conscious suffering—even his conscious cleverness *about* the suffering of "ordinary-looking" fish who get so bloated eating too many bananas in a "hole" they shouldn't have been attracted to in the first place.

In the same way, not only does the entertaining surface of *Franny and Zooey* depend on the conscious appealingness and youthfulness and generosity and sensitivity of Seymour's brother and sister, but Salinger himself, in describing these two, so obviously feels such boundless affection for them that you finally get the sense of all these child prodigies and child entertainers being tied round and round with veils of self-love in a culture which they—and Salinger—just despise. Despise above all for its intellectual pretentiousness. Yet this is the society, typified by the "Fat Lady" (symbolically, they pictured her as their *audience!*), whom they must now force themselves to think of as Jesus Christ, and whom, as Christ Himself, they can now at last learn to love.

For myself, I must confess that the spiritual transformation that so many people associate with the very sight of the word "love" on the printed page does not move me as it should. In what has been considered Salinger's best story, "For Esmé with Love and Squalor," Sergeant X in the American Army of Occupation in Germany is saved from a hopeless breakdown by the beautiful magnanimity and remembrance of an aristocratic young English girl. We are prepared for *this* climax or visitation by an earlier scene — the Sergeant comes upon a book by Goebbels in which a Nazi woman had written, "Dear God, life is hell." Under this, persuaded at last of his common suffering even with a Nazi, X writes down, from *The Brothers Karamazov:* "Fathers and teachers, I ponder 'What is hell?' I maintain that it is the suffering of being unable to love."

But the love that Father Zossima in Dostoevsky's novel speaks for is surely love for the world, for God's creation itself, for all that precedes us and supports us — that will outlast us and that alone helps us to explain ourselves to ourselves. It is the love that D. H. Lawrence, another religious novelist, spoke of as "the sympathetic bond" and that in one form or another lies behind all the great novels as a primary *interest* in everyone and everything alive with us on this common earth. The love that Salinger's horribly precocious Glass characters speak of is love for certain people only — forgiveness is for the rest; finally, through Seymour Glass's indoctrination of his brothers and sister in so many different (and pretentiously assembled) religious teachings, it is love of certain *ideas.* So what is ultimate in their love is the love of their own moral and intellectual excellence, of their chastity and purity in a world full of banana fish swollen with too much food. It is the love that they have for themselves as an idea.

The worst they can say about our society is that *they* are too sensitive to live in it. They are the special case in whose name society is condemned. And what makes them so is that they are *young,* precocious, sensitive, different. In Salinger's work the two estates — the world and the cutely sensitive young — never really touch at all. Holden Caulfield condemns parents and schools because he knows that they are incapable of understanding him; Zooey and Franny and Buddy (like Seymour before them) know that the great mass of prosperous spiritual savages in our society will never understand them.

This may be true, but to think so can lead to a violation of art. Huckleberry Finn (so often cited as a parallel to the hero of *The Catcher in the Rye*) was two years younger than Holden, but the reason he was not afraid of an adult's world is that he had respect for it. He had never even seen very much of it until he got on that raft with a runaway Negro slave he came to love and was able to save. It was still all God's creation and inspired him with wonder. But Holden and, even more, the Glass children are beaten before they start; beaten in order not to start. They do not trust anything or anyone but themselves and their great "idea." And what troubles me about this is not what it reflects of their theology but what it does to Salinger's art.

« 4 »

Frank O'Connor once said of this special métier, the short story, that it is "the art form that deals with the individual when there is no longer a society to absorb him, and when he is compelled to exist, as it were, by his own inner light." This is the condition on which Salinger's work rests, and I should be sorry to seem unsympathetic toward it. It is an American fact, as one can see from the relative lack in our literature of the ripe and fully developed social novel in which the individual and society are in concrete and constant relationship with each other. But whatever this lack, which in one sense is as marked in the novels of Scott Fitzgerald as it is in Salinger's emphasis upon the short story, it is a fact that when Fitzgerald describes a character's voice, it is because he really loves—in the creative sense is fully interested in—this character. When Salinger describes a character's voice, it is to tell us that the man is a phony. He has, to borrow a phrase from his own work, a "categorical aversion" to whole classes and types of our society. The "sympathetic bond" that Lawrence spoke of has been broken. People stink in our nostrils. We are mad with captious observation of one another. As a friend of mine once said about the novels of Mary McCarthy, trying to say with absolute justice what it was that *shocked* her so much in them—"the heroine is always right and everyone else is wrong." Salinger is a far more accomplished and objective writer of fiction than Mary McCarthy, but I would say that in his work the Glass children alone are right and everyone else is wrong.

And it is finally this condition, not just the famous "alienation" of Americans from a society like our own, that explains the popularity of Salinger's work. Salinger's vast public, I am convinced, is based not merely on the number of young people who recognize their emotional problems in his fiction and their frustrated rebellions in the sophisticated language he manipulates so skillfully. It is based perhaps even more on all those who have been released by our society to think of themselves as endlessly "sensitive," spiritually alone, gifted — and whose suffering lies in the narrowing of their consciousness to themselves, in the withdrawal of their curiosity from a society which *they* think they understand all too well, in the drying-up of their hope, their trust, and their wonder at the great world itself. The worst of American sophistication today is that it is so bored, so full of categorical aversion to things that writers should never take for granted and never close their eyes to.

The fact that Salinger's work is particularly directed against the "well-fed sunburned" people at the summer theater, at the "section men" in colleges parroting the latest fashionable literary formulas, at the "three-martini" men — this, indeed, is what is wrong. He hates them. They are no longer people but symbols, like the "Fat Lady." No wonder that Zooey tells his sister: *Love* them, love them all, love them anyway! But the problem is not one of spiritual pride or of guilt: it is that in the tearing of the "sympathetic bond" it is not love that goes, but the deepest possibilities of literary art.

[1961]

Brendan Behan: The Causes Go, the Rebels Remain

ALTHOUGH the twentieth century is almost three fifths over, it often seems to outsiders, at least, that the Irish manage to live in the nineteenth. Other small countries have not been so lucky. The real predicament of these countries is not how to get freedom from the old imperial states, but how not to be torn apart from within by the long-repressed masses and from without by the great power conflict. But the Irish seem to be where the Italians were during the *risorgimento*. Not only are the six northern Irish counties still out of the Free State, but the world fame of all those Irish writers who could never live at home now sustains among young Irish intellectuals the legend of an Irish literature that is romantically rebellious

Borstal Boy, by Brendan Behan. New York: Alfred A. Knopf, Inc.

in the nineteenth-century style. James Joyce dead means more to young Irish writers than James Joyce alive ever meant to their fathers, and the fact that he is on the Index makes the forbidden fruit exciting if not lethal. After all, in many parts of the world it is not books that are banned but the writers themselves. Perhaps it is not injustice the Irish suffer from so much as it is frustration. Causes go; at least they change; the rebels remain.

For Irish writers who were too young for the "troubles" but who are never out of the militantly Irish context, this cultural lag, this constant living in the past, is a real problem; and at least one new Irish writer, Brendan Behan, has capitalized on cultural myths that he himself plainly feels are out of date.

Brendan Behan was born in 1923 to a solidly working-class Irish Republican family with a long tradition of anti-British activity. His father saw him for the first time from a prison cell during the Civil War, when the Irish Republicans fought against the settlement with Britain; thousands were arrested, and many of them were excommunicated for their adherence to the Irish Republican Army. The Behan men were house painters, and the solidly gregarious, tough, and racy life of the Catholic Irish working class — an experience not shared by the Protestant Yeats or by Joyce, whose father had so many middle-class pretensions — is the element that plunged Brendan Behan into terrorist activity from the age of thirteen and that got him arrested in Liverpool at the age of sixteen. Yet the same background gave Behan the hilarious and cynical freedom from literary convention that is the most rousing thing about his prison memoir, *Borstal Boy*, and his two remarkable plays, *The Quare Fellow* and *The Hostage*. Behan's literary interest lies in his sense of living speech, in his joyous hamming of the Irish personality; he turns his prison memoirs into pure talk, and both plays, somber and even sinister as the situation of a condemned prisoner is, are also hilarious.

The major reason for his present significance lies in the detached sense of himself as a professional young Irishman surrounded by the ghosts and corpses of old causes. His exploitation of this role reminds one of the late Dylan Thomas, who was also a deliberate ham in a world full of literary old ladies who expected every Welshman to sing and to be rapt. What Behan has done, coming in too late to participate in the Irish literary renaissance, is to identify himself not with the abstract cause of art but with the profane and explosive speech of the streets, the saloons, the prisons. In books, this speech is a literary invention like any other, and Behan, who on principle is excessive in everything, certainly gets tiring. "I was no country Paddy from the middle of the Bog of Allen to be frightened to death by a lot of Liverpool seldom-fed bastards, nor was I one of your wrap-the-green-flag-round-me junior Civil Servants that came into the I.R.A. from the Gaelic League. . . . No, be Jesus, I was from Russell Street, North Circular Road, Dublin, from the North-side where, be Jesus, the . . . whole of this pack of Limeys would be scruff-hounds would be et, bet, and threw up again — et without salt." But only in this way can he perpetuate his disdain of the English middle class, of English severity and gentility and hypocrisy. At the same time, with a sardonic awareness of the contradictory loyalties that a sensitive intelligence is likely to hold, he can mimic in certain overpious Irish Republican diehards their dread of thinking beyond their comfortably stagnant prejudices.

Behan is a complicated and tortured writer, as anyone in his double situation must be. No one who reads *Borstal Boy* with admiration for its open style, its raciness, its savagery, should miss for a moment the ordeal to which this sixteen-year-old boy put himself. He was quite aware of how useless and dangerous his own mission was in planning to bomb English naval installations during the war; yet one cannot easily forget his misery in the Liverpool prison, when he was denied the sacraments by the chaplain because of his refusal to oppose the Irish Republican Army. If people would not automatically think of Brendan Behan as the stage Irishman he himself sometimes tries to be, if they would read his autobiography not as the undiluted eloquence it strives for but as the illuminating self-portrait of a young man born out of his time, they would realize better not only the real power in this book but also its subtle literary limitation, for Behan's work is created by will.

These contradictions, the conflict in his heart, explain why Behan trusts to speech for the representation of everything. *Borstal Boy* is an autobiography based on dialogue — an extraordinary feat not so much of memory as of control. By putting every reminiscence into speech, Behan avoids a formal evaluation of experience in favor of rudimentary characterization; it is his way of suspending final judgment, of retaining his contradictions. It is not only Behan's dramatic flair, his obvious feeling for everything that has to do with the stage, that is important to his dialogue; it is the inescapable impression he leaves of mimicry. He is the clown of his own Irishness. *Borstal Boy* opens with his landlady shrieking up the stairs that the police have come for him: "Oh God, oh Jesus, oh Sacred Heart. Boy, there's two gentlemen to see you." Five pages later, we are told that "This landlady was mean and barren as a bog. Her broken windows would be a judgment on her for the cheap sausages and margarine she poisoned her table with, for she was only generous with things that cost little in cash . . . you would think half the men in Liverpool were running after her, panting for a lick of her big buck teeth."

« 2 »

Yet *Borstal Boy* is a memoir; the author is his own most important character, and not only is everything seen through himself as the center, but everyone else is a mere shadow, described as a passing type. There are no developed characters in Behan's work—not even in his plays, wonderfully dramatic as they are. It is typical of Behan's generation that his sense of other people is hurried and sardonic; people, though they are given names, are passing Englishmen, warders, laborers, convicts, and the rest. This dense sociological crowd, this mass and mess of people—this is how a truly contemporary eye often does see human beings today. And given the Irish sense of fun, which creates in mimicry the parody of one's outworn but unaltered cultural role, the result is a yeasty mixture: deflation of the pompous, a slightly hysterical reaching after the obscene, and, what is most solid in Behan's work, the Irish workingman's sense of what life is really like. He describes the doctor in the Liverpool prison; while Behan had to stand naked before him, he "set his lips and spoke through them, like an English officer in a film about the Khyber Pass," and a warder gave him a rectal examination "with the usual appearance of British official detachment." His description of the prison itself is decisive:

> All the time it was cold and black. In the morning the slate floor was freezing cold, and over the whole huge wing was a cold smell of urine and bad air, like a refrigerated lavatory.

It seemed to me the English were very strong on washing and cold, but not so much on air and cleanliness. Like the well-tubbed and close-shaven looks of the screws — cruel and foul-spoken, but always precise and orderly.

From his own position, as a professional Irish rebel, he can see the fun of people being carried away by their roles. The prison chaplain got so enthusiastic talking about the Christmas spirit to the half-starved convicts that he pictured for them plum pudding, cigars, and the "foaming" glass of ale; in describing the Borstal (in England, a reformatory) institution to which he was finally sent, Behan reports a speech by the local colonel who forgot that he was addressing young prisoners and talked to them as if they had all been at Eton together. It is this instinct for the ridiculous that gets into his mother's account of why Oscar Wilde was sentenced to prison; apparently she did not know what Wilde had done and described him as another Irish revolutionary whose sexual passion had given the English an excuse for disgracing him: "His downfall — they brought him down the same as they did Parnell." Behan, always looking for "a read," saw in prison a copy of Gibbon: "I'd heard it was on the Index, but that is not always a recommendation, I'd discovered, for so was *The Cricket on the Hearth*." The professional pugnacity that got him into trouble for defending the I.R.A. against the prison chaplain — "Me blood was up and me country in me knuckles" — has, on its other side, a shrewdness and a refusal to carry a quarrel beyond human limitations: "In two months Walton Jail had made me very anxious for a truce with the British. I had come to the conclusion, not only that everything I had ever read or heard in history about them was true, but that they were bigger and crueler bastards than I had taken them for, lately."

The description of the Borstal institution itself, the North Sea Camp, is relatively peaceful and idyllic; here Behan was in a remarkably well-run institution, and he had a chance at physical labor such as he was used to, with workingmen of his own class. Describing a young upper-middle-class English boy in the camp who tried to run away, Behan notes shrewdly: "He was dead lonely; more lonely than I and with more reason. The other fellows might give me a rub about Ireland . . . and I was never short of an answer, historically informed and obscene, for them. But I was nearer to them than they would ever let Ken be. I had the same rearing as most of them, Dublin, Liverpool, Manchester, Glasgow, London. All our mothers had all done the pawn — pledging on Monday, releasing on Saturday. . . . As the middle class and upper class in England spend so much money and energy in maintaining the difference between themselves and the working class, Ken was only getting what his people paid for but, still and all, I couldn't help being sorry for him, for he was more of a foreigner than I."

This working-class heritage, by drawing Behan to his mates in prison, deepened his sense of irony about the political Irish cause; returning to hard physical labor gave him an exhilarating sense of reality again. He describes himself at work in the fields in a line that might have come out of one of Dylan Thomas's poems: "The sweat came from me, easy and freely, and I breathed with my stroke like a swimmer." The workingman's sense of his job, the feeling that people who work with their hands have earned a respite from genteel convention — it is this, and not the professional Irishness, that so often gives the authentic vitality to Behan's book. In his eyes it is perhaps only the workingman who still knows what real life is; other classes just play roles.

« 3 »

In Behan's new play, *The Hostage*, a disenchanted old Irish revolutionary, Pat, explains why he jeers "at the boys": "The H-Bomb. I'm nervous of it. It's such a big bomb it's after making me scared of little bombs. The I.R.A. is out of date and so is the R.A.F. So is the Swiss Guard and the Foreign Legion, the Red Army, the United States Marines, the Free State Army." When a crazed old Irish patriot (significantly half-English) comes in playing the bagpipes and talking Gaelic, Pat laughs: "That's Irish. Isn't it great for them that has an Oxford University education. God help me, I'm only a poor ignorant Dublin man. I wouldn't understand a word of it." And when a young whore is shocked by his raillery of the old cause, Pat says: "Why are you getting so upset about Ireland? Where the hell were you in nineteen-sixteen when the real fighting was going on?" She answers, "I wasn't born," and he throws up his hands: "You're full of excuses!"

Behan's evident cynicism extends even to his new profession, literature. It is clear from the jeering theatrical shrewdness with which he sets his plays, as from the "Irishness" of style in his memoir, that Behan's future is unpredictable. Just as *Borstal Boy* tends to peter out, so the plays, powerful in stagecraft as they are, tend to be too manipulative and deliberate. There is a constant suggestion in Behan's work that the laughter which supports despair does not always hide despair. But Behan's is the despair of an authentic predicament, of the actualities of life at the present time. He is our true contemporary. Though he has come to realize how many faiths are outworn, he is to be saluted for his honesty and power — and above all, for his gaiety in the face of so many cultural and human losses.

[1959]

How Good Is Norman Mailer?

PERHAPS more than any other book since Scott Fitzgerald's *The Crack-up*, this book reveals how exciting, yet tragic, America can be for a gifted writer. It is a remarkably full book; all of Mailer up to now is in it; and that is exactly what is wrong with it. For at thirty-six, after following up *The Naked and the Dead* with an artistic failure, *Barbary Shore*, and one ambiguous *succès de scandale*, *The Deer Park*, Mailer (now embarked on a very long and extremely ambitious novel that may take many years) has obviously been hungry to make his mark again in one big smashing outrageous way. He has put together an anthology of all his works, from undergraduate short stories to two sections of the novel in progress, that includes his columns from a Greenwich Village weekly, social and political comment, his now famous essay on "The White Negro" and other socio-sexual themes, stories, spoofs, interviews, poems, and some shrewd but essentially subjective evaluations of his literary generation. In the "advertisements" to the different works he talks about himself and Hemingway, himself and marijuana, himself and sex, himself and Eisenhower's America. By the time you get

Advertisements for Myself, by Norman Mailer. New York: G. P. Putnam's Sons.

through what is often a very brilliant if screamingly self-conscious book, you feel that Mailer has worked so hard to display everything he has done and everything he knows that it has all collected on the surface. Mailer's performance here reminds me of the brilliant talker who impresses the hell out of you at a cocktail party but who, when he turns his back to go home, seems vaguely lost.

« 2 »

Yet *Advertisements for Myself* is a remarkable performance, and it is clearer to me than ever that Mailer is a powerful, courageous talent admirably provoked by our culture. I admire him because he is naturally a radical, strong, and exuberant talent; this book is full of more penetrating comment on the America of Eisenhower, television, suburbia, and J. D. Salinger than anything I have seen in years. But as Mailer says, "I have been running for President these last ten years in the privacy of my mind," and he is probably the only Jew who has been. He wants to be not just a good novelist but the Hemingway of our period. Hemingway obsesses him (and ignores him); Faulkner once made fun of him for saying that whites are always jealous of Negro sexuality; the publisher who made so much out of *The Naked and the Dead* finally turned down *The Deer Park*; there are actually good writers in America who pay no attention to him.

In short, like many another American radical, desperado, Reichian stalwart of sexual frankness, Norman Mailer has been driven crazy by an affluent and greasily accommodating society which not only doesn't oppose him but which turns even his disgust and frankness into a form of literary capital. Just as the hipsters, whom Mailer admires, are not outlaws, not radicals, but the slobs and remittance men and spoiled brats of a society so wasteful and indulgent and satiated with normal sex that it has to discover new thrills all the time, so the secret burn of Norman Mailer is that a book like this, which is meant to slap respectable America in the face, may not sell as much as it could. Like every American writer whose name is an instant password, who can support himself by his writing, who knows himself a celebrity because he moves largely in the company of celebrities, Mailer can no more stay off television or move back to Brooklyn than, being an honest and intransigent spirit, he can admire television or sentimentalize the Brooklyn which, as he says, is not the center of anything. Anyone who reads this book with as much attention and admiration as I have just done can, nevertheless, see that what obsesses Norman Mailer is not just the swarminess of our culture, the repressiveness of our official morals, the flabby gentility of our ruling intellectuals, but the fact that this same America is itself constantly coaxing Norman Mailer to share in the take and join the fun.

What makes this society so marvelous for the gifted rebel, and so awful, is that, lacking all standards by which to counter or to question the new, it hungrily welcomes any talent that challenges it interestingly — but then holds this talent in the mold of its own shapelessness; the writer is never free enough of his neighbors and contemporaries to be not simply agin the government but detached from it. Mailer, who like all his generation has had to work against the overpowering example of Fitzgerald and Hemingway and Faulkner, now thinks that these older fellows had it easier, that our society did not drag them into its maw as compulsively as it does present writers. When I recall how desperately out of fashion Fitzgerald and Lewis and Anderson and Cather felt at the end of their careers, I doubt that the literary competition has ever been less punishing than Mailer obviously feels it to be. What has changed since the 1920s is first that there are more and more writers, as there are more and more people. Even "advanced" literature is beginning to get as crowded as the mass media, and Mailer cannot be sure, now that he has dismissed Bellow, ignored Malamud, and ruled out all women writers as unreadable, that there isn't someone in South Dakota who may yet outdistance him.

More important, Hemingway (of whom Mailer seems constantly to dream and to curse in his dreams) was still based enough on the old "inner-directed" Protestant culture to measure his need of courage against the moral abstractions of courage, duty, grace, etc. Mailer measures himself against others. Symbolically, Hemingway got his great experience in the first world madness by volunteering for the Italian Army long before Americans were in the war. Mailer in 1943 had to keep from becoming a clerk, for only as a rifleman could he collect the experience for the great Hemingwayish novel about the war that he was already prepared to write. And only in the Pacific, as he brilliantly estimated again, would he be able to gather experience for a really provocative novel, since there the growing reactionary tendencies in American life would be manifest.

Without his egotism, no writer is likely to carry much weight. But granted that he must fight for himself and push himself, what reserves of thought and imagination are left? A writer is not only what he knows himself to be, what he consciously fights for and hates and loves — he is the book he makes, the book that must surprise him in the making, the book that somewhere within itself is always greater than he is. Scott Fitzgerald's *The Crack-up*, moving as it may be, has less of Fitzgerald than *The Great Gatsby*. The question all over this book is: How good is Norman Mailer? — and the trouble is that Mailer thinks that he can answer it in terms of available competition. Only a highly self-conscious and rather stormily competitive fellow would have tried so hard to win the prize by dismissing so many writers whose books he hasn't read. This performance calls up the comment on the famous French writer who boasted in his journal that sexually he was more gifted than other men: "How does he know?"

Still, *we* have a right to ask, How good is Norman Mailer? How good are his books? Quite apart from the deleterious influence of our government, our publishers, our official morals — and apart from all the obscene words about television and the cowardice of the "squares" and the marvelous sexuality of Negroes and the necessity of Hip — how good are Norman Mailer's novels? My answer would be that *The Naked and the Dead* is a good novel, though too literary, with worked-up army detail that is thin compared with James Jones's *From Here to Eternity*, and with only one real character in it, the General, who is too obvious a villain; that *Barbary Shore* is hysterical politically and a bad novel by a writer of obvious talent and guts, so that everything in it makes its mark, but not as a work of art; that *The Deer Park* is an extraordinarily uneven and somehow sick book with something peculiarly closed and airless about it. I felt this painfully when I read the novel, and Mailer says in *Advertisements* that he rewrote the novel under marijuana. I am neither shocked by this nor moved to admire Mailer because of it; I do think that *The Deer Park* is not what Mailer thinks it is. It seems to me ridiculous for Mailer to push his novel so hard in this book, since the question is not what Rinehart or the critics did to the book but what Mailer did.

How good is Norman Mailer? The answer varies from work to work, sometimes from page to page. Some of his new work, particularly a torrid story wholly about sexual intercourse, "The Time of Her Time," seems to me remarkable; the opening of his new book, "Advertisements for Myself on the Way Out," a lot of wind. Not only can Mailer not know how good he is; he is himself one of the most variable, unstable, and on the whole unpredictable writers I have ever read. He has a remarkable intelligence, and this book shows it; a marvelously forceful and inventive style; great objective gifts as a novelist. On the other hand, his intelligence, though muscular, has no real ease or quietly reflective power; he is as fond of his style as an Italian tenor of his vocal chords, and he sometimes tends to overpower when the more manly thing — if I may touch on a major concern in this book — would be to convince; his sense of reality, though boldly critical, is often obsessive in its self-consciousness. On the whole, Norman Mailer is very, very good indeed — not better than ten million other fellows, as he thinks one has to be, but good.

But what will become of him God only knows, for no one can calculate what so overintense a need to dominate, to succeed, to grasp, to win, may do to that side of talent which has its own rule of being and can never be forced.

Truman Capote and "the Army of Wrongness"

THE HEROINE of *Breakfast at Tiffany's* is of the type made famous by Christopher Isherwood's Sally Bowles. She is the adorable immoralist, the completely free spirit in a world whose dominating types are usually disgusting; where her true friends — the narrator. who speaks as Truman Capote himself, and a lovable old bartender

Breakfast at Tiffany's: A short novel and three stories, by Truman Capote. New York: Random House.

— can only watch in helpless admiration as she is whirled away from them to one bed after another.

The lovable strumpet, as Isherwood showed, is a setup for a clever novelist with a good ear and a flair for highly polished comedy, and Capote's accurate sense of both the speech and the night life of upper Bohemian New York shows itself in the way he combs in detail after detail of Holly Golightly's life against the background of a fly-by-night apartment in the East Seventies. The time is 1943, not because the war really enters into this society of fashion photographers, South American diplomats, degenerate millionaires, and animal-like Hollywood agents, but because the date symbolizes a society wholly in flux. No one else, however, has the charm of the lady of the story, who is nineteen, devastingly honest, and in this cold, often phony world can find comfort only in Tiffany's. When she gets the "mean reds," which are far worse than the blues, "What I've found does the most good is just to get into a taxi and go to Tiffany's. It calms me down right away, the quietness and the proud look of it; nothing very bad could happen to you there, not with those kind men in their nice suits, and that lovely smell of silver and alligator wallets. If I could find a real-life place that made me feel like Tiffany's, then I'd buy some furniture and give the cat a name." She has steadily refused to give her cat a name. "'Poor slob,' she said, tickling his head, 'poor slob without a name. It's a little inconvenient, his not having a name. But I haven't any right to give him one: he'll have to wait until he *belongs* to somebody. . . .'"

This profound instinct for nonattachment, mixed with a certain wry tenderness for those who would like to be attached (the cat, the narrator, the elderly bartender), is the "serious" side of the book, and one that ultimately raises doubts about Capote's ability to bring off the story he intended to write. But the purely external side of Holly's character, as seen before one gets to know her or by those who never do, is skillfully done. Capote has caught perfectly the professional accent of New York, the trigger-tenseness of a speech that is always excited, declamatory, on the make. Miss Golightly alone seems to keep cool — Miss Holly Golightly, who can never hold on to her key and, coming home in the dead of night with a new gentleman, cheerfully rings other people's bells so that they will let her in. She is impulsive, she is direct, she is generous — and while she does not get *paid* for anything, she judges a man by his "chic." "Any gent with the slightest chic will give you fifty for the girl's john, and I always ask for cab fare too, that's another fifty." When she discovers that the narrator is a writer, she is reminded that she has never been to bed with a writer, and demands the ages of the more famous. "I can't get excited by a man until he's forty-two. . . . I simply *trained* myself to like older men, and it was the smartest thing I ever did."

A horrible old Hollywood agent ("Tufts of hair sprouted from his ears, from his nose; his jowls were gray with afternoon beard, and his handshake almost furry") reveals that Holly gave up her big chance in Hollywood. "She says you got to want it to be good and I don't want it, I say Well, what the hell do you want, and she says When I find out you'll be the first to know." There is a cocktail party at Holly's. "Except for a lack of youth, the guests had no common theme, they seemed strangers among strangers; indeed each face on entering had struggled to conceal dismay at seeing others there." At the party is a pro-Nazi millionaire, and it is worth quoting the first description of him, for it conveys the acidulous, "social," and hard manner of Capote at his best:

> He was a middle-aged child who had never shed its baby fat, though some gifted tailor had almost succeeded in camouflaging his plump and spankable bottom. There wasn't a suspicion of bone in his body; his face, a zero filled in with pretty miniature features, had an unused, a virginal quality: it was as if he'd been born, then expanded, his skin remaining unlined as a blown-up balloon, and his mouth, though ready for squalls and tantrums, a spoiled sweet puckering.

This is good writing, and — what one should not miss in Capote when he has his eye on a character, not on his own "style" — it is angry writing. For as the narrator reflects, "If Holly could marry that 'absurd fetus,' then the army of wrongness rampant in the world might as well march over me."

Holly doesn't marry him, but the end of the story is as inconsequential as its background. It turns out that Holly is really a hillbilly who was married to a Texas farmer at thirteen or so and played stepmother to his many children before she ran away. The hoped-for tenderness that Capote tries to build up as a significant part of her life fails, and because of this failure the story turns sentimental when it is no longer clever. The fact is that it is impossible to believe anything of Holly but what we can see before us. Without her patter, her legion of boy friends, her cat, and her guitar, she is nothing. And the failure to make her background convincing starts from the curious doubleness that afflicts Capote's writing. Either he builds up a witty line of social details, seen from the outside, or he collapses into tender and mawkish details that are really private symbols. As Holly herself says about the narrator, he does a lot of "Yearning. . . . He wants awfully to be on the inside staring out," and she pictures him with his "nose pressed against a glass."

The lovable old bartender in the story, the narrator's fellow in respectful admiration of Holly, insists that it is possible to love a woman without sex. "You can love somebody without it being like that. You keep them a stranger, a stranger who's a friend." Yet *Breakfast at Tiffany's* is a love story; the point of the story lies in the narrator's attachment to one who can be attached to nobody, and who, when she gives up her cat in the end, suddenly realizes how frightened you can get from "Not knowing what's yours until you've thrown it away." The trouble with the narrator's kind of love is that it is too easy; it presents us with an image of the loved one that cannot be proved; it gives us the outline without the woman, a "character," not a person.

Whenever Capote tries to suggest the inner life of his heroine, the writing breaks down. The image of the starving hillbilly child never comes into focus behind the brightly polished and eccentric woman-about-town in her black dress, pearl choker, and sandals. The reason is that the narrator can show us only his "admiration," not his passion, and one of the serious faults of the story is that we are meant, for the explanation of certain passages, to think of the narrator as Truman Capote the author, the sad little devil whose picture is always so prominent on the back of each book. This kind of extraliterary reference violates the imaginative unity of the story; yet in one sense the story has never been unified at all, for the emphasis has been alternately on Holly as a town character and Holly as a Southern waif — never on Holly as a woman. This double vision was a limitation of Isherwood's portrait of Sally Bowles, but what gave *Good-bye to Berlin* its lasting quality was the documentation of Germany on the eve of Hitler, and the humility with which Isherwood recorded the oncoming disaster. For Truman Capote the "armies of wrongness" are indiscriminate: the "absurd fetuses" are really everybody. They are the enemies of those who are truly poor in spirit, like Holly. But we cannot take these "armies of wrongness" too seriously, for between Capote's pity for the hillbilly child and his instinct for the smart Madison Avenue manner, some deeper tone than either — the tone of actuality, which comes from the portrayal of people in truthful relationship with each other — has been lost.

It is a great pity, for Capote is not only a writer of admirable talent, but he has an eye for human weakness, a feeling for those who really are oppressed, that could be devastating. He is not a superficial writer; no one should miss how much he has aimed for in this clever book. But he is a writer for whom the world is all society or all self, public vice or private tears.

[1958]

The Essays of James Baldwin

Recently, a scholar investigating the Negro novel in America discovered that of sixty-two Negro novelists writing between 1853 and 1952, forty published only one novel; eleven published only two; only eleven published more than two. Certainly one reason for this situation is the economic difficulties that so many Negro writers have had, a lack of encouragement from publishers and a lack of audience among Negroes as among whites. But surely another reason is that too often a writer turns to the novel not because his talent lies in fiction, not even because he wants to write fiction, but because he hopes to make his experience seem as individual and artistically realized as possible. To many writers in this country the novel seems the only badge of "creativity," and it is understandable

Nobody Knows My Name: More Notes of a Native Son, by James Baldwin. New York: Dial Press.

that a Negro would aim for the novel as a way of gaining distinction for his individual experience.

This is a kind of thinking that operates among many minorities in this country, for one of the incidental blows to a writer's self-respect is the belief that everybody knows about his background anyway, and that the only way for him to get out of the rut of Harlem or the East Bronx is by transmuting his experience into a conscious work of art. But of course the deliberate transmutation of one's own experience into "fiction" works badly. The book doesn't really hang together on its own terms, as the novel of a genuine novelist does. So after the first, transparently autobiographical novel, the second requires a wholly imaginative conception that often isn't there. And even among the pros, those who write novels because they think in narrative, there is often a strained and "hypothetical" quality, to adapt the title of one of James Baldwin's essays, that suggests the writer is trying to do certain things in and with the novel to show that he can do them. Baldwin himself, who is certainly a good novelist and is likely to become an even better one, nevertheless strained pretty hard in *Giovanni's Room* to show that he could write a novel entirely about a sexual conflict among white people. That was a "hypothetical" situation, and in some respects the novel remained hypothetical too.

When I read Baldwin's first collection of essays, *Notes of a Native Son,* I realized that the tortured intellectual consciousness I felt behind his fiction could be turned into the self-representation of an absolutely first-class essayist, reporter, and social critic. *Notes of a Native Son* is one of the two or three best books ever written about the Negro in America, and it is the work of an original literary talent who operates with as much power in the essay form as I've ever seen. I'm sure that Baldwin doesn't like to hear his essays praised at the expense (seemingly) of his fiction. And I'm equally sure that if Baldwin were not so talented a novelist he would not be so remarkable an essayist. But the great thing about his essays is that the form allows him to work out from all the conflicts raging in *him,* so that finally the "I," the "James Baldwin" who is so sassy and despairing and bright, manages, without losing his authority as the central speaker, to show us all the different people hidden in him, all the voices for whom the "I" alone can speak.

Each of his essays in this new book is a facet of this different experience, each is a report from the battlefield that is himself, that he sometimes feels may be *only* himself: he is in Paris as an American writer, he attends a congress of "Negro-African" writers where he certainly doesn't feel altogether at home, he indignantly describes a slummy housing project in Harlem, he speaks up for the Negroes who broke up the U.N. meeting by protesting against Lumumba's murder, he goes South for the first time in his life, he is in Stockholm to interview Ingmar Bergman. No doubt other writers could have done all these pieces coolly, as correspondents from another shore to us; for Baldwin, each of his subjects represents a violent conflict in himself.

The extraordinary thing about these essays is that he can give voice to all his insights and longings and despairs without losing control — indeed, without ever missing his chance to dig in deeper. Speaking now with the moral authority of the future, now with the bitterness of Harlem, now with the sophistication of the perennial American abroad, now with the toughness of the adventurer who knows the slums and messes of Paris, now as the dopester on Gide's marriage, now as the literary celebrity moving in the company of other celebrities, he somehow manages never to enjoy things so well that he will get heedless, never suffers so constantly that he will lose himself. He is bitter yet radiantly intelligent as he seizes the endless implications in the oppression of man by man, of race by race. To be James Baldwin is to touch on so many hidden places in Europe, America, the Negro, the white man — to be forced to understand so much! He has a relatively weak essay on Norman Mailer and other white friends who romanticize the Negro sexually. But Baldwin himself, in what is probably his best piece, "Fifth Avenue, Uptown," can say: "The Southerner remembers, historically and in his own psyche, a kind of Eden in which he loved black people and they loved him. Historically, the flaming sword laid across this Eden is the Civil War. Personally, it is the Southerner's sexual coming of age, when, without any warning, unbreakable taboos are set up between himself and his past. Everything, therefore, is permitted him except the love he remembers and has never ceased to need. The resulting, indescribable torment affects every Southern mind and is the basis of the Southern hysteria."

The humiliation and worse that the Negro remembers can also become an issue of hysteria — and it is extraordinary how Baldwin can manage so often to suggest both the Negro's impatience for the future and his own despair in the present, both the understanding made necessary by despair and the futility of intelligence in the face of so much despair. What the "Negro-African" writers in Paris "held in common was their precarious, their unutterably painful relation to the white world." This is often the endless subject of the American Negro's life. But powerful and lashing as Baldwin can be when he accuses the white man, he also knows that oppression has worked its way into his own character. What ultimately makes these essays so impressive and moving is not merely the *use* Baldwin makes of his conflicts but the fact that this personal form is an urgent necessity. This is the book of a deeply troubled man, the spiritual autobiography of someone who hopes, by confronting more than one beast on his way, to see whether his fear is entirely necessary.

« 2 »

When one is a Negro always in the path of this juggernaut of hate and suspicion and exclusion, how can one say where the social cruelty ends and one's private weaknesses begin? Who can say just how much the Negro as actor, the Negro as dissembler in the white man's world — how much of this has been made by "society" and how much by family hatred, love, and jealousy? Of all the many things I admire about Baldwin's essays, I think what I admire most is this: more than any other Negro writer whom I, at least, have ever read, he wants to describe the exact place where private chaos and social outrage meet. He wants to know just how far *he* is responsible for his unhappiness. Of course he can sum up the social paranoia of Southern racists "who are quite incapable of telling you what it is they are afraid of. They do not really know what it is they are afraid of, but they know they are afraid of something, and they are so frightened that they are nearly out of their minds." But he can also say generally, remembering his experiences in Europe, that "In America, the color of my skin had stood between myself and me; in Europe, that barrier was down. . . . It turned out that the question of who I was was not solved because I had removed myself from the social forces which menaced me . . . The question of who I was had at last become a personal question, and the answer was to be found in me."

The answer, perhaps, but not the cause. Baldwin will face what has become a personal condition, but of course he will not let off history, society, man in general. He is too intelligent to rest on the soft and psychological cliché that allows so many middle-class white Americans to absolve the society that feeds them. He knows that in certain crucial areas we are all under the same pressures. "The one thing that all Americans have in common is that they have no other identity apart from the identity which is being achieved on this continent." And the fact that Baldwin, a preacher's son, ends every essay with a plea that something be done to make us more human, that this is the job for which we really and at long last must look to each other — this expresses the American hope about as obstinately as I've seen it done in our languishing time. And how funny and touching and like Baldwin it is that these sermony endings should follow on as ruthlessly deep an analysis of American incapacity as we are likely to get. "In short, I had become an American. I had stepped into, I had walked right into, as I inevitably had to do, the bottomless confusion which is both public and private, of the American republic." No wonder that the range of feeling, the vibration of so many conflicts, puts this book as close to us as any personal document can be.

[1961]

Tough-minded Mr. Roth

SEVERAL WEEKS AGO I was awakened, while reading the *New Yorker*, by Philip Roth's "Defender of the Faith," a story with such extraordinary guts to it that I went around for days exhilarated by the change in the literary weather. Mr. Roth's story described the agonizing moment of decision in the life of Sergeant Nathan Marx, a combat veteran sent back to the States in 1945 to train troops. Sergeant Marx found himself being cajoled into obtaining special favors for three Jewish recruits until, lied to once too often, he

Goodbye, Columbus, by Philip Roth. Boston: Houghton Mifflin Company.

punished the ringleader with deliberate harshness. The story ended with a picture of troops preparing to go off to the Pacific, "trying as best they could to accept their fate. Behind me, Grossbart swallowed hard, accepting his. And then, resisting with all my will an impulse to turn and seek pardon for my vindictiveness, I accepted my own."

It was this conscious acceptance that particularly interested me in the story, for the narrator, reluctantly exploited by Jewish fellow feeling throughout most of the action, rose to an unusual level of moral complexity in affirming his own deliberate hardening of heart. In punishing the soldier so severely, Sergeant Marx was affirming his own — not altogether admirable but candidly mature — acceptance of his own raw human limitations, and the reader was left with a deepened sense of the necessary and painful decisions on which life rests.

This is a note that Jews, in writing about other Jews, do not often strike; the appeal to raw human nature, to the individual in his human complexity and loneliness as a mere human creature, is less common than the grand collective themes of Jewish life, of Jewish solidarity in the face of oppression. Even the most gifted and profound writers among Jews tend to describe love and hate, misery and savagery, as if they were merely symbols of the depth and range of Jewish experience. The unusual thing, Mr. Roth's achievement, is to locate the bruised and angry and unassimilated self — the Jew as individual, not the individual as Jew — beneath the canopy of Jewishness. I admired Mr. Roth's story because he had caught perfectly the drama of personal integrity in the face of group pressures that is so typical of American literature, and I was not surprised to learn that Mr. Roth's story had aroused the darkest displeasure among some readers of the *New Yorker* and that he had been called in and worried over by at least one professional Jewish organization.

Yet in turning to this collection of his stories, I can see that Mr. Roth's favorite theme is not the anarchical self struggling with its natural loyalties — which might be the story of George F. Babbitt — but romantic and credulous youth defeated in love by a brutally materialistic society, like Fitzgerald's Gatsby. The long, hilarious, but sharp-edged title story tells of a poor Jewish boy from Newark who fell in love with a rich Jewish girl from Short Hills, and lost her.

It is so much the story of the boy's romantic infatuation versus the girl's bourgeois calculatingness that no reader should be fooled by Roth's Jewish material into thinking that he is interested exclusively in its local color. The story is brilliant, and in a culture like ours the symbols are national. Neil Klugman, the poor boy from Newark, works in the public library; his parents are nobodies, and the aunt with whom he lives is a gross Yiddish immigrant. He falls in love, rapturously, with Brenda Patimkin, who goes to Radcliffe, whose father can spend a thousand dollars on each nose operation for his children, and whose brother Ronald, six feet four, once a football hero at Ohio State, is marrying Harriet Ehrlich of Milwaukee. Harriet was "a young lady singularly unconscious of a motive in others or herself. All was surfaces, and she seemed a perfect match for Ron, and too for the Patimkins . . . she nodded her head insistently whenever anyone spoke. Sometimes she would even say the last few words of your sentence with you, though that was infrequent; for the most part she nodded and kept her hands folded. All evening, as the Patimkins planned where the newlyweds should live, what furniture they should buy, how soon they should have a baby — all through this I kept thinking that Harriet was wearing white gloves, but she wasn't."

The tone of voice in which Neil Klugman describes the Patimkin family seems perfect to me. He is rapturous as well as satirical, aloof but envious of their grossness, constantly amazed by their height, their girth, their appetities, their profusion. Ron Patimkin, lying in bed rapturously listening to a record of the football crowd at Ohio State saying good-by to the town and the college years, "goodbye, Columbus," is the thickest, dumbest, solidest, most amiable American football hero yet; Neil, watching him swim, "looked back to see Ron taking the length in sleek, immense strokes. He gave one the feeling that after swimming the length of the pool a half dozen times he would have earned the right to drink its contents."

That tone is Mr. Roth's particular achievement. He is acidulous, unsparing, tender, yet more than anything else he is *young,* he sees life with a fresh and funny eye; in the midst of the tense romance between poor boy and rich girl, one catches lampoonings of our swollen and unreal American prosperity that are as observant and charming as Fitzgerald's description of a Long Island dinner party in 1925. Boy and girl are physically unrestrained with each other, yet when they talk birth control they express a horror of Mary McCarthy's daring descriptions of fornication in *Partisan Review*, of old-fashioned moral defiance and Bohemian adventurism, that itself is funny in its wryness. Yet comic as "Goodbye, Columbus" is, hilarious as the rich, overstuffed, overbearing Patimkins are, it is made increasingly clear that the gap between poor Jewish boys and rich Jewish girls in modern American society can be final. Even before the romance crashes, the theme is pushed home in the protection that Neil Klugman extends to a little Negro boy who visits the Newark Public Library to look at a book of Gauguin reproductions, instead of taking it home, because "I *likes* to come here. I likes them stairs." There is a bond between the poor Jew and the little Negro boy that will never be felt between Neil and the Patimkins. When Brenda, perhaps unconsciously, allows her mother to discover that she has been sleeping with Neil so that the family itself can decisively end the romance, the betrayal is felt by Neil as a betrayal not only of his love but of his dignity as a human being who comes from the slums. He has gone up to Cambridge to see Brenda, and bitterly standing outside the beautiful Lamont Library after everything is finished, he feels like throwing a rock through the glass. Like Gatsby, he has not only been betrayed by the girl he loves, he has been made to feel that his origins alone are at fault. His humiliation is complete.

Yet brilliant as this story is, it is not nearly as deep, as many-sided, as moving as *The Great Gatsby*. It is all a little too sharp-edged, too much in control, indeed all too much in the *New Yorker* mode. The best of the *New Yorker* story writers, like John Cheever, always make me feel that, keen as they are, there is a whole side to their observations of American society that is entirely fantastic, imaginative, almost visionary, and so belongs to themselves alone. Roth, though emphatically not tailored to the *New Yorker*, involuntarily fits it because of a certain excess of intellectual theme over the material. There are too many symbols of present-day society, too many quotable bright sayings; the stories tend too easily to make a point. I don't like "The Conversion of the Jews," the story of an independent little boy who, by threatening suicide, made his rabbi and his mother more tolerant of non-Jewish beliefs. The point —"You shouldn't hit me about God, Mamma. You should never hit anybody about God"—is altogether too clear; there really isn't a story apart from it. Something like this can be said about the last story, "Eli, the Fanatic." A group of prosperous young Jews in a suburb are embarrassed by an old-fashioned Talmudical school in their midst, and particularly by one of the teachers who walks about town in East European rabbinical dress. They commission a young Jewish lawyer to get these unwelcome foreigners out of town, or at least to make the uncouth stranger change to American clothes. But the lawyer, already mentally overdriven by the pressure to conform, is suddenly seized by a vision and, exchanging clothes with the teacher, walks about town in fur hat and caftan until he is locked up as a mental case.

The story, though appreciable social commentary, adds up only to its theme; it is all too easily paraphrasable, and in its own way as shallow as the psychoanalytical clichés that Eli's wife is always throwing at him. I admire the edge and fierceness of Mr. Roth's mind, but his book leaves me worried about his future. For he has put so much of himself into being clear, decisive, straight, his stories are consciously so brave, that I worry whether he hasn't worked himself too neatly into a corner. He shows himself too anxious in each story not only to dramatize a conflict but also to make the issue of the conflict absolutely clear. He has intelligence and courage aplenty; what he needs is more of the creative writer's delight in life for its own sake, in figures that do not immediately signify a design.

[1959]

V
The European Current

The Plant, Man, Is More Robust and Large in Rome than Elsewhere

From the time he first saw the country, when he was seventeen, with Napoleon's conquering and liberating armies, until his last years, as French consul at Civitavecchia, Stendhal had so uncontrollable a passion for Italy that, as Benedetto Croce was to say, even Stendhal's dreams came dressed up as Italy. He constantly visited it, wrote about it, held it up as an example to France. Italy was the embodiment of his own passionate and romantic nature in a world that had forced him to disguise it, and it is this that explains the dominating role of Italy in all his work. Italy, for Stendhal, was more than a pleasure; it was an idea, and it was because of this idea that he enlisted himself in the struggle against the reactionary spirit in Europe after Napoleon's downfall.

The most obvious thing about Stendhal's strength as a novelist is that he always serves an idea. It would have seemed preposterous to him that a time would come when novelists would aim at "truth" for its own sake, as if they were laboratory technicians recording the behavior of another species. Stendhal, although one of the first consciously "psychological" novelists in history, would have suspected that it is only when novelists cease to believe in the importance of ideas, when they come to think of fiction — as so many young writers do now — as wholly psychological, that they become subjective and uninteresting. What saved Stendhal from the obsession with himself to which his erratic and emotional temperament exposed him was the historical fact that he belonged to a revolutionary generation that had come to life under Napoleon and, like Stendhal himself, in Napoleon's armies. After Waterloo — which for him signified the end of revolutionary Europe — Stendhal could never believe that conservatism in any field was anything but devitalizing. And in this drama of opposition between the spirit of Na-

A *Roman Journal,* by M. de Stendhal. Translated by Haakon Chevalier. New York: Orion Press.

poleon and the world that had so fearfully succeeded him, between the imperial tradition of audacity and those who tried to re-establish the *ancien régime* — "candle snuffers," as Stendhal called them — Italy was, to Stendhal, the most important part of the symbolic landscape of sensuousness, colorfulness, carelessness, joy.

It is this intense and brilliant appreciation of Italy that gives significance to Stendhal's old "guidebook," *Promenades dans Rome*, which has been translated into English by Haakon Chevalier under the title *A Roman Journal* and published by the Orion Press in a large and handsome edition sumptuously decked out with prints of the period. Although *A Roman Journal*, like so many of Stendhal's minor works on Italian subjects, would probably have been forgotten if he had not held a winning ticket, as he predicted he might, in the "lottery of fame," the book has a special interest for us, both because it is a portrait of Rome under the temporal rule of the Papacy and because of Stendhal's incomparable sassiness on this subject and every other. Stendhal could not sit down to any book, not even to a guidebook done purely for the money, without making his intelligence and verve felt on every page. The book was written in 1828 and 1829, in a hotel room in Paris, when Stendhal was at a low ebb, broke, and — as usual — at the end of a love affair. He thought a good deal about suicide, and in one year he made seven wills. But such was the hold Italy had on him that even though the book was an astonishingly personal exposition of Rome, it nevertheless served as a useful guidebook in an era when people traveled in Italy on the advice not of Baedeker but of travel books by Goethe and Mme. de Staël. The form of *A Roman Journal*, a fictitious day-by-day tour of Rome by Stendhal and a group of friends, is of no particular significance in itself, since Stendhal was the kind of writer who would have intruded his own personality if he had written the Book of Genesis. But it is an indication of Stendhal's longing for his other country that in grinding out his guidebook in Paris he wrote it as if he were actually walking about Rome.

Stendhal's passion for Italy was literally a passion, explicitly connected in his mind with women. Just as he attributed to Italian men a libertine boldness that, he felt, bourgeois morals and manners had checked in France, so he identified with Italian women in particular that perfect warmth and tenderness which all his life he sought in an unbelievable succession of love affairs. Stendhal's mother died when he was seven, and from the time he first saw Italy, a young officer excited by the brilliance of Milan, he seems to have personified the country as the face and body of that ripe older woman, permissive, loving, indulgent, whom he portrayed as the bewitching Countess Sanseverina in *La Chartreuse de Parme*. And in his other great novel, *Le Rouge et le Noir*, a dominant figure is an older woman, Mme. de Rênal, who extends to the young Stendhalian hero a protectiveness that enables him to pursue a woman of his own generation. It has been pointed out by Mr. Frank O'Connor, in a recent book on modern novelists, that if Stendhal associated the softness and ease of Italy with his mother, he identified with France his harsh and despotic father, whom, quite simply, he called "the Bastard."

The most peppery side of *A Roman Journal*, as in everything Stendhal wrote about Italy, is the contrast between that country and France, which for him was the contrast between the heart and the mind, between the pleasure principle and the repressive instinct. When he emphasizes "that passionate sensibility without which one is unworthy of seeing Italy," one can guess how many Frenchmen, in his eyes, lack it. He writes that "in Rome, clever people have *brio*, which I have observed only once in a man born in Paris. One sees that the superior men of this country despise affectation. They could well say, 'I am like myself: so much the better for you.'" He cites a cardinal in Italy who, aged ninety-two, is "constantly in society, busy . . . addressing subtle remarks to young women." In France, he complains, you have to be solemn in order to succeed, and while the country is moving toward liberty "along an extremely dreary path," there is "nothing of this kind in Rome; everyone is looking for a good time." Frenchmen are petty, care only for public opinion, bother their heads with political nonsense. Italians are bold, indifferent to opinion, swashbucklers—and besides, the country is full of real paintings, unlike the art shops of Paris, with their "painted curios." "An Italian who loves a painting hangs it opposite his bed so as to see it on awakening, and his salon remains without ornament. Here people want pleasures that are real, and *appearance* is nothing."

Such observations (or, rather, inventions) made up Stendhal's contrast between France, which oppressed him, and Italy, whose greatest charm was that he found it easy to adore what he did not respect. The effect of Italy on all travelers is the effect not merely of the climate and the physical beauty of both the country and the inhabitants, but of their supposed primitivism, which has enabled so many writers to describe the country as if they were on holiday from tiresome moral restrictions. Although Stendhal had a good deal of contempt for the ignorance in which the Italian people were kept, he was able to write with admiration, with relief, "What can one not dare in a country that has had only a glimpse of modern civilization from May 17, 1809 [when Rome was annexed by Napoleon], to April, 1814 [when it was restored to the Pope]?" That "what can one not dare" was especially exciting to Stendhal, who often wrote about Italy as if it existed chiefly to please his sexual imagination. Like a great many other writers, he openly enjoyed the violence of Italian life. He complained that Christianity had spoiled the "sweet delight" of sitting in the Colosseum and watching wild animals put to death, and that civilization, by "etiolating" the passion and poetry that had once distinguished martyrs in Rome, "will destroy cruelty." The more he despised the self-conscious prudence of so many people in the France of the 1820s who were afraid of risking further revolutionary upheavals, the more he delighted in the spectacle of the papal city, where corruption and indifference seemed to walk hand in hand. Everywhere else, people appeared to take politics too seriously, but in Rome there was not even a pretense that popular opinion mattered, and in such a climate people looked more colorful, more passionate, more truly alive. Nowhere in Stendhal's many pages on Italy did his admiration find better expression than in his "the plant, man, is more robust and large in Rome, than elsewhere."

From other books of his, one learns that Stendhal actually liked Rome far less than he did Milan, and he described the two cities as women — Milan his special love, Rome "her elder sister . . . a woman of grave, austere worth, without music." But in A *Roman Journal* he shows how much he could suspend his passion for the metropolitan gaiety of Milan and submit fully to Rome, a city so full of historical ghosts, the city that for Stendhal represented the violence and bloodiness of the Renaissance — and that was full of the Raphaels he particularly loved. Rome in the grip of the Vatican dramatized perfectly for Stendhal the extremes of Italian despotism and superstition that seemed to him in such colorful contrast to the self-satisfied common sense of the French. Rome was a city where the dead were carried down the main street late at night, with heads exposed — "an atrocious spectacle that I shall not forget so long as I live, but that makes one think of death, or rather that strikes one's imagination with it, and in this sense a spectacle highly useful to those who reign in this world by making people fear the other." In the leading churches of the city, there had been gravely shown to the faithful a portrait of Jesus Christ painted by the Saviour Himself, the ark of the covenant, Moses' rod, Aaron's rod, the marble table that had been prepared for the sacrifice of Isaac, one of the pieces of silver received by Judas. The Franciscan monks of the church of Santa Maria in Aracoeli, the famous church next to the Capitol, "have the power to attract to their church every year all the devout of Rome and the surrounding countryside by putting on view a doll that is called *il santo Bambino*. This child of olive-wood, magnificently swaddled, represents Jesus Christ at the moment of his birth. This is what is being done in 1829 to pick up a little money, on the spot once revered by the masters of the world as the center of their power."

No one loved the tale of a juicy Renaissance murder as did Stendhal. Although he was describing a tour of contemporary Rome, he reached for every bit of historical gossip or scandal. In the "heyday of poisoning," as he admiringly calls it, "about 1650, it was possible to cut a peach into two halves with a gold knife poisoned only on one side. This peach would be shared with the woman who had made one jealous; the half that had been touched by the sound part of the knife could be eaten without danger; the other half was fatal." Stendhal, who praised brigands and highwaymen for their defiance of society, found in authority a defiance of the people that excited him by its very outrageousness. He describes some of the treasures of the magnificent Vatican library, full of manuscripts that the Popes have collected because of their rarity but that at the same time are considered heretical, so in the Vatican library itself there are areas "into which one cannot enter without being excommunicated *ipso facto*." He reports with glee that among the paintings in the Vatican is one showing the assassination of Admiral de Coligny, the leader of the French Protestants who were slaughtered in the St. Bartholomew Massacre. No wonder that once Stendhal got into the swing of things in Rome, he wrote, "If I were not afraid of shocking moral people, I should confess that I have always thought, without saying so, that a woman really belongs to the man who loves her best. I should be inclined to extend this blasphemy to paintings."

The fact that the Pope had temporal as well as spiritual power seemed to Stendhal highly entertaining, an example of the unreal world that had been foisted on Europe by Napoleon's conquerors. But because it was unreal, it appealed to his sense of the absurd. He felt that in Rome he was watching an opera, and although he was an unrelenting critic of existing society, he had such misgivings about the onrush of the middle-class future that he decided to enjoy the revival of the past while it lasted. The antithesis to the squalid magnificence of Italy was the sterile virtuousness of Protestant England and America. One of the funniest things in the *Journal* is his campaign against the English, whom he has standing about Rome like morose savages, and he can never refer to the United States without attributing to all of it the frigid goodness of a Sunday school. Since the disorder and roughness of nineteenth-century New York might have stimulated him, it is entertaining to find him writing that although the country around Rome is infested with bandits and "this country could be civilized in eighteen months by a French or English general, [it] would thereupon be as estimable as it was uninteresting; something like New York. . . . In this highly moral country, boredom would put an end to my existence in a very few months."

In Rome, by contrast, even cardinals come dressed like Bartolo in Rossini's *Barber of Seville*—"a black habit with red braids and red stockings." He has the Pope attending Mass, sitting behind the altar on a throne, sucking at the Saviour's blood with a gold straw. He reports that from the upper stories of the Colosseum "one can look down on the arena and see the Pope's convicts working while they sing." He often describes "this Roman revery, which seems so sweet to us and makes us forget all the interests of active life," and he sees Romans spending "whole hours in mute admiration, leaning on a window of the Villa Lante, on Mount Janiculus." But sensitive as he is to these purely peaceful impressions of "Rome, where the dome of St. Peter's is outlined against the exquisitely pure glow of an orange-hued twilight surmounted high up in the sky by some star that is just appearing," he never allows the Eternal City to blunt his sensuality or to melt his anger at what the world has become.

[1958]

Sholom Aleichem: The Old Country

THE WAY TO READ Sholom Aleichem is to remember from the outset that he is writing about a people, a folk: the Yiddish-speaking Jews of Eastern Europe. There are a great many Jews and non-Jews who resent the idea that the Jews are a people, for they think this requires all Jews to speak the same language and to live in the same territory. But Sholom Aleichem's characters already are a people. They are a people not merely because they speak the same language, Yiddish, or because they live in the Pale of settlement that the Czarist government kept Jews in. They are a people because they think of themselves as a people. And what is most important, they are a people because they enjoy thinking of themselves as a people.

This is the great thing about the Jews described by Sholom Aleichem. They enjoy being Jews, they enjoy the idea of belonging to the people who are called Jews—and "their" Sholom Aleichem, perhaps more than any other Jewish writer who has ever lived, writes about Jewishness as if it were a gift, a marvel, an unending theme of wonder and delight. He is one of those writers whose subject is an actual national character, a specific type—the Jew as embodied in the poor Jew of Eastern Europe. In a way he does remind us of Mark Twain,* who was so entranced with a new character, the Western American, that he was always trying to weigh

* Sholom Aleichem was so often called "the Jewish Mark Twain" that Mark Twain, on meeting him, referred to himself as "the American Sholom Aleichem."

him, to describe him, as if he, Mark Twain, had discovered a new chemical element. When Mark Twain writes of "the calm confidence of a Christian with four aces," we know that the pleasure he gets in writing that is, in part, the satisfaction of knowing that no one but an American could have written that sentence. It is an artistic pleasure, not a chauvinistic affirmation or a defensive maneuver: it is the pleasure of presenting certain local traits, feelings, habits, jokes, even certain biological characteristics, as a physical *substance,* a living addition to the world of nature — something that you can smell and taste and enjoy. You find this kind of artistic substance in Shakespeare's presentation of a lower-class character like Pistol; in Dickens's Cockneys, who walk off the streets of London, delighting us with their pleasure in being Londoners, in their physical relish of their identity as people of that place and time (and who are proud that they spring straight from the imagination of Charles Dickens). Americans, in their attempt to endow a new country with a specific national type, have contributed very largely to this art of national character. But, generally, this kind of pleasure in one's own national being is, I should say, more European than it is American. I have often noticed the difference in the greater pride with which Europeans tend to project their own language, as opposed to our more functional and careless use of English. I have seen it particularly in the Neapolitan dialect theater of Eduardo de Filippo, and in Italian movies, where a type will appear that instantly captivates the audience because he is recognizable, a symbol of the country's human wealth, a tangible re-creation of the life of ordinary experience.

« 2 »

It is this European, seasoned, familiar pleasure in the national circle of one's own people, that lies behind Sholom Aleichem's stories. But what kind of enjoyment can these people derive from being Jews, since they are incessantly harassed by the Russian government and surrounded by peasants who are usually anti-Semitic and can easily be goaded, with the help of the usual encouragement from the government itself and a lot of vodka, into making pogroms? What is it, in short, that makes for *enjoyment* in these local terms? The answer is that one enjoys being a member of a people because one shares in the feast of their common experience. You share in something that is *given* to you instead of having to make every institution and every habit for yourself, out of nothing, in loneliness and with exertion. The secret of this enjoyment consists not so much in physical solidarity and "togetherness," in the absence of loneliness, as in the fact that a deep part of your life is lived below the usual level of strain, of the struggle for values, of the pressing and harrowing need — so often felt in America — to define your values all over again in each situation, where you may even have to insist on values themselves in the teeth of a brutish materialism. We enjoy things only when we can commit some part of our daily life to tradition, when we can act ceremonially, ritualistically, artistically, instead of having to decide in each case which act to perform and how to go about it and what we are likely to get out of it. What we enjoy is, in fact, nothing less than the unconscious wealth of humanity, which is its memory.

This is the fabled strength of "the old country," which deprived the Jews of Eastern Europe of every decency that we take for granted, but allowed them to feast unendingly on their own tradition — and even to enjoy, as an unconscious work of art, their projection of their fiercely cherished identity. The very pen name "Sholom Aleichem" is an instance of this. (His real name was Solomon Rabinowitz; he was born near Kiev in 1859 and died in the Bronx in 1916.) *Sholom aleichem* is the Hebrew greeting, "Peace be unto you," that is technically exchanged between Jews. It is said with more lightness and playfulness than you would guess from the literal translation. Its chief characteristic, as a greeting, is the evidence it gives of relatedness. Now Solomon Rabinowitz, who actually belonged to the prosperous and more "emancipated" middle class of Russian Jewry (he even married into its landed gentry), took this pen name precisely because he found in the phrase an image of the sweet familiarity, the informality, the utter lack of side, that is associated with the Yiddish-speaking masses of Eastern Europe. A Yiddish writer who calls himself *Mister* Sholom Aleichem tells us by this that he has chosen cannily to picture himself as one of the people and, modestly, to be a register or listening post for his people. Sholom Aleichem! The name's as light as a feather, as "common" as daylight, as porous to life as good Yiddish talk: it is the very antithesis of the literary, the mannered, the ornate. If you didn't know anything else about Mister Sholom Aleichem (several of his characters address him so when they bring their stories to him) you should be able to guess from the name the role that he has chosen to play in his own work. He is the passer-by, the informal correspondent, the post office into which Jews drop their communications to the world. All he does, you understand, is to write down stories people bring him. He invents nothing. And need one say—with that name, with that indescribably dear, puckish, wrinkled face of his—that you will never learn from him *what* he has invented, that he has all Yiddish stories in his head, that any one story people bring him will always be capped with another?

In the world of Sholom Aleichem, nothing has to be made up, for the life of the Jews, to say nothing of the Jewish character, is an unending drama. Nor can it be said of anything that it's never been seen or heard of before. The Jews have lived with each other for a very long time, and they know each other through and through—and this, often enough, is what they enjoy. Their history, alas, has too often been the same, and everything that you see in Kasrilevka (the little Jewish town which is all little Jewish towns) or Yehupetz (Kiev, the big city) can be matched from something in Mazeppa's time, which is late seventeenth century, or that of Haman, who tried to kill all the Jews in Persia in the fifth century B.C. Nor, indeed, is anything ever said just *once*. Everything is real, everything is typical, and everything is repeated.

You must understand, first, that Sholom Aleichem's characters possess almost nothing except the word—the holy word, which is Hebrew, and the word of everyday life, which is Yiddish. They are "little" people, not in the sense that they are poor little victims, but in the sense that they are unarmed, defenseless, exiled, not in the world, not in *their* kind of world. All they have is the word. They talk as poor people always talk—because poor people live near each other, and so have a lot of opportunity to talk. They talk the way the European poor always talk—Cockneys or Neapolitans or Provençals: they talk from the belly; they roar, they bellow, they grunt, they scream. They imitate the actual sounds that life makes, and they are rough and blunt. But most of all, they are poor Jews talking, i.e., they find an irony in language itself. Their words strive after the reality, but can never adequately express the human situation.

This sense that the letter strives after the spirit, but can never fully capture it — this seems to me the essence of the historic Jewish consciousness, with its devout and awestruck yet faithful obedience to some overmastering reality. We are all familiar enough with the Hebrew psalmist's despair that he can find the word, the deep, deep word still lacking to human speech, that will convey the bounty of God. But Yiddish, which is particularly the language of the exile, of the long Jewish wandering, is identified by these poor Jews with the contrast between the Jewish situation in the world and the large and inextinguishable hope of another world which they profess. They do not "despise" Yiddish because it is the tongue of everyday life, and one which they themselves call a vernacular: they love it; it is theirs. But by identifying it with their reduced situation, with their exile, with their isolation, they embody in it a historical moment, the present and its desolation, rather than the world of eternity which is mirrored in Hebrew. Yiddish is the poor Jew's everyday clothes rather than his Sabbath garment, Hebrew. But in the Jewish consciousness it is precisely the life of everyday that is contrasted with the divine gift of the Sabbath, and it is this awareness of what life is actually like (seen always against the everlasting history of this people and the eternal promise) that makes the very use of Yiddish an endless commentary on the world as found.

And it is a commentary on the spirit of language itself. One of the things you get from Sholom Aleichem is this mockery of language, a mockery which — need I say it? — carries a boundless pleasure in language and a sense of the positive strength that goes with mighty talk. The mockery may indicate the inadequacy of words when describing the vastness and strangeness of Russia, in which Yiddish-speaking Jews felt lost: "They all began to tell each other stories about spirits and ghosts, incidents that had occurred right here in Zolodievka, in Kozodoievka, in Yampoli, in Pischi-Yaboda, in Haplapovitch, in Petchi-Hvost, and other places." It conveys, over and over, a mild, loving, but positive irony toward the Creator. "How cleverly the Eternal One has created this little world of His, so that every living thing, from man to a simple cow, must earn its food. Nothing is free." The mockery may indicate despair at reproducing a really odd face: "In appearance Shimmen-Eli was short and homely, with pins and needles sticking out all over him and bits of cotton batting clinging to his curly black hair. He had a short beard like a goat's, a flattened nose, a split lower lip, and large black eyes that were always smiling. His walk was a little dance all his own and he was always humming to himself. His favorite saying was, 'That's life — but don't worry.'" Sholom Aleichem leaves the rest to the imagination. Only the imagination can do justice to the rest.

Or the mockery may, as in a familiarly shrewish tirade by a wife or mother-in-law, mean not only the opposite of what it seems to mean (i.e., it may actually hide affection, though no one but the husband-victim should be expected to know this); but, even more, it will be a commentary — to put it gently! — on the world which a woman cannot always act in, but which, with tongue and blazing eyes, she implacably judges. The husband is always in a direct line of fire, since he is a ne'er-do-well, a *schlemiel*, a genius at bad luck, a *schlimazl*. But it is not the husband's failures alone that are scorned; it is the folly of the world itself — for daring to think of it as *the* world (i.e., a place where human beings can live). Thus Menachem-Mendel ("In Haste"), who tries his hand at everything in the big city and succeeds at nothing, and who, precisely because his ambition is exceeded by his innocence, illustrates the cruelty of the great world in which he naïvely tries to get a living. The particular joke just now is that he has become a professional matchmaker. Home for Passover, first off he sees in the yard his mother-in-law engaged in furious housecleaning for Passover:

When she saw me, she managed to control her joy. She kept right on with her work, muttering to herself:

"Well, well! You mention the Messiah — and look who comes! Here he is, my bird of Paradise. . . . If he doesn't spoil, he'll find his way home. Goats run away, chickens get lost, but men always come back. . . . The only place they don't return from is the Other World. Now I know why the cat was washing herself yesterday, and the dog was eating entrails. . . . Oh, Sheine-Sheindel, daughter, come here! Welcome your ornament, your jewel, your crown of gold and diamonds! Your holy of holies. . . . Quick, take the garbage away!"

At this point my wife runs out, frightened, and sees me. Her welcome is more direct.

"Tfui!" she spat out. "You picked just the right time to come. All year long you roam around that dirty city, lying around in all the attics, engage in every idolatry — and here you come fluttering in on Passover Eve, when we're busy cleaning up and there is not time to say a word to each other. . . ."

An irate man says of a stranger he doesn't like: ". . . comes all the way from Zolodievka and fastens himself to us like a grease spot." Sholom Aleichem says of Kasrilevka itself (*the* very embodiment of all little Jewish towns, the poor man's town): "From a distance it looks — how shall I say it? like a loaf of bread thickly studded with poppy seed." He remarks, in passing, that "the real pride of Kasrilevka is her cemeteries." The wonderful, the lovable Tevye, Tevye the dairyman, the poorest and most faithful and most touching of all Sholom Aleichem's poor Jews, remarks in passing: ". . . with God's help I starved to death." And when he comes through the woods from Boiberik to Kasrilevka, late, so very late that he has to say his evening prayers on the spot, the horse runs off and Tevye runs after his wagon — saying his prayers as he runs. Characteristically, he regrets that he cannot, now, *enjoy* saying his prayers. "A fine way to say *Shmin-esra!* And just my luck, at a moment when I was in the mood to pray with feeling, out of the depth of my heart, hoping it would lift my spirits."

In this world, the extreme is a matter of course — and yet, from a Jewish point of view, an understatement. For these people have much to think about, much to live with; much, much, to live through. In the lovely lyric story, "A Page from the Song Of Songs," which portrays the closeness to nature, to ordinary sensuous enjoyments that these Jews so rarely experienced, the boy cries out, in the rapture of Passover, of spring: "What delights the Lord has provided for his Jewish children." But Tevye the dairyman, who loves God with all his might, can still remember, as he runs after his horse — "chanting at the top of my voice, as if I were a cantor in a synagogue" — he can still remember to add private comments on his prayer. "*Thou sustainest the living with loving kindness* (and sometimes with a little food) *and keepest thy faith with them that sleep in the dust.* (The dead are not the only ones who lie in the dust; Oh, how low we the living are laid, what hells we go through, and I don't mean the rich people of Yehupetz who spend their summers at the *dachas* of Boiberik, eating and drinking and living off the fat of the land. . . . Oh, Heavenly Father, why does this happen to me?) . . ." And coming to the part of the evening prayer which asks, *Heal us, O Lord, and we shall be healed,* he cannot help adding under his breath: "Send us the cure, we have the ailment already."

For Tevye and his people the word is not the beginning of things, the foundation of the world; it is a response to the overmastering reality — to the world and the everlasting creation, the eternal struggle and the inestimable privilege of being a Jew.

[1956]

Thomas Mann: or The German as Novelist

I ONCE SAW Thomas Mann plain. It was in Hollywood, of all places; and of all things, it was at a wartime rally of "progressive" movie stars and "united front" scriptwriters. John Garfield was an usher, and I found myself sitting next to Thomas Mann. He told me how much he liked movies, and I soon discovered that the culture lovers who produced pictures at Paramount and M-G-M would solicitously send new films out to his house in Pacific Palisades. Tall, inexpressibly grave yet unmistakably arch, he hid his thoughts behind his well-known disguise: the German professor. The contrast with himself and the scene in hand was delicious. The businessmen who made movies all talked like intellectuals and even tried to look like intellectuals, but the author of *Buddenbrooks, Death in Venice, The Magic Mountain,* and how many other lightly demonic works of creative intelligence looked like a highly patrician bourgeois or the scholarly chief of the German General Staff — anything, that is to say, but a "writer."

This contrast between the conservative social self and a mind so

The Ironic German: A Study of Thomas Mann, by Erich Heller. Boston: Little, Brown and Company. An Atlantic Monthly Press Book.

complex that his real opinions were always elusive — this was Thomas Mann's situation, his strategy in human relations as well as in his books, and often enough the very theme of his novels, which in one guise or another are concerned with "ordinary," bourgeois, conservative men rising to the challenge of an utterly unsettling and unpredictable universe. Mann, the creative peer and contemporary of great experimental novelists like Proust and Joyce, is easier to read but actually harder to grasp through the external conventionality of his form and the heavy load of German philosophic apparatus. He is so continuously double-sided, so "safe" in manner and so subversive within, so much the pompous German pedant in his literary manner and in his substance so representative of his esthetic, nihilist, decadent generation, that it is almost impossible to do justice to the range and elusiveness of his mind. Either one makes too much of only one side of him or one imitates his own tiresome Olympian irony, the suavely self-protective use to which he put his doubleness by effectively concealing his real opinions.

Perhaps no one but a European critic could do full justice to the complexity and genial deceitfulness of Thomas Mann's mind. American critics have often written acutely about him, but without full awareness of his marvelous imposture, his self-referring irony. Yet even European intellectuals, writing out of the full emotional vibration of what modern Germany has meant and done to the world, have either celebrated in Mann the conservative German decencies that Hitler hated, or attacked in him the German pretentiousness that Hitler made use of. It is hard to see the many sides of Mann without taking sides, and Erich Heller's book, which brilliantly does the first, should interest American readers not only for its passionate defense of Mann but also because its intelligence, its emotion, and its learning represent unforgettably the debate of a cultivated European mind with itself.

Erich Heller, now a professor of German in Wales, comes from Kafka's country — the German-speaking minority in old Bohemia who once were Austro-Hungarian, then Czechoslovakian, then German, and who have lived inside such a maze of national contradictions, have seen so many artificial political constructions destroyed, that the German language and the German intellectual tradition have come to seem their only real fatherland. "The background to my writing," Heller has said, "is the political and cultural catastrophes of this century, and my attachment to the things overtaken by them. My aims: to preserve the memory of the things I love, to be truthful to them. . . ." His first book in English, a masterly study of German literary thought, was significantly titled *The Disinherited Mind;* his second, *The Hazard of Modern Poetry;* a key chapter in this book on Thomas Mann is called "The Conservative Imagination." Heller is a traditionalist first because he is a literary scholar and critic, with a deep and urgent sense of the norm to which contemporary works are to be joined or compared; it is probably impossible to be a literary scholar at all — concerned with the development of literary forms, with the analogy between books — without a deep sense of tradition. But Heller is not a conservative in the native, deeply rooted sense in which Thomas Mann seems to him to be one: Heller is a writer who feels himself "disinherited," exposed to "hazard," looking for "order." And it is precisely this urgency, the civilized but remarkably intense commitment to "order" — which, he once wrote, "is neither behind us nor before us. It is, or it is not" — that gives his writings their extraordinary web of cultural detail, their moving quality of invocation, and, above all — remarkably so for a man writing in an adopted language — their pith and style.

« 2 »

The best side of Heller's writing is the fact that he recalls the essentially philosophical nature of literary criticism when it is not shop talk written by poets, dramatists, and novelists. Literary criticism is technical only when it illuminates a technique that one practices oneself; nobody can "explain" what makes a book good, or even what a book wholly is, least of all if he cannot write a book like it. A critic like Heller not only makes no pretensions to that phony *explication de texte* which has fooled so many half-literate American undergraduates into thinking that talk about "metaphors" gets into a "work of art," but, standing his own ground, he shows us that criticism is essentially speculative discourse concerned with ideas and values of life. The better the critic, the more he will contribute to our understanding of life in general; but he must do this in the critic's own way, solidly commenting on the text before him.

As a reader of Mann's works, Heller is superb. Anyone who appreciates criticism for the passionate intelligence it can display, who recognizes it as a classic form of literary activity, will derive great pleasure from this book. In its learning, its wit, its steadiness and ease of tone, in the gaiety and sharpness of its critical asides, it is not only exciting but, as only really seasoned and disciplined European writers can be, truly satisfying, for it stems from a European awareness of the difficulty and the tragedy — but also the satisfaction — of life when it is interpreted by the intelligence. Yet because Heller's book is written from so strong a personal emphasis on the importance of tradition, it seems to me to overvalue the externally "bourgeois," conventional *form* of Mann's thought over that purely mischievous and artistic side of him which represents the intelligence of Thomas Mann the novelist, not Thomas Mann the German thinker.

This is a book on a novelist that has nothing to say about the novel as a general form. Heller has much to tell us about Mann's relationship to Schopenhauer, Nietzsche, Wagner, *et al.*, but nothing about his lack of relationship to Joyce, Proust, Lawrence. After all, Mann interests us in the outside world because he was *not* simply another heavy German thinker but a superb novelist and storyteller. There have been so few writers in Germany wholly committed to the novel that Mann's genius in this form, though it can be demonstrably related to the dramatic side of Nietzsche or the literary side of Wagner, surely asks for some further explanation in itself. The "conventional" side of Mann's outward manner as a novelist (which he himself, no less than Dr. Heller, opposed to the great iconoclasts and experimentalists like Joyce) may be due simply to the lack of the novelistic tradition in German literature. Just as Kafka writes novels with the chilling simplicity of a man who has none to imitate, so Mann writes them with the ponderous complexity of a man imitating every literary form except the novel.

Mann's indebtedness to German philosophers and composers is indeed the story within the story of his life. To anyone brought up outside this German literary tradition, the fascination of Thomas Mann's career, ending in a whole series of extraordinary novels, is as complete as the sensation of being outside it. Just as German poets and composers seem to have more in common than, say, Beethoven has with Rossini, so in reading Heller's book our sense of this German tradition makes us feel that we are witnessing a cultural phenomenon that is not only complete in itself but which, in its union of philosophy and art, of religion and style, seems constantly to ache for the projection of its completed image.

Erich Heller's literary criticism is deeply grounded in the German tradition, even to the characteristic of being most deeply critical of it; he seems constantly to yearn for a world that no longer is, for "order" to be restored to a world that long ago lost it. This particular emphasis in Heller's work is not so very different from what one finds in German philosophy, music, criticism, and even fiction. In the German tradition, he seems to yearn for philosophical absolutes, he longs for "sense" to be restored to the world, though he bases himself entirely on a cultural (not a religious) tradition which is already full of the particular German sense of self-contradiction and inner conflict. In Heller's work there is a constant effort to reach beyond the "chaos" of modern literature to what, in the German tradition, is itself nothing but the felt "chaos" of modern thought, modern Germany. Perhaps it is this longing for an explicit spiritual solution, which reminds one of the entreaty in the last quartets of Beethoven and the last poems of Rilke, that explains why intellectuals in the German tradition find it difficult to take the novel seriously as a form in itself. For the genius of this form is precisely that it works against the explicit solution and even the "spiritual," when it is hugged too tightly.

My objection is not that Heller wishes so urgently to make sense of the world, to return to a spiritual order, but that he may possibly exaggerate Thomas Mann's own desire to do so. I have the impression that Mann, more solidly rooted in the nineteenth century and the old bourgeois way of life, may have been concerned with the mundane side of life more than is Erich Heller, who attributes to Mann a religious quest that tells more about Heller than about Mann. The fact is that Mann's famous "irony" is not only a matter of eating one's cake and of having it too — from the plaudits of Hollywood producers in 1944 to those of East Germany in 1954 — but it is typical of the kind of solid taste for the details of life from which one writes *novels*. There is a degree of spiritual urgency that novelists need not make explicit. In the same way, Germany as a country meant literal and material things to Thomas Mann that the literary tradition of the German language cannot mean to Erich Heller in Wales.

[1959]

The Saint as Schlemiel

WHEN I first read "Gimpel the Fool" (in the quick and pungent English of Saul Bellow) I felt not only that I was reading an extraordinarily beautiful and witty story, but that I was moving through as many historical levels as an archaeologist at work. This is an experience one often gets from the best Jewish writers. The most "advanced" and sophisticated Jewish writers of our time — Babel, Kafka, Bellow — have assimilated, even conquered, the whole tradition of modern literature while reminding us of the unmistakable historic core of the Jewish experience. Equally, a contemporary Yiddish writer like Isaac Bashevis Singer uses all the old Jewish capital of folklore, popular speech and legendry, yet from within this tradition itself is able to duplicate a good deal of the conscious absurdity, the sauciness, the abandon of modern art — without for a moment losing his obvious personal commitment to the immemorial Jewish vision of the world.

Perhaps it is this ability to incarnate all the different periods that Jews have lived through that makes such writers indefinably fascinating to me. They wear whole epochs on their back; they alone record widely separated centuries in dialogue with each other. Yet all these different periods of history, these many *histories,* represent, if not a single point of view, a common historic character. It is the irony with which ancient dogmas are recorded, the imaginative sympathy with which they are translated and transmuted into contemporary terms, that makes the balance that is art.

Gimpel himself is an example of a legendary Jewish type — the saint as *schlemiel.* The mocked, persecuted and wretched people, who nevertheless are the chosen — chosen to bear a certain knowl-

Gimpel the Fool and Other Stories, by Isaac Bashevis Singer. New York: Noonday Press.

edge through a hostile world — are portrayed again in the town fool, a baker who is married off to a frightful slut without knowing what everyone else in town knows, that she will bear a child in four months. Gimpel is *the* fool of the Jews: a fool because he is endlessly naïve, a fool because, even when he does learn that he has been had, he ignores his own dignity for the sake of others. His wife's unfaithfulness, her shrewishness — these are not the bourgeois concealment, the "cheating" on one's spouse that it would be in another culture, but a massive, hysterical persecution. The child she already has she passes off as her "brother"; Gimpel believes her. When she gives birth to a child four months after the wedding, Gimpel pays for the circumcision honors and rituals, and names the boy after his own father. When he cries out that his wife has deceived him, she deliberately confuses him, as usual, and persuades him that the child is "premature":

> I said, "Isn't he a little too premature?" She said that she had a grandmother who carried just as short a time and she resembled this grandmother of hers as one drop of water does another. She swore to it with such oaths that you would have believed a peasant at the fair if he had used them. To tell the plain truth, I didn't believe her; but when I talked it over next day with the schoolmaster he told me that the very same thing had happened to Adam and Eve. Two they went up to bed, and four they descended.

The humor of this is always very real, for these people are rough old-fashioned village types who know their own. The town boys are always playing tricks on Gimpel, setting him on false trails; he is mocked at his own wedding — some young men carry in a crib as a present. His wife, Elka, is a living nightmare, a shrew of monumental proportions, a Shakespearean harridan. Yet in Gimpel's obstinate attachment to her we recognize, as in his customary meekness, the perfection of a type: what to the great world is folly, in itself may be wisdom; what the world thinks insane may, under the aspect of eternity, be the only sanity:

> She swore at me and cursed, and I couldn't get enough of her. What strength she had! One of her looks could rob you of the power of speech. And her orations! Pitch and sulphur, that's what they were full of, and yet somehow also full of charm. I adored her every word. She gave me bloody wounds, though.

One night, Gimpel comes home unexpectedly and finds another man in bed with Elka; this time he has had enough, and he separates from her. But the town mischiefs take her side and persecute him, while Gimpel worries whether he *did* see the man:

> Hallucinations do happen. You see a figure or a manikin or something, but when you come up closer it's nothing, there's not a thing there. And if that's so, I'm doing her an injustice. And when I got so far in my thoughts I started to weep. I sobbed so that I wet the floor where I lay. In the morning I went to the rabbi and told him that I had made a mistake.

Elka has another child and "all Frampol refreshed its spirits because of my trouble and grief. However, I resolved that I would always believe what I was told. What's the good of *not* believing? Today it's your wife you don't believe in; tomorrow it's God Himself you won't take stock in."

Even his superstitions — Singer uses local demons and spirits as dramatic motifs — become symbols of his innocent respect for the world. One night, after covering the dough to let it rise, he takes his share of bread and a little sack of flour and starts homeward:

> The moon was full and the stars were glistening, something to terrify the soul. I hurried onward, and before me darted a long shadow. It was winter, and a fresh snow had fallen. I had a mind to sing, but it was growing late and I didn't want to wake the householders. Then I felt like whistling, but I remembered that you don't whistle at night because it brings the demons out. So I was silent and walked as fast as I could.

He returns home to find his wife in bed with the apprentice. Characteristically, he suffers rather than storms; characteristically, "the moon went out all at once. It was utterly black, and I trembled"; characteristically, he obeys his wife when she sends him out of the house to see if the goat is well; characteristically, he identifies himself tenderly with the goat, and when he returns home, the apprentice having fled, the wife denies everything, tells him he has been seeing visions, shrieks prodigious curses. Her "brother" beats him with a stick. And Gimpel: "I felt that something about me was deeply wrong, and I said, 'Don't make a scandal. All that's needed now is that people should accuse me of raising spooks and *dybbuks*.' "

So he makes his peace with her, and they live together for twenty years. "All kinds of things happened, but I neither saw nor heard." When his wife dies, she tells him that none of their children is his, and the look on her dead face seems to say to him — "I deceived Gimpel. That was the meaning of my brief life."

Now Gimpel is tempted by the Spirit of Evil himself, who tells him that it is all nothing. " 'What,' I said, '*is* there, then?' 'A thick mire.' " And, succumbing to the devil, Gimpel urinates into the risen dough. His dead wife comes to him in a dream — and, when he weeps in shame at his act, "It's all your fault," she cries — "You fool! You fool! Because I was false, is everything false, too?"

When the mourning period for his wife ends, he gives up everything to tramp through the world, often telling stories to children — "about devils, magicians, windmills, and the like." He dreams constantly of his wife, asks when he will be with her; in his dreams, she kisses him and promises him that they will be together soon. "When I awaken I feel her lips and taste the salt of her tears."

The last paragraph of the story, Gimpel's serene meditation before death, is of great beauty. It sums up everything that Jews have ever felt about the divinity that hedges human destiny, and it is indeed one of the most touching avowals of faith that I have ever seen. Yet it is all done with lightness, with wit, with a charming reserve — so that it might almost be read as a tribute to human faithfulness itself. "No doubt the world is entirely an imaginary world, but it is only once removed from the true world. . . . Another *schnorrer* is waiting to inherit my bed of straw. When the time comes I will go joyfully. Whatever may be there, it will be real, without complication, without ridicule, without deception. God be praised: There even Gimpel cannot be deceived."

« 2 »

Singer's story naturally suggests a comparison with I. J. Peretz's famous "Bontsha the Silent," who was offered everything in heaven, and meekly asked for a hot roll with fresh butter every morning for breakfast. One thinks also of Sholem Aleichem's Tevye the dairyman, who recited his prayers even as he ran after his runaway horse. But in his technique of ambiguity Singer speaks for our generation far more usefully than the old ritualistic praise of Jewish goodness.

While Bontsha and Tevye are entirely folk images, cherished symbols of a tradition, Gimpel — though he and his wife are no less symbols — significantly has to win back his faith, and he wins it in visions, in dreams, that give a background of playfulness and irony to this marvelously subtle story.

This concern with the dream, this everlasting ambiguity in our relations with the divine — this is a condition that our generation has learned to respect, after rejecting the dogmas first of orthodoxy and then of scientific materialism. This delicacy of conception unites Singer to the rest of imaginative humanity today: Man believes even though he knows his belief to be absurd, but what he believes represents a level of imaginative insight which shades off at one end into art, at the other into Gimpel's occasional self-doubt, the thought that he may be "mad."

It is the integrity of the human imagination that Singer conveys so beautifully. He reveals the advantage that an artist can find in his own orthodox training — unlike so many Jews who in the past became mere copyists and mumblers of the holy word. Singer's work *does* stem from the Jewish village, the Jewish seminary, the compact (not closed) Jewish society of Eastern Europe. He does not use the symbols which so many modern writers pass on to each other. For Singer it is not only his materials that are "Jewish"; the world is so. Yet within this world he has found emancipation and universality — through his faith in imagination.

His case is very much like that of Nathaniel Hawthorne, who also grew up in an orthodoxy against which one had in some sense to rebel in order to become a writer at all. Only a Jewish writer in the twentieth century could make one think of Hawthorne, who said that although his ancestors would have been shocked to see him become a writer of storybooks, his values would not have surprised them. Singer illustrates the extraordinary ubiquity of the Jewish writer in time: the demons, the spirits, even the fools belong to the woodland past, the dark mythological background of modern life. At least one of his stories, "From the Diary of One Not Born," could have come out of Hawthorne's stories, for Singer is concerned with the same theme of temptation that led Hawthorne to fill up New England woods with witches. But the positive way in which Singer makes one feel that he has a conviction (very different from Hawthorne and, indeed, from most Jewish writers today) shows the burden of spiritual responsibility that his work carries. The Jews have been so long kept from art that it is interesting to see, at least in Singer, how much respect there is for orthodoxy. For him, at least, it nourished the secret of art — the revelation of the truth that lies in imagination.

[1958]

Facing It

Last year there was published in this country a remarkably brilliant novel, Muriel Spark's *Memento Mori,* whose highly original and unexpectedly funny characters are all in their seventies and eighties. Each of them is frequently called to the telephone to hear a voice — in each case a different voice — saying, "Remember you must die." They go to the police, but already a few of them realize that the caller is not a sadistic prankster but Death, who evokes a different picture of himself in each one he calls.

The very old are very much with us just now. People live longer, and even in extreme debility they are kept alive. A longer life is felt by everyone as a real possibility — and why not, since the better life for all seems just around the corner? Imagine missing Utopia after we have waited so long! Yet at the same time so many millions have been done violence to, so many millions have been put to death, so many have to live every day with the sense of possible world catastrophe, that we have all, so to speak, come to live on the brink. Our rationalistic thinking about everything forces us, when we predict so much else, to be constantly aware of our future. And if you add to the general anxiety the profound skepticism that the scientific revolution has planted even in the minds of people who think of themselves as believers, you come up with an extraordinarily large number of human beings having to think about death. And it may be that more of us now view death in lonely stoicism and with conscious bitterness about the end than, on such a scale, human beings have previously had to do.

The Big Ward, by Jacoba Van Velde. Translated from the Dutch. New York: Simon and Schuster.

It is these peculiarly contemporary feelings that seem to me the essential background of Jacoba Van Velde's very honest and moving novel about an old Dutch lady dying in a "home." The most striking thing about the book is its studied bleakness. It is hard to believe that in less disillusioned times a novel could concentrate so narrowly, so devastatingly, on death. Miss Van Velde, who lives in Paris, has surely been influenced by those French writers who have confused their civic hopelessness with "the human condition" in general. The Dutch themselves, like everyone else in Europe between 1939 and 1945, saw so many betrayals that in reading Miss Van Velde's novel, I often asked myself whether her deliberately gray and toneless description of human weakness reflects powerlessness before death so much as it does a general disgust with the state.

The most impressive single scene occurs when a government welfare worker calls upon the old lady's daughter, who is married to a young artist in Paris. The official explains that whenever patients in the home cannot pay for their entire care, the children are obliged to pay the difference. "'And supposing the children don't earn much?' I asked. 'Then they pay pro rata. We have cases where they only pay one guilder a week.' 'If these people have to pay so little,' I said, 'perhaps a guilder means a lot to them.' 'Yes,' he said, 'we sometimes have great difficulty in getting it out of them. It involves a lot of administrative work.'" The very tone of this insertion in the narrative is pure Kafka, as is the fact that since the daughter cannot pay anything, the state sells the old lady's furniture. The state does not need the pittance the furniture will bring, but keeping the old lady alive demands that it get something back as a matter of form. In the same way, keeping people alive becomes a matter of form. The routine is always impersonal, and the individual patient has no more *reason* to complain against the administrative setup than she has against the logic of circumstances that has brought her there. If patients are awakened at 5:30 every morning, that is because the night staff goes off duty at that hour. If the toilet door no longer has a lock, that is because a lady once died there after she had locked herself in.

This is the peculiar pitilessness of the situation: since there is nothing logically wrong in any of this, not even in the state's selling a few sticks of furniture, there is nothing, in logic, to complain of.

The situation of the very old in the modern welfare state reminds me of the Russians who confessed in the Moscow Trials to crimes they could not have committed. Since they had been argued into accepting the trials as necessary to the party and the state, they logically had to pretend to their guilt. Once you agree to the premises of these larger powers, you must agree to their conclusions, even if it means assenting to your execution.

So it is with death in *The Big Ward.* The old lady has no *reason* to see her life any differently from the value placed on it by the people around her. She has always been peculiarly meek, and since the death of her husband she has felt more than usually powerless. Her daughter, who has far more spirit and has always raged against her mother's softness and gentleness, nevertheless has no more hope than her mother does. "Human beings are so terribly alone, my darling Mummy. Most of them don't realize it. Only occasionally do they have an inkling of it when they are in great distress, and neither man nor reason can help. But they usually forget it again, and perhaps that's for the best. For how could we go on living if we all recognized our loneliness and the awfulness of our condition? Would we not all become panic-stricken, like people in a concentration camp?"

No wonder that the mother places herself "in the black tunnel whose end I could not see . . . Is there nothing left to help me? No, I am all alone. No human being can do anything more for me." The daughter, though she does not realize it, cannot give her mother the slightest hint of an alternative. The mother, in the "big ward" that is our society, is surrounded by people not one of whom can offer her a crumb of faith, of hope, even of personal love; so mild and meek, she is not likely to disagree with anyone around her.

This, it seems, is the last horror of the lonely crowd — that we should be argued into hopelessness for lack of the mental independence, the courageous idiosyncrasy, with which to see human destiny any differently. We are all joined to each other these days by an infinitely shallow common sense. We agree about so many of the main issues of life and death that it must be hard, especially when we are weakened by age, to court unpopularity by disagreeing with most of our contemporaries in the big ward where we have to live. Miss Van Velde's old lady is obviously a symbol of the frail, vulnerable, essentially disbelieving human being in our time who has no resource against the state, loneliness, death. I found her infinitely touching, and the book itself is immaculately and intelligently done. Yet it is not so much a novel as a performance—a brilliant but perhaps too artfully detached performance. Like so many purely sophisticated performances, it is too aware of the mistakes it doesn't commit to engage the subject at an unexpected level. *The Big Ward* is a performance because there are really no people in it, just symbols of our condition. We are not symbols; we are flesh and blood, and what we feel most about our condition, we do not always know and cannot easily say. Each one hears differently the voice of Death. What makes Muriel Spark's *Memento Mori* so remarkable is that she follows the difference into each of the people themselves, and so shows some of them preserving in the face of death a quality of faith, and even of humor, that encourages us.

[1960]

A Condemned Man: Albert Camus

THIS SELECTION of essays, editorials, and manifestoes, made by Camus himself, represents in an oddly tragic way his last word. I don't mean that the selections are all from his last period—the book opens on his wartime editorials from the underground paper *Combat* and with his well-known "Letters to a German Friend"; no doubt there will be other books by him. But what the present selection conveys most of all is the last stand that Camus took on a whole variety of political and generally contemporary subjects that, like Algeria, divided him from others and from himself.

Often enough it is not the stand that he made but his attempt to fix a position in moral terms alone that makes the book dispiriting. It brings home the side of Camus's literary character that underlay the artist—and that outlasted the artist.

Resistance, Rebellion and Death, by Albert Camus. Translated by Justin O'Brien. New York: Alfred A. Knopf, Inc.

In the last years of his life Camus was at odds with both sides in Algeria, with Sartre, with the apologists of Soviet totalitarianism. Even his silences were recognized as evidence of his struggle with himself. As a child of the French working class in Algeria, he could sympathize neither with the Algerian nationalists nor with the reactionary *colons;* and long before the Algerian crisis had reached its present intensity, Camus had been involved in polemics arising from his criticisms in *The Rebel* (*L'Homme Révolté*) of the French revolutionary tradition. He was inevitably the victim of many malicious literary attacks after the Nobel Prize award in 1957. In addition to the independent, wholly moral "third force" position he took on so many political issues dividing French opinion, he talked of a moral "renaissance" vaguely based on solitary inspiration like his own.

Intellectual polemic is, of course, more familiar in France among imaginative writers than it is in this country—where a Hemingway derides a Melville for caring about ideas. In itself, there was nothing unusual about the fact that during the war Camus wrote his first novel, *The Stranger,* along with many noble editorials for *Combat;* after the war, the author of *The Plague* also wrote editorials commemorating the Spanish Republic, pleading for an end to capital punishment, denouncing Eastern Europe's "socialism of the gallows." But step by step he became almost wholly a moralist, a definer and upholder of *formal* values.

Looking back on his work as a whole, one can see that even his fiction consists of short moral anecdotes. The extraordinary success of his first "*récit*" and most unqualified artistic success, *The Stranger,* surely rests not on the kind of powerfully sufficient image of life that is the imaginative artist's challenge and delight, but rather on an explicit idea of life. *The Stranger,* in itself Camus's one "nihilist" work of fiction (and succeeded by the antinihilistic *The Plague*), owes its great popularity to the fact that it speaks for widespread feelings of alienation from social cant. Vivid and acridly ironic as many details in the book are, the hero of *The Stranger* represents the bitterness of the early Camus rather than the bewildered and self-pitying clerk that Meursault is supposed to be. The beautiful last pages, in which the condemned man welcomes death as freedom, can only be read as Camus's own austere philosophical testament.

The very titles of his books — *The Stranger, The Rebel, The Fall* — denote stages in one man's struggle for moral clarity, while the curt simplicity and tense balances of his style represent, in fact, that need to embody a position, to fix a value, which is typical of those for whom a moral, once defined, is a lesson to be followed. It is typical of Camus, who, I think, did not read English, that he was instinctively drawn to Emerson, the author of so many moral "gems" and epigrammatic conclusions about life, and that he was always quoting Emerson's admirer Nietzsche, whose writing is probably the most brilliant example of this genre that we have had in modern times.

The moralist is always one who tries to prescribe for life, for whom man has a destiny that he can put into words. The background of Camus's concern with this is significant: it is his awareness of death, of war, of the afflictions rained on our generation by totalitarianism. All the finest essays in this book, like the famous wartime editorials on man's duty to the spirit of life, the lament for a poet-friend shot by the Germans, the magnificent attack on capital punishment, the rage against Kadar and his hangmen — all these reflect the writer who was one year old when his father was killed at the Marne, who from a very early age saw the human violence as well as the natural beauty in North Africa, who thought that he would himself die young of tuberculosis, whose most famous story describes the senseless killing of a native by a "Stranger" who at the end of the book awaits his own death. All his life Camus felt himself surrounded by death — his death and that of a whole generation. As he said so movingly in his debate with left-wing intellectuals, each of us today can expect some day to be condemned to death for political reasons, "whereas that eventuality would have seemed ridiculous at the beginning of the century."

Camus was aware of death at home, death in the verminous hovels of Algeria and on the beaches, death in Spain during the Civil War, death in France itself from the Nazis, death in Poland, Hungary, East Germany. At the end of his life, when he was so exhausted and driven by the effort to be "reasonable" on Algeria (for him hardly an "objective," political question), he wrote hopelessly, like a man engulfed by the unreasonableness of politics. Finally it was Algeria itself, with all its memories for him, that he might also have to lose. It hardly needs to be emphasized that the violent death that Camus anticipated all his life, the death that seemed to glare out at him from every political crisis of his time, finally did find him — in an automobile accident as violent and yet as "absurd," as typical of man's uncontrol over his mechanical creations, as any of the larger defeats that Camus brooded over in our era.

« 2 »

Albert Camus wrote like a condemned man. To me, it is this desperate emphasis on the value of life that is the key to his moral urgency. In his best essay, the one against capital punishment, he felt no complication in his way; he had nothing to plead for but life itself. The key images in all his best books are of "strangeness," death, violence to the human person. Like his adored Dostoevsky, he was haunted by the scaffold. And like all people who feel themselves condemned, who look to a new teaching to lead them back into life, Camus, with his shattering background in working-class poverty and family misfortunes, in political defeat and intellectual isolation, came to identify life with certain values alone. It was this that made him, even when he became world-famous, preach before non-Communist workmen on the "union of labor and culture"; he could not bear to divorce himself from the experience in which he had first come to his values. The more genuinely philosophical radicals like Sartre, now implacably opposed to Camus's "soft" principles, seemed to isolate Camus from the class he came from, the more Camus, in calling attention to Soviet totalitarianism, tried to create a "moral" solidarity. The more he fell away from fashionable left-wing ideologies, the more he had to explicate and to reason and to prove what his own particular values were. The life that Camus had so painfully grasped from death he had to re-establish as absolute clarity about life.

This clarity is the great value of Camus's essays — as, indeed, it is the great thing about the ending of *The Stranger* and of key passages in his plays, novels, and essays. It is the quality of the man who has set his teeth, as it were, in the face of the absurdity that overhangs life in the shape of death. It is the "Spanish" quality (his mother was Spanish) of grace under pressure. It is the style of the man who has set his focus on what is possible, on the portion that belongs to man, on man's consciousness of himself, and on man's duty to himself. Although Camus was careful to declare himself in principle an atheist, he rejected even the fashionable term "humanism" for his personal philosophy. It is this grim wariness at the expense of every illusion but hope itself that gives Camus's essays the fundamental quality of French moralism — which is to recognize a limit, to define a need, to posit some small specific hope. Clarity of this kind is clarity won for oneself and out of oneself, the clarity that helps one to live. This is seen in the terse, true exactness of many passages in these essays. Camus, in his wartime "Letters to a German Friend," speaks of them as "a document emerging from the struggle against violence." Of the new French militancy in the Resistance, he says, "In order to face up to you, we had first to be at death's door." And shrewdly, to his friend turned German nationalist: "What is spirit? We know its contrary, which is murder. What is man? There I stop you, for we know. Man is that force which ultimately cancels all tyrants and gods. He is the force of evidence. . . . Man must . . . create happiness in order to protest against the universe of unhappiness."

Camus's essays are full of aphorisms, and they make one wonder if the truest monument to Camus would not be one of those collections, such as has been made from Proust, which convey the French *moraliste's* sense of fact. "Nothing is given to men, and the little they can conquer is paid for with unjust deaths." Speaking at a Dominican monastery: "If Christianity is pessimistic as to man, it is optimistic as to human destiny. Well, I can say that, pessimistic as to human destiny, I am optimistic as to man."

Yet precisely because this is such arduous knowledge and has been won with such desperate honesty, because it is so grimly self-created and forever self-conscious, because it is so unsure of everything but what man can discover moment by moment, it is somehow without avail. It is rhetorical. The only thing you can do with a principle, in this kind of writing, is to repeat it. And Camus does, in lecture after lecture, in interview after interview. The liberty, ease, and joy — of either a great belief or a great imaginative talent — are denied him. We are left with the impression of a painful sincerity and of a nobility that expresses itself only in definitions, not in the activity of imagination. The secret of conquering a greater world than himself is not known to him.

I read these essays with constant agreement and respect and yet with pity, for Camus's life was harder than even he thought it was. Camus thought that truth will live for man if only he defines it closely and truly enough. But truth is never something that man controls. And the very closeness with which Camus tried so hard to condense the truth is one of the most poignant things about his life. There was a fundamental distrust that he could not conquer, a space across which his imagination could not carry him. He hugged life close, as he hugged his style close. And so the felicity and brilliance of these essays remind one all too sadly of the world that has to be conquered with each sentence — but which, with each sentence accomplished, is as quickly lost.

[1960]

The Least of These

OF ALL THE CRIMES by the Nazis, surely the most unforgivable is the internment and murder of so many children. It has been calculated that a million Jewish children perished during the war. Yet many children managed to survive years in the death camps, and now, only in their late twenties and early thirties, have turned out to be the most effective personal historians of life under the Nazis. This is the generation of Anne Frank (who would now have been thirty-one), and the young Spaniard Michel del Castillo, who in that unforgettable memoir A *Child of Our Time* described what it was like to be a child in Buchenwald.

Children who went through such experiences and survived have more than anyone else been able to express the fundamental violation of human dignity committed by the Nazis. The battle-weary soldiers, the superficially experienced journalists, the hardened politicals — none of these has been able to convey, with the same innocence, the full atrocity of the camps. And perhaps only a few of

Night, by Elie Wiesel. Translated from the French by Stella Rodway, with a foreword by François Mauriac. New York: Hill and Wang.

the children themselves felt innocent enough, after constantly being told that they were guilty of being outside the German law, to resent the Nazis at all. But what has made a few good books possible is the fact that some of these children were still so impressionable and trusting that the terrible experiences of the camps were stored up subconsciously in their minds. Only now, in our relatively "peaceful" period, have such memories risen to the surface. Yet such experiences can become curiously unreal even to people constantly obsessed by them, and remarkably vivid as these memoirs are, they often betray the writer's fear that he may be describing a hallucination.

The author of this piercing memoir of life in Auschwitz, Birkenau, and Buchenwald was only sixteen when the war ended for him in April, 1945. By that time he had been separated from his mother and sisters, whom he never saw again; he had seen his own father, after surviving so many "selections," smashed to death. He had lived in Auschwitz with the constant odor of burning human flesh; he had seen children, still alive, thrown into the crematoria; he had seen starving men, in the cattle cars transporting them from one camp to another, fighting each other to death over pieces of bread negligently tossed them by German civilians. There are details in his book which can be read only with fresh astonishment at the unflagging cruelty of the Nazis and the peculiarly sadistic frivolity of those who directed this vast system of human extermination. The infamous SS doctor, Mengele, who quickly "selected" those who were to be gassed from the terror-stricken crowds running and stumbling before his eyes, would motion people to death with a conductor's baton! And there is one particular scene which has already made this book famous in Europe. A young boy, after days of being tortured in an attempt to make him reveal where a Dutch prisoner had hidden arms, was put up on the gallows to be hanged. His body was too light and so he kept strangling in front of the thousands of prisoners who had been summoned to watch the execution and who were marched past the gallows. As they went by, Wiesel heard a man asking, "Where is God now?" And he heard himself thinking: "Here He is — He is hanging here on this gallows . . ."

It is this literal "death of God" as absolute emptiness in the soul, the blackness that in his mind means that there is no longer any light from a divine source, that Wiesel experienced most in the endless night of Auschwitz. What makes his book unusual and gives it such a particular poignancy among the many personal accounts of Nazism is that it recounts the loss of his faith by an intensely religious young Jew who grew up in an Orthodox community of Transylvania. To the best of my knowledge, no one of this background has left behind him so moving a record of the direct loss of faith on the part of a young boy.

Night is about a world so unreal that often indeed it reads like a nightmare. Wiesel would be the first to admit its seeming unreality; often enough it must seem unreal to him. But the book satisfies us as a human document; it brings us back to the world we all know, through the crisis of faith that it describes. The Book of Job is the most universally understood part of the Bible, and the young Wiesel's embittered interrogation of Providence unites, as it were, the ever-human Job to the history of our own time; it recalls that peculiarly loving and scolding intimacy with God which is the most powerful single element in the history of the Jews.

« 2 »

It was Wiesel's religious background that originally interested the French Catholic writer François Mauriac in this book. When Wiesel, now an Israeli newspaperman, came to interview Mauriac, the latter described the ineradicable impression that had been made on Mme. Mauriac as she watched the trainloads of Jewish children being deported from Austerlitz Station in Paris. When Mauriac spoke of how often he thought of these children, Wiesel replied, "I was one of them." Mauriac's preface to the book is singularly beautiful, and though a devout Christian, he describes the martyrdom of the Jews in terms reminiscent of the death of Christ. He too sees the Jewish experience under Nazism in Biblical terms. He describes young Wiesel as "a Lazarus risen from the dead," and, recalling Nietzsche's cry that "God is dead," expresses his compassionate understanding of why a boy in Auschwitz should have thought that "God is dead, the God of love, of gentleness, of comfort, the God of Abraham, of Isaac, of Jacob, has vanished forevermore, beneath the gaze of this child, in the smoke of a human holocaust exacted by Race, the most voracious of all idols." Mauriac's preface is written with that charity and intellectual passion which is the particular mark of French Catholic writers. The magnanimity and literary distinction of his few pages puts into relief the rather delicate literary achievement of Wiesel himself, who in recounting these atrocious early experiences makes one realize how difficult it is for a victim to do full justice to the facts.

Yet Mauriac's preface, beautiful as it is, misses the dramatic human element, the Job-like accusations that actually unite Wiesel to the religion of his fathers. On the Jewish New Year service in Auschwitz, when ten thousand prisoners said with one voice, "Blessed be the name of the Eternal," the young boy defied the Divinity, Whom he had come to think of as blind and deaf: ". . . but why should I bless Him? In every fiber I rebelled. Because He had had thousands of children burned in His pits? Because He kept six crematories working night and day, on Sundays and feast days? Because in His great might He had created Auschwitz, Birkenau, Buna, and so many factories of death? How could I say to Him: 'Blessed art Thou, Eternal, Master of the Universe, Who chose us from among the races to be tortured day and night, to see our fathers, our mothers, our brothers, end in the crematory?' . . .

"This day I had ceased to plead. I was no longer capable of lamentation. On the contrary, I felt very strong. I was the accuser, God the accused. My eyes were open and I was alone — terribly alone in a world without God and without Man . . . I stood amid that praying congregation, observing it like a stranger.

"The service ended with the Kaddish [prayer for the dead]. Everyone recited the Kaddish over his parents, over his children, over his brothers, and over himself."

To Mauriac, this loss of faith seems unnecessary as well as tragic, and he wishes, in effect, that Wiesel could see all these immense losses in our time from a Christian point of view. Mauriac feels that the deportation of children touches upon "the mystery of iniquity whose revelation was to mark the end of one era and the beginning of another. The dream which Western man conceived in the eighteenth century, whose dawn he thought he saw in 1789, and which, until August 2, 1914, had grown stronger with the progress of enlightenment and the discoveries of science — this dream vanished finally for me before those trainloads of little children." Mauriac is a great soul in our time. But less gifted, less hopeful, and even pathetic as the young Wiesel is, there is a positive strength to his complaints against God that Mauriac may have missed.

The accusation of God is of someone very real to Wiesel. The dialogue continues. It is exactly because of a child's demand for justice, because of his demand on God, because of his insistence that the consummation has not yet been reached and that history remains imperfect, that the book is so effective. Faith is often hard to talk about. Franz Kafka even said that he who has faith *cannot* talk about it. What counts may be not always one's explicit assent to faith or to non-faith, but the immense confrontation of history, the demand that we make of it as the only ground on which justice may yet show itself. I don't think that I shall soon forget the picture of this young boy standing on a mound of corpses, accusing God of deserting His creation.

[1960]

No Sky for Renaud

A YOUNG PARISIENNE is in a provincial town to claim an inheritance. At the hotel, she opens the wrong room and discovers a suicide attempt. The man is taken to the hospital in time, and the young woman, visiting him out of a sense of duty, finds herself physically so fascinated by a man who constantly spews out his contempt for everything and everyone that she moves him into her Paris flat, gives up her studies, and goes through most of her capital keeping him in drink.

Renaud is not just an alcoholic; he is a brilliant and devastating unbeliever who, brought back to life by Geneviève against his will, feels that it is up to her to keep him alive. If she doesn't, he will simply go under again, and without the slightest concern. And since he can barely be bothered to get out of bed, he is constantly accessible to the mistress in whom he has awakened a capacity for

Warrior's Rest, by Christiane Rochefort. Translated from the French by Lowell Blair. New York: David McKay.

violent passion. Renaud jeeringly makes love to her as if anything else were too much trouble.

Suicidal, drunk, and cynically lecherous, Renaud is the "warrior" of the title — a warrior for the hard truth against the softening illusions, a warrior personifying the human condition in our day against those who would minimize its bitterness. And the real jolt of the story is that the warrior is brought low, brought to his "rest," by the mistress who despite all her abandon with him and her boundless sympathy for him cannot help but betray a skepticism she cannot share. This acidulous little novel, which was a best seller in France and has largely been ignored here, goes to the heart of a quarrel that seems to be on in all countries just now, between the angries and the squares. In France this quarrel tends to dwell with more deliberate bitterness on the emptiness of contemporary life than it does in the United States — where Renaud would promptly be packed off to a psychiatrist and saved by the love of a good woman, or at least by a passionate one. In this book Renaud is not "saved" but surrendered; he even helps to surrender himself by falling in love with the woman when he can no longer keep up his anger with the world. After the last jolting paragraph, you are meant to go back to the book and to recognize that it is the woman's unwearying stress on love and desire that robs him of his anger, of his unwearying complaint against man's lot. "My love is stronger than you, Renaud. The finish line is coming closer and closer, and that's why you are so panicky, you're kicking out in all directions. Do whatever you like, you won't wear out my patience, and you'll consent to happiness at last; soon you and I will find peace, we'll rest. We'll rest."

There is no belief stronger in America just now than that love is best. In fact, there is virtually no other belief. But it is an old European conviction that what is decisive is man's relationship to transcendent truth — to the gods, when there are any — and not what Americans now value as the "security" of being loved. This first conviction (which may help to explain why current French novels, though not great, are so much more interesting than current American ones) makes Christiane Rochefort's novel particularly telling. For the warrior is as a human being utterly impossible, loathsome, and "difficult," yet you are meant to recognize what he is fighting for even when he seems just to be fighting everyone. The hypocrisy of our civilization on the brink of possible world disaster revolts him, but the increasing meaninglessness of a life lived in mindless self-absorption terrifies him. What makes the story so biting is the fact that the woman won to him by his very intransigence, by the immobility that expresses his contempt and despair, nevertheless destroys him with a love that is unconsciously selfish because she lacks his principles.

This is a brilliant novel rather than an important one; it is brilliant in the testimony given to Renaud, whose speeches denouncing contemporary life run away with the book, and brilliant in the rhythm and pace of the narrative. It is nimble, amazingly rapid and subtle in the way the story springs out of the heroine's thoughts; and because the hero is deliberately powerless everywhere but in bed, it brings much forgotten humor back to the act of sex. Artistically, it lacks extension, reverberation, the sounds of humanity moving about in the world; it is *small*, like so many good novels of today content to tell a single story well. But it is truly a contemporary novel, a novel that speaks to our condition — one might almost say to our hidden condition.

The difference between Renaud and those "beat" characters whom he would seem to resemble in being "difficult" is that Renaud is dying of what ails him. His intelligence has been stricken, one could say insulted, by the lack of significance, of depth in which to move — a lack covered up by a postwar generation anxious to swill up the brief moment of peace it may have. Renaud's mistress, telling the story, cries out: "Who ever heard of a madman with all his wits about him? I couldn't understand him. A man couldn't live that way . . . There was no sky for him, no outside. Time didn't flow, the days didn't follow one another, there was only one homogeneous, continuous day, one indefinite hour that wiped away everything as it passed; his life left no trail, he was always dying and forgetting himself along the way . . . I had him constantly, yet it seemed to me that I possessed nothing." He touches her, but she cannot help him. One day, when she allows him to walk out on her, she panics and finally catches sight of him at a crossing: "He'd stopped. He didn't know which of the four directions to take. He didn't know where to go. The earth was round. Round. He had nothing. He had no one. He stayed there. He might die there." Here is a woman utterly possessed by sexual passion for a man she has constantly but who tells her: ". . . Sex isn't important to me. Don't look surprised, it's obvious. If anything is absent from me it's sexuality. It means nothing to me. What matters in an orgy is the god, not the pleasure, and the god was always absent."

What makes the novel too tight, a brilliant demonstration rather than a moving narrative, is the fact that, since it is told by the woman herself, she can convey only her own changes of mood, of thoughts. She communicates her humanity but we see the leading character only through her — a woman voraciously in love — and so we miss his humanity and get only his intelligence. Once in a while the irony of her own eventual betrayal of him comes through, as when she complains that "he went on sinking as though I'd sacrificed nothing." For the rest, we see him from a distance; as if in his rages, his drunkenness, his sloth, he appeared improbable to us, an "idea" rather than a human being, an idea that she possessed and one that eventually she will crush. But the ideas themselves, as Renaud speaks them, are the passion of truth, and it has taken the fine French hand of Christiane Rochefort to find words for the complex disgust that may fill an intelligent man in this year of our Lord:

"Ah, snows of yesteryear that never were and never will be! The snow was warm in those days, I was there. But those days never were, and we won't go back to the source because there was no source; the rivers come from the sea and Bach is dead. I won't survive him . . . The whole conscience of the world is gathered here, but it's only useless love without an object, hopeless love, a drop of water in the desert, now do you understand at last why I get so thirsty? . . . I'm very tired. Rest me. You're the warrior's rest, the cowardly warrior's rest, the slacker's. . . . I want to sleep-die, and a woman is the best way to do that. Love is a kind of euthanasia . . .

". . . I'm resigning from the job of being an idealist in a vacuum. You can't keep grace without faith, my love, it was an illusion . . . hope can't be invented. . . . I'm tired of playing the part of a fugitive whose place is nowhere, I want . . . to enter the Great Washing Machine; help me, you know how it's done."

[1960]

VI
Places

Gastprofessor für Amerikanistik

[Cologne: 1952]

From my back porch, I look out to the trolley barns across a wild and dreary clump of matted fern. The stucco wall is dotted with fine little holes, as if it had been lightly brushed by machine-gun fire. Actually, not many bombs fell on this corner of Cologne; this is just suburbia, mildly rotting away of itself at one end of the gutted city. And here I sit every morning in fine weather, rereading my American texts until it is time to go the university and give my lecture. Yesterday, looking up something in an anthology of American prose, I discovered that an Indian chief named Red Jacket had said this to a missionary who had come to Buffalo in 1805: "Brother, listen to what we say. There was a time when our forefathers owned this great island. Their seats extended from the rising to the setting sun. The Great Spirit had made it for the use of the Indians. All this he had done for his children because he loved them." When the noon whistle blows up from the factories, I take up *Representative Selections from Emerson*—or is it *Walden* I am lecturing on today, *Moby Dick, Light in August?*—am bidden an obsequious "*Guten Morgen, Herr Professor!*" by the aged refugees from East Germany who live in the attic, and head for the Number 15 tram to Albertus Magnus Strasse.

It is dreary living at this end of the city. Whenever I want to go anywhere at all, I have to go the whole length of Cologne all over again. But as my assistant, Dr. C., always says, I am lucky to have a room at all; out in Ehrenfeld, hundreds of people still live in bunkers, and the other day I heard from a young doctor who visits in the poorest quarter that he found one family living underground in a cellar made out of old airplane parts. "The automobiles here live better than the people," he says; the garages of the new-rich have windows, the people underground have none. The shiny neon-lighted prosperity of the new "American-style" buildings rises out of so many ruins that it reminds me of the pink skin grafted into the faces of so many former soldiers. Every day I go past all the ruins again. I begin every journey from the carbarns, and if I want so much as a whiff of the Rhine, or to get the Paris edition of the *Herald Tribune* at the railroad station, I have to go clear across town. And the trolley always takes so long, so long: I wear out my days on the hard yellow benches of Number 15 looking at ruins. First I wait in the rubble around the newsstand until the driver and conductor finish their smoke; I look at German imitations of *Life, Look, Click* and *Pic;* at the German edition of *Reader's Digest* and at the *Amerikanische Zeitung in Deutschland;* at Rita Hayworth smiling up at me from the corner of the *Illustrierte;* at a skeleton in a German army helmet warning me against the perils of Marxism from the front page of *Der Stahlhelm.* Then the men look up at the clock, put their little pipes away into their green army jackets, and with a great lurch and a crash, while the brick dust blows in from the remains of the nearest houses, we're off on my daily tour of the ruins.

"Straight through?" the conductor asks. "Straight through!" most of the passengers answer. For only thirty pfennig, Number 15 will conduct you across Cologne, straighter than Virgil conducted Dante, from ashes to cinders. Only, after the first three days, you don't really notice any more. Block after block after block, the same squashed houses with their insides open to the street; block after block, the loose mounds of brick blowing up the same yellow dust. Two blocks from where I live now, the whole outside wall of a house caved in one night in 1943 or 1944 or 1945 and then slid halfway down the street. The house is still there, just about to topple, its old girders twisting out from under it; the great black mass of broken wall looks as if the pavement itself had reared up in fright. In the cars, all passengers stolidly occupy their seats, staring straight ahead. That sticky-looking German blond hair, unmistakable, and always long at the back. A somber people, an absorbed, industrious and somber people. Only the conductor ever laughs as he walks up and down heartily collecting his thirty pfennig. The cars are full of the blind and the near-blind wearing the three-dotted yellow armbands that will alert people to their condition; are full of young men wearing the black glove over the stump of a hand; are full of faces so burned and blasted that the inserts of pink new skin grafted over their mouths give them a strangely babyish and pleading look. . . . It's all like a hospital: they say that the German army surgeons during the war rarely tried to save limbs; they just cut and cut. What with the ruins outside the cars and the ruins inside the cars, the slightest bit of color and gaiety in these streets suddenly makes you giddy. The other day, I saw a Corpus Christi procession from the trolley, and the vestments and banners startled me by the bright colors they jauntily raised against the ashen city everywhere around them.

In front of the miserable little movie house on the Zulpicher Strasse, a large poster shows John Garfield advancing on a blonde with a gun; next week, Roy Rogers. My young doctor friend, who spent the war years in Switzerland and is very eager these days to show me the art and historical monuments of his city, drove me far out the other day to point out a Roman monument. *Colonia Agrippinensis!* The doctor was so eager, indeed, that he drove me there at night, and lighted up his little Roman icon for me in the brights of his car. But despite the Emperor Claudius, who founded this *colonia* in A.D. 50, here I sit in a Cologne trolley car reading Emerson. A century ago, Ralph Waldo came to Germany to learn; but I, if you please, have come here to teach. This is how an American writer now gets to Europe; he teaches. Sometimes I go out to Bonn to see Ernst Curtius, who has read everything except, possibly, the three or four young writers since Truman Capote he thinks he needs to read; so I teach even him. I wanted to ask this great scholar about his friend Proust, but he most respectfully asked me about *my* friends. Once I had a beer at the local *Stübe* with my landlady and her husband, who wanted to know all about American merchandising; I have also been asked to tea by all the scholars in the Rhineland who are writing papers on Melville and Faulkner. The other day, while sitting in my office next to the "American Library," a young man rushed in and requested of me, in meters, the exact length of Brooklyn Bridge. When I assured him that I didn't know, he looked incredulous. Ach, what it is in the new Germany a *Gastprofessor für Amerikanistik* to be! Not American literature, notice; not even American history: but *Amerikanistik*. They want it all, and they want it in a quick dose: *Amerikanistik*.

H. in New York assures me that in old Germany she never heard the word, and I suspect that, like the word, the product it sells hereabouts is also made up to look more sellable than it is.

Still, when you talk about dear old Emerson and Melville and Henry James, you discover that one touch of American literature makes the whole world kin. My students speak and write English (sometimes even pointedly *American*) with what I can only call efficiency, and they're amazingly like nineteen-year-old undergraduates in Minneapolis, Cambridge and Washington Square, and except for the fact that they're oh-so-respectful to teacher and grimly industrious, the topics and the papers themselves are all the same just now: *Symbolism in "The Scarlet Letter"; Vernon Parrington and D. H. Lawrence as Critics of American Literature; The New Criticism; The Verse Technique of Walt Whitman; The Symbolism of "Light in August."* My assistant, Dr. C., who knows Gothic and Anglo-Saxon and Church Latin but who doesn't seem to understand much American literature, doesn't have this eager good will, this innocent receptivity, toward American texts; he was a Nazi and is too old. But the really young ones among my students, and more especially the young intellectuals in this Catholic city, who feel strong cultural connections with Italy and France, are as deeply attracted to American writing now as those German poets and intellectuals who fell in 1914 with *Leaves of Grass* in their packs. It's funny to give a viva-voce exam here in the local coffeehouse (I hadn't realized what a Big Thing this was) and to hear an eager young student confess how much E. E. Cummings has come to mean to him. Funny and sad, for if only it were E. E. Cummings or Frost or Eliot whom he praised, and not "your open American way of doing things"! I hadn't realized that the national product, even in poetry, was all that much of the same manufacture, and it makes me uneasy to have these very attractive and eager-minded kids looking for *this* much salvation in *Amerikanistik* — or for this much *Amerikanistik* in me!

« 2 »

How the wheel does turn. When I walk into my lecture hall and hear this mob of students pounding with their feet on the floor, I have to remind myself that in their local fashion they are welcoming teacher, not hooting him out. But at the same time this very eagerness for the American word, almost for any American word, excites anticipations which not the United States, not our dear old American classics, and certainly not this *Gastprofessor* can ever fulfill. But as soon as you even hint of this to your students, in comes one of those professional Americans from Texas, and "sells" America to them as if it were toothpaste. I had been doing Frost's "Two Tramps in Mudtime" with my seminar, and as if the poem in its last lines weren't sententious enough, in walks Professor X. and interrupts to announce that "You can tell what a straight-shooter Robert Frost is." Why is it that nowadays the biggest dopes are so attracted to American literature? And why is it that this horde of half-literate nativists, fundamentally as ignorant of Europe as a congressman, are regularly assigned to tour Europe in behalf of the American way of life? *Amerika, du certainly hast es besser.* The other day D. turned up in behalf of the Daddy Warbucks foundation and generously ordered venison. It seems to me in peculiar taste to lap it up amid so many ruins; but as he says, Germany inspires cynicism, doesn't it? If only these professional Americanists consistently believed that America was still a revolutionary culture with which to leaven the Old World! If only they understood even half the implications in the material they are always dishing out! Then one could at least credit them with ingenuous good will — or with the private need to "defend" America against all comers which the sons and even the grandsons of immigrants so often feel in Europe when faced with the locusts of the French Communist party screeching about germ warfare in Korea. But the trouble is that these professional Americanists now get over to Europe only to get themselves over. With the intellectual flabbiness that you might expect of people who have worked long and exclusively on the minor poets of Nebraska, they are now unable to understand either America or Europe, and look slack-jawed at cathedrals until they have their chance, by gum, to praise Robert Frost as a real straight-shooter.

« 3 »

I was asked to dinner by an official of the university, and after making my way with some difficulty through bombed-out streets still full of ruins, arrived to discover that although the lady of the house was ill and the host could manage only sandwiches, there would be more than enough to drink. Also on hand was a professor of economics, with English that flowed as uninterruptedly as the wine; but there was so much wine in proportion to the food that after a while they relapsed into German and then into an argument on some moot point about the fighting on the Russian front. They had both been officers, and, it turned out, had heard considerable shooting of civilians by the S.S. The house got darker, the wine flowed madly, and when I finally excused myself to go home, the professor of economics, seeing how enraged their conversation had made me, insisted on accompanying me. A canny man, full of all the right liberal attitudes, he somehow couldn't bear to see me go home without some further conversation on *the* topic. "Yes, we heard them shooting, but we were regular army, and had nothing to do with it." Nobody had anything to do with it — neither the doctor, who was in Switzerland; nor my landlady's husband, who was in England; nor the professor of economics, who was a lieutenant colonel on the Russian front, and heard other people shooting. But *I* have everything to do with it still, and so in the dark Cologne night, amid so many ruins, I get myself back to my room and my *Representative Selections from Emerson* for the morrow.

By the waters of Cologne, there we sat down, yea, we wept, when we remembered Zion.

« 4 »

Boppard-on-the-Rhine, conference of local Americanists and Anglicists. The local American adviser for education sits at the head of the table with a sleek young German interpreting into his ear, and although the adviser is a round and amiable dean of education from Kentucky and the discussion couldn't be more Teachers College-ish, I seem to see him as a proconsul sent out from Rome to one of the conquered provinces, sitting in a box at the local games, while an obsequious native fills him in. It is really extraordinary, despite this fantasy, how academic the discussion is. Now that the raging madness of the Nazi years is officially lifted, the officious conservatism and bustling propriety of the professorial class reveal themselves as the most solidly entrenched of local passions. An official of the Bonn government, in charge of educational matters —

very tweedy, twinkly and relaxed-looking with red rose in buttonhole — nevertheless grows white with anger as he listens to unheard-of tales of slackness among students, and fixes his jaws with determination each time he comes to the magic phrase: "They must learn . . . to . . . *work!*" It fascinates me that, after everything that has happened, the old-fashioned pedantry and narrowness should have survived like those caryatids you see in downtown Cologne still bent under the weight of buildings that no longer exist. Although the English language is fluently in use and *Amerikanistik* is obviously the coming thing, the old familiar easiness, flexibility and accommodatingness of the American mind are not much in evidence. It comes as a bit of a shock to hear from the linguist E., who has been much influenced by Parrington and who intervened briefly this morning in favor of a more realistic understanding of the social background of literature: "My promotion will never come now. I used the word *belletristic*. My superiors won't stand for it."

We were taking a turn along the Rhine when this happened, and with my usual sense of double vision in Germany, I thought of the contrast between the idyllic scene before me and the atmosphere of bitterness which E. described for me. Like many German scholars of literature who have studied in the American seminar at Salzburg, or in the states, he has been genuinely affected by the plurality of views and the radical-democratic bias he has discovered in American literature. But it is quite clear, without his explicitly saying so, that he regards the academic study of literature in Germany as hopelessly idealistic, generalized and abstract. Suddenly the almost too familiar bias of Parrington, so overdone in the thirties and so *vieux jeu* now to the young scholars at home, becomes — in the Germany of 1952 — as fresh and provocative a form of literary intelligence as Randolph Bourne or Van Wyck Brooks gave to the America of 1915. Even the great Ernst Curtius has taken to writing articles on the German classics and world literature for the newspapers; he feels that he must do whatever he can to get the Germans out of the sick circle of their cultural isolation. And I must say that my assistant, Dr. C., who knows so many head-breaking languages and doesn't in the least understand the revolutionary and fraternal impulse behind so many nineteenth-century American writers, is a depressing example of how little literary scholarship of the most formal kind can do for you in this country. Obviously to be a professor of literature in Germany is in some mysterious way to feel yourself a vestal virgin tending the pure, pure flame of scholarship — scholarship on the kind of subject that could be rendered safe and indestructible even during the Hitler years. I can see that the profound instinct to play it safe and to keep oneself above the herd has been redoubled since the war by the need at least to live with professional dignity amid so many ruins. But it is a shock to come upon Professor S., who informed me that discussion of the concentration camps was "vulgar." How little we understand minds so encased in professional dignity that they can still, after the "worst episode in human history," think of themselves as above the battle, living in an unhistorical world protecting timeless values. It is only when you are in Germany, living among German professors, that you realize how frightfully easy it is for them to idealize things. I didn't realize that I was upsetting any rules by inviting my students to the coffeehouse, but I can see now that to be a professor is, by God, to be something. In discussing the bombings of Bonn, Ernst Curtius, who really *is* somebody, pointed to a black bust of himself that stood at the other end of his library and said, in describing the havoc: "Why, my own bust flew across the room!"

In Puerto Rico

[1959]

LONG BEFORE the ice-cream man comes down the block (twice a day) you can hear his truck playing Brahms's "Lullaby" over the loudspeaker, and after he is gone, the sweet and gluey tones (a little like the tasteless local ice cream itself) still linger maddeningly on the air. Over and over and over, the music box repeats the treacly phrase — tum-te-*tum*, tum-te-*tum*, tum-te-*tum tum tum tum!* — and you think, probably that's what Chinese water torture used to be like, used to be like, only you didn't think it would come to the cadence of Brahms's "Lullaby"! But finally he takes himself down the street of identical pink and blue stucco houses, and the nothingness of the long day takes over.

Time is longer here than elsewhere; the day begins early, as it does in all the hot Latin countries; at 7 A.M. people are already walking across the garbage-strewn fields next to our house that are a short cut to the 65th Infantry Road and the highway to the airport; they are beginning to lay out streets on these fields; soon there will be more identical pink and blue stucco houses; the men are already at work. And already it's hot: the even late-summer heat of Puerto Rico that before noon clamps you around the back and chest, and that will go on all day and late into the evening, interrupted only by the sudden rains that stop as quickly as they come, and that end always in the same heavy clamping late-summer heat.

The day begins early and it begins indistinguishably from the rest of the day and from all the other days. Across the empty fields back of Street Number 1, house Number 14 (there are so many new developments in Puerto Rico that they no longer bother to give names to such streets), the brown-faced men and women are already going to work, and as you look at the faces, the curious stillness is already on them — the stillness that always seems inertness in the presence of the "continental," the "American," the stillness that in my students at the university I can no longer tell from a deeply resistant shyness. "Feed my lambs." . . . There is a lamb in the official seal of the Commonwealth of Puerto Rico, and in truth these people *are* lamblike. We laugh when an outbreak of rapings in Santurce calls out headlines in the *Island Times:* "NEW-YORK-TYPE GANGS"; but as they say, there *was* no such violence here until Puerto Ricans came back to the Island. I believe them, for their famous docility (which can also be interpreted as the apathy of tropical countries and the Step'n Fetchit sloth in the presence of Americans barking questions in the language they do not know and no longer even pretend to know) shows itself all day long and every day in a variety of silences and withdrawals. Even on the road — and they are the most erratic drivers in the world, with a sickening record of accidents — they will commit every fault but that of excessive speed. They drive, in fact, as if they were on muleback; they drive *en famille,* arms perpetually hanging out of the car, talking and eating as if they were home; but they are not aggressive. They are used to waiting on life, waiting on other people; they are used to taking orders; they are "sensitive" beyond endurance, but not stormy. The long long hot day long ago took them over, and the sudden rainstorms — to say nothing of the Spanish generals, the Spanish bishops, the Spanish slaveowners and feudal owners, and now. . . . And now the bishops are still never Puerto Ricans but are American Irish, and the girl behind the automatic cash register at the *supermercado* (run by Grand Union, development by Laurance Rockefeller) may not speak English but has learned to say "Okay, you bet, next aisle please," and *my* lambs are reading Emerson and Thoreau, you bet! "In transcendentalism is implied that there is knowledge of transcendental elements. In these three passages are implied in the following way: Emerson: During these days the people is getting rid of the traditional feelings. . . ."

Are they "docile" because someone has always taken them over — or are they just docile? To me they are the waifs and wards of big power politics, the submerged colonial mass incarnate, the emerging masses in Africa and South America and the East Indies — the mass just getting itself up through the crust of poverty, racism, and the bush, which, as it gets up, is immediately handed a television program and a subscription to *Confidential*. The Puerto Ricans are always being reformed, educated, studied, analyzed, worked on, "developed" by others. Just now they are being worked on by the most intelligent and social-minded administration in Latin America, and thanks to the massive infusion of American capital and the rapid industrialization of the island, Puerto Rico is now the most prosperous and fastest growing economy in this area. But as I see from the complaints of Puerto Rican students who have been to the States, they are very quick to suspect, to misunderstand, to be hurt — and somehow I hear from them more of what they have suffered from Americans than of what they *think* of Americans. It must be this passivity that explains the hilarious number of anthropologists and sociologists forever prowling this island. I am told that there is still no really good history of Puerto Rico. But let a young American loose with a foundation grant and a manual of behavior patterns, and he doesn't need to know any history, for he can always look into breast-feeding patterns in the purely Negro areas, or study spiritualism.

It's all such a gold mine, either for the American sociologist or the American chain store — two and a half million Puerto Ricans, waiting to get into Woolworth's, Franklin's, Kresge's, Grand Union; as they wait, they can get their resources counted and their "patterns" studied. They won't object: why should they? The boy who stands all day long outside the big hotel on the Avenida Norte trying to get rid of the few coconuts he brought down this morning will before long move into the hotel and learn to serve ten different kinds of rum drinks to the *alrightniks* in the swimming pool — and he will still have the same far, faraway look on his face. The *alrightniks* will never *see* him, any more than they see his cousins and brothers in New York; and truth to tell, he doesn't have the information and undoubtedly lacks the curiosity with which to see *them*. The Puerto Ricans live on an island in every sense of the word: they are here, and their minds don't roam around much. Talking with university students about American writers, I have been struck by their refusal to visualize New England landscape or wintry weather. It's not simply that they haven't seen snow: neither had the young heroine of Carson McCullers' novel who so longed to see some. It's that they are here and cannot easily imagine anything too different from their island, their town. For centuries they were wrapped round in the torpor of the Spanish Empire, and their island was never of major significance to the Spaniards themselves. Puerto Rico was largely the taking-off place for Spain, the "rich port," in which anchored the galleons bearing the gold back to Spain from Mexico, a last place to which Spanish royal troops retreated from South America after losing to Bolívar.

« 2 »

Richard Morse, head of the institute at the university for regional studies of the Caribbean, has written a paper on "The Deceptive Transformation of Puerto Rico" in which he points out that there was less transplantation of Spanish society here than anywhere else in Latin America. This explains why even the most ignorant foreigner somehow senses the lack of any real cultural tradition here, of any firm national identity. Not only was there no strongly organized society here under the Spaniards, says Morse, but Puerto Rico even lacked the spontaneous spirit of organization and economic thrift which produces a flourishing class of independent farmers. No wonder that there have been no real group identities here for the sociologists to seize on, not enough "rituals of celebration": even Catholicism has never been an all-dominating cultural force here, for the Spanish priests were always regarded as agents of Madrid, and evangelical Protestantism has taken hold here as it has nowhere else in Latin America. Morse believes that the island itself has always been passive to history, that it has usually been subject to violence from without, whether by hurricanes or buccaneers or French, British, or Dutch invaders. It has *always* depended for its sustenance and progress upon more highly organized institutions and societies abroad, and even in the heyday of the Spanish Empire depended on a periodic financial subsidy from vice-regal Mexico (the famous *situado*), on contraband trade with European ships and with the plantation islands of the Lesser Antilles. Now it depends on the skills, capital, and industrializing organization of the United States.

Morse's paper, which I discovered thanks to sarcastic comments on it by a columnist in the *Island Times*, explains a good deal of what troubles me about Puerto Ricans — as much here as in the United States. If there is no strong local tradition on the part of migrating groups, if there is no articulated and positive ideal in their own history for which they seek expression and fulfillment in the new country — as was true of the Irish with their longing for political emancipation and religious tolerance, of the German democrats and liberals who loved the republican idea, of the land-hungry Italian peasants and the oppressed East European Jews — then it follows that some of these "newcomers," as Oscar Handlin calls them, will not consciously seek any real attachment with American culture. Handlin thinks that for Puerto Ricans the "break of migration" is not "as sharp as it had been for Europeans. . . . Such newcomers did not feel the complete and total sense of foreignness that overwhelmed the European immigrants, and, therefore, did not feel called upon to create the institutions which were the response to the shock of separation." But in Puerto Rico itself one discovers on every hand that these cultural institutions have never existed, and so cannot arbitrarily be created in New York. As many a schoolteacher in East Harlem has learned, Puerto Rican kids are often as illiterate in Spanish as they remain in English; and judging from the frenzied missionary effort of the Catholic Church to reclaim Puerto Ricans in New York for the faith, they often arrive without any real religious traditions at all. Handlin thinks that Puerto Ricans have a sense of connectedness with the United States because they are already American citizens. But I think that it is because citizenship has simply been granted *en bloc*, because they have not had to earn it as a voluntary and individual act, that they lack connectedness with the United States and even with its language. During the Korean war many Puerto Ricans in the American forces were killed, Dan Wakefield says in *Island in the City*, almost as a direct result of not knowing English, and he suggests that the American Army was at fault in not assigning these troops to officers who could give orders in Spanish. But it must be a powerful feeling of separation from the United States that will keep a soldier from learning enough English to keep himself alive, as so many refugees did. And lecturing in English here in Puerto Rico, I can testify that this feeling of separation exists; I have taught American literature all over Western Europe, but have never had such trouble communicating with my students as I do here. The United States figures here simply as Big Brother, and my boys and girls don't quite believe in what I am saying — or in its possible relevance to them. The more prosperous ones do, of the class from which José Ferrer came. In 1949, when Ferrer was given the medal of the National Academy of Arts and Letters for the best diction by any actor on the American stage, I heard him deliver a bitter and powerful attack on intolerance against Puerto Ricans, and truly, *his* diction was beautiful. But his complaints against the inhumanity of the city don't help me much when I go over a page of Thoreau or Melville with my students. I have never cared for the humor of H*Y*M*A*N K*A*P*L*A*N, but he tried, didn't he? Yes, yes, my students try, too, and the babble from the speech clinic is all around me as I teach. But let us say that they try without hope; they don't really believe, as J. Robert Oppenheimer once said of his German-born father, that being an American citizen is the greatest privilege in the world. And why don't they believe it — because individuals among them are treated with disrespect, as are individuals among Negroes, Italians, Jews, California-born Japanese? It is because they see themselves as wards of the state — as colonials, not as immigrants; it is because they are "associated" with the United States, not attached to it. They are in no position to see what they can make of the United States; they are in position only to suffer from it.

Historically, the great achievement of the United States as a civilization has been its creation not of a tradition but of a promise; it has been extraordinary in its ability to suggest to all peoples the fulfillment of their particular hopes. If anything, it has promised the fulfillment of too many: this is why immigrants jokingly curse Columbus, for having prepared the frustration with the promise. There is a kind of bitterness about America which is the other side of the universal and infinite hopes connected with it. As F. Scott Fitzgerald said, France was a land and England a people, but America, "having about it still that quality of the idea, [is] harder to utter." Even Mark Twain, who like all his generation in the West was an immigrant from a fabulous natural world to the era of Mark Hanna and Rockefeller, spoke like an immigrant when he said crossly that wonderful as it was to discover America, it would have been more wonderful to lose it. No country can disappoint like America, for no other country has aroused so many hopes. But such hopes can arise only from an identity of one's own and a specific tradition sharp enough to arouse the possibility of its fulfillment in this country. Otherwise there is no spiritual marriage at all between America and its newcomers, and the great epic of immigration simply becomes a picture of the lesser breeds attached to the white Protestant majority.

Richard Morse says that the essential lack of direction behind the "spillage" of American capital and techniques into Puerto Rico has merely perpetuated and deepened the instability of the Puerto Ricans, and that the industrial boom has significantly lacked any counterpart in agriculture or education or city planning. Now "the hard shell of top-level technocrats covers an underbody of soft institutions." Needless to say, Governor Muñoz Marín is worried about this situation, and now that massive industrialization, "Operation Bootstrap," is so brilliantly under way, he has called for "Operation Serenity," for a massive cultural and spiritual effort to close up the gap behind Puerto Rico's industrial progress. If Puerto Rico is "the Formosa of the New Dealers," Muñoz Marín — and his equally brilliant wife — are certainly not the Chiang Kai-sheks. Muñoz Marín's salary is astonishingly modest; he has refused pay increases, and he is as imaginative and dedicated to the welfare of his people as an administrator can be. The United States would be fortunate indeed if it were led with half as much imagination and eloquence as Puerto Rico is by the present commonwealth government. But in Puerto Rico all such operations, whether toward industrialization or "serenity," seem to percolate downward; and Luis Muñoz Marín, with his warm heart and his quick brain, is still in the tradition of a famous father and of the Puerto Rican intellectual elite, a teacher and reformer from the governor's palace. And because he represents so much of what is best in the American Democratic party, New Deal wing, his friends worry over what may happen to Puerto Rico in Washington — where its fate has so often been decided — if the Republicans, some of whose leaders have repeatedly expressed their contempt for Puerto Rico and all its works, win again in 1960.

When a people has never had a chance to work out a deep national identity of its own, when its experience has fundamentally been that of dependency, when even in its religious practice it shows an inner mutinousness against the beliefs imposed by the conqueror — then it must seek in external political solutions at least the sign of the independence and unity it has lacked in the past. Whether under the Spaniards or under the Americans, the Puerto Ricans have always debated the same problem — whether to be "associated" with the larger country, or to be independent of it, or to become directly part of it. The Puerto Ricans were granted autonomy within the Spanish Empire just as the Spanish-American war broke out. Since this was followed by American domination of the island, Puerto Ricans think that the everlasting problem of their political status might have been solved if it had not been for the war of 1898. But even if one grants the closer ties to Spain, it is obvious, from the continued restiveness of the Puerto Ricans under commonwealth status and a native administration, that Muñoz Marín's hope — to deflect the agitation for purely formal solutions into a massive effort to raise living standards — has in the first respect not succeeded. The Puerto Ricans are very busy debating statehood versus commonwealth status, and there is still a core of intellectuals with strong faith in Puerto Rico's national culture who are simply for independence, while the hard-bitten extremists who tried to kill Truman and shot up Congress are still represented by the Nationalist party. Muñoz Marín, who was once simply for independence and now of course strongly backs commonwealth status, tried to detour the statehood movement by coming up with a new formula: there would be time to consider statehood only when the per capita wealth of the islanders reached that of the poorest state in the union (Mississippi); it was calculated that this would happen in the 1990's. Without directly opposing statehood, Muñoz Marín managed to give the pro-commonwealth forces a handle against it, and the next day the *New York Times* editorially applauded Muñoz Marín for his brilliant and thoughtful solution. But while the *Times* drew a sigh of obvious relief at being able to put the problem off for thirty years, at least a few Puerto Rican intellectuals pointed out that even considering statehood wholly in economic terms was distinctly not complimentary to the United States.

The demand for statehood is probably strongest in the prospering new middle class. Now that they travel like Americans between San Juan and New York, or gaily study psychoanalysis in Iowa City and the theater arts in Dallas (unlike the poorer and darker-skinned Puerto Ricans, who arrive on the hideous economy flight that seems to be the airlines' effort to duplicate the steerage in mid-air), many businessmen and doctors and lawyers are all for statehood, and you can see in the rear windows of the newer and bigger cars stickers asking for admission of Puerto Rico as the fifty-first state. But obviously statehood is spiritually inconceivable to Governor Muñoz Marín and many other Puerto Ricans — and how else should it be? They are Latin Americans; their language is Spanish; and Governor Muñoz Marín, one of the principal advisers to Washington on Latin American policy, is, as head of the Commonwealth of Puerto Rico, a far more dignified and significant figure than he would be as head of just another American state. Understandably, since by now many Puerto Ricans feel closer to the elites on the mainland than they do to the peasants in the hills, statehood promises more secure personal status. So with one thing and another, the everlasting argument about what Puerto Rico is to be still boils over. And how it fascinates and enthralls! How many stickers in the back of how many cars! What endless excitement! Like the Russians of the nineteenth century debating Slavophil against Westerner, the Puerto Rican may yet discover that debates about which culture to join up with are a symbol of national powerlessness. But in Puerto Rico these debates cannot conceal the fact that there is no positive, rich, and glowing national past either to save from the Americans or to affiliate with them.

« 3 »

To make the situation even drearier, the American businessmen and technical experts and supermarket designers, who in typical American fashion have *expertise* without culture, who no longer have any intellectual convictions of their own with which they can either challenge, or adopt, or reject the culture of others, are now all "liberals" to a man, sympathetic to Puerto Rico as a matter of course, and sit around the bars discussing affiliation versus independence as if this gummy question were one that *they* could answer. If ever proof were needed that Americans do not have enough pride and self-knowledge even to think of themselves as "imperialist" custodians of the "lesser breeds," it can be found in Puerto Rico. The manager of a soft-drink company told me that he thought the United States should "hold on" to the island, whatever the cost to us, only in order to show the world how beneficent and richly devoted to the welfare of other peoples we can be. This would show up Russia in the eyes of the world and give us a higher score in the cold war. Most of the Americans I meet here don't even think of themselves as "holding on" to Puerto Rico. The intellectuals at the university, many of whom came expecting a breath of Latin culture, a whiff of the mother continent, by now either feel like Puerto Ricans or just feel sorry for them; whereas the technical experts, the airlines personnel, and the journalists find it all too easy not to think beyond their jobs. This in part I can understand, since the heat, the perpetual need of a lift, the lack of the more oppressive stateside taxes on liquor and the bathfuls constantly being flown in from the free ports of the Virgin Islands — to say nothing of the fact that you can conveniently buy your liquor in the *supermercado* and that the rum is cheap and the local beer excellent — make this place a perpetual New Year's Eve party. The swimming pool is never far from the bar, and all you need to cover your nakedness is a credit card.

Of course there are other Americans who do not drink at all. There is a whole group of evangelical young American physicians who have given up big incomes in the United States to build up medical stations like Castaner, in the middle of the island — which can be reached only by mountain roads so winding that people in small cars often take dramamine. And there are young writers and artists at the university in Rio Piedras who are there out of a deep interest in Hispanic culture, who know their Lorca and their Machado as well as they know their Hart Crane, and so are not as homesick as I am when I read my students' papers on *The Great Gatsby*. They do not believe in the press-agent talk of Puerto Rico as a "hybrid" of two cultures; they are there for the Spanish, like the wonderful Spanish Loyalist scholars you run into at the university. But between the young American officers here and in the Virgin Islands, who like the medical scientists here seem virtually the last Americans with a keen professional edge to their lives, there is a whole group of Americans who have come here in flight: from broken marriages, from the lifelong stigma of having once belonged to the Communist party, from . . . the difficulties and pains of not being better than they are. An American Somerset Maugham could do a picturesque novel on the drifters, the ex-radicals, the drunks, the queers, the invalids seeking the sun, the missionaries, the Southern crackers who have gravitated here as a matter of course and interestingly have learned to be civil to their Negro neighbors. And what I mind most about Puerto Rico is not that this island absorbs so many Americans, but that it enervates them, gives them no mark to shoot at, nothing hard, clear, perfect of its kind to be equal to. The torpidity I mind as I mind it anywhere, whether in Latin America or in those parts of the United States where insularism makes itself felt, sooner or later, in the same peculiarly thin, two-dimensional quality of a society wholly "modern," without tradition and without ideas.

The Spanish Republicans in Puerto Rico do not have this peculiar sensitiveness without pride, this readiness to take offense from a stranger; the Englishwoman at the University speech clinic, who has spent much of her life teaching Latin Americans, does not have it. But with Puerto Ricans, one always finds oneself discussing their feelings and their sufferings, never their ideas and their hopes.

And so history always repeats itself here as the sterile tale of the bigger nation and its Puerto Rican victim. Unfortunately, there is not as much time left for Puerto Ricans as there used to be, for as everything moves faster and faster even as the subject nations and peoples come forward, there is barely a chance to make up for the centuries of intellectual numbness before the smoothing out process of mass culture takes over. Independence will not create in Puerto Ricans the past they lack; statehood, should it ever be granted, will not automatically create the self-respect they seek; the present commonwealth status of "association" will continue to symbolize the uneasiness that must persist so long as the people do not know what to hope for — or the direction from which their hope is to come.

From a Russian Diary

[1959]

Our new interpreter talks perfect American with a very slight, almost teasing Cockney accent, looks like a Brooklyn taxi-driver, and asks us to call him Georgie. Although he talks the lingo so well that he boasts of fooling American tourists at the Intourist hotels, he is 150 per cent patriotic, a true-blue Bolshevik, a model of the smiling, happy youth on the face of the Soviet calendar who used to cry, "Thank you, Comrade Stalin, for giving us such a happy childhood!" Georgie is the son of a Red Army colonel who fell in the Battle of Kiev. I have heard — not from Georgie, certainly — that the Red Army was wiped out at Kiev because Stalin obstinately, insanely insisted on the troops making a stand when the Nazis were already on the other side of the Dnieper. But when Georgie talked to me of Stalin's death in 1953, of the hushed and shaken crowds, he referred to him only as "the old man."

"Cried like a baby," said Georgie reminiscently. "Couldn't help it. What he meant to us!"

And at one point, when I asked him to tell me something about the "doctors' plot" and the open drive against Jews in Stalin's last days, I joked, "Don't worry, the chauffeur doesn't understand English." Georgie turned to me and said with hauteur: "Before 1953 I would not have talked to you *at all*; now I would not be afraid to talk to you about *anything*."

Georgie is a Jew. All our interpreters have been Jews, and unfailingly Jews pop up as assistants to the editor, translators, technical personnel in most of the literary establishments we are taken to. And since I seem to be one of those Jews whose very presence brings up discussion of Jews — if I ever touch at the North Pole, the first Eskimo running up to me will ask my opinion of Ben-Gurion — I am not surprised to have a disconcerting effect in a culture that is so notoriously and visibly nervous about Jews — no one more so than the "official" Jews here in Russia themselves. In Leningrad, I heard one of them mimic the "Jewish" accent of various writers we met, and in Kiev the Jewish writer Gregory Plotkin, who has written an unforgettable series of articles for Soviet papers about the coercion of Jews in Israel, explained that only a few "riffraff" Ukrainians participated in the Nazi massacres of the Jewish population of the Ukraine.

When I lectured before the "American literature specialists" in Moscow on our recent writing, the Jewish professors tore me limb from limb on the grounds that a book I had edited on Dreiser had no discussion of Dreiser's "Marxist" book of reportage on the Thirties, *Tragic America*.

The fact is unmistakable here: Jews embarrass. I am struck over and over by the extraordinary significance attached here to being a Jew, and I am almost ashamed to have to put down now what happened to me, at the hands of Georgie, when we were all in Tashkent.

It was a hot day, and coming out of the local park of "culture and rest," we hurried to the car to take us back to the hotel. The Oriental street was full of women in veils, vendors of *shashlik*, bazaars. The other members of the delegation were already in the car when I noticed with interest exactly such a glimpse of the Orient as I had dreamed of seeing all my life — an aged blind man with a magnificent Muslim beard, like a muezzin, being led along the street by a lady swathed in veils. "Ah," I said appreciatively to

Georgie, "how Oriental they are!" He looked sour. "They're not Orientals," he said curtly. "They're Jews." When I expressed a desire to meet them, Georgie shrugged his shoulders and declined to assist me. I went over and introduced myself as an American and a Jew, and asked if they would be good enough to converse with me.

Would they converse with me! In the middle of the hot Uzbek street the old man let out a great cry, *"Blessed be the Lord!"*, threw his arms around me, and to my astonishment engulfed me in such a scalding, weeping, tumbling account of everything they had gone through since they had left Odessa in 1941, just ahead of the Nazis — he had been blinded by a machine-gun bullet from a Nazi plane that had shot up evacuation ships crossing the Black Sea — that I could barely keep up with everything he and his wife were trying to tell me. They spoke at once, they blessed me in Hebrew at every other sentence, they crowded the experiences of sixteen years into a few minutes, and they lost me altogether in an involved story of a Jewish leader in the Tashkent community of evacuees who had betrayed certain people to the police.

As I stood there, listening with the deepest emotion — after all, they could very well have been my grandparents — I felt someone pulling at my elbow. It was Georgie. Looking at the two wretched old people with what seemed to me appalling condescension, he informed me that my fellow delegates in the car wished to return to the hotel and that I was being asked to return with them immediately. Perplexed by this, I went back to the car, discovered that everybody else was asleep, and returned to the conversation. After a few minutes, Georgie pulled my sleeve again. Would I *please* terminate this interview *immediately;* my presence was most *urgently* requested back at the car. I waved him aside, and went on listening, and then to my amazement found Georgie pulling me to the car. The blind old man, who had already seemed mentally disturbed, took his wife's hand, and in the glaring sunlit street they took up their stand behind an old sentry post at the entrance to the park, trying to conceal themselves. I took my place in the car.

« 2 »

Surely I was here in a former life. There is so much that I recognize on sight — that bustling Russian propriety in offices and hallways, the pillows piled high on my bed, the flash of golden teeth, those square (yet somehow round!) Russian females, always in transparent blouses over pink slips, bodies into which have been poured tons of crusty yellow wheat bread, borsht, and kvass — bodies strong but agile on a concrete foundation that seems to say, *No nonsense here!* — bodies which say, Only a sincere Russian love could win *me*.

Always the smell of furniture polish, always the covers over the sofas and the chairs, always the many Russian readers. In the clean Russian parks — under the statues of Lomonosov and Lenin, Gorky and Lenin, Pushkin and Lenin, Lenin and Lenin — on the clean and dear Russian slat benches under which there is not a speck of old bourgeois dirt (for all day long old women in white aprons with white cloths tied around their hair walk about with brooms and scourges, as in a Russian bath, scouring our parks clean of all dirt) — in the dear and meditative Russian parks, sage and staid readers in crushy soft Panama hats sit reading Stendhal and Balzac, Tolstoy and Mark Twain.

"And in your country?"

Clean as clean as clean is our old dear Moscow with its many banners — *Forward in the Battle for Peace!* And at each Russian desk before the old-fashioned penholder and glass inkwell and curved blotter with a handlepiece, we sit at attention, serious and studious.

That Russian propriety, that Russian schoolmistressy exactness and solemnity, that Russian straightforwardness! Our own delegation shocks by its levity, its loud internecine disagreements, its unheard-of lack of interest in agricultural fairs, its interest in drinking vodka. Our official Soviet hosts, the Foreign Commission of the Union of Soviet Writers, should be an object lesson to us all.

Four Russians sit at one side of the greenclothed table and four Americans sit across from them. On the walls, pictures of famous writers — Anna Seghers, Martin Anderson Nexø, Pablo Neruda, Louis Aragon. Alexey Surkov, poet, formerly head of the Union of Soviet Writers and now head of its Foreign Commission — orients us. In the Soviet Union, literature is produced in some sixty languages — even more, perhaps. . . . Is sixty languages, is thousands of magazines, is hundreds of thousands of copies of any book, is millions and millions of readers! Is not printing enough copies of any book, so great is the demand! . . . Poetry! Long lines outside the dozens of bookshops the day the edition is coming out! We are honoring your great American writers, Jack London and Mark Twain . . . celebrating just recently sixtieth birthday of your great Ernest Hemingway!

"And in your country?"

Surkov is a man with a mighty voice, a great Russian wind instrument. Its boom effortlessly fills the room, and as he recites literary statistics I get the impression that he is as awed by the sound of his voice as we are. It is a great voice, an authoritative voice, rich and deep — it works with relish on the crunchy Russian consonants. It is the voice of the man born to be the branch chairman, the district organizer. He *knows.*

But he can be genial. When we ask to see Pasternak, he leans over to a colleague and grins — "Now it's out in the open!" — and then turns to us with the remark, "Between Pasternak and ourselves there is, as you might say, a state of peaceful coexistence." He laughs at the abstract paintings he has seen at the American exhibition. Maybe that contorted female depicted in the garden is the American woman! Hah! Hah! He will now imitate an American *avant-garde* painter at work. Closes his eyes, throws paint about. Grins. When we come back to literature, their treatment of Pasternak is up again — and the obvious contrast with our handling of Ezra Pound. Surkov explains that the psychiatrists who originally put Ezra Pound into St. Elizabeth's did so because they were all in sympathy with Pound's Fascist views.

« 3 »

Tea with Ilya Ehrenburg and his wife at his *dacha* in the country. We had heard a good deal about Ehrenburg's "post-Stalin" novel, *The Thaw,* and about two long recent essays, one on Stendhal and the other on Chekhov; the latter has references to the Dreyfus affair which have been interpreted as a partly veiled defense of Pasternak; and Ehrenburg's recorded passion for both Stendhal and Chekhov has been taken as a stand against the crudities of official Soviet realism. On the way over, I remembered that Ehrenburg during the war became the most celebrated of the many Soviet writer-correspondents, and despite Stalin's dislike of Jews, one of his favorite writers. I had heard a good deal, too, about Ehrenburg's wealth — he is said to own a Rembrandt and in his Moscow apartment keeps a notable collection of modern French paintings — and so was rather startled, when we were welcomed at the large and splendid country house, by his lack of teeth.

Wrinkled, clever, haughty, sad face. They say that Ehrenburg has much to be sad about, for it was he who first signalized, with his attacks on "rootless cosmopolitans," the roundup of Jewish intellectuals slain in the madness of Stalin's last days. Ehrenburg is now in his sixties. But how many Ehrenburgs there have been already — the Ehrenburg who once wandered over Russia as a tramp, the Ehrenburg who fled the Revolution, the Ehrenburg who lived so long in Paris, the Ehrenburg who at one time thought of becoming a Benedictine monk, the Ehrenburg who returned to Russia in 1940, the Ehrenburg who is still faithful enough to his origins to speak out against certain well-known literary anti-Semites in Russia.

Which Ehrenburg sits before me now?

Exquisite wooden house, sturdy blond Russian wood, style severe and bracing. Rooms as thick with greenery as a jungle scene by Henri Rousseau. Outside, flowered terraces. There is an unmistakable atmosphere of civilized good living about the Ehrenburgs — cigars from Havana, cognac from Paris, and Madame has so obviously bought her dress in Paris rather than in Moscow that she looks like a visitor from another planet.

Conversation begins a little nervously, however, when my colleague from the *Atlantic Monthly*, taking out a memorandum book to make a note, is startled by a scream from Madame. She has seen her maiden name, Kozintsev, written in the book and now cries out, "Why have you my name written in your book? I ask you, why?" The name is that of a prominent Soviet film director whom we had met in Leningrad, and who turns out to be Madame Ehrenburg's brother. Perplexed by her suspiciousness but fascinated by her English, which she learned in India when her former spouse was attached to the Soviet Embassy.

Meanwhile, Ehrenburg opens up with a sharp attack on the misuse of his recent books in the United States. I've never read *The Thaw*, but he loudly complains that the novel, after being turned down by his publisher, has been brought out by a right-wing house in Chicago, and that the edition includes an anti-Soviet postscript, added by the publisher himself, which puts Ehrenburg in a false position. By his account of the matter, he has been badly used; and we all agree that since the cold war, many of the best Soviet writers have been strikingly absent from the lists of American publishers.

Ehrenburg becomes more and more cordial — perhaps because he is launched on a monologue that will outlast the rainstorm that drives us indoors from the veranda. Fascinating performance. Ehrenburg manages to run down most of his Soviet critics and to establish his popularity with Soviet readers — especially the younger ones. His main point: "Today the grandfathers and the grandsons have more in common than either has with the fathers." Those who grew up with the revolution (like Ehrenburg himself) and those who have come of age since 1945 understand one another far better than they do those who grew up between the wars. (This is a point confirmed in conversations with young Soviet intellectuals, who are now undoubtedly more skeptical and easy than their Stalinist fathers.) Still, it is ironic to hear Ehrenburg belaboring this point, for he is reaping the advantage of survival. He has written from so many different positions, he has survived so many purges, that by now he has caught up with a Russia naturally evolving toward a more sophisticated culture. Actually, he has probably never been an ideological fanatic himself, and in his company, you know that you are not far from the cafés of Paris.

Yet how wily he is! He happens to be the only survivor of the Anti-Fascist Jewish People's Committee, organized after the Nazi invasion to enlist Jewish support for the Soviet war effort — all the other members were shot or disappeared. Apart from distrust of him inspired by his many shifts, Ehrenburg's literary reputation has suffered in recent years; I heard several of the younger writers here complain that his recent novels tend to make a topical point and then to peter out. But no doubt there is some resentment in everything said about him. Whatever his literary limitations, he understandably feels himself a man of the world and thus a cut above the party hacks and trained literary seals who unwearyingly chant the same slogans. Ehrenburg's scorn for the "rank and file" in the Writers' Union* is well known. To us, he pointedly emphasizes the work of some younger poets, and suggests that this turn to poetry is more significant than the novels of "Soviet construction" so much better known abroad. He makes many analogies between literature and painting. And unlike a more solidly talented and relatively uncomplicated realist such as Mikhail Sholokhov — still the most popular novelist in the Soviet Union and probably the best — Ehrenburg finds it necessary to demonstrate his popularity with young people.

This demonstration of the writer's audience is becoming tiresome, both as personal boasting and as a proof of the writer's national standing. "The people" are brought up again and again as the highest audience that a Soviet writer can reach — and as the only possible material for the writer. Soviet writers seem always to be dashing off to new industrial cities being built in Siberia, or staying at home engulfed in thousands of letters, suggestions, and criticisms from their readers.

Dear Ilya Grigorievitch:
We have read your last story, with its description of our cement factory, and want, in a comradely way, to tell you that your portrait of the foreman is lacking in Socialist verisimilitude! With love . . .

This insistence that the writer be constantly in touch with the people, always in tune with the national purpose — this is so dominating that even a foreign visitor finds himself feeling a bit heretical if he talks shop for a moment. Still, it is apparently easier in the Soviet Union than anywhere else in the world for a writer to know if he's made it or not. Like a television star in the United States, a Soviet writer always knows his rating. The people are always right — especially when they write letters!

I wonder if commonplace literature here does not have the role that advertising does with us. The good writers here, like good writers everywhere, probably work on a deeper level; but since the situations are often identical, it is hard, listening to Ehrenburg talk

* At the last Writers' Congress a delegate from Orel said that once there had been only three writers from Orel: Turgenev, Bunin, and Leskov. Now, however, there were seventy-nine members of the Writers' Union from Orel.

about how many letters he gets each week, to suppress thoughts of movie stars, and TV comedians, and other "personalities" equally beloved by the audience. Of course it was not wholly out of vanity that Ehrenburg dwelt so long on his popularity; there has always, in Russia, been a traditional image of the writer as the teacher of the people, a guide to the young. But it is also clear that every bushel of letters received by Ilya Ehrenburg helps to stave off the many grievances against him personally — to say nothing of complaints that his recent novels have been unsatisfactory.

When not engaged in special pleading, Ehrenburg's considerable intelligence has all the famous Russian bluntness. That old Russian alertness to the spiritual weakness of the West has become under Soviet Communism a hard and brilliant instrument of denunciation. Describing a visit by Alberto Moravia, Ehrenburg dwelt mercilessly on the morbidity of Moravia's fiction. (I wonder, however, if Moravia was pompous enough to say, "None of my characters is as intelligent as I am.") Ehrenburg has the easy raconteur's skill of a good journalist, and by the time tea was over I felt that I knew all his best stories. I can't see that these *always* point up the optimism of Soviet civilization and the corresponding demoralization of the West. Ehrenburg quoted his friend Picasso: "I do not search. I find." I believe Picasso does just that. But what is the bearing of this on Ehrenburg's own writings, on the immediate scene around us?

Later, he showed us around his gardens and told us something about the immediate district — Chekhov had practiced here as a young doctor, and across the plain stands the house of the millionaire Morosov, who had been the friend of Chekhov and Gorky and who had supported the underground Bolshevik paper *Iskra*. He eventually committed suicide. Grinning with pleasure at his own mot, Ehrenburg remarked that the history of the Morosovs was the history in brief of Russian capitalism — the grandfather a peasant, the father a magnate, the grandson (Chekhov's friend) a patron of arts. It occurred to me that this seemed to be the case with certain very wealthy American families as well, though perhaps the sympathy with the arts so noticeable in the more recent Guggenheims and Rockefellers did not, as a historical necessity, lead to suicide. Ehrenburg did not want anyone to take him up on this. He had made his joke. One does not discuss social analogies between Russia and America; to do so might make us all a little more forbearing with each other.

On the road back to Moscow, we stopped to see Chekhov's old house. It had been burned by the Nazis, and the ruins have pointedly been left by the Soviet authorities. A bust of Chekhov stands before the charred door.

Pasternak's Wake

[1960]

Boris Pasternak died on May 30. From Moscow, next day, the *New York Herald Tribune* correspondent Tom Lambert revealed that "neither the state-controlled Russian press nor radio has yet reported Mr. Pasternak's death. . . . Relatives, friends and admirers of the kindly and talented writer—he still has many of the latter despite the official attitude here toward him—will gather at his house Thursday afternoon for the traditional Russian Orthodox 'Panikhida' (farewell to the dead) service. . . ."

One of the first friends to call, the correspondent continued, was "Konstantin Paustovsky, a writer who was Mr. Pasternak's supporter even when Moscow's Communist Party-directed writers were baying his deportation abroad and the then chieftain of the Young Communist League was likening the great writer to a pig."

I had never heard of Konstantin Paustovsky until I went to the Soviet Union last August with an American literary delegation to meet Soviet writers. In the plane going over I read up on the speeches that had been made at the recent Soviet Writers' Congress, and was staggered to come across Paustovsky's hard, clear, contemptuous remarks on Soviet literary timeservers. Most literary pronouncements in the Soviet Union, as I was to discover even in personal meetings with lesser writers, are composed in an officially correct and fawningly patriotic style that seems designed to avoid saying anything dangerous. No wonder that at the congress Khrushchev admitted his boredom with Soviet literature and contemptuously told the writers not to take their "squabbles" (like the Pasternak case?) to him.

Paustovsky's speech at the congress was about "Ideas — Disputable and Indisputable." Since it is always in order in the Soviet Union for a writer to write up a new tractor works in Sverdlovsk as if the news story put him "in touch with every heartbeat of our people," he began by saying that a writer never fools his readers, and that they can tell instantly whether he is writing from "pureness of thought or, on the contrary, timeserving adaptation, [from] breadth of horizon or a sinister paucity of ideas . . ." The writer, he went on, gets from the people the appreciation he deserves. "All literary people and critics who take on themselves the right to speak in the name of the people should keep this in mind. . . .

"We are lucky that Leo Tolstoy managed to write *Anna Karenina* before [the current] tradition appeared. He did not have to make a bow to anyone, even the publisher; he could allow Anna to break up her family and pass out of life from purely private, and consequently impermissible, considerations.

"It is not our custom to write of [Soviet] shortcomings . . . without making in advance an apologetic bow and bringing to mind our achievements. . . . One might think that one had to drive home to every Soviet reader the advantages and superiority of our system to the capitalist system — in the forty-second year of the revolution, mind you!

"There is nothing so cruelly affronting as hypocrisy in a writer. . . . Why do we tolerate . . . bureaucratic and Philistine language? . . . Language is being turned into a bureaucratic jargon from top to bottom, beginning with the newspapers . . . and ending with every minute of our ordinary everyday life."

These are the words of a faithful, decent person — not a great writer, I gather, probably not anywhere so accomplished and subtle a writer as Pasternak was in his greatest poems, but at the same time a less complicated, more open, and exuberantly generous nature. Paustovsky is actually cherished in the Soviet Union for his charm, and the same lady official of the Writers' Union who told me out of a blue sky that Pasternak was "awful" pressed on me an English translation of Paustovsky's literary autobiography, *The Golden Rose*.

Paustovsky is a descendant of Ukrainian Cossacks, and after early schooling in Kiev worked as a laborer, sailor, and reporter, then fought in the civil war. He has tramped all over Russia, and in his almost sentimental ardor for the Russian land, and in his loyalty to early associations, his book reminds me a little of Gorky's marvelous reminiscences of his life in the lower depths, *My University Days*. Paustovsky tends to be an impulsive, rambling writer, but his respect for the private human experience, for genuine feeling of any kind as opposed to official orthodoxy, is unmistakable.

One of his most charming stories is called "Loaf Sugar." A strange old man, a wanderer who has taken refuge for the night in a farmhouse far to the north, is asked to show his papers by a fat little bureaucrat carrying "a shabby briefcase . . . stuffed with reports and accounts." When the old man explains that he has papers "but they weren't written for you, dear man," the bureaucrat calls in a militiaman. The old man tells the story of *his* grandfather, whose famous singing voice the poet Pushkin loved so much that when Pushkin was killed in a duel, the grandfather sang over his coffin, in the freezing cold, until he lost his voice forever. His illiterate grandson, the old man of the story, goes about collecting folk songs and tales. The militiaman is so moved by the story that he presents some sugar for the old man's tea. "Ah, the pity of it," the old man says. "There's nothing worse than for a man to have an arid soul. Those kind of people make life wither as grass withers from the autumn dew."

Paustovsky's generous act of homage to Pasternak is liberating. It reminds me of the traditional respect that the great Russian writers and thinkers have always known how to show each other despite intense differences of opinion. (Paustovsky is unmistakably more in sympathy with the October Revolution than Pasternak was.) Paustovsky's gesture reminds me of the dying Turgenev writing to Tolstoy after years of estrangement: "I am writing to you particularly to tell you how glad I am to have been your contemporary." He calls up Gorky's unforgettable tribute to Tolstoy: "I am not an orphan on earth so long as this man lives on it." Even Lenin, the author of the system that finally outdid itself in calumniating, blackmailing, and isolating one introverted, highly literary symbolist poet, knew how to pay proper tribute to his Menshevik opponent Martov. As the old man in Paustovsky's story sang over Pushkin's body in the freezing cold until he lost his voice, so Pasternak was among the first to rush to Mayakovsky's flat when the poet committed suicide in 1930. So, in the steady Russian cold, many a Russian poet, many a Russian reader of poetry would, if he could, mourn over Pasternak today.

« 2 »

In Russia last summer, it was not the American visitors but the Russians who kept bringing up Pasternak. Every time they abused him in public, they would look around at each other as if to make sure that they were reciting their lessons well. The talented novelist Pavel Nilin gratuitously, at a public reception, told us not to be misled by the example of *Mister* Pasternak. The old Stalinist boss of the Writers' Union, Alexis Surkov, ranted that Pasternak had betrayed him personally by publishing *Doctor Zhivago*, and that the great aim of *his* life was now to write an "Anti-Zhivago." Even the charming and urbane novelist Konstantin Fedin, who had been made first secretary of the Writers' Union to replace the impossible Surkov, had to denounce the "traitor" during the campaign against Pasternak. Pasternak was Fedin's neighbor in Peredelkino. Last summer, four American writers had dinner with Fedin at his *dacha*, and we talked of many things. But Pasternak, who lived so near, was not mentioned. He could not be mentioned. Officially, Boris Pasternak was already dead.

At Ease in Zion

[1960]

ALFRED NORTH WHITEHEAD, that singularly clear mind, observed that even in Jesus's evasive "Render therefore unto Caesar the things which are Caesar's," one sees that the Jews had no independent state to govern; "the absence of such responsibility has been a characteristic of the Jews for centuries. That is one reason for their unpopularity."

We are certainly more "popular" now — especially with ourselves. I came here in the plane of the Jewish state; under the great blue-and-white shield of David I rode the skies from New York to Paris to Rome to Athens to Lydda; and though even at twenty thousand feet some details, like the boiled chicken at dinnertime, are all too familiar, "responsibility" puts them into a new setting and gives them a new look — as witness the immigration inspector at Lydda airport who, in the exact duplicate of a British officer's uniform and a British officer's handlebar mustaches, makes little cracks in Yiddish to relieve the impatient, baggage-laden and weary crowd. Even the local bobby-soxers running and squealing after Harry Belafonte in the slightly too posh hotel complete with pool remind one that Israel is now an established center of international show business — while Helena Rubinstein's splendid museum assures us that here, too, we have the *haute couture* of modern art. The blissful normality of *La Dolce Vita* in Hebrew! The established international hotel style that serves as well in Tel Aviv as in Caracas and Omaha! No wonder that Shimon V., the burly taxi-driver outside our hotel who looks and talks like a barrel-chested Lancashire trade-union secretary, boasts to us that he never gets a foreign visitor into his cab without working on him to settle in Israel. He rides us around Tel Aviv shouting, roaring and boasting about his conquests of Canadian businessmen in a tone that plainly says: "*I* am at home and *I* am normal! *We* are at home here and *we* are all normal! I am the most normal taxi-driver in Israel, and Israel is the only place for normal people!"

Smiling and at ease in Zion, Dr. Kaplan, head of the new, not yet opened museum of antiquities in Jaffa, shows us around the first proud exhibits in what was once a Turkish prison. The squat pillars and high grated windows in this great vault must once have been as ominously full of shadows as one of Piranesi's prisons. But now the gleaming whitewashed walls bear neat museum placards identifying the friable clumps of earth and potsherds that can still be traced to ancient Israel. What meticulous and exhausting effort, what delicacy of touch and obstinate resolution to keep these shards and brown clusters of earth from crumbling back into the anonymity of earth! Dr. Kaplan reads out the old Aramaic, Greek and Latin inscriptions left in the stones, pillars and roads. Starting from the bottom of recorded time, he reads his way up the ladder of Israel from Biblical times to the present. For though the present is of course not exhibited in this museum of antiquities, it is Israel today that has crowned and sealed the past as leading up to the state of Israel. And as we stand in what was once a Turkish prison and is now a museum, the obstinate Jewish insistence that history does have a design and purpose would seem to be confirmed by the fact that we are here, looking at the relics of ancient Israel dug out of the local soil. But Dr. Kaplan, charming and delicate-spoken man, is too absorbed digging up ruins and deciphering monuments to draw a moral and point a conclusion; he is preoccupied with the white lettering in the dim stone recovered with such effort from the earth. And closing shop to go home to lunch in his rattly old car, he points with his ignition key to the cellar below the museum, where through the grated window just above the ground we can see old people, on a special reclamation project, weaving cane seats for chairs.

« 2 »

Jaffa, ancient Joppa, is now only a borough of Tel Aviv, and though there are fewer Arabs around than there must have been, the hovels built into the rock overlooking the Mediterranean are still plainly Arab. The old Arab quarter is a mass of ruins; "we had to blow up the houses because they were in a state of collapse and unsafe," the guide from the municipality gravely tells us, and gravely we look at each other. There can be no doubt that being in power eliminates many a doubt and a shudder. But my pleasure at finding so much normality in Israel is considerably enhanced as we make our way past a Moroccan whore with a Jewish star around her neck, who is, the guide reluctantly admits, discussing last night's business with her greasy colleagues. The guide blushes but gamely translates to the end, adding the wistful comment that these "new elements" have brought Israel its first experience of prostitution. My constant sense in Israel that the rungs of history are still plainly marked in the stone comes back to me now as we go up and up the narrow winding staircases from the harbor. It was from somewhere below that poor old Jonah set sail for Tarshish. At each landing here, Jewish history gets a millennium more sophisticated. Consider that at the bottom, at the old harbor that was Joppa, poor Jonah slunk aboard the ship from which he was to be flung overboard into the belly of the great fish, while the landing above already has immoral Oriental bazaars openly trafficking in flesh, and above *that* is a vaguely beatnik night club, and above *that* the studio of a German-born sculptor who works in abstract forms! These little cubicles built into the rock remind me of a Roman tenement, they are so deeply wedged into each other, and the landings are full of the unending babble of people crowding into the open. But despite the cactus plants on the landings, the faintest possible tang of lemon and eucalyptus in the air, despite the shining blue Mediterranean everywhere in front of our faces, there is not a hint of the *dolce far niente,* or *das Land wo die Zitronen blühn.* The Arabs themselves look too much of the earth to be epicurean about it — their faces are the color of earth and look as neutral as earth. The Jews, of course, are not here to moon over the landscape; they are absorbed in higher things, crucial affairs of state, the everlasting life-and-death questions. So that even when I suddenly see cypresses on far-off hilltops and for a moment remember the Tuscan countryside, the white ashy powder left in the ruins of exploded houses and the sour smell of the rotting stone bring me back to where I am. You do not "relax" in Jaffa, you do not "enjoy" — the debris of time itself in this country (to say nothing of war and continued bitterness), the soft continuous breaking-up of the stone into dust, are as obvious today as they were to Herman Melville in Palestine a century ago when he found that the Hebrew inscriptions on the tumbled heaped-up graves "can hardly be distinguished from the wrinkles formed by time." How old everything is in this land, and how unsparingly time itself stares us down from the wrinkled and jagged rock suddenly rising out of the sand.

‹ 3 ›

Shraga Friedman of the Habimah players, driving us out to lunch in Herzlia with other members of the troupe, purrs over his new little car, his patrician-looking beautiful blonde wife, his American guests, the gleaming seaside road to Herzlia. He has only recently learned to drive, and in this, as in other things, he is a new man, a Polish brand saved from the burning. He is alive and happy, he has worked his way across the world to Israel and up from the Habimah school to its regular troupe, with which he now tours every *moshav* and kibbutz in the country. As we sit at lunch, Shraga beams like the Sabbath. There is nothing stagey about him at all; with his round and plump bridegroom's smile, he could be anything but an actor, and his easiness and staidness remind me more of certain bashful Jewish mathematicians than of the actors I have known. Even the two older and well-known members of the troupe, Shimon Finkel and Aharon Meskin, look like the "quiet" uncles from out-of-town at the wedding feast. These are actors? Meskin, who had been waiting a bit too long in the lobby for us to arrive in Herzlia, smilingly admits that he's not too hungry — "Took a little something at the house" — while Finkel, whom I remember so well in the great Habimah production of *The Dybbuk*, reveals only in the quick observant turns of his eye the professional attention to gesture, the swift and mobile body which I remember from his slidings and cavortings around the stage in *The Dybbuk*. The Habimah is getting on — the old Habimah players are — and there is a placid hands-in-lap contentment about these prime actors that makes our pleasant lunch in the new hotel by the wide-shining sea, in the town named after the patron saint of Zionism, rather stiffer than I had expected of actors. It is all very pleasant, and just the faintest bit too formal — for though we *are* the "kinsmen," so to speak, from the other side, we haven't, after all, seen each other before, and as on all such visits, the family news is quickly exhausted. But as we get up from the table, Shimon Finkel comes up to me and, proud to have just received it, shows me a letter from Gordon Craig enclosing a new photograph of the famous old theater director and designer. Gordon Craig is now eighty-eight years old, and in his long seclusion in Corbeil, in Southern France, has been engaged in re-editing his works and in writing his memoirs. Off there in France, surveying the greatest theatrical experiences of his life, the famous son of Ellen Terry, the theatrical mystic *par excellence*, feels suddenly linked to Shimon Finkel in far-off Israel and has to tell him so — for of course the Habimah was one of the gratifying moments in his long and often bitter career.

And now Shimon Finkel has really something to talk to me about!

No longer the slightly bored Jewish uncle dragged out to sit with company, he is the passionate man of the theater, and as he talks about Craig, his eyes light up, his fingers start to mold a half-remembered figure out of the past. Though he shrugs his shoulders as he recounts examples of Craig's well-known intransigence—after all, this is the visionary who gave up the theater as impossible, the absolutist of theater who said that "the *real* theater, the theater which is an art in its own right like music and architecture, is yet to be discovered and may not come for several generations"—you can see how touched and pleased Finkel is to have had this message from the still exalted theater name that is synonymous with experiment and the international art-crusade of the past.

« 4 »

Of all things to pick up again in Israel—Kafka's *Letters to Milena.* It was to this great love of his earlier life, to this extraordinary Czech patrician who long after Kafka's death was to be a prisoner and to save so many lives in Auschwitz, that Kafka once wrote: "In the evening I talked to a Palestinian Jew. I believe it's impossible in a letter to make you understand his importance to me—a small, almost tiny, weak, bearded one-eyed man. But the memory of him has cost me half the night." After all, as Kafka said on another occasion, "It is not necessary to fly right into the middle of the sun, but just to crawl to some clean spot on the earth on which the sun sometimes shines and where one can warm oneself a little." Kafka lived in a mental dungeon inside a ghetto that was inside the maze of ancient, crazy, doomed Prague—but from the dungeon that was his neurosis as well as his genius, from the Prague where the Jews of modern times could no longer call up the Golem to help them, he asked just to crawl to a bit of sun and warm himself a little. The prophets of modern Israel, I venture to think, are not just the Zionist statesmen and the socialist statemakers, but also those artists and originals, like Kafka, who had in the endless exile of their own minds become small, almost tiny, weak, one-eyed men. They dreamed of the sun—and here is the sun. From my window overlooking the sea at Herzlia, where in the golden light the last swimmers are slowly coming in, shrugging the light-beaded drops of water from their shoulders, I seem to see not the usual health club but Kafka and Babel, Modigliani and Rosa Luxemburg — all those Jews of whom Khrushchev has complained that "They are all individualists and all intellectuals. They want to talk about everything, they want to discuss everything, they want to debate everything — and they come to totally different conclusions!" And — bent, one-eyed, tiny — they hear the new state of Israel: "Come to us and be happy at last."

Last night we were seated after dinner on the terrace of the hotel. X., of the Foreign Office, who had come out with flowers, rippled along in that standard British accent which among Israel diplomats tends, like a waxed but defective Daimler, to stop short at the oddest moments. X. is a handsome fellow, accustomed to please, and purred along just splendidly until he came to the subject of the American poet, freshly divorced, who on his visit to Israel got off the plane complaining about his ex-spouse, and went from Dan to Elath telling everyone about his sufferings! X. was honestly shocked at so much raw American self-concern. To arrive in the Promised Land and talk only "personal problems"! It smacks of the vanities and fleshpots of the Diaspora. Sitting on this elegant terrace overlooking the sea and sipping cool drinks (the lights kept going out every five minutes, and our hosts groaned and apologized at each lapse as if the national honor were at stake), I could not help thinking that although all the literary people I've met in Israel admire the American writer and wistfully add that they've no one quite so brashly imaginative and wildly intelligent, he would never make it here. The anarchic force of his personality is just too strong and cuts through all the life lines of cousinship thrown out by the friendly new state. Yet just as Kafka's sisters live, or have lived, in Israel on the world-wide royalties accruing to his work, so I believe that eventually many people in Israel may live on the gifted and extreme individualists who have never seen Israel or who would never live here.

« 5 »

At Caesarea, along the Mediterranean, there is a fisherman's kibbutz. There are remains along the shore of a Crusaders' fort — and just outside these empty stone shells I saw some students from Ghana and young kibbutzniks taking turns riding a white horse. In the harbor, just outside the remains of the old seawall and staircases, there rode at anchor the yacht of a wealthy scientist who has been digging for the treasures left in shipwrecked Roman ships. Farther inland, deadly quiet among the sands, is a new excavation site where has been uncovered a Roman mosaic floor and several headless but regal statues. The deep quiet of the ancient past is absolutely uninterruptable here: even the minute rustling of grass in the hot wind adds to the intensity of a silence here which is more than the absence of sound. What unexpected ruins these are — where the very chalk letters on the walls of the fort, unless I am mistaken, say *Ben-Ari loves Miriam,* and where, though the rubbish in the corners of these deserted shells lets out the same sour smell of damp stone, these students from Africa wait to ride the kibbutz's white horse! None of the boys, not even the local girls, bother with a saddle; and, as they plod along the sandy ruts of the beach, the colors of the sea and the colors of the rigging on the ship and the intense, almost blue blackness of the Ghana students on the white horse raise hot new colors against our eyes.

« 6 »

To be a small country these days is to be at last in the center of things! At the Hias hostel in Beersheba, I was struck by the group of young French engineers, in army shirts and chino pants, who were knee-deep in charts and blueprints, and I was touched to see, in the restaurant attached to the hostel, Walter Lowdermilk, the famous soil conservationist — who though past seventy and with so much work behind him in Israel, likes, I hear, to "hang around" still. I have been fascinated by the fluent international gossip of Israeli officials, who may change from Epstein to names more Canaanite-sounding, but who can now reel off for you the exact mistakes American diplomacy has made in the Congo and give you the lowdown on the damnedest things in the Soviet Union. On the top level, at least, it is obvious that to be in charge of a small country intensely ambitious for technical development is to acquire a fabulous range of information.

Surely not much of this sophistication gets down to the mass of new arrivals in their special housing areas. But it seems to me that this inevitable division in small "backward" countries between the administrative elite and the submerged mass points up in Israel the traditional gulf between the patriarchs and prophets — who with their special vision feel that they have been chosen by God and are answerable to God — and the poor old children of Israel, who trudge grumblingly through the desert, from time to time are taken with false gods, and have always to be brought back sternly to the business of reaching the Promised Land — under the gifted leaders who are irascible with their charges, weary to death of these masses, but who have sworn to God to Finish The Job.

Shortly after the war I met on shipboard a relative-by-marriage of Chaim Weizmann's; his sense of personal superiority, especially on the subject of the Jews, startled and fascinated me; I guessed that it was borrowed. His pompousness was of the kind that you often find among dull men with advanced degrees, but his sense of irony about the Jews, coming from such a source, interested me. His conceit could not have been all his own; it must have reflected a more complex position, for he made you feel that he was reluctantly committed to "this peculiar people to whom we happen to belong." And in Israel I have come to understand why, of all the famous Zionist leaders past and present, only Chaim Weizmann has deeply interested me. For Weizmann, so gifted as a scientist and as a man who could charm even the British Foreign Office, evidently felt that like the infant Samuel he was pledged to the Jewish people. But just as Freud, so much more self-centered and less attractive a human being, sought to enlighten the humanity that he distrusted, so Weizmann, moving on the highest echelons of modern science and diplomacy, sought to raise up a people whom he often despaired of.

Weizmann is supposed once to have complained to Vladimir Jabotinsky that the Jewish masses were "the dust of the earth." And though Jabotinsky replied with moving appropriateness that "God made man out of the dust of the earth," it is obvious from many accounts of his personality that Weizmann, that first-class mind among Zionist leaders, felt that he had to stoop to the dust. At the Weizmann Institute in Rehovoth, where so many of Weizmann's relics and personal papers are exhibited, you can see how he longed for quieter pursuits but steadily pressed on, through the fifty years in the desert of Zionist congresses and of courting the English that it took to realize the Jewish state. Of course Weizmann loved the Jews; all his manifest charm and humor reflect his emotional participation in their lives. But, more than the Jews, he loved the Jew: the Jew's historic destiny, the Jew's idea of the Promised Land, the Jew's idea of himself as creatively and morally the advance guard of humanity. So it was Chaim Weizmann's duty, as a scientist and national leader, to guide and instruct and reproach those whom God had chosen. It was the sacrifice of himself that he gloomily expected in the new state. But greater than the state was the historic promise and its task, and greater than the presidency of the state was his place among all the Jewish patriarchs who have guided the "children" to their appointed place. In his ironic and unceremonial way, this organic chemist was more consciously a believer in Providence than many a ritualist in the synagogue. But just as the patriarchs dwelt apart, so it was from the silken recesses of the Dorchester in London that Weizmann looked down to the trade-union activists who were actually making the new state. "What a bound*er!*" he is supposed to have complained of one cabinet minister.

In Weizmann's private study at the Institute, there are just two photographs on his desk. One is of Fritz Haber, who won the Nobel Prize for chemistry in 1918, was head of the Kaiser Wilhelm Institute, and invented the famous Haber process for converting atmospheric nitrogen into ammonia and nitric acid that was so important to Germany in the First World War. The other photograph is of Richard Wilstaetter, who won the Nobel Prize for chemistry in 1915. Both were Jews who occupied the highest scientific posts in Germany and were thrown out by Hitler; both were constantly beseeched by Weizmann to settle in Palestine, and both died in Switzerland — Haber was actually on his way to Palestine when he died.

These were Weizmann's particular admirations — and both these German Jews, so gifted, so dedicated to science and to Germany, so reluctant to embrace Weizmann's Zionism, must have seemed to Weizmann particular examples of the fate of intellect in mass society. For of course Weizmann found himself a mere figurehead of the new state, not consulted and not needed. And by contrast, it is surely for Ben-Gurion's shrewdness and toughness, not for his pretentious and unreadable efforts to play the intellectual leader, that the prime minister of Israel is actually admired.

I would guess, from such interviews as I have had with the new Israeli administrative and scientific elite, that they have Weizmann's proud sense of *expertise* — and of course Weizmann's passionate sense of duty to the people — without Weizmann's mystic sense of Jewish destiny or of the leader as necessarily lonely in his prophetic role. At the Weizmann Institute I picked up an account of Weizmann's last days, significantly entitled *Hollow Glory*, by the Israeli newspaperman Samuel Shihor.* It is extraordinary to read Weizmann's recorded observations to Meyer Weisgal: the dying man, speaking in his first language, in the Yiddish of the East European Jews, talked of the Jews with the bitterness of a father who has tested his sons and found them not altogether satisfactory. "My greatest difficulty in lying here in this helpless condition is to watch and see all the mistakes that are being made in this country. . . . The Jews are a small people, a very small people . . . but also a great people. An ugly people, but also a beautiful people, a people that builds and destroys. [A] People of genius, and at the same time, a people of enormous stupidity. . . . We can do a fine thing, a very fine thing, which can become an honor to ourselves and to the whole of mankind. But we must not turn it into an ugly thing. Because we are an impulsive people we mess things up and often we destroy that which has taken generations to build up. . ." He does not flatter the Jews! He judges them as severely as did the prophets, who saw in them the instrument of the divine purpose. Weizmann, who gave his life to the Jews, obviously felt, chemist and skeptic as he was, that he too spoke for God — that is, for the truth.

Where in this new Israel that Weizmann could be "president" of, but could no longer influence, is the leader with his kind of moral imagination — devoted to the vision of man's necessary future, not to just another national cause? Perhaps the times make it impossible. For the future is already here; everything predicted in purely material and external terms is clearly on its way. But it is ex-

* Translated from the Hebrew by Julian L. Meltzer. New York: Thomas Yoseloff.

actly this unexpected realization of *all* the national causes and material hopes that makes the world so strange to Jews; Israel is now just another small country. Israel was re-established, but not until the cruelest and most apocalyptic pagan dreams of revenge against the Jews had been realized in the gas chambers. The Yemenites in great airplanes have returned to the Holy Land "on the wings of silver eagles," exactly as was prophesied in scripture. But the Mohammedan prophecies are also being fulfilled, of a great new power for the descendants of Ishmael — while in Russia even old believers have found that the Communist theology has made their dreams for Russia come true. Soon each country in Asia and Africa and Latin America will have its Promised Land, its seat in the U. N., and its own atom bomb. No wonder that in this age of redemption, amid the strange and literal fulfillment of so many ancient hopes and prophecies, it is hard not to sympathize with those who, unlike the great men who merely dreamed the future, now have to live in it. The unregenerate nineteenth-century prophets are now quite superfluous, but, among the practical people running things, one looks for those who represent a more humane age without trying artificially to recapture it.

« 7 »

One of the most interesting people I have met here is Zalman Aranne, the former Minister of Education, and thus predecessor to Abba Eban. Aranne's accent is Russian, not Yiddish, and he *looks* Russian; in his stiff double-breasted suit and the rather stiff lecture, over fruit and soft drinks in his Jerusalem apartment, when he explained Israeli schools to us, he retains the pedagogical Russian manner. Only a Russian could look so solemn while sipping a soft lemon drink through a straw; and, at first, listening to Aranne on the educational problems of his country, I worried: was there an exam in this course? There was a charming young Sephardic Jew from Greece with him, a former assistant in the ministry, who would gracefully help out with a word whenever Aranne's English bogged down. The contrast between the ease of the assistant and the sternness of his old superior made me recall Matthew Arnold's lesson of the Hellenes and the Hebrews — except that this Hellene was a Hebrew and this particular Hebrew very much a Russian! I was interested to hear of Aranne's talks with visiting Soviet personalities — among them a group of sailors off a merchant vessel, and a diplomat who noted icily that Israel spent in proportion far more on schoolchildren than the Soviets did. Aranne, who as a democratic Socialist during the Provisional Government had enjoyed "the one period of absolute cultural freedom that the Russians have ever known," decided, with the increasing repression of the early 1920s, to leave for Palestine. He crossed the border in deep winter, wearing white to camouflage himself in the snow; at one point, twisting and hiding in the woods, he found himself eating an apple and laughing with joy as he said out loud to himself in the woods: "I'm going to *Eretz Yisroel!*" When he finally got there, he worked as a laborer on the Haifa docks; then, gradually making his way up to the inner circles in the Histadruth and Mapam, eventually joined the cabinet as Minister of Education. I've heard, without being able to check it, that Aranne left this ministry to make room for Abba Eban's entry into Israeli politics. No doubt, as the pioneer generation of Russian-born Israeli leaders yields to the young sabras and the standard British accents, someone like Zalman Aranne will perhaps seem almost as old-fashioned in Jerusalem as he is in New York, and was long ago in Moscow.

But how the world will miss these fiery old Jews — and how I will miss them! Far from being the stiffly creaking Russian academic that at first I feared he might be, Aranne turned out to be the most intensely eager intellectual that I found in official circles. Our first meeting wasn't enough; we had to go on with it next day at dinner at the King David. In the great dining room I naturally looked around for British officers carrying swagger sticks and Sternists with bombs under their Arab cloaks; but Otto Preminger had hired them all to make *Exodus,* and all I could see was Miami Beach, complete to the mink stoles in the Near Eastern night. The only exception was a church group, just in from Jordan no doubt and on their way to Egypt, the lucky Methodists!

Aranne at dinner ignored them all; he even ignored the dinner, to the intense mortification of the headwaiter, who in his stiff shirt and swallow-tail coat may have to bring out boiled chicken, but does it with an air. Aranne looked at the mounting dishes with the most intense distraction in his noble eyes, and, pushing everything away, implored us to send our children to Israel, not to cut ourselves off from the new, struggling, beleaguered Jewish state. He was interested in us; we were a brand *he* wanted to save from the burning. Naturally a Jew brought up in the old Russia thinks that his very survival depends on a Jewish homeland, and views with mistrust our old-fashioned and obstinate hope that the lion and the lamb may yet lie down together in our part of the world. But it is not a self-righteous patriotism that drives Zalman Aranne. He told us that one night during the "war of liberation," when the siege of Jerusalem was at its worst, he saw a soldier coming off duty and stumbling with fatigue down the streets. The soldier was loaded with tommy gun, hand grenades, bayonet, trench knife; he must have looked like a walking arsenal. Suddenly, to Aranne's amusement, there walked past the soldier an old, bearded, ultra-orthodox Jew, probably from the Mea Shearim "quarter of fanatics," dressed in white stockings, caftan, and shiny furred hat. Many Israelis were shocked and disgusted by the refusal of these fanatically pious Jews to support the new state. And Aranne was annoyed to see the orthodox Jew suddenly stop in front of the exhausted soldier and look him over from head to toe in the most condescending way. Then the old Jew said savagely and bitterly, dancing around the poor soldier in his rage: "*You're* the Messiah? You?"

VII

Freud and His Consequences

Sigmund Freud, 1856-1956: Portrait of a Hero

THE FRONTISPIECE to Volume II of Ernest Jones's biography of him shows Freud in 1906, age fifty. With his arms militantly folded across his chest, the everlasting cigar in one hand, only one somber eye visible in this profile of his tensely reflective face, he sits for the photographer with such immense conscious self-possession that it is impossible not to see this calm but vibrant look of mastery as the goal of Freud's maturity and the manifestation of his intellectual authority. This, we say to ourselves out of the midst of Jones's almost thousand pages on Freud—this is what has persuaded so many who do not believe his science; this is the face of the founder, the father of his subject and the father in spirit to so many of his disciples; this is the face not of the pleasure principle but of transcendent consciousness; this is the man who in his dreams identified himself with Joseph, in his writings with Moses. This is the look that wins respect for the Jews and the deepest resentment—for this man lived apart from the greater world around him, and yet claimed to understand everything inside it. This is the look which I, living all my life among the Freudians, the disciples, have never seen in the flesh. For this is the face of a great man—a man who taught us not only to see, but, as he said, to "tolerate a piece of reality." This man transformed our sense of things. He is the only *kind* of man that ever works magic in our lives. By devotion to his task, he becomes the most aloof of men—the hero.

Ordinarily, the early life of a hero is not really significant. For what counts with him is not, as with us, the search for "maturity," for "integration," but the tales of his mastery over the secret and the forbidden, the recital of his ability to make nature yield up its secrets. The early struggles of the hero may have a purely dramatic element. For we who know what he must become can still watch with suspense as a Freud discovers cocaine and does not develop his

The Life and Work of Sigmund Freud, by Ernest Jones. New York: Basic Books.

discovery, or comes to the verge of discovering the neurone without fully realizing it. His destiny lies elsewhere, and generally these early struggles are decisive only as they lead to the discovery of his true vocation. But in a man like Freud, whose interest so peculiarly was the self, and who even formally documented his science from his own dreams and self-analysis, this early period becomes the very material which the hero will rework into the fully forged personality he needs for his appointed work. For this reason the intensely Jewish background of Freud did not, as critics of psychoanalysis often say, simply act to limit his knowledge to idle repressed ladies of the Jewish bourgeoisie in Vienna; it served (a Jewish background often does this for certain thinkers) as a microcosm of the world, a guide to that larger reality in which he did not share. Such confidence may not be valid. The point is that a Jew can think that it is, if he sees an essential unifying principle of identity running through human experience. The very mark of Freud's ability to speculate so largely on the basis of what would seem very restricted evidence is, indeed, a measure of his ability not merely to come to terms with himself — to suffer so many early anxieties and to rise above them — but to *use* these disabilities as a guide to the elucidation of many larger problems.

This, for me, is the fascination of Jones's first volume. And it is a measure of the unforced but remarkable artistic tact of Freud's biographer that even the second volume, which carries us to Freud in his sixties, should close so beautifully, like a musical *da capo*, on those probable childhood musings by the little Freud about his complicated family situation, which, Jones thinks, explains Freud's passion for the truth and his aggressive independence in seeking it out.

This link between early sexual curiosity and the passion for knowledge is, of course, standard Freudian doctrine. Freud applied it to the scientific side of Leonardo da Vinci, and Jones centers Freud's curiosity, finally, on his need to ferret out the truth about his half-brother Philipp, who was so much older and given to "joking" about the difference in their ages that he could be thought of as the mate of Freud's own mother. As Jones speculatively works it out, the little Freud thought that Philipp "evidently knew all the secrets," but that he could not be trusted to tell the truth about them. And so perhaps it was "this insignificant little man," Jones surmises, who "through his mere existence . . . fortuitously struck the spark that lit the future Freud's determination to trust himself alone, to resist the impulses to believe in others more than in himself. . . ." This explanation of Freud's inquisitive genius is something that one may be permitted to doubt in favor of the intrinsic gift of curiosity itself. And yet the decisive fact in Jones's account is exactly Freud's confidence that in his own situation he could find the nucleus of reality.

This kind of confidence reminds one of Thoreau's saying that a poet learns to watch his own moods as narrowly as a cat. It displays that gift for being convinced of the significance of one's experiences that seems to me the essence of being an artist. But this confidence may also signify that spiritual ability to generalize on the basis of restricted experiences which seems to be an essential of Jewish consciousness. Nothing is so astonishing in the history of the Jews as this disparity between their history of exile, of marginal existence, of worldly inexperience in the ghetto — which by contrast with Western civilization looks like a long sleep — and their belief that reality is consistent, all of one piece. Where *they* are is perspective enough on the "world," on the world's great, and on the issues of heaven and earth. Indeed, one might even say that one can measure the degree of originality one finds among Jewish intellectuals by this ability to trust themselves. Where this faith in the essential correspondence between themselves and the world is at once intense and yet clouded by self-doubt, as in Kafka, the effect in their work is significantly morbid even when the achievement is very great.

Now Freud would have assented to this "gift of conviction," as I call it, but would have located it not in the Jewish genius but in the scientific conviction of the biological identity of mankind. The mechanistic school of physiology in which he was trained under Brücke was the school that supplanted Schelling's romantic view of nature and established, in a succession of vital discoveries, basic examples of cause-and-effect in the body. Indeed, Freud was so wedded to positivism that in the absence of any empirical evidence he had to pronounce God an "illusion." But in point of fact this kind of empirical evidence is not always present in psychoanalysis either, for even where certain "confirmations" exist, they lie under the suspicion of being culturally instigated by psychoanalysis itself. The "proofs" that Freud found for his theories lay not so much in evidence — for some *part* of this evidence, by the very nature of the material, must always be beyond proof — *but in his way of reasoning solidly about material which only he could see.* It is precisely this enormous honesty and carefulness that make so curiously impressive a book like *Moses and Monotheism,* which is not merely unfounded on evidence, but at times preposterous because of Freud's suggestion that he may be just about to find evidence at any minute. Yet the book is anything but preposterous; indeed, it is strangely persuasive. The basis of this, I submit, is the wholly sane, orderly, scientific way in which Freud reasons, and which is so compelling in Freud's work that he convinces us of the reality of what he is discussing. When you look back, you can see that this air of leading us step by step to the truth, of considering all possible objections, is not always justified, for Freud often merely appears to consider objections. But the point is that Freud had an honest persuasion and that once he saw his subject, he opened up its possibilities honestly. Not everyone who is wedded to positivistic explanations has an instinct for the unexplored, and people who go in for Freud's kind of material rarely bother to reason at all. But he had the kind of mind that has both an instinct for the reality behind phenomena and a moral determination to find a cause for everything. And it is no accident that in him the wish for fame represents not only a hunger for success but a desire to find a reputation that will express the immense role he had to play.

Now this kind of mind, I feel, represents in Freud the Jewish belief in the essential logic of human experience, and it is this, as I see it, that enabled Freud to seize with such *conviction* — the essential mark of genius — on the basis of his early childhood experiences. Freud, by attributing inquisitiveness in general to early sexual curiosity, tended, if anything, to make this principle too hard-and-fast. For all biological explanations of human curiosity are too general to account for a Leonardo, a Newton, an Einstein, a Freud. But the sense of the presence of larger things within the restricted family circle, of things which we dare not think are real but which *are* real to us — this seems to me the essence of Freud's early struggles to accept his gift of divination. The drama, then, is not that Freud was eager for fame because he was "insecure," as so many people who in our age recognize only the "integrated," "well-organized" personality seem to feel, when they express their *surprise* that the great man had so many anxieties. Freud was indeed eager for fame, so much so that he was always looking for solutions in different fields that would make his name. (In the golden era of positivism, all subjects seemed to be laid out, so that it seemed that only keys were needed to the various locks; Freud characteristically inaugurated a new *field.*) The point about his early discoveries and near-discoveries, surely, is not only that Freud was trying desperately to become famous so that he could get some money to marry on and rise despite the usual restrictions against him as a Jew. He was so aware of his unfulfilled gifts that he was trying to find the occasions that would allow him to discover just what they could do for him. Hence, as we see in all these early scientific efforts, he was either too impatient, as in the cocaine episode, where he recklessly tried it out on everyone, or, as in the neurone episode, too cautious, for he missed out, says Jones, by "not daring to pursue his thoughts to their logical — and not far-off — conclusion." In the account of his early scientific experiments we feel, indeed, that Freud had to a remarkable degree the gift of intellectual venturesomeness, but we feel, too, that it is precisely this gift of believing too easily on too little evidence, of *plunging* — as it must have seemed to his teachers — too recklessly from one field to another that shocked his innate scientific probity, pulled him to just short of the final prize, and then stopped him, probably more puzzled than anything else that he had not gone through to the end of his "hunch." In this early period, at least, he was, to the extent that he was inwardly the boldest of men, equally uncertain. He was shy about his boldness and ignorant, as yet, of where he would triumph. "I have often," he wrote once, "felt as if I had inherited all the passion of our ancestors when they defended the Temple, as if I could joyfully cast away my life in a great cause. And with all that I was always so powerless and could not express the flowing passions even by a word or a poem. So I have always suppressed myself and I believe that people must notice that in me."

This instinctive self-trust of the gifted man is, paradoxically, a gift that he can mistrust. Freud, then, had good sanction for mistrusting his, since his whole training in the school of Brücke was to avoid the kind of speculation he was prone to make. Indeed, it was just this tendency in himself that probably attracted him to that utterly speculative character, Wilhelm Fliess, who was so busy working out a system of biological time on the basis of the menstrual cycle, and whose attraction to Freud, and Freud's to him, was so obviously founded on their common tendency to intellectual guesswork. But since Freud distrusted this tendency until it could be put on a scientific footing, and Fliess distrusted his own not at all, it is understandable that the relation between them broke down — as was to happen later with the equally speculative Jung. Although Freud was a "son" to Fliess and a "father" to Jung, one can see that, despite the enormous difference between Fliess and Jung, Freud had to assert in both cases not merely the originality but the felt reality of his hypotheses.

In both cases, however, we see that Freud is inherently not the plodder he has been trained to be: he is not a man who will always be abashed by an older and more authoritative type like Fliess. On the contrary, the man who conceived psychoanalysis, who reached into the unconscious, who generalized so confidently from his own dreams and Jewish jokes, was the same man who, in his earlier period, was so excited by the possibilities of cocaine that he tried it on his own fiancée; who caught fire on seeing a particular case of hysteria; who later was to insist that Moses was an Egyptian and that there is a death wish. Obviously this man had the bold reach, the speculative power, the gift of forming radical and breathtakingly fundamental hypotheses to an extraordinary degree. But how typical it was of him, too, to say in a letter, when he was preparing himself to write *Totem and Taboo:* "I am reading thick books without being really interested in them since I already know the results; my instinct tells me that. But they have to slither their way through all the material on the subject. In that process one's insight gets clouded, there are many things that don't fit and yet mustn't be forced." We can see that he was reading these books not for the kind of external proof of his theories, based on someone's research, which in the case of *Totem and Taboo* would have been more formal than real; he was reading in order to make sure that he was not flying in the face of the facts and, I suspect, in order to see whether anyone had thought along this *subject* before. In that case, we can be sure, he would have checked. He was original, not irresponsible.

This is the essential Freud of the portrait — the speculative, the experimenter, the plunger, all of whom add up to the highest scientific rectitude. It is the adventurousness in Freud that explains his break with his old teacher Breuer, with whom he had written the cardinal first book in psychoanalysis, *Studies in Hysteria*. But Breuer was frightened of "sexual studies" and withdrew. On the other hand, with a younger man like Jung, we can see that the break occurs precisely because Freud is wary of what he called in Jung the "mystical" element. Now what is the difference, someone might well demand, between Freud and Jung, since they are both theorists in a highly speculative field and each may be equally right? The difference lies in the extent to which things are real to one. Freud said, my theories are *true*; Jung, my theories are *possible*.

This is not the place for a discussion of Freud and Jung, except as their early association and later quarrel affected the founder of psychoanalysis. But I will say that even someone who is far more sympathetic to the religious imagination than Freud is can hardly help a feeling of revulsion when he compares Jung's *Modern Man in Search of a Soul* with Freud's *The Future of an Illusion*. Freud's book, though limited, sounds as if he is talking about something he believes; while Jung's — "sincere," far more supple and sympathetic to the modern yearning for a faith, for any faith! — has about it the unmistakable suggestion: try it, it may be good for you. One rejects an *illusion*; the other offers us a *search* — for an illusion? The difference between these two books is that Freud thinks like a scientist, and is concerned with what he knows; Jung thinks "psychologically": *i.e.,* he is concerned with what man *needs*; Freud is concerned with what he sees as *truth*.

« 2 »

It is this passion for the sharp edges of truth that makes Freud a hero. It prepares you for whatever surprises in the shape of tigers and jaguars may spring out at you from the underbrush of the human soul. Jones emphasizes this feeling for the truth as the greatest single mark of Freud's mind; and I must confess, as someone who is not a Freudian, that whatever the obscurities and unprovabilities of Freudian doctrine, one gets an overwhelming sense in Freud's own work that he is a man who seeks truth. In Jones's psychoanalytic terms, to seek truth is already to show that one has an instinct for truth; but Freud's sense of reality was surely an individual gift, a mark of unique insight. What a man sees, that is what he is; but he has really to *see* it, as Cézanne saw the apple, and as so many highly theoretical Americans do not see the thing they tell us they are writing about. The more a man really sees, the more absurd and reckless he will seem to those who can see only what the intellectual fashion gets them to see. Freud's sense for the truth is not nullified by the highly speculative character of his mind. Indeed, the two go together: the condition being what I do not find in Jung: the persuasion that these things are unutterably real to the man himself.

Such a mind walks on the thin edge of an abyss. On one side of you is not only all that is unknown, and perhaps unknowable, indescribable, frighteningly obscure and vaguely obscene — but, for a man as religiously trained in science as Freud was, and for whom science was, indeed, a religion, there is the danger of seeming to fly off beyond the sanctioned limits of science. And this danger Freud incurred, as he incurs it still. One leading German psychiatrist stormed at a scientific meeting, when psychoanalysis was brought up, that it was a subject "for the police." At the Academy of Medicine in New York, Freud was denounced as a typical "Viennese libertine." Freud, the most laborious sublimate of men, the man whom his lifelong associate Jones calls "quite peculiarly monogamous," was identified with the Vienna of *La Ronde*. (On the one hand his findings were scoffed at because so many of his first patients were repressed Jewish ladies; on the other hand he was denounced as an example of Viennese immorality.) The German neurologists were so entirely united against him that at one meeting, when Sadger read a study of the influence of his mother in C. F. Meyer's life, a Dr. Braatz cried out that German ideals were at stake and that something drastic should be done to protect them. Freud had hoped that Jung's important place in the early psychoanalytic movement would save it from being thought of as a "Jewish national movement." But Jung withdrew. And similarly, though Jones does not label the point, one can see from his account of Freud's struggle for a hearing that some of the most violent attacks on him came from Jewish doctors. One could wish, however, that the well-known Freudian tactic of showing up every opponent and critic as badly in need of treatment were not so marked even in someone so humanly impressive as Dr. Jones. The opponent Oppenheim has to be labeled a neurotic, and "furthermore, his wife was a bad case of hysteria." Another opponent "was a curious man, a doubtful personality with a shady past." Freud's old teacher Meynert, who had turned unfriendly, is in his turn revealed as a sick man. The heretics in the Freud circle — Adler, Jung, Stekel, Rank, and how many others — are all exposed, more or less regretfully, but with unmistakable certainty. "Nor did it surprise Freud that the so-called arguments brought forward by his opponents were identical with his patients' defenses and could show the same lack of insight and even of logic. All this was therefore in the natural order of things and could neither shake Freud's convictions nor disturb him personally."

So, despite the violent attacks, he persisted (and he never replied; only the disciples do). Why did he persist? Because he believed it. Had psychoanalysis been entirely a subject susceptible to proof, like Newton's or Pasteur's, the early hypothesis might have been confirmed and the discoverer's continuing belief in it would have seemed less remarkable than it does. Nevertheless, all discoveries, all works of art, begin in this gift of conviction, long before experimental confirmation or even realization is possible. And the test of it is always the same: a piece of reality that no one else sees is real to someone, and he makes us see it. In the same way, the original insight is either so real that you can convincingly work it out, or it is no insight at all. The brilliant but marginal thinkers, from Fliess to Rank, end up as episodes in someone else's life. The give-away is always in Jung's suggestion that God may not exist, but that He is good for you.

In Freud's kind of conviction lies the principle of the hero; it is this that gives him his character. Seen from the outside, a life like Freud's, ending as it did not merely in the loss of so many talented disciples, but in his suffering as an old man at the hands of the Nazis, in the loss of his library, in the cancer of the throat that so agonizingly killed him, represents, as we feel, a remarkable ordeal. And the tendency of most Americans who are sympathetic to psychoanalysis is probably to complain, as David Riesman does in *Individualism Reconsidered,* that Freud believed in arduousness, that he could see anything good only as the reward of extreme effort. By contrast with the sloppiness which was a Viennese joke and self-indulgence and boast, Freud's grim laboriousness must have aroused further dislike and hostility. It was *after* seeing patients all day and after writing up his notes and correspondence that he would sit down, after nine in the evening, to his own books. This routine went on day after day, interrupted only by a walk and one evening a week playing cards with his cronies. (Only when he was sixty-five, Jones tells us, did he allow himself a cup of coffee at five o'clock. He rarely drank even wine.) But what both the corrupt society of Vienna, and Americans who think that any extreme kind of moral exertion is somehow unhealthy—what both miss is the extraordinary hold that conviction of the truth has upon such a man as Freud, dominating his life, holding him to his desk late into the night, forcing him at the end, when he was dying of cancer in London, still to see patients. And need it be noted that this was probably not a merciful gesture, that Freud was not so much a healer as a scientist, that his patients were the one laboratory in which this man could confirm and advance his theories? The hero is a hero because he has an heroic destiny, and the very mark of such a destiny is that no one chooses it; it chooses the man it shall be embodied in. The destiny is a cause, an essential idea behind the perplexing surface of things. Just as it chooses the hero, its oracle, its voice to the world, so in this knitting-together of hero and cause lies the essence of a suffering that he cannot reject any more than he could, anticipating the cost ahead, not have chosen it. But truth, choosing him, pledged him to endure what had to be. And it is in this sense of the inescapability of the truth that the characteristic devotion of the hero is found.

[1956]

Psychoanalysis and Literary Culture Today

THERE IS a young Englishman on Broadway who shouts every night that he is angry, very angry. Yet when we open John Osborne's play

Look Back in Anger and try to find out just what he is angry about, we make a curious discovery: he is not angry on specific grounds, as people often are; he is angry at his inability to feel anger, angry that he lacks a cause to be angry about. At one moment, after complaining that "nobody can be bothered. No one can raise themselves out of their delicious sloth," he says, very wistfully indeed for an angry man, "Was I really wrong to believe that there's a — kind of — burning virility of mind and spirit that looks for something as powerful as itself? The heaviest, strongest creatures in this world seem to be the loneliest. Like the old bear, following his own breath in the dark forest. There's no warm pack, no herd to comfort him. That voice that cries out doesn't *have* to be a weakling's, does it?"

This is the truest note in a play which emotionally and artistically seems rather contrived. It is not intensity of feeling but the longing for this intensity that is behind Mr. Osborne's confused and rather forced emotions. And equally, this same pseudo-violence, expressing the dearth rather than the excess of feeling, has struck me in several contemporary literary works that parade an air of militancy and rebelliousness — Norman Mailer's *The Deer Park*, Jack Kerouac's *On the Road*, Tennessee Williams's *Camino Réal* and other plays, the books of essays that Henry Miller has published from California, Allen Ginsberg's *Howl*. What puts all these works together in my mind is the fact that this essential lack of feeling, of direction and point is accompanied by the same extreme yet abstract violence of sexual activity and description. I am reminded of the Marquis de Sade, that famous sexual rebel, that supposed martyr to the cause of sexual freedom — when one actually opens his books, he turns out to be not a rebel at all but a fantasist whose idea of sexual pleasure is always something so extreme, perverse and complicated that only the mind can imagine it — as only the mind can stage it. This is the situation in Norman Mailer's *The Deer Park*, a book that was acclaimed by some left-wing critics as an indictment of Hollywood, and is based in part on the enforced exile from the industry of Communist directors and writers who would not give the names of party members to the investigating committees. One discovers very soon in reading his book that Mailer is not interested in the political significance of his material, though he feels that he *should* be; he is concerned with sex as an ultimate expression of man's aloneness.

The Deer Park takes place mostly in a famous desert resort, and despite the urbanities of luxurious American living, I had the sensation that these people really were in the desert, and with nothing to talk about, nothing to think about, nothing to feel, they were like Eskimos whiling away the eternal boredom of the igloo with unending sexual intercourse.

The sensation of claustrophobia, of something profoundly cheerless and inhuman that I got from Mailer's book was intensified by his article in *Dissent* — "The White Negro: Superficial Reflections on the Hipster." Mailer's theme is that the Negro has been forced by discrimination into an outlaw state in which he has developed the primitive and uninhibited sexuality that white men are not allowed to indulge. As modern capitalist society becomes inwardly more demoralized, certain advanced sectors of white society — the more naturally rebellious, intelligent and unafraid — become white versions of the Negro, seek to become hipsters (spiritual outlaws) rather than "squares" (conventionally conformist men and women). On the model of the Negro, they can find in the sensations of unprecedented orgasm that direct, blazing, ultimate contact with reality of which so many people are deprived by conventional, inhibited middle-class life.

Anyone with experience in Marxist literature will recognize immediately in this essay the adaptation to the hipster of the myth of the proletariat. Mailer's essay is a completely Marxist-revolutionary essay. Although the characters are the same, their names are different; and although the plot is really the same, too, the real difference is that the play is not on the boards, nothing is really taking place except theoretically. There *was* a proletariat once, and a bourgeoisie; people did suffer from starvation, inhuman hours, physical violence. But Mailer's picture of the Negro and of his revolutionary, unprecedented orgasms gives even the interested and sympathetic reader the sense that all this is being relayed to him from far away, for it is all a mental construction. Nothing here is taken from the real life of struggle, from life as actual conflict; it is an attempt to impose a dramatic and even noble significance on events that have not genuinely brought it forth. So desperate is Mailer for something to be revolutionary about, as Osborne is, that after telling us contemptuously that modern psychoanalysis merely softens the patient up by adapting him to modern middle-class society, he says that, by contrast, two strong eighteen-year-old hoodlums beating in the brains of a candy-store keeper do have courage of a sort, "for one murders not only a weak fifty-year-old man but an institution as well, one violates private property, one enters into a new relation with the police and introduces a dangerous element into one's life. The hoodlum is therefore daring the unknown, and so no matter how brutal the act, it is not altogether cowardly."

Jack Kerouac is a far less gifted and intelligent writer than Mailer, but in his recent best-seller, *On the Road,* one finds this same loneliness of emotions without objects to feel them about, this same uprush of verbal violence which, when one looks at it a little closely, seems to be unnaturally removed from the object or occasion. Kerouac, indeed, writes not so much *about* things as about the search for things to write about. When he celebrates the "kick" of ecstasy brought about by drink, drugs and jazz, it is the relief of having so strong a sensation that impresses him, not his communion with some object in ecstatic relatedness. And it is significant that his highest praise is for "the mad ones, the ones who are mad to live, mad to talk, mad to be saved, desirous of everything at the same time, the ones who never yawn or say a commonplace thing, but burn, burn, burn like fabulous yellow roman candles exploding like spiders across the stars and in the middle you can see the blue centerlight pop and everybody goes 'Aww!' "

Though it may seem a far step from the raucous and self-advertising propaganda of Kerouac's Bohemian group to the professional theater world of Tennessee Williams, the very subject of Williams's plays is always this same loneliness. When Williams, minus the stage lights and hocus-pocus of his director, is read for himself, as in his execrable fiction, *The Roman Spring of Mrs. Stone* and the stories collected in *One Arm,* one discovers that his subject is not merely the fantasy world of the utterly lonely, but that in fantasy even the sexual fulfillment of his characters has a brutal and mechanical quality, as if one mental category dully followed another without any stimulus or color from direct experience. In one of the stories in *One Arm,* a Negro masseur not merely violates his white patient, but literally butchers him; this same hellish oppression of sexual fantasy, like a nightmare from which the dreamer may never escape into the unpatterned relief of the real world, dogs us in some of the more violent stories of Carson McCullers, in the most recent novel by Nelson Algren, *A Walk on the Wild Side*, and in the last section of Paul Bowles's *The Sheltering Sky*, where a young American wife, maddened after her husband dies in the desert, is captured by an Arab and added to his harem.

I wish I could describe some of these new novels and plays in greater detail, for what is most striking about so many of them is the fact that despite the surface sexual violence, they seem little concerned with sex itself, with the *physicality* of sex; in many of these books there are simply not enough people about, in actual human relation of any sort, for sexual activity to take place. On the contrary, many of the newer writers use sex exactly as a drunken and confused man uses profanity — as a way of expressing anger, irritation, exasperation, and thus of breaking through the numbing despair of isolation. And indeed, isolation of the most crippling and stupefying sort is the really significant experience behind this literature — the kind of isolation that makes it impossible to break the lockstep of one's thoughts, the isolation that imagines anything because it has contact with nothing, but which, in the imagination of loneliness, cannot give us the color, the tactile feel of anything, only the abstract category to which the experience belongs.

Yet this loneliness does not call itself that; it calls itself revolutionary. In a long and now celebrated American poem simply called *Howl*, the young poet Allen Ginsberg has taken Whitman's long line and has described an hallucinated tour of America that reverses Whitman's celebration and becomes an exultant nightmare of denunciation:

I saw the best minds of my generation destroyed by madness, starving hysterical naked,
dragging themselves through the negro streets at dawn looking for an angry fix,
angelheaded hipsters burning for the ancient heavenly connection to the starry dynamo in the machinery of night,
who poverty and tatters and hollow-eyed and high sat up smoking in the supernatural darkness of cold-water flats floating across the tops of cities contemplating jazz,

who bared their brains to Heaven under the El and saw Mohammedan
angels staggering on tenement roofs illuminated . . .
who cowered in unshaven rooms in underwear, burning their money in
wastebaskets and listening to the Terror through the wall,
who got busted in their pubic beards returning through Laredo with a
belt of marijuana for New York.

Now this abstractness contrasts very sharply with the lyric and sensuous imagery with which sexual desire or activity used to be described by writers who were famous for their prophetic, unconventional concern with the subject. I have not the space to spell out in its required and fascinating detail the kind of imagery which one finds in Whitman's "Out of the Cradle Endlessly Rocking," in the love scenes of D. H. Lawrence's *Sons and Lovers,* in the glorious pages of Colette, who could portray sex as the union not only of man and woman but of man and the whole physical world of earth sounds and earth smells, of colors and nuances; in those pages of Proust where, despite the pain of Swann's jealousy of Odette, one feels the gasping sharpness of real desire and the excitement of the great city that is its background and stimulus. Perhaps I have made it too easy for myself by contrasting so many classically sensuous writers with American writers who have never had the same tradition of art as the celebration of the natural world. But as Albert Camus confessed in his recent Nobel Prize speech, even someone brought up in the pagan and sunlit world of North Africa finds himself unable to describe the sensuous joy of life as he once did. As man increasingly loses his connection with the world, the great world, the only world, he finds himself playing the moralist and the revolutionary as part of the same imposture — the purpose of which is to perform *some* action, to see oneself performing any role.

« 2 »

Much of the fiction and poetry I have been describing has been influenced by the theories of Wilhelm Reich, and in the terms in which I have been describing them, illustrates the use of psychoanalytical terminology for the sake of an utterly hypothetical rebelliousness, in which a gangster beating out the brains of an old storekeeper is seen as the ritual of a revolutionary terrorist destroying the old order. Turn to the enormously fashionable and influential literary criticism written under the inspiration of Dr. Jung, and you find in academic and philosophical circles the use of psychoanalysis not as socialism but as religion. In a recent effort to summarize the Jungian conception of literature — the book takes its very title from the loneliest character in American literature, Melville's Ishmael — James Baird explains that what orthodox Christians regard as sacrament is really symbol, and that since art itself deals with symbols, art itself may be viewed as a religious ritual. To anyone who has followed the development of literary criticism since the vogue of neo-orthodoxy began with Eliot, this is old stuff; phrases like symbol, symbolic action, ritual, myth, are the mainstay of fashionable academic criticism. But the themes I have been stressing in this paper — isolation and forced rebelliousness — are paralleled in the pseudo-metaphysics of the following. For just as art is really a religious ritual, so religion is really art; sacrament, says Mr. Baird, is symbol "representing corporateness in which the individual is subsumed, and ultimately these new compensatory symbols transcend the artist in the collective of the archetype."

> The abstraction of his created form as sacrament singularly envisions the corporateness of man in a religious act. . . . Each man worships alone on his island. The sacrament which he creates invokes for his comfort and his "salvation" a world of the ideal where what he remembers of lost symbols is mixed with what his heretical allegiance to non-Christian (Oriental) custom supplies. Whether this custom, displayed to him through the aperture of his Oriental journey as experience, was mastered or merely "sampled" cannot very much matter. His symbol suggests the possibility of a new sacramental corporateness. As a maker of sacramentalism he belongs to an unconscious artistic community of his age because, as artist, he is like other workers who find art a better means of affirmation than existential courage. He has cast off convention and traditional theology, and in his act of creating, he descends to the true primitivity of religiousness; he returns to the authority of primitive feeling and the emotive life.

There is not a phrase here which refers to anything real; neither art nor religion, neither the so-called primitive feeling nor the emotive life means anything in this context. But Mr. Baird is not bogus: he is not pretending that he believes in God; he is pretending that out of something which is not religion, religion may come again, so that human beings who have lost the traditional objects of their belief, but not the habit of belief, may have something to believe in again. Just as the Reichians want to believe in Socialism again, because they don't, so the Jungians write as if religion could be had back for the asking. It is all so easy, so fatally easy — this Socialism that carefully avoids society; this religion that dares not say that God exists. It is easy because everything is based on what the self wants, what the self needs or thinks it needs, and nothing on what the world is really like. The world — the surrounding and not always friendly reality of nature, history, society — has disappeared for these writers, and has taken with it everything which has given measure and definition to man's struggles in the world, everything which has given man a sense of his possibilities and his limits, of his guilt as well as his desire, of his tragedy as well as his happiness. These writers are not concerned with winning over nature, with forcing it to yield up its secrets; they are searching for a world they can believe in again, and get angry at again. They are tormented not by the pains of heroism, but by the inability to feel heroic — and often by the inability to feel anything. The human catastrophes visited upon our generation by totalitarianism seem too great to understand, to describe, to cope with. History has become meaningless to them, and private life a search for sensations — either of unprecedented orgasm or of God — that may make them feel real to themselves.

« 3 »

This pervasive sense of unreality is authentic, and, as usual, the writers — those whom Ezra Pound saluted as the "antennae of the race" — see ahead of everyone else. For the middle-class world which all of us have depended on so long has itself, as a value system, ceased to exert any real authority, to arouse real respect. The sense of unreality that I have been describing arises naturally out of the bewilderment of people who recognize that history has taken still another turn, and that the solid middle-class virtues on which so many of us depended, so that we could meaningfully oppose them, are no longer believed in seriously enough for opposition to mean anything. The real tragedy of our time, as Nietzsche correctly foresaw, is a nihilism so total, so pervasive, so defeatist even in the midst of the greatest luxury our world has ever known, that it is no wonder that unimaginative people try to turn back the clock of modern science, to blame Marx and Darwin and Freud for robbing us of the illusion of our omnipotence in the universe. These people are hopeless, yet there is one element of tragic truth in their indictment of the modern spirit: more and more people lack the sense of tradition with which to assimilate the endless shocks and changes of the twentieth century. Just as Marx could not anticipate heirs who would completely lack his culture and tradition, who in the name of his great insights into capitalist society would create a society far more tyrannical and unjust, so Freud, himself so rooted in the Hebraic tradition, the English tradition, the nineteenth-century tradition, the scientific tradition, could not have predicted the destruction of Western civilization at Auschwitz, Maidenek, Belsen. He could not have imagined a psychoanalytically oriented psychiatry divorced from the humanistic and moral tradition, a psychiatry that would be used for market research in consumer motivation and even for the manipulation back to "normal" of political deviants. Psychoanalysis depended enormously on the intellectual and literary tradition out of which it arose, and of which it is an essential part. Now that this tradition of cultivation and intellectual freedom no longer commands allegiance as it used to, one sees an increasing divergence between writers, who are concerned with the tradition itself, and therefore with Freud's classic insights, and those psychoanalysts who, lacking the needed cultural reference, foolishly and self-indulgently suppose that they are living in the same world of bourgeois morality which made Freud grasp the necessary reactions of repression, guilt and shame. In the last few years, the kind of psychoanalytical comment on literary works which used to be so arresting and valuable has come to seem a wholly mechanical jargon. Significantly, it has become the staple of the most pedantic and academic research, unrelated to living literature; for, as with all things academic, this perspective is based on admiration of the static, the enclosed, on the literary tradition that neatly folds itself up and files itself away.

Equally, the use of psychoanalysis as a kind of pampering to merely bourgeois tastes and self-delusions, to the lapdog psychology of Americans whose only problem is to reduce and to save on income tax, is in itself a literary scandal. In this connection I would point to several things. One: the myth of universal "creativity," the assumption that every idle housewife was meant to be a painter and that every sexual deviant is really a poet. From this follows the myth that these unproductive people are "blocked"; whereupon how easy for the hack and the quack to get together! Second: the use of psychoanalytical jargon as a static description of the personality of the artist. There is no doubt that although neurosis can cripple creative artistry or hinder it entirely, talent is always quite separate in function — if not in theme — from the emotional chaos of neurosis, which provides no clue whatever to the reality of creative life. But perhaps the theme I have been stressing in this paper — the contemporary use of psychoanalysis in order to find identity rather than freedom — is seen here, too, since the more unreal people become to us, the more we try to pin them down with a descriptive formula, usually gained these days from psychoanalysis. If we approach literature exclusively by way of the writer's personality, psychoanalytically considered, we not only get even farther away from the real experience of literature than we were before, but we obliterate even the fundamental cultural respect for the health of the creative self in our eagerness to label the writer ill.

A recent example of this is the introduction by Mrs. Diana Trilling to a new selection of the letters of D. H. Lawrence. Mrs. Trilling confesses that Lawrence no longer means as much to her as he did in rebellious youth, and one believes her, since her analysis of Lawrence's work is based not on his real and marvelous creativity, but on an Oedipal conflict which she insists is the root of his ultimate failure as a novelist. More than one great poet, or poetic talent, has known the same kind of failure, which is probably rooted in the gap between the poetic realization of reality, which is always fundamentally "personal," and the kind of novelistic instinct which specializes in *story* — an instinct that Lawrence never really had. But instead of paying the homage to him that his genius deserves — and calls for — homage that would at least see Lawrence as possessing the defects of his genius, Mrs. Trilling regales us with the kind of clinical hindsight which, divorced from literary humility and appreciation, has made this kind of writing a terror to anyone who simply cares for literature.

I think it was this institutionalized conjunction of sex and love that threw Lawrence into the despair of the war years. The conflict raging in the world was an externalized expression of the private sexual struggle which was to absorb so large a part of his emotional energies for the rest of his life.

This is no irrelevant private point I'm making, no psychoanalytical advantage I'm trying to take of Lawrence, need I make that clear? The conflict which was crystallized in Lawrence when he and Frieda finally married seems to me to be the essential conflict, and contradiction, that runs through all his work.

This may not be an irrelevant private point, but it shows an attitude toward literature which has nothing to claim for literature itself. It is odd that the very people who are so quick to see suppressed and wasted creativity in people who are merely emotionally ill should always wish to deny the fundamental creativity of the greatest writers, like Kafka and Lawrence and Dostoevsky — a mistake that, in the case of the latter, Freud pointedly refrained from making. Yet the reason for this relentless psychologizing of art, so often equally irrelevant to both art and psychology, is that it gives the analyst, whoever he may be, the chance to share in the creativity of his subject. There is a sad perversion here of what, in genuine literary criticism, *is* an act of appropriation. Henry James said that the true critic is so much in love with art that he tries to "possess" it — to include it in his personal experience, which means to increase his power of enjoyment and understanding, and thereby of instruction to others. But as Ernst Kris has pointed out, the rise of a wholly "esthetic" attitude toward life — I should call it pseudo-esthetic in effect — is an attempt to appropriate not the work of art, which does exist so that we may possess it, but the artist himself. It exists so as to give us "status" and "prestige" in a world where the old bourgeois claims of money and social position, though they support the life of art, are felt not to be as real in advancing one's prestige as creativity itself. And the myth of creativity, the endless search for it in modern times, is simply a search for identity on the part of people who believe that they can find it in an experience, that of the real creator, utterly foreign to themselves.

I could go on here to speak of many related aspects: of "taste," of corruption, of the demonstrable fact that while psychoanalysis has added nothing to the creation of art, it has added a great deal, perhaps too much, to our modern concern with art. But in conclusion it is more important to note that the most signal fact about our experience today is that it is utterly unprecedented. The protagonist of middle-class literature, from Goethe to Thomas Mann, from Blake to D. H. Lawrence, from Rousseau to Proust, naturally saw life as a struggle against convention. Under the slogan of nature as freedom and truth, man saw himself as a hero reuniting man to the natural destiny of which he had been robbed by the gods. If there had been no profound tradition of repression, no moral code to bind us, Don Juan could never have been a hero or Anna Karenina a heroine; there would have been no guilt to suffer and no rebellion to honor. But the great human symbol of contemporary literature, I suggest, is no longer the rebel, since there is no authoritative moral tradition that he can honestly feel limits and hinders his humanity. It is the stranger — who seeks not to destroy the moral order, but to create one that will give back to him the idea of humanity.

[1958]

The Lesson of the Master

Philip Rieff's book is a brilliant and beautifully reasoned example of what Freud's influence has really been: an increasing intellectual vigilance about human nature. So far as I can tell, Freud has been marvelous for intellectuals and a bit confusing to everyone else. The art of loving (even oneself) seems to be as difficult in the Freudian era as in any other; and the intelligence with which certain writers can get to work on Freud's ideas — sorting them out, pairing them off, relating them to previous ideas and to our sense of crisis — is only further proof that the Eden of our undivided human nature is far behind us, and that, like the Master himself, many an intellectual today has no greater passion than to write a good book.

Freud's own life was quite extraordinarily laborious, ascetic, and intellectual. Despite his concern with civilized man's oppression and

Freud: The Mind of the Moralist, by Philip Rieff. New York: Viking.
Sigmund Freud's Mission, by Erich Fromm. New York: Harper & Brothers.

denial of his instinctual nature, Freud himself believed that this repression is essential to "culture." And in describing human nature as a fundamentally insoluble conflict between two different provinces of human need, Freud was not merely describing human nature but actively interpreting it. Like every true investigator of human nature, he showed that man's difficulties already represent ethical ideas and can lead to new ethical choices. In short, Freud was a moralist, drawing "lessons on the right conduct of life from the misery of living it."

This starting point leads Mr. Rieff really to examine the implications and consequences of Freud's ideas; and the examination is exciting, for Mr. Rieff has not only a sociologist's alertness to the cultural implications of Freud's doctrine but also acute resources — and knowledge — as a student of intellectual history. Fundamentally, his motive in writing the book would seem to be the Freudian motive in so many intellectual enterprises: to lay bare, to disentangle, to establish contradictions and to unveil significances. Just as psychoanalysis has become for many writers what it was for Freud all his life long — an intellectual adventure, a constant sense of discovery related to problems rather than to patients, who merely furnished the problems — so Mr. Rieff's own excitement in the book is to make elegant distinctions, to uncover the mind of this moralist as a descendant and correction of modern thought. Mr. Rieff has a superb last chapter on "Psychological Man" — who has replaced the Political Man of antiquity, the Religious Man of the Middle Ages, the Economic Man handed down by the Enlightenment, and who produces the kind of cultural self-concern that is so characteristic of our period. Once you realize, as Mr. Rieff does, that men live by distinct values and choices, whether they know it or not; that they go from role to role in history as expressions of the philosophy they live by — then you have a sense that our fate depends on the soundness and correctness of the ideas we have now. An intellectual critic like Mr. Rieff can get to work, minutely retracing the implications and correlations of the Freudian world view, as if every step of thought were the only meaningful action for man today.

In a sense this intellectual vigilance duplicates the psychoanalytical session itself, which constantly offers up to the patient the minute significances and implications of his self-interpretation. In analysis, these follow from what Mr. Rieff brilliantly underscores as the Freudian distrust of everything that is not the inner life, private conduct, the self. But what the analyst does for the patient — present the terms for his new choices as a human being — Mr. Rieff does in respect to the cultural significance of Freudianism. His style has the same closeness, the same undertone of hypertense alertness. Again and again he makes brilliant points. Although everyone knows that Freud's ideas are in direct descent from the Romantic poets and philosophers, who valued "that which cannot be described," no one, to my knowledge, has analyzed this relationship as well as Mr. Rieff has. He points out that since Freud "refused to treat mind except as in historical process," no thought or feeling is self-explainable to Freud, and he develops this latter in showing how pitilessly Freud assumed that everything in the psyche is for use, how little he accounted for apathy. This wholly dynamic psychology led Freud to show things in too "emphatic" a setting, to enlarge on purposes and conflicts, equivalences and denials. But "as Freud's sense of the compelling social nature of love grew upon him, he became more aware of sexuality — the secret act of the private individual — as a safeguard to the de-individualizing functions of love as authority."

Mr. Rieff's most moving insight is that "we can measure the speed and distance of the modern retreat from a political doctrine of freedom by this touting of whatever appears refractory in human nature, as if freedom were thereby being proclaimed as inherent in the life-giving act itself." In the particularly brilliant last section of the book, analyzing the increasing privacy with which the individual views his role today, he shows why "the popular drift of psychological science aims at freeing the individual most of all from the burden of opposition" and remarks that "Freud was . . . unable to perceive that our own culture might become highly permissive in the sphere of . . . sexual morals — the better to enforce its public repressions."

The real value of Mr. Rieff's book is that it shows to what extent contemporary thought has assimilated Freud's ideas; the complexities and contradictions he has uncovered in Freud's thought — these are now everyone's, and the only way in which we can conceive getting the better of them is in extending our intellectual vigilance over human nature, in the kind of thoughtfulness which Mr. Rieff's book exemplifies.

« 2 »

By contrast, Dr. Erich Fromm's little book, essentially a hostile analysis of Freud's personal asceticism and authoritarian personality, renders its own points ineffective precisely because of the slightness and discursiveness with which he tries to express in such short space criticisms of Freud's personality and the moral implications of his doctrine. Such criticisms have to be made minutely and thoroughly to have any significance at all.

The trouble with the "revisionists" of Freud, like Dr. Fromm, is not so much in their ideas — many of which, emphasizing the social molding of human nature, are valuable in contrast to the unrelieved solitude of the Freudian arena in which the self struggles for light. It is the utter lack of any system, of intellectual coherence, of decisiveness; the neo-Freudians seem to live intellectually from hand to mouth, and they offer corrections of Freudian doctrine that are not unsound so much as they are inconstant. Dr. Fromm's criticisms of Freud's harsh and puritanical personality would be more significant, surely, if one did not see in his impatient style that he is looking for any stone to fling against this Goliath. Much of what he says about the dismal nineteenth-century bourgeois in Freud is perfectly correct. "The whole mystery of sublimation, which Freud never quite adequately explained, is the mystery of capital formation according to the myth of the nineteenth-century middle class. Just as wealth is the product of saving, culture is the product of instinctual frustration. . . . Freud speaks of . . . love as a man of his time speaks of property or capital." This is an important point, but it is a point in passing; it does not follow from any whole point of view that Fromm offers us in rebuttal to Freud.

Freud's overwhelming influence stems from the fact that he does offer us a new point of view, that with him one goes from idea to idea, from subject to subject. In the same way, the great intellectual systems of the past exerted their appeal by really lighting up the world, by explaining things in extent, by showing the relationship of man to the world and of man to himself. Mr. Rieff, though no disciple, shows the thoroughness and coherence of Freud's system by the closeness with which he is able to analyze every side of it; his book, tight and complete, is the best possible tribute to the comprehensive nature of Freud's genius. Dr. Fromm, who seems to have learned the intellectual caprice of his adopted country, gives away the fundamental eclecticism of his view by trying to evaluate so fundamental a theme as Freud's austerity in this short space. Freud's theory may be more useful to the intelligence than to the passions, but it does answer to certain fundamental requirements of the intelligence.

[1959]

The Conquistador: or Freud in His Letters

EVEN IF the life of Sigmund Freud had been less arduous and heroic, his character less complex, the present selection from his personal letters, edited by his son Ernst, would still have a special claim on our attention. For psychoanalysis was founded not merely by Freud, but in a very real sense *on* him. Freud found the meaning of dreams in his own dreams, and was led to formulate the Oedipus complex by being the favorite of a mother who was twenty years younger than his father. Even at the end of his life, when he had been driven into exile, his enduring conception of himself as a lonely prophet made him cast the Moses of *Moses and Monotheism* in his own image. No one who has read Ernest Jones's marvelously informative biography, or the more purely scientific letters (to Wilhelm Fliess) which have been published as *The Origins of Psychoanalysis,* can miss the dramatic and significant involvement, in the theory of psychoanalysis itself, of Freud's intense puritanism, his anxiety about money, his colossal ambition, his domineering attitude toward women (and in a very real sense his inability to understand women).

Psychoanalysis certainly bears the imprint of Freud's own character. Yet harsh and overstrained as his personality was, it has always puzzled me that "revisionist" critics of Freud like Erich Fromm,

The Letters of Sigmund Freud, selected and edited by Ernst L. Freud. New York: Basic Books.

armed with a wholly social notion of what a "healthy" personality should be, can attribute the excesses and mistakes of orthodox psychoanalysis exclusively to Freud's personal faults. For the cardinal thing about Freud, seen against the history of psychology, is how gifted he was. Without the peculiarly compelling insight that enabled him to grasp what was *typical* in his own experience, Freud would now be as dead as any of the Wundts and Lombrosos who were such great men in their time. There has been very little original insight among Freud's rivals — or, for that matter, among his own followers. Freud stands out not because he was always right, but because he tended, on the whole, to have real insight — to see *some* things as they really are.

Ironically, it is the very indiscrimination with which psychoanalysis has been taken up in this country that makes it so much harder for people to appreciate Freud's real qualities. We now tend to evaluate people as if they were inherently alike, but differ only in their upbringing. We do not share in the intellectual tradition out of which Freud came, and so we cannot recognize what Freud took from it and how he added to it. We overlook the significance of Freud's gift for discovery — that which adds new territories to our awareness. A great intellectual gift is the human element that is most strange to the thinker himself and that makes him strange to us. He *sees* differently. Somehow his life and character get hitched up behind his peculiar intellectual urgency in such a way that he has a more pressing commitment, a sharper impatience with ordinary relationships, than do others.

What interests me in Freud is that side of himself that he called the "conquistador" — the momentum of originality, the driving force in carving out a wholly new field, that makes such a man peculiarly the teacher of others. It is the quality, when all allowances have been made, that unites the great religious teachers, the great poets, the primary scientists. It is clearly his conception of truth as something hidden, repressed, driven underground, but to which he had come closer than others, that made Freud, despite his belligerent positivism, go so far beyond the materialism of his generation in science in saluting the great novelists and poets. Surely it was this sense of truth as a "mystery," to be revealed as the illumination of one's own experience, that made Freud venerate those who like

Joseph could uncover dreams, or like Moses, see God in fire. To have a vision of truth as profound because hidden, hidden by the force of convention, is to see nature as a constant challenge. The "conquistador," the intellectual pioneer, can never rest, for he alone sets his standards and has no one with whom to compromise. To have such a conception of oneself is to embark on a lonely, hard destiny, to be always at war with conventional society and yet not be able to take it seriously. It is to need love more, perhaps, than do other people, and at the same time to believe less in the significance of love.

These are the qualities, as I see it, that lie behind Freud's constant sense of his own arduousness, of his lack of ease and accommodation. At the end of his life he was able to acknowledge these traits in himself with a certain resignation, but even at the end he could not relent. There is this extraordinary passage from a letter of 1929:

> All I know is that I had a terribly hard time; the rest followed as a matter of course. It could also have been very much better. I was only aware of the objective, not of myself. My worst qualities, among them a certain indifference to the world, probably had the same share in the final result as the good ones — *i.e.*, a defiant courage about truth. In the depths of my heart I can't help being convinced that my dear fellow men, with a few exceptions, are worthless.

He recognized that he had a peculiar disposition to take life hard; and in fact he did have to wait four and a half years to marry his fiancée, constantly suffered the extreme anti-Semitism of Vienna, and as soon as he had published his first great theories, found himself ostracized. In 1886, when he was studying in Paris under Charcot, he wrote to Martha Bernays, his future wife:

> I think it is my great misfortune that nature didn't grant me that certain something that attracts people. When I think back over my life I realize that I would have needed little more than this certain something to assure myself of an easy existence. It took me such ages to win my friends, I had to struggle so long for my precious girl, and each time I am introduced to someone I realize that the new acquaintance is led by some impulse, which defies analysis, to underestimate me. . . . I believe people see something alien in me and the real reason for this

is that in my youth I was never young and now that I am entering the age of maturity I cannot mature properly.

Certainly there were "motivations" enough to justify the grimness that Freud always felt about life and himself. No one reading these many letters can doubt why Freud felt constantly that he had to persuade, to cajole, even to beat down, a host of enemies. Once, in a train where all the windows were tightly closed, he had only to open a window to find himself shrieked at, "He's a dirty Jew!" He recounts how the famous Koller, one of the great innovators in eye surgery, found himself, after disagreeing on a scientific point with a colleague, being publicly insulted and having to fight a duel. Freud had to worry about money all through his youth, and no sooner had he begun to feel a little secure than the First World War came in, ruining the Austrian middle class. He lost a beloved daughter when she was still in her twenties. Even after he had become world-famous, he could not get his professorship until a friend virtually bribed a minister. By the Second World War, he had to give up his library, his savings, and barely made it to England. During this period, he suffered atrociously from cancer of the jaw, and underwent a whole series of operations. Four of his five sisters, all too old to escape from Austria, were gassed by the Nazis.

Freud waited for his fiancée, for security, for fame, with the special bitterness of the Middle European Jew who is not at home with himself or the society around him. He suffered from cultural claustrophobia and the lack of fraternity that Kafka and so many others had identified with the Austro-Hungarian Empire. He felt that he was living in a crazy-quilt of nationalities, cut off from the more liberal and humane culture of England and France that he admired. One of the most touching moments in the letters comes when he writes to Martha, during the long exile of his engagement (she was living near Hamburg): "Have you seen the sea yet? Please give it my best regards — we will meet yet."

No wonder that with these many deprivations and postponements, this constant isolation and antagonism, these repeated blows, Freud wanted a marriage that would give him security on at least one flank. During the long engagement, he flew into a rage because his meek, good little Marty refused to stop seeing a certain Fritz Wähle of whom Freud was jealous. (She soon gave way, and

Freud duly congratulated her: "I was patient and finally you did me justice. . . . You will eventually agree with me more fully on this point.") Later, when he had established the psychoanalytic movement, he was almost pathetic in his eagerness for Jung to be his chief lieutenant, and wrote in 1907: ". . . You are more suitable as a propagandist, for I have invariably found that something in my personality, my words and ideas strikes people as alien. . . ." As early as his student days in Paris, Freud had sat at a performance of *Carmen* feeling utterly detached from the pleasure-seeking "masses" around him. The peculiar loneliness of his experience at the opera led him to formulate (in a letter to Martha) a positive value in the repressions. This makes ironic reading for us who have been brought up to distrust repression and to seek satisfaction as our destiny.

. . . The mob gives vent to its appetites, and we deprive ourselves. We deprive ourselves in order to maintain our integrity . . . we save ourselves for something, not knowing for what . . . we strive more toward avoiding pain than toward seeking pleasure. . . .

Surely it was out of this awareness of what life had cost him that Freud learned to calculate, in every life, the balance that a person must strike between the pleasure-principle that we instinctually seek and the reality-principle to which we must learn to submit. But to an American, living in a culture in which more and more people seek at any price to avoid pain, at all times to be comfortable, cherished, secure, Freud's letters make strange reading. They virtually ask the question: Need his life have been so grim? Would Freud have benefited from a good psychoanalysis? Couldn't the man have arranged things better? Freud, who was certainly aware of not being on the sunny side of life, would not have taken very seriously this proposal to limit and to temper his life. To look too deliberately for happiness — this fear of pain would have reflected to him nothing but the emptiness of our intellectual environment. It is a pleasant irony that, misusing his name, a watered-down psychoanalysis, seeking above all to adjust man to his society, has proved especially pervasive.

Whatever Freud's personal "grimness," to repeat the word that seems central to any discussion of his character, he was concerned not so much with himself as with the "objective." He had a pressing sense of actualities which he could not overlook and which certainly did not overlook him. Freud's despair of his fellow men, his disbelief in their official ideals — all this compared unfavorably in his mind with his own "defiant courage about truth." No wonder that with this stern sense of opposition between his own intellectual virtue and the treacherous, inimical world, he clung, despite his belligerent declaration that he was an "unbeliever," to his Jewishness. He joined the Jewish fraternal organization, the B'nai B'rith, when at the outset of the psychoanalytic movement he found everyone in Vienna against him. In his golden period, the mid-Twenties, when Vienna under a Socialist administration was at last prepared to honor him, he wrote fiercely that "as a Jew I was prepared to be in the opposition and to renounce agreement with the 'compact majority.'" This constant sense of defiance is perhaps more characteristic of the great prophets than of the usual Viennese professor.

Freud saw in the relationship between man and the truth something of the quality which is found in the Biblical confrontation of man and God — a quality at once persistent, tragic, despairing, and exalted. It might have been Moses outraged by the Golden Calf who wrote, as Freud did about the Viennese public: "Truth is unobtainable; humanity does not deserve it." It is true that Freud "had a terribly hard time." But surely the real hardness of his life, the deepest urgency behind it, lay in his commitment to the truth. Men are led by a mysterious destiny that is no less terrible when its moving power, as Freud thought, is our hidden nature, ourselves alone.

[1960]

The Language of Pundits

It is curious that Freud, the founder of psychoanalysis, remains the only first-class writer identified with the psychoanalytic movement. It was, of course, Freud's remarkable literary ability that gave currency to his once difficult and even "bestial" ideas; it was the insight he showed into concrete human problems, the discoveries whose force is revealed to us in a language supple, dramatic, and charged with the excitement of Freud's mission as a "conquistador" into realms hitherto closed to scientific inquiry, that excited and persuaded so many readers of his books. Even the reader who does not accept all of Freud's reasoning is aware, as he reads his interpretation of dreams, of the horror associated with incest, of the Egyptian origins of Moses, that this is a writer who is bent on making the most mysterious and unmentionable matters entirely clear to himself, and that this fundamental concern to get at the truth makes dramatis personae out of his symbols and dramatic episodes out of the archetypal human struggles he has described. It is certainly possible to read Freud, even to enjoy his books, without being convinced by him, but anyone sensitive to the nuances and playfulness of literary style, to the shaping power of a great intellectual conception, is not likely to miss in Freud the peculiar urgency of the great writer; for myself, I can never read him without carrying away a deeply engraved, an unforgettable sense of the force of human desire.

By contrast, many of the analysts who turn to writing seem to me not so much writers as people clutching at a few ideas. Whenever I immerse myself, very briefly, in the magisterial clumsiness of Dr. Gregory Zilboorg, or the slovenly looseness of Dr. Theodore Reik, or the tensely inarticulate essays of Dr. Harry Stack Sullivan, or the purringly complacent formulas of Dr. Edmund Bergler, or even the smoothly professional pages of Dr. Erich Fromm, I have a mental picture of a man leaping up from his chair, crying with exultation, "I have it! The reason for frigidity in the middle-aged female is the claustrophobic constitution!," and straightway rushing to his publisher. Where Freud really tried to give an explanation to himself of one specific human difficulty after another, and then in his old-fashioned way tried to show the determination of one new fact by another, it is enough these days for Dr. Bergler to assert why all writers are blocked, or for Dr. Theodore Reik, in his long-winded and inconsequential trek into love and lust, to announce that male and female are so different as to be virtually of different species. The vital difference between a writer and someone who merely is published is that the writer seems always to be saying to himself, as Stendhal actually did, "If I am not clear, the world around me collapses." In a very real sense, the writer writes in order to teach himself, to understand himself, to satisfy himself; the publishing of his ideas, though it brings gratifications, is a curious anticlimax.

Of course, there are psychoanalyst-writers who aim at understanding for themselves, but don't succeed. Even in Freud's immediate circle, several of the original disciples, having obtained their system from the master, devoted themselves to specialties and obsessions that, even if they were more than private *idées fixes,* like Otto Rank's belief in the "birth-trauma," were simply not given the hard and lucid expression necessary to convince the world of their objectivity. Lacking Freud's striking combination of intellectual zeal and common sense, his balanced and often rueful sense of the total image presented by the human person, these disciples wrote as if they could draw upon Freud's system while expanding one or two favorite notions out of keeping with the rest. But so strongly is Freud's general conception the product of his literary ability, so much is it held together only in Freud's own books, by the force of his own mind, that it is extraordinary how, apart from Freud, Freudianism loses its general interest and often becomes merely an excuse for wild-goose chases.

Obviously these private concerns were far more important to certain people in Freud's own circle than was the validity of Freudianism itself. When it came to a conflict between Freudianism and their own causes (Otto Rank) or their desire to be uninhibited in mystical indefiniteness (C. G. Jung), the body of ideas which they had inherited, not earned, no longer existed for them. Quite apart from his personal disposition to remain in control of the movement which he had founded, Freud was objectively right in warning disciples like Ferenczi, Rank, Adler, and Stekel not to break away from his authority. For the analyst's interest in psychoanalysis is likely to have its origin in some personal anxiety, and some particularly unstable people (of whom there were several in Freud's circle), lacking Freud's unusual ability not only to work through his own neuroses but to sublimate everything into the grand creative exultation of founding a movement, committed themselves fruitlessly to the development of their unsystematic ideas, found it impossible to heal themselves by the *ad hoc* doctrines they had advanced for this purpose, and even relapsed into serious mental illness and suicide.

Until fairly recently, it was perfectly possible for anyone with a

Ph.D. (in literature or Zen or philology) to be a "psychotherapist" in New York State. I have known several such therapists among the intellectuals of New York, and I distinguish them very sharply from the many skillful and devoted lay analysts, with a direct training in psychoanalysis, who are likely to have an objective concern with the malady of their patients. The intellectuals with Ph.D.'s who transferred from other professions to the practice of psychoanalysis still seem to me an extreme and sinister example of the tendency of psychoanalysis to throw up the pundit as a type. Like modern intellectuals everywhere, intellectuals as self-made analysts are likely to have one or two ruling ideas which bear obvious relation to their private history, but which, unlike intellectuals generally, they have been able to impose upon people who came to them desperately eager for orientation in their difficulties. In short, the ruling weakness of intellectuals, which is to flit from idea to idea in the hope of finding some instrument of personal or world salvation, has often become a method of indoctrination. All the great figures in psychoanalysis have been egotists of the most extreme sort; all the creative ones, from Freud himself to the late unfortunate Dr. Wilhelm Reich, were openly exasperated with the necessity of having to deal with patients at all. They were interested only in high thinking, though Freud at least tempered his impatience enough to learn from his patients; the objective power, the need to examine symptoms in others, never left him.

By contrast, the intellectual who is looking for an audience or a disciple has often, as a psychotherapist, found one in his patient. And the obvious danger of exploiting the credulous, the submissive, the troubled (as someone said, it is the analyst's love that cures the patient, and certain intellectuals love no one so much as a good listener), which starts from a doctrine held by the analyst in good faith but which may be no less narrow-minded or fanatical for all that, seems to me only an extension of the passion for explaining everything by psychoanalysis which literary intellectuals have indulged in so long. When I think of some of the intellectuals who have offered their services as therapists, I cannot but believe that to them the patient is irrelevant to their own passion for intellectual indoctrination. My proof of this is the way they write. Ever since Freud gave the word to so many people less talented than himself, it has become increasingly clear that, whatever psychoanalysis may have done for many troubled people, it has encouraged nonwriters to become bad writers and mediocre writers to affect the style of pundits. For the root of all bad writing is to be distracted, to be self-conscious, not to have your eye on the ball, not to confront a subject with entire directness, with entire humility, and with concentrated passion. The root of all bad writing is to compose what you have not worked out, *de haut en bas,* for yourself. Unless words come into the writer's mind as fresh coinages for what the writer himself knows that he knows, knows to be true, it is impossible for him to give back in words that direct quality of experience which is the essence of literature.

Now, behind the immense power and authority of psychoanalytical doctrines over contemporary literature — which expresses itself in the motivation of characters, the images of poetry, the symbol hunting of critics, the immense congregation of psychiatric situations and of psychiatrists in contemporary plays and novels — lies the urgent conviction, born with modern literature in the romantic period, the seedbed of Freudian ideas, that literature can give us knowledge. The Romantic poets believed in the supremacy of imagination over logic exactly as we now believe that the unconscious has stories to tell which ordinary consciousness knows nothing of. And just as the analyst looks to free association on the part of the patient to reveal conflicts buried too deep in the psyche to be revealed to the ordinarily conscious mind, so the Romantic poets believed that what has been buried in us, far from the prying disapprovals of culture, stands for "nature," our true human nature. A new world had been revealed to the Romantics, a world accessible through the imagination that creates art. And Freud, who also felt that he had come upon a new world, said that his insights had been anticipated by literary men in particular; he felt that he had confirmed, as scientific doctrine, profound discoveries about our buried, our archetypal, our passionate human nature that philosophers and poets had made as artists.

Had made as artists. Nietzsche, who also anticipated many of Freud's psychological insights, said that Dostoevsky was the only psychologist who had ever taught him anything. No doubt he meant that the characters Dostoevsky had created, the freshness of Dostoevsky's perceptions, the powerful but ironic rationality of Dostoevsky's style had created new facts for him to think of in comparison with the stale medical formulas of psychiatry in his time. Similarly, Freud said of Dostoevsky that "before genius, analysis lays down its arms," indicating that with the shaping power of the artist who can create characters like old Karamazov and Prince Myshkin, with the genius that in its gift of creation actually parallels life instead of merely commenting on it, analysis cannot compete. And in point of fact we do learn more about the human heart from a stupendous creation like the Karamazov family than we ever do from all the formulary "motivations" of human nature. Just as each human being, in his uniqueness, escapes all the dry formulas and explanations about human nature, so a great new creation in imaginative literature, a direct vision of the eternal like William Blake's or an unprecedented and unassimilable human being like old Karamazov, automatically upsets and rearranges our hardened conceptions of human nature.

There is no substitute for life, for the direct impression of life; there is no deep truth about life, such as writers bring home to us, that does not come in the form of more life. To anyone who really knows how rare and precious imaginative creation is — how small, after all, is that procession which includes Dante's Paolo and Francesca, Shakespeare's Othello, and Tolstoy's Natasha — how infinitely real in suggestion is the character that has been created in and through imagination, there is something finally unbearable, the very opposite of what literature is for, in the kind of metallic writing which now so often serves in a novel to "motivate" a character.

Maybe the only tenable literary role which novelists and poets, as well as critics and psychologists, now want to play is that of the expert — the explainer, the commentator, the analyst. Just as so many psychoanalysts want to be writers, so many writers now want to be analysts. And whenever I rise up at intervals from my dutiful immersion in certain specimens of contemporary literature, I find it hard to say who has less to contribute to literature, the psychiatrist who wants to push a few small ideas into a book or the novelist who in the course of a story breaks down into writing like a psychoanalyst.

« 2 »

The deterioration of language in contemporary fiction into the language of pundits is not often noticed by critics — perhaps because the novelists have taken to writing like critics. But it is by no means the highbrow or intellectual novelist — like Mary McCarthy, who in a single story for *Partisan Review* is likely to produce so many deliberate symbols — who is the only offender against art. John O'Hara in *From the Terrace* wrote, of the mother of his hero, that "What had happened to her was that she unconsciously abandoned the public virginity and, again unconsciously, began to function as a woman." Of the Eaton brothers, O'Hara made it clear that "If William slapped Alfred or otherwise punished him, the difference in ages was always mentioned while William himself was being punished; and each time that that occurred the age separation contributed to a strengthening of the separation that was already there because of, among other considerations, the two distinct personalities." This is a novelist? Frankly, I have the impression that many of the younger novelists have learned to write fiction from reading the New Critics, the anthropologists and psychologists. I cannot begin to enumerate all the novels of recent years, from Ralph Ellison's *Invisible Man* to Vance Bourjaily's recent *Confessions of a Spent Youth*, which describe American social customs, from college up, as fulfilling the prescription of tribal rites laid down by the anthropologists. But whereas an angry and powerful novelist, as Ellison is in *Invisible Man*, whatever helpful hints he may get from psychiatrically oriented literary critics, will aim at the strongest possible image of Negro suffering and confusion in a hostile society, Vance Bourjaily, in his recent novel, has his hero preface his description of a business smoker by apologizing that "it would take the calm mind of an anthropologist to describe objectively the rites with which the advertising tribe sent its bachelor to meet his bride."

I don't know what repels me more in such writing, the low spirits behind such prosiness or the attempted irony that is meant to disguise the fact that the writer is simply not facing his subject directly but is looking for something to say about it. No wonder that a passage like this sounds not like fiction but a case history: "I had a good time with Vicky during those two or three months; at the same time, I was learning about the social structure of the town and that of the school which, with certain exceptions for unusual individuals, reflected it; Vicky was more or less middle middle. As a friend of hers, since my own status was ambiguous, it seemed to me that I must acquire hers by association." And Mr. Bourjaily's book *is* a case history, though so meanderingly self-absorbed, for the most part, that it comes splendidly alive when the hero describes a visit to his relatives in the Near East; for a few pages we are onto people whom Mr. Bourjaily has to describe for us, since they are new types, and then we get free of the motivational analysis that is the novelist's desperate response to people who he thinks are too familiar to be conveyed directly. This is a curious idea of a novel — as if it were the subject, rather than the point of view, which made it boring.

The true writer starts from autobiography, but he does not end there; and it is not himself he is interested in, but the use he can make of self as a literary creation. Of course, it is not the autobiographical subject that makes such books as Mr. Bourjaily's flat; it is the relatively shallow level from which the author regards his own experience. The mark of this is that the writer does not even bother to turn his hero into a character; he is just a focus for the usual "ironic" psychological comment. If the writer nowadays sees himself as a pundit, he sees his hero as a patient. What, in fact, one sees in many contemporary American novelists today is the author as analyst confronting his alter ego as analysand. The novel, in short, becomes simply an instrument of self-analysis, which may be privately good for the writer (I doubt it) but is certainly boring to his readers.

« 3 »

The deterioration of language in contemporary "imaginative" literature — this reduction of experience to flat, vaguely orphic loose statements — seems to me most serious whenever, in our psychiatrically centered culture, spontaneity becomes an arbitrary gesture which people can simulate. Among the Beat writers, spontaneity becomes a necessary convention of mental health, a way of simulating vitality, directness, rough informality, when in fact the literary works produced for this pose have no vitality, are not about anything very significant, and are about as rough as men ever are using dirty words when they cut themselves shaving. The critic Harold Rosenberg once referred scathingly to the "herd of independent minds"; when I read the Beat and spontaneous poets en bloc, as I have just done in Donald Allen's anthology of the "new" American poetry, I feel that I am watching a bunch of lonely Pagliaccis making themselves up to look gay. To be spontaneous on purpose, spontaneous all the time, spontaneous on demand is bad enough; you are obeying not yourself but some psychiatric commandment. But to convert this artificial, constant, unreal spontaneity into poetry as a way of avoiding the risks and obligations of an objective literary work is first to make a howling clown out of yourself and then deliberately to cry up your bad literature as the only good literature.

The idea of the Beat poets is to write so quickly that they will not have to stand up for the poem itself; it is enough to be caught in the act of writing. The emphasis is not on the poem but on themselves being glimpsed in the act of creation. In short, they are functioning, they are getting out of the prison house of neurosis, they are positive and free. "Look, Ma, no hands!" More than this, they are shown in the act of writing poems which describe them in the act of living, just about to write poems. "*Morning again, nothing has to be done/ maybe buy a piano or make fudge/ At least clean the room up, for sure like my farther / I've done flick the ashes & buts over the bedside on the floor.*" This is Peter Orlovsky, "Second Poem."

Elsewhere, the hysterical demand for spontaneity as an absolute value means that everything in the normal social world becomes an enemy of your freedom. You want to destroy it so as to find an image of the ecstasy that has become the only image of reality the isolated mind will settle for. It is a wish for the apocalypse that lies behind the continued self-righteous muttering that the world is about to blow up. The world is not about to blow up, but behind the extreme literary pose that everything exists to stifle and suppress and exterminate us perhaps lies the belief, as Henry Miller plainly put it in *Tropic of Cancer,* that "For a hundred years or more the world, *our* world, has been dying. . . . The world is rotting away, dying piecemeal. But it needs the *coup de grâce,* it needs to be blown to smithereens. . . . We are going to put it down — the evolution of this world which has died but which has not been buried. We are swimming on the face of time and all else has drowned, is drowning, or will drown."

The setting of this apocalyptic wish is the stated enmity between the self and the world, between the literary imagination and mere reality — a tension which was set up by Romanticism and which Freudianism has sharpened and intensified to the point where the extreme Romantic, the Beat writer, confesses that the world must be destroyed in order that the freedom of his imagination proceed to its infinite goal. Romanticism put so much emphasis on the personal consciousness that eventually the single person came to consider himself prior to the world and, in a sense, replacing it; under Romanticism, the self abandoned its natural ties to society and nature and emphasized the will. The more the single conscious mind saw the world as an object for it to study, the more consciousness was thrown back on itself in fearful isolation; the individual, alone now with his consciousness, preoccupied in regarding himself and studying himself, had to exercise by more and more urgent exertions of will that relationship to the world which made consciousness the emperor of all it could survey — the world was merely raw material to the inquiring mind.

Freud, himself a highly conservative and skeptical thinker with a deeply classical bias in favor of limitation, restraint, and control, could not have anticipated that his critique of repression, of the admired self-control of the bourgeoisie, would in time, with the bankruptcy of bourgeois values, become a philosophy for many of his followers. Freudianism is a critique of Victorian culture; it is not a prescription for living in the twentieth century, in a world where the individual finds himself increasingly alienated from the society to which he is physically tied. Freud once wrote in a letter to Romain Rolland: "Psychoanalysis also has its scale of values, but its sole aim is the enhanced harmony of the ego, which is expected successfully to mediate between the claims of the instinctual life [the id] and those of the external world; thus between inner and outer reality.

"We seem to diverge rather far in the role we assign to intuition. Your mystics rely on it to teach them how to solve the riddle of the universe; we believe that it cannot reveal to us anything but primitive, instinctual impulses and attitudes . . . worthless for orientation in the alien, external world."

It was the Romantics who handed down to modern writers the necessity to think of the world as "alien and external." By now so many writers mechanically think of it this way that it is no wonder that they look for a philosophy of life to the "primitive, instinctual impulses and attitudes," though, as Freud knew, they are "worthless for orientation in the alien, external world." Man cannot cheat his own mind; he cannot bypass the centrality of his own intelligence. Yet is not sole reliance on the "primitive, instinctual impulses" exactly the *raison d'être* of so many Beat poems and novels; of neurotic plays dealing with people whose only weakness, *they* think, is that they are repressed; of literary studies whose whole thesis is that the American novel has always been afraid of sex? What is wrong with such works is not that the single points they make are incorrect, but that they rely upon a single point for a positive philosophy of life. It is impossible to write well and deeply in this spirit of Sisyphus, pushing a single stone up the mountain. It is impossible to write well if you start from an arbitrary point of view, and in the face of everything that is human, complex, and various, push home your *idée fixe*. It is impossible for the haunted, the isolated, the increasingly self-absorbed and self-referring self to transcend itself sufficiently to create works of literature.

Literature grows out of a sense of abundant relationships with the world, out of a sense that what is ugly to everyone else is really beautiful to you, that what is invisible to many men is pressingly alive and present to your writer's eye. We can no longer, by taking thought, transcend the life that consists in taking thought. The English novelist and philosopher Iris Murdoch has recently helped clear the air of desperate self-pity by saying that "We need to return from the self-centered concept to the other-centered concept of truth. We are not isolated free choosers, monarchs of all we survey, but benighted creatures sunk in a reality whose nature we are constantly and overwhelmingly tempted to deform by fantasy. Our current picture of freedom encourages a dream-like facility; whereas what we require is a renewed sense of the difficulty and complexity of the moral life and the opacity of persons."

By now the self-centered mind fashioned by romanticism, constantly keeping itself open only to adjurations of absolute freedom and spontaneity, has traveled about as far along the road of self-concern as it can; it has nothing to discover further of itself but fresh despair. The immediate proof of this is in the quality of so much of the literature that has been shaped by Freudianism — only because all other creeds have failed it. It is not possible to write well with one's own wishes as the only material. It is not possible any longer to think anything out without a greater reality than oneself constantly pressing one's words into dramatic shape and unexpected meaning. All our words now are for our own emotions, none for the world that sustains the writer. And this situation is impossible, for it was never the self that literature was about, but what transcended the self, what comes home to us through experience.

[1961]

VIII
The Puzzle of Modern Society

The Uses of Experience

LESLIE FIEDLER'S *An End to Innocence*, a first book, is a collection of literary and political essays that seems to have been published with the particular encouragement of leading members of the American Committee for Cultural Freedom. (The book is in a series edited by the executive director of the American Committee for Cultural Freedom, and features special testimonials by two officials of the committee.) In an extremely self-conscious preface, Mr. Fiedler tells us that he feels "just a little misrepresented by a first book so largely political," that he is primarily a literary person, but that he has been forced, like all our generation, through a crisis in liberalism which seems to him "a major event in the development of the human spirit." It is on this reluctant note, of a man sadly committed to a public service, but who would rather occupy himself with purely literary studies, that Mr. Fiedler exposes "the age of innocence." He reviews the Hiss-Chambers case, with Chambers emerging a Dostoevskian hero, unattractive but desperately honest; he analyzes the death-house correspondence between Julius and Ethel Rosenberg, showing how unbelievably fanatical they remained on the eve of execution; he insists that McCarthy is a complex and far more ambiguous figure than certain naïve intellectuals believe; he brings together, into his memories of a Fulbright year in Italy, his indignation at how little Europe knows America and how deliberately, indeed, it misrepresents us. There is a brilliant literary essay on Whitman's reputation, and a very acute piece on how the West (Mr. Fiedler teaches in Montana) commercializes the literary myth of itself. There is also a piece of claptrap, "Come Back to the Raft Ag'in, Huck Honey!", showing that *Huckleberry Finn* is about homosexual love, and some bright remarks, not very conclusive nor very true, pointing up Scott Fitzgerald as a failure and informing us that the American novel has graduated from its former adolescence into its present maturity.

Mr. Fiedler is a very clever writer; he has an engaging gift of

An End to Innocence, by Leslie A. Fiedler. Boston: The Beacon Press.

candor, and he learned long ago not merely to accept himself as a Jew, an intellectual, a writer passionately interested in political events and a political critic essentially dedicated to literature, but, wherever possible, to throw his "tragic" knowledge at people in such a way as to embarrass them. He tells us that his essay on *Huckleberry Finn* has outraged the homosexuals, and adds — "This, I suspect, is success." This may be success, but I'm afraid that it is only the kind of success that can come from such deliberate provocativeness — this air of talking, talking brightly, brashly, penetratingly, all the time, no matter what the subject or whom he embarrasses. This provocativeness is not the sort of bravado which is so marked in a really interesting writer like Randall Jarrell; it is more a kind of fatalistic, "merry," desperate acceptance of Fiedler's fate in our society, of himself.

This candor, this aggressive superiority to other people's "innocence" and delicacy, is the distinguishing mark of what Mr. Fiedler writes. It explains why, when anyone else would have ignored the correspondence between the Rosenbergs — published, after the execution, by the Communist defense committee — Mr. Fiedler not only rushed in to examine, in remorseless detail, all their sickening disingenuousness on the eve of death, but now adds surprise and dismay that anyone could have missed the pain that he himself experienced in *having* to write this article. Similarly, it is this same, this really unbelievable insistence on his own forthrightness in saying what so clearly needs to be said that leads him to write that "There is scarcely a Montanan who does not at one remove or another share in the hoax and in the take; who has not, like the nightclub Negro or the stage Irishman, become the pimp of his particularity, of the landscape and legend of his state." Or to explain that "Katherine Anne Porter and Eudora Welty . . . began the process of taming and feminizing Faulkner . . . making possible the ingrafting of Henry James which produces the true Magnolia Blossom or Southern Homosexual style." It is this, again, that compels Mr. Fiedler to admit that he was the one believing Jew in Rome at Passover and that he is the one intellectual in Montana not afraid to call things out there by their right names. His review of *From Here to Eternity* is called "Dead-End Werther: The Bum as American Cultural Hero."

Candor is an important, and sometimes a great, literary device, but with all the feelings that a man may have as a Jew, as an intellectual, as an American who has passed through the delusions of the Thirties, Mr. Fiedler seems to me shrewd rather than desperate in the way he has exploited his experiences. To what purpose, encouraged by officials of the American Committee for Cultural Freedom, has he shown us that Hiss was guilty and that the Rosenbergs were Communists; that Scott Fitzgerald was a failure, Whitman not what he seemed, and that we, God bless us, have come through to "maturity" in the American novel? Granted that American liberalism did pass through a period of self-deception, that we are now less the dupes of certain theories than we were in the Thirties. What are the uses of experience in fiction today that allow us to be superior to those poor old "innocents" who wrote *Winesburg, Ohio, An American Tragedy, The Great Gatsby, The Sun Also Rises?* What are the uses of experience on the American Committee for Cultural Freedom, that organization dominated by ex-Marxists who are also so careful to let us know that they have repented of their past? What, since Mr. Fiedler is at such pains to tell us that he is a faithful Jew and believes that the Jews are the chosen people — what has he learned from his religious experience that would take the form of not sneering at the Jews of Rome, who hardly know what Passover means?

What are the uses of experience, this sad wisdom that Mr. Fiedler has come to, his stern and reluctant acceptance of capitalist America, his tragic acceptance of the fact that "we are an embodiment of the least palatable necessities of history?" Is it Mr. Fiedler's outrageous calculation that *we* murdered only two Rosenbergs, whereas *they* can shoot millions without arousing the same indignation? Is it the insight that while the intellectuals were wrong, "the buffoons and bullies, those who *knew* really nothing about the Soviet Union, were right — stupidly right, if you will, accidentally right, right for the wrong reasons, but damnably right?" Is it the habit of describing the most painful realities of our epoch only in literary types, so that, brave man that Mr. Fiedler is, he can give us this portrait of Dean Acheson: "his waxed moustache, his mincing accent, his personal loyalty to a traitor who also belonged to the Harvard Club; one is never quite sure that he was not invented by a pro-McCarthy cartoonist?" Is it this description of the evil in McCarthy as "not the reactionary blackness of the oil interests or of the Catholic Church, but of something in the American people which grows impatient with law and order, with understanding and polite talk, when it feels it has been betrayed?"

Despite the encouragement which the book has received and the air of AT LAST TELLING THE TRUTH ABOUT THE RED DECADE, Mr. Fiedler's book is not at all the book of an ex-Communist — of someone who, like Whittaker Chambers, may be said to have passed through a profound experience. This book is wholly a literary concoction, in the sense that it has been plainly put together in order to give Mr. Fiedler a rallying theme for a collection of his essays, and, through his bright and provocative talent, to give a literary publicist to the American Committee for Cultural Freedom. It is this situation, I suppose, that explains the unnatural and strident reiteration of the theme of "innocence" in the book — the worst of which is Mr. Fiedler's utterly unconscious patronizing of any creative talent as "innocent," compared with a really knowledgeable critic like himself. And in the political realm, it is not a sense of former innocence but of actual loss, of a painful nostalgia, as Chambers's book clearly shows, that the hardened veterans of the Communist Thirties really feel. Mr. Fiedler impresses me as not being half so indignant about the "age of innocence" as he tries to feel; frankly, I don't think he cares this much at all, and it is this that makes his book so peculiarly disagreeable. But he has found a fashionable thesis, a rallying cry for his first book, and what an irony it is that this book, so carefully planned, so eager to startle and to provoke, may already be out of date.

[1955]

Old Revolutionists: Dwight Macdonald

DWIGHT MACDONALD'S one-man magazine, *Politics*, meant a good deal to me during its brief lifetime (1944-1949), and for years I have

Memoirs of a Revolutionist, by Dwight Macdonald. New York: Farrar, Straus and Cudahy.

stubbornly held on to certain back issues because of an inarticulated feeling that here, at least, was a sign that radical intellectuals were not always so empty, so nationalistic and so obsessed as many of them have come to be. I was not only in sympathy with Macdonald's unashamedly ethical attacks on political realism, on the "science" of Marxism, on the falseness as well as the stupidity of the liberal weeklies and the "progressive"-New Deal front, but I was grateful above all for the continuing astringency of his notes on the American scene. Unlike so many ex-radicals, who seemed to have given up everything in Marxism except its cocksureness, Macdonald not only kept up his irritable alertness to all that was becoming increasingly stultifying in American culture, but wrote like a man who was honestly trying to understand a world that had outrun the expectations of *all* social "science."

Politics, from my point of view, was a refreshing contrast to the petty egotism and dogmatism of those intellectuals who had grown up inside the radical movement. Macdonald's capacity for dissent from the majority point of view, his almost physical resistance to war slogans, made him oppose particularly the liberals' indictment of Germany as a whole, the silly conceit and even sillier optimism of the New Dealers as world regulators. In addition to this, he had the humility to present to his readers, who certainly needed some fresh ideas, the insights of European witnesses (and victims) of totalitarianism: Simone Weil, Bruno Bettelheim, Nicola Chiaromonte, Victor Serge, Albert Camus. Despite the hysteria of certain contributors and the sometimes intrusive personal moodiness of the editor, the magazine gave one the feeling, in those critical war years and after, that *Politics* signalized and encouraged a definite effort to think one's way back to the humanism, the experimentalism and the universalism of pre-Marxist and anti-Marxist socialisms.

Yet with all this, there is some question in my mind as to just what purpose a collection of Macdonald's back pieces can serve right now. Much of the excitement of *Politics* consisted in its European contributors. *Memoirs of a Revolutionist* is not a systematic study or the kind of memoir that Edmund Wilson likes to do, where the center of interest is not so much in the period as in its confrontation by a wholly literary imagination. Macdonald is neither a historian nor a theoretician; he is essentially a cultural critic, a born "magazinist," as he describes himself, who cannot write a book in cold blood, but who is stimulated by a speech, a slogan, a book, to do quick slashing analyses of the issues it raises. Unfortunately, many of these issues no longer seem very real ten years later — at least not in the wholly polemical terms in which Macdonald likes to attack them. Macdonald's chief concern during the war period is epitomized by his section on "The Responsibility of Peoples" (the original title of this book); he fought constantly against wartime hysteria and the idea of "total" German guilt. In 1943-1945, it took some courage and independence — if not necessarily a knowledge of Germany — to take this position. But Macdonald's irritability on this question has, for obvious reasons, no great relevance at a time when the (West) Germans are the richest and smuggest people in Europe today, and when it takes real courage to insist that the Germans were responsible at all for the unspeakable mass murders of civilian populations.

If we take the book as cultural criticism — as an example of the kind of literature made famous in this country by Mencken — the book may seem to justify itself in the way that old volumes of Mencken's *Prejudices* do. General Patton's pearl-handled revolvers are about as interesting just now as the antics of William Jennings Bryan, but Macdonald on Patton is lively and vitriolic in the style of Mencken on Bryan. Although Macdonald's often solitary fight against the "war idols" made one think of Randolph Bourne, Macdonald's best work is always negative and slashingly critical, like Mencken's. Like Mencken, Macdonald has an instinctive sense of the phoniness and absurdity on the American scene, and he can always spot cultural pretension. It is a pity, in this connection, that he did not include in this book his memorable *New Yorker* attack on Mortimer Adler and the "Great Books" syntopicon. Macdonald there illustrated a kind of cultural criticism that is rarely done in this country, for we have so few people who combine any kind of cultivation with real freedom of manner. But despite this alertness to the inflated and the absurd, Macdonald is not very much like Mencken. For Mencken was not only a nimble satirist and a very funny writer, but he was detached, cold as ice, brutally smug. Macdonald is writing here about events and ideas in which he was passionately implicated up to the limits of his capacity, and he gets angry and abusive in a way that Mencken never could.

In the end, then, the book has to be read as the autobiography of an idea — it belongs with those memoirs of the Marxist left which in American writing correspond to memoirs of the early Progressive period. It takes its place on the shelf with the memoirs of other old revolutionists; it has the immediate quaintness of material to which the author himself looks back with incredulity, as who should say: Was *I* there, in Paterson, in Passaic, at the time of the great strike? Was it really *I* who wrote that pamphlet appealing to the workers and peasants of the Bronx?

It is this extraordinary and unexpected irrelevance of the "radical" experience that is so striking in Macdonald's book. In retrospect, it is the unreality of old issues, old quarrels, the utter insignificance of American Communism, Lovestoneism, Weisbordism, Trotskyism, that is the most profound impression he leaves. But why is the impression so much of triviality, boredom and fatigue? Actually, the irrelevance of the radical tradition to current politics is far less obvious than the insignificance of the conservative tradition. And in any event, the editorials in the *New Republic*, the fights on *Partisan Review*, the letters-to-the-editor in the *New International* — all this, though it seems to him now only vacuous, must have been important enough to Macdonald, since an essential part of his life was invested in it. Yet vigilant and unsparing as he is about himself, eager to be honest, to avoid exaggeration, he writes as if he cannot disguise from himself the utter meaninglessness and triviality of what it means to be an old "revolutionist." The feeble irony of this word, borrowed from the Russian (or from the English of Russians), illustrates the self-consciousness, the unease, the absurdity that he feels about his position. Nowadays there are many other old revolutionists — for some Marxism was not an adventure but part of one's very upbringing — who also feel that the experience was essentially accidental, sentimental, absurd; for them the Young People's Socialist League, the branch meeting, correspond to Sunday schools and to the Epworth League.

But despite this personal impression of triviality, there remains the dogmatism, the materialism, and sometimes the very real corruption of many old revolutionists. Macdonald points to this in passing, in an excellent commentary on the *New Leader's* shameless flattery of politicians in power. Macdonald could have spared us some of his esthetic youth at Exeter and Yale and have used the space to comment on some of the professional patriots and religionists who have been thrown up by the left. Saint-Beuve once remarked that in France people remain Catholics long after they have ceased to be Christians. Certain people in America today have remained "revolutionists" long after they have ceased to believe in anything whatever. In one of Macdonald's best chapters, his "letter" to Henry Luce on the *Time*-sponsored "cultural" magazine that William Schlamm was to edit, there is a pointed indication of what Schlamm — and later, the *National Review* — represents. But how much more could we have said about those other old "revolutionists" who, whether they take to Americanism, or to Judaism, or to Richard Nixon, or to the Catholic Church, are all "revolutionists" still, eternal ideologists, unrelenting fanatics. Macdonald is wrong in thinking that the left has lost all its potency and power. It is from the ranks of old revolutionists that have come labor advisers to Eisenhower, brain trusters to union racketeers, dopesters for McCarthy, "salesmen" of American democracy abroad, expert consultants to Hollywood on the Red Menace, professional informers to smut magazines.

The truth is that in this country, where there are hardly any genuine conservatives in power, old revolutionists constitute not a party but an information service. They are the ones who "know" — or who knew first; it was they who once saw the totalitarian beast face to face. After such knowledge, what forgiveness? Of themselves, their past? Of the "liberal," "innocent" world that still does not know? One path for the old revolutionist is that of power; another, Macdonald's, is that of personal confession, of vigilant truth-telling, no matter how absurd one sounds. Macdonald is not a Machiavellian old revolutionist, but he has the equally unprofitable illusion that "candor" is the same as truth. Although no one has been more critically and attentively concerned with the reconstruction of human values on the left, he is the kind of man who would rather sound foolish than take thought, who identifies honesty with self-deprecation, impatience with wit. It is a measure of our horror of certain impersonal slogans and antihuman dogmas that this sense of the individual person should be so anguished. But one would have liked from Macdonald less autobiography in this sense and more reflections on the history, the character, the possible future of the old revolutionist as a force in our culture. It is this lack of thoughtfulness, of objective concern, that gives his book so immediately transient a quality. The book would have been far more durable if it had been more openly and humbly the study of a generation, for it is a fact that, despite Macdonald's impatient assertiveness of his identity, his experiences seem to be almost completely "political," symbolic of a whole generation. If he had been able to think of his subject as the plight of a representative group of intellectuals, his book would have had a less self-conscious quality and a more obvious purpose. The "radical" experience, however unimportant, humorous, incredible it may seem to be, needs to be studied with detachment—for it has shown itself, in many hands, to lead to goals which are the very opposite of those which radicals profess.

[1958]

Edmund Wilson on the Thirties

One of the many things that I miss in American writing today is the frankly "literary" reportage of national events that used to be done by writers like Theodore Dreiser, H. L. Mencken, John Dos Passos, Edmund Wilson. One reason for the decline of this kind of journalism is the assumption by writers that there is nothing to investigate, that ours is the dead calm that comes after or between wars, that the literary man on a news story belongs only to a blazing time of troubles. The younger writers complain that they are too far from the peaks of power to be able to say what is really happening. Some of the writers who came out of the 1930s have reacted so sharply against their youthful radicalism that they now have a vested interest in contentment. The only Victorians left in the world

The American Earthquake, by Edmund Wilson. New York: Doubleday and Company.

today are the exhausted, guilt-ridden, tediously accommodating ex-radicals who want peace at any price. Some years ago an English magazine edited by such intellectuals announced in its very first issue that the mood of the present period could be summed up as "After the Apocalypse." This was on the eve of the H-bomb, the revolts in Eastern Germany, Poland, Hungary, and the intercontinental ballistic missile; but veterans of the 1930s, as we know from the example of Whittaker Chambers and how many other ex-revolutionaries, project their sense of depletion into the world itself.

Still, it cannot be denied that writers turn to reportage in times that are warlike — times when issues are wholly on the surface, when society is visibly in flux, when there are disturbing social tensions which everyone feels in his own life. The 1930s, an era of incessant social violence, depression, revolution, war, lent themselves to reporting because writers felt themselves carried along by history. So much happened in the 1930s, from the depression to another world war, from Roosevelt to Hitler, from the Japanese attack on Manchuria to the Spanish Civil War, that it can be said of a great many writers that nothing has happened to them since. If the nineteenth century did not end until 1914, the twentieth did not fully begin until the 1930s, for it was then that we began to see even in our innocent and long-protected country the onset of the all-powerful state, the security police, the governmental manipulation of mass opinion, the establishment of the "common man" as an absolute good — all of which have become so much part of our lives, especially since 1945, that we no longer recognize how much we have changed. But in the 1930s all these things emerged out of the unexpressed admission that the crisis was permanent and uncontrollable; in America, virtually the last symbol of pure capitalism, one could see the old order of ideas actually disintegrating, while millions of people sought salvation from the welfare state, Communism, Father Coughlin, Dr. Townsend, Huey Long. And if this continuing ferment made so many writers turn to reportage, so there arose, under the whiplash of now unbelievable despair, that dependence on the state which by now has made the state the only loyalty that people profess.

But we are all wise after the event. The 1930s were not only a fearful beginning to our characteristic mid-century world but an immediate shock; while a great many people understandably lost their heads, no one now can admit it — one is supposed to have looked at fifteen millions unemployed, the country desperate, Hitlerism and Fascism overriding Europe, without feeling anything. The tragedy of so many radicals of the 1930s is precisely that they believed in justice, in freedom, in co-operation. They were not prepared for politics as tragedy; Americans so rarely are. It is easier to rewrite history now, to portray Franklin Roosevelt as more calculating than he really was. So the New Deal appears, in the works of John T. Flynn, Whittaker Chambers, James Burnham, as planned, theoretical, coherent; and the picture becomes really grotesque in the last works of Charles A. Beard, who saw Roosevelt tricking the Japanese into attacking at Pearl Harbor, so that the United States would have an excuse for coming to the aid of the British Empire.

Such interpretations of the New Deal show a remarkable forgetfulness both of the mass suffering which no government during the 1930's could entirely have overlooked and of the confusion, amazement, and powerlessness of those in office. If the 1930s mark the beginning of the contemporary history — the century of mass society — it is because in the 1930s anyone could apply to society Henry Adams's saying that modern man has mounted science and is run away with. With the 1930s, one could see in force the unavailingness of intelligence and good will in a world where political order is continually flying apart under the pressure from ideological new states. Men like Roosevelt, who fundamentally lacked ideas, were able to give the impression that they were planning or plotting a new society, when actually their greatest gift was one of charismatic leadership, the ability to hold up images of stability and national tradition during the storm.

« 2 »

It is this quality of flux, of storm, of violent change, that Edmund Wilson has summoned back so vividly in *The American Earthquake*, a literary expansion of his articles from the *New Republic* about the 1920s and his book reportage of the depression.

It may be that the impression of chaos and intellectual helplessness that Wilson ascribes to the New Deal appeals more to the literary imagination than it does to political historians. Arthur Schlesinger, Jr.'s, recent book on the background of the New Deal (*The Age of Roosevelt: The Crisis of the Old Order; 1919-1933*) presents a picture of intellectual foresight which Wilson, drawing on his actual writings in the 1930s, obviously does not share. And perhaps the gift for seizing and holding personal impressions, the capacity for swift observations and revealing contrasts, gives Wilson an over-sensitized capacity for descriptions of social change. Writers like Wilson, with their instant feeling for the literary image that will convey the feeling of social crisis, for the scene that will instantly evoke a historical moment, are so strong on history as literature, on swift and brilliant passagework, that they tend to impress upon us, as Carlyle does, a picture of history as a series of picturesque accidents. The stream of time bursts into iridescent foam for a paragraph or two, then retires into brutal inconsequence again.

But on the other hand, Wilson's chronicle is so unflinchingly personal, it presents so dramatically the confrontation of the period by a mind obviously unused to social ugliness, that it catches perfectly the revolutionary and unsettling impact of the 1930s on those who were least suited to it. The shock of the times comes through in the reactions of someone like Wilson, whose instincts are always for culture and tradition, and who never ceases to think of himself as an unattached man even when he comes closest to Marxism. It is the radicals who committed themselves intellectually who now have to revise history, for it is themselves that they have to disengage from the past. Similarly, it was never the "proletarian" novelists who caught the drama of the 1930s — they lost themselves in the general hysteria. Much of the Communist writing done in the 1930s, by people who were honest enough but who gave away such brains as they had, now looks like the fever chart of a patient *in extremis*. Such writers are now wrecks of the 1930s, writers who fell to pieces under the last disillusioning blow of the Soviet pact with Hitler, precisely because they had no culture to abdicate from, no wit to surrender. The pseudo science of Marxism gave them all the ideas they ever had, worked on them like strong drink; and their personal confusion was stepped up by incessant political manipulation and propaganda. It was precisely these Communist writers, who saw the 1930s as a time when everything was breaking up and who deliriously joined in the *Götterdämmerung* of "bourgeois" values, who became the real victims of the period. It was not a lack of integrity that doomed so many of these writers. It was a lack of background and perspective, an inability to see that their movement, too, would have its natural and inevitable end.

Wilson's cultural imagination saved him from this loss of perspective. If anything, he had too much of it, and his extraordinary gift for turning every assignment into a superb literary article is a symbol of his inability to lose himself, as many writers did, in a purely human situation. The reins are always tight, and the horses always go the same way. On the other hand, Wilson's detachment certainly never made him incurious. The secret of his durability as a writer is his patient, arduous effort to assimilate, to clarify for himself and for others, subjects from which he feels excluded by temperament. The same hard-won intellectual triumph that as an agnostic he gets out of the Dead Sea Scrolls Wilson used to get, also as a bystander, out of descriptions of the Ziegfeld Follies, police beating up Communist marchers at New York City Hall, the Scottsboro case, the career of Henry Ford, the miseries of depression Chicago. Amid the laziest minds in the world, he is the most Puritanical of intellectual students, the most exacting in the correctness of his language and his learning.

Unsympathetic critics like to portray Wilson as a popular writer who sacrifices the ambiguity and complexity of his subjects. In truth, all his strength comes from the fact that he seeks to understand, to know; and it is his habit of willed attention, of strained concentration, that explains the exciting luminousness and tension of his prose.

Wilson is not a reporter but a literary artist driven by historical imagination — like Henry Adams and Carlyle. Such writers are lightning-quick to see the many metamorphoses of modern man. In Europe, where the succession and contrast of different epochs can be seen on every hand, writers who appeal to the historical imagination can be read for their merit as artists. But in this country, where we are likely to overvalue single traditions as such but to overlook the beauty of history itself, the creative side of such writers is unappreciated. Wilson's sense of historical contrast is documented entirely from his own life and that of his family in relation to America. The points of the compass for him are "the old stone house" of his ancestors in upstate New York that he describes so movingly in this book; New York, the great symbol of the cosmopolitan 1920s, a city that he always describes with distrust; and the ancient greatness embodied in Lincoln.

Only someone who has read much of this old material before can recognize how fine a work of art Wilson has made out of his records of the 1920s and 1930s — based always on the overriding fact of American instability. To see this as coldly as Wilson does, without for a moment allowing oneself to become cold to America, is to have the gift of perspective. When Wilson writes about a buccaneer of the 1920s, "Sunshine Charlie" Mitchell of the National City Bank, he notes that "the boom produced its own human type, with its own peculiar characteristics." When he writes about "the old stone house" in Talcottville, New York, he writes with appreciation of the old farmers that "they were very impressive people, the survivors of a sovereign race who had owned their own pastures and fields and governed their own community."

The section on the solitaries in his family significantly ends with a tribute to Herndon's unsentimental biography of Lincoln, and when Wilson writes about Lincoln, his prose rises to an uncontrollable emotion and we understand why, in the face of so much misery, so much helplessness, thinking of Lincoln inspires him "with a kind of awe — I can hardly bear the thought of Lincoln."

If the historical imagination lives on metamorphosis, it expresses itself as personal impressions. Wilson writes cultural reminiscences as novelists and dramatists write scenes and dialogue. His strong suit is never ideas as such (any more than ideas as such were the strength of Carlyle or, despite his pretensions to philosophy, of Henry Adams); the end of the book, with its halfhearted approval of Beard's thesis on the war, simply emphasizes Wilson's stubborn and romantic isolationism. What makes Wilson's reporting good is the impression of actual experience brought to white heat on the page; it is the re-creation of a scene that relates Wilson to history, not the significance of history in itself. Wilson's writing depends entirely on the strength and flexibility of his style, and its unusual quality lies in the coupling of his intellectual tense style with the lower depths, the city junk heaps and bread lines, the strikes and demonstrations, the agony of mass fear.

The subtler achievement of the book is in the rapid succession of these sketches, which are run together to create a sense of history in motion. In Wilson, reportage becomes a series of impressions united only by the writer's temperament. Like all writing that is fundamentally personal, it depends almost too much on the writer's spirits, his wit, his virtuosity of style. Once the tone flags, the whole threatens to become commonplace. This is what above all things it dare not become, since it is so close to life that only the personality of the writer keeps it from relapsing into meaninglessness. Nothing in such a book dare appear in its objective crudity; everything must be assimilated by imagination. Nothing is held too long, for when the attention is fixed so sharply on cultural detail, it may easily tire, and in any event, the essential point has usually been made swiftly. But the assembling of details, the movement of ideas — these give us the orbit, the "spread" of life in a particular time, the picture of history behaving organically, through a hundred filaments and cells of the social body, lighting up together.

[1958]

The Ghost of Leon Trotsky

It is almost nineteen years since a GPU agent put a pickax into the brain of Leon Trotsky, and during that period Trotsky's interest for everyone has certainly diminished. Despite the usual acknowledgment of his brilliance and literary gifts and a certain abstract sympathy for his fate, it is impossible, now, not to blame him for many features of the terror system that murdered him and several of his children. Between 1940 and now there have emerged the worst horrors of totalitarianism — Russian as well as German. The once electrifying figure of the outstanding intellectual and military organizer of the revolution, the historian and European *homme de lettres* — always so admired by intellectuals in particular, who found their beau ideal in this very incarnation of revolutionary intelli-

The Great Prince Died, by Bernard Wolfe. New York: Charles Scribner's Sons.

Trotsky's Diary in Exile: 1935. Cambridge: Harvard University Press.

gence and energy — now looks at worst like a self-deluded ideologue who mistook his "laws" of history for reality, and at best like the admittedly tragic figure who, with the highest confidence in his ideas, his rectitude, and himself, managed step by step to prepare his own destruction.

The memory of Trotsky stirs up embarrassment among those who admire his intellectual gifts and militant spirit. No man ever destroyed so many people so loftily, so idealistically, so self-approvingly while watching his face in the mirror of history; and it is because he was at the same time a tragic anachronism, a nineteenth-century scientific intellectual at the mercy of the twentieth century, that he elicits embarrassment. Every intellectual is to some extent a dupe of his own rationality, of the belief that reality is as logical as one's thoughts about it. But to think that the most brilliant, the most high-minded, the most cultivated of the Russian Communists never understood his Communist opponents, never for one moment conceded that his dogma was in part the author of his impending fate — this is indeed to be embarrassed for one's vanity as an intellectual.

« 2 »

In 1937, Mr. Wolfe, only twenty-one, was for eight months a member of Trotsky's secretariat in Mexico, and he says that it has taken him the better part of twenty years to develop the necessary emotional distance toward his old hero. This early attachment to Trotsky was at the time characteristic of intellectuals, for whom he personified the highest intransigence and brilliance; and an essay Mr. Wolfe has added to his novel shows so many complicated feelings, all of them intense, that one is not surprised to find him escaping into attacks on the lingering sentimentality for Communism among European intellectuals like Sartre. But what makes Mr. Wolfe's novel itself unsatisfying is the fact that he exhibits all the passionate, noble, and contradictory feelings about Trotsky that his former admirers are still likely to feel; they will reproach him with every mistake, charge him with any crime, so long as they can slip in the suggestion that he was a great man. Far from giving up this opinion, Mr. Wolfe has even created a fictional character, Victor Rostov, who has all of Trotsky's intelligence without his acerbity, all his obstinacy without his fanaticism, and who adds to Trotsky's vision of the revolution a certain softness, an evident self-doubt, that — whatever Trotsky's actual despairs in the last period — are plainly foreign to the everlastingly self-righteous man whose diary of 1935 has been published by the Harvard University Press.

Mr. Wolfe says that in a novel full of invented or transformed incident, it would be improper to call a fictional creation by the name of Trotsky. True, but this does not change the fact that Victor Rostov, a rather kindly and verbal man, makes a much nicer Trotsky than the real one. In his diary, he compared himself to a doctor who could cure people but who is not allowed to practice and must yield to quacks and charlatans. "That would approximately be the way I feel as I watch the criminal work of the 'leaders' of the French proletariat. Conceit? No, a deep and indestructible conviction."

There is the real Trotsky — the man who so combined intellectual sweep and moralistic Bolshevik arrogance that he could say of a harmless French novel that its "eroticism . . . smacks of the police blotter"; who picked up an Edgar Wallace and shouted that "by this book alone you can judge to what a degree enlightened England (and of course not England alone) remains a country of cultivated savages"; who with his precious "dialectic" was just as credulous and mystical as any communicant but for whom the news that the Pope had sent a blessing by radio to Lourdes was enough to call out a frenzy of contempt. "And what could be more absurd and disgusting than the union of proud technology with the sorcery of the Roman chief druid? Indeed, the thinking of mankind is bogged down in its own excrement." Trotsky was a superb writer, and the Stalinist hacks who sent so many of his comrades to death were vulgar careerists; but this Bolshevik passion for invective, for phrases that are merely arrogant but that pose as principles — this unites Trotsky with a Vishinsky far more closely than his admirers would have admitted twenty years ago.

Mr. Wolfe is concerned with a fictional creation named Victor Rostov, not with this savagely polemical and compulsively contemptuous intellectual. But actually Rostov is at times too soft, too yielding, already too weakened with "guilt" to support the brilliant historical career — Trotsky's own — ascribed to him. And, equally, Rostov's staff in Coyoacán are themselves so riddled with disillusionment that Mr. Wolfe has had to leave out a whole dimension of feeling for him — intellectual emulation, always very characteristic of Trotsky's immediate following. Years ago I heard Trotsky's leading American disciple deliver a two-hour lecture to an audience of half-literate working people that was such a shameless display of personal erudition and intellectual operatics that he seemed more interested in catching the Master's personal style than in any working-class problem.

In Mr. Wolfe's novel, the immediate entourage is already virtually anti-Trotskyite. Mr. Wolfe has not only imposed on the characters of 1940 the current craze for psychology and the apolitical outlook of so many ex-radicals today, but he has often "made" fiction by dramatizing his ideas of things rather than the things themselves. Despite many felt scenes and an irresistible sympathy that the reader will extend to a writer so intelligent and full of *brio*, the overwhelming impression his novel makes on me is of how *intellectual* it is. In scene after scene we find Mr. Wolfe translating into actions, into phrases, into colors, his prior notion of human motivations. Even in his style the author depends heavily on free-association images that are really ideas, heavily psychological and self-conscious. This reliance on quick formulas of description seems to me unfortunate, a basically inartistic quality in a book that asks to be judged on the level of creative imagination. Yet the very phrasemongering, the rapidity of the formula with which people's lives are summed up, the alertness and aggressiveness of intelligence — these qualities in Mr. Wolfe are familiarly attractive in themselves and explain why "Rostov" can talk endlessly in the same style of political monologue. Other people's unconscious may be dark and stormy; Rostov's is all politics, phrases, sharp edges. At one point he says to the Mexican police chief whose criticism of the moral failure of the Russian Revolution has stung him, "If you want guarantees, don't try to make history; invest in three per cent bonds." There is the authentic voice of the leader, the man who from the tribune of the victorious Soviets told the Menshevik leader that "You now belong to the dustbin of history." Phrases, phrases! Yet each phrase is a concept, an idea, a notion; and the chain of these phrases, moving in a surge, is what gives Trotsky's writing its firmness. In reading his monumental *History of the Russian Revolution*, one actually feels that the phrases and epithets are the very rhythm of history moving on to its appointed destiny. And in an age when the language of literature seems to refer only to private emotions (in conflict, not passion) rather than to the quickening sound of history as it is made by men, one feels again the reason for his enduring hold on intellectuals.

But at what a cost! For the sense of power that with one hand Trotsky creates in his *History*, where language seems the very sound of history in motion, he took away with the other, by assuming that words were not only signs but absolute realities. He could actually conclude his *History* by stating that where Czarism introduced into world parlance such barbarisms as "czar," "pogrom," "knout," the October Revolution has internationalized such words as "Bolshevik," "soviet," and "piatiletka." "This alone justifies the proletarian revolution, if you imagine that it needs justification." In short, where "October" once stood for a date or an insurrection, it now stood for reality: the word had become flesh, and if you didn't believe it, you were pulled out of the human community and off the face of the earth. Trotsky himself always lived by words; for him the word stood not for the thing but had become the thing itself, which is why his precious "October" still signified the possibilities of human brotherhood even when this same revolution — in "the wrong hands," of course — was knocking the pickax into his brain.

[1959]

The Historian at the Center

SOME YEARS ago, during the Truman era, when Arthur Schlesinger, Jr., began thinking of *The Age of Roosevelt*, he understandably felt that it was a bad time to be writing about Roosevelt. Whatever Truman's endearing personal qualities, his administration certainly did

The Age of Roosevelt, Vol. II; The Coming of the New Deal, by Arthur Schlesinger, Jr. Boston: Houghton Mifflin Company.

not add to the reputation of the New Deal; and Truman's weaknesses as the heir of the Roosevelt administration so quickly made him the sacrificial goat when the Republicans in the McCarthy period came up with their retrospectively long knives that Schlesinger must have felt that he was writing dead against the spirit of the times. Moreover, Eisenhower, at least in those now far-off first months when he seemed to be coherent and occasionally even sage, offered up so powerful a glamour in opposition to F.D.R.'s that it intensified the disenchantment with Roosevelt that had set in with Stalin's obvious exploitation of Allied victory.

But a work of history takes so long to produce that it sometimes sees changes — either in the public taste or in the historian himself — that make for an ironic reversal of expectations. The Truman era may have been a bad time to begin *The Age of Roosevelt*, but the last years of Eisenhower's have certainly made it a good time for publishing it. By 1957, when Schlesinger published his first volume, *The Crisis of the Old Order*, it was impossible not to see parallels on every hand between the obstinacy of Hoover and the obtuseness of Eisenhower.

No wonder Schlesinger's account of how the first New Deal emerged has proved so unexpectedly rousing. Not only was the depression the most significant social experience of the generation now increasingly in the ascendancy; it so colored its experience of the war that anyone who came of age in the 1930s recognized not only that war is politics carried on by other means but that the war was in some sense an extension of the depression. Everything since 1933 has taken place outside the domain of the "normal," the traditionally hopeful American experience. The increasing weakness of middle-class standards and traditions, of the faith in progress and of the habitual insistence on freedom; the increasing frivolity of popular culture; the political nihilism and cynicism of which McCarthy was the largest postwar symbol — all this had its beginnings in the bitterness of the depression and the intellectual bankruptcy of business leadership. It is the great merit of Schlesinger's history that he describes the breakdown of public order, then the first excitement of the New Deal and the hoped-for revival of the national faith, with complete emotional authenticity.

This is because Schlesinger really believes in the New Deal as a tradition, a political idea, a historical legacy. He believes that it was one of the great expressions in our time of historical intelligence and moderation, that it symbolizes the vitality still possible at the center. Schlesinger believes in the New Deal even more than do most of the New Dealers, for whom it represented a whole series of inconclusive compromises. He is sure that as a philosophy the New Deal has coherence and that as a national tradition it has distinct shape. This, while historically debatable, is so deeply felt a conviction that he includes among the dramatis personae of the New Deal the ancestral figures of many American social philosophers with whom Roosevelt had no intellectual connection.

Schlesinger has conviction, and what among so many historians is merely a liberal prejudice is for Schlesinger a way of separating all sheep from all goats. Very few American historians have a real point of view. The amorphous liberalism of so many intellectuals works with particularly numbing force on historians who are so full of American history (i.e., *modern* history) that they are too much a part of what they are writing about to describe it with required force and edge and interest. American historians are deficient in ideas. Whether their lack of perspective is due to their lack of general historical interests or whether it is the other way around, they need a gimmick, a tool, a formula. (No wonder that the conservative and Catholic de Tocqueville is always invoked by American historians; he knew what he thought.) But the gospels are all contradictory — de Tocqueville, Turner, Beard, Marx, Freud — and now Riesman. Schlesinger, whose ease embodies some of the characteristic glibnesses of the present historical guild, certainly has a point of view. It was this, in a period when few historians will try a "big" book, in the grand style, that led him to attempt the whole age of Roosevelt. One reason for this is his evident wish to re-create, as an intellectual tradition, the New Deal for the Democratic party. But even more, Schlesinger's book represents an interest in history as seen from the top, from the inside, among the policy makers — and it is this, actually, that gives the book its old-fashioned *literary* interest, for the great nineteenth-century historians also wrote as if they were operating from the center of things.

« 2 »

Schlesinger's notable sense of literary organization and drama, his ability to describe the Washington scene and the New Dealers as episodes in a historical drama — these have distinct literary overtones (there is even a reminiscence of John Dos Passos's style in the early portrait of Hoover's childhood) and literary value. Because Schlesinger writes as a partisan, with enormous confidence in his cause, he lacks the literary freedom of a Van Wyck Brooks or Edmund Wilson; but he is also free from the mawkish and desperate psychologizing of the academic historian who feels that he writes from the outside, far from the centers of power. Schlesinger's history embodies the admiration of an American intellectual, who feels himself part of a new elite outside the business ethos, for the one great recent American leader who was also outside it. Radicals are usually interested in ideology, not politics; liberals tend to see themselves as sympathizers, not leaders. Schlesinger has reversed this pattern among American historians, just as he believes that F.D.R. reversed it in government.

It was Roosevelt the "country squire," who was patrician in tradition and in fact undistinguished at both law and business, who became the idol of all those people in this country — minorities, labor, Southern peons and Southern aristocrats, intellectuals — who also felt themselves outside the business community as an activity and a tradition. In particular, Roosevelt gave new sanction to those academic intellectuals and theorists who, until the New Deal came along, had always been baffled by their inability to make use of, even to test, their explicit analysis of modern society. The more the businessmen hated Roosevelt because, as they correctly thought, he despised business as a way of life, the more the intellectuals and academicians clung to him. They had all been thrown together by their common exclusion from "normal," commercial, American experience. The Roosevelt haters were wrong when they charged that Roosevelt hated business because he had failed in it. Schlesinger quotes a remarkable letter Roosevelt once sent to a Harvard dean: he really thought business "absurd." It was this freedom from the most powerful tendency in American life that gave Roosevelt his inner freedom; it is this, surely, that gave him his sense of the dramatic, of the "forward" movement in American life at a time when the old order, in Schlesinger's phrase, was not merely in crisis but had actually collapsed.

Schlesinger's first volume, *The Crisis of the Old Order*, though highly partisan and sometimes downright unfair in its black-and-white scheme of values, was exciting because it represented the actual drama in the passing of the old order. *The Coming of the New Deal* is far more technical in its detail and minutely carries the history of the administration up to the 1934 elections. It is not merely his sense of historical responsibility, it is his New Deal mystique, as it were, that has made Schlesinger in this volume stick so closely to the inner history of the new reform agencies — the AAA, the NRA, the PWA, and all the rest. Yet the image of Roosevelt is always in the reader's mind, obviously because it is in the author's. The book concludes with a character study of Roosevelt in office that is an extension of the biography of Roosevelt with which the first volume ended; I suspect that future volumes in *The Age of Roosevelt* are likely to close on this same magnetic human image.

« 3 »

The administrative point of view, I have suggested, is a brilliant literary and dramatic device that gives the reader the old-fashioned sense of commanding history as a drama and a spectacle. The conflict of administrators, the sensitivities of Henry Wallace, the prickliness of Harold Ickes — all these become problems of policy, as they must have been to Roosevelt; and, like Roosevelt, we feel ourselves to be patient, sage, endlessly resourceful. The trouble with this is that while it gives us a sense of being at the center and almost in command of things, it tempts Schlesinger into sacrificing the truth that cannot be fitted in, the jagged edges that would detract from the straight frame and the smooth design. From the center of the administrative web, all things appear in relation to itself. The historian in this position, like the President, gets a sense of the whole that is exciting, but some things look flatter to him than they need to; he must cover too much in a hurry; he cannot help being a little condescending and mechanical. Just as Roosevelt said "my old friend" too easily, so Schlesinger is a little offhand in describing a New Deal politician as "irresistible and penetrating."

More serious is the intellectual unctuousness that comes from thinking inside the position of power. It is true, as Schlesinger says in his moving portarit of Roosevelt, that "the American system remained essentially a presidential system; in the end, all things came to the man in the White House." But the White House is more likely to hear of things than it is to initiate or even to understand them, and here Roosevelt's famous "pragmatism," his lack of ideas, has turned out to be far more sterile and even dangerous than Schlesinger's account of Roosevelt in his favorite image of himself — the "quarterback," the shifting center of operation — suggests. Roosevelt's freedom from the business ethos was more an accident of birth and a quality of personality than a matter of personal philosophy. When one recognizes the intellectual poverty and spiritual thinness with which he defended democracy during the war — has there ever been so notable an American leader whose public papers are so insignificant as political literature? — and remembers how Wilson, by contrast, always had historical reasons for what he did and recognized the historical tragedy of what he was forced to do, one sees the tragedy of a diminishing democratic leadership that Schlesinger, who sees F.D.R. always in winning human terms, does not bother with. Wilson, demonstrably a failure in his own terms, a "foolish" and obstinate idealist, nevertheless left behind him concepts that the Democratic party could think about. The use of a political philosophy, after all, is that it be carried on. Roosevelt's pragmatism, which his enemies thought opportunism and which in Schlesinger's book becomes an exciting democratic vitalism and pluralism, was in fact conducted so far beyond the limits of "normal" politics that it signified neither the bankruptcy that his enemies saw nor the inspired common sense that Schlesinger sees. It represented the extreme of administrative maneuvering, Roosevelt's only knowledge, in a world in which — as with Stalin at Yalta — gestures and smiles and personal charm deceived the actor far more than they did his audience. It had been Roosevelt's great good luck that he was socially an anachronism, but by the end of the war he was really one politically: only his growing inaccessibility inside the web permitted him not to realize that stratagems had replaced principles.

The New Deal did not destroy the old order. Like all modern

revolutions, it came in after the old order had collapsed. It operated, as all governments must operate nowadays, under the shadow of extremes, in a world of improvised solutions. But Roosevelt could not know how much he had gone beyond the traditional morality, the clear sense of good and evil, that at least left Woodrow Wilson historically lucid.

It is this failure to show the growing uncontrol within and behind the New Deal, the hidden dimension of moral extremism, that I object to in Schlesinger's new book. He writes as if, by recounting on so minute a scale the first year of the New Deal, he were reporting from some irrefutable center the established truth. Actually, it has become increasingly clear that the New Deal represented, against the will and sometimes without the knowledge of many people who participated in it, a series of adventures in a void that was created by the decay of tradition.

When Roosevelt was asked once for his philosophy, he replied testily: "I am a Christian and a Democrat." This was the legacy passed on to him, and was purely personal; it was not one he could hand on to his successors. And in fact, he has no disciples, only admirers. Since, in Schlesinger's total argument, the New Deal represents a philosophy of moderation, a middle way between *laissez faire* and the Communist specter, I think that one clear intention of his book — to create a canon, to show the New Deal as a viable tradition — is an illusion. What makes his volumes so notable is really their literary sense, their dramatic organization, their feeling for the personalities of administrators who were swept up by the times as by a tidal wave. It is in such pages that Schlesinger shows his awareness of the plight of democracy, of the increasing pressure of mass society on the eighteenth-century machinery of American government. Schlesinger's book, which becomes thin in its complacent New Deal references, is actually exciting and moving whenever, in seeking to render the facts, it hints of the permanent crisis that is the truth of our times.

[1959]

The Education of T. S. Matthews

AUTOBIOGRAPHY used to be a success story: "In 1890 I founded the Doolittle Metal Works, which, I am happy to say, employs 39,000 industrious and smiling Americans; after my retirement, my third son-in-law took charge of the main office." Now it tends to be written by people, of any age and material condition, who know that they haven't altogether made it. For them autobiography is frankly an effort to arrive at an encouraging new definition of themselves, a way of analyzing themselves through the relentless and public confrontation of their own experience.

In our shaky world people who can even talk about themselves as "successes" tend to be third-raters; so it is a temptation to believe in those people who have every material reason to feel successful, but don't. But there are as many bad, trivial, and private reasons for feeling oneself a failure as there are distinguished reasons — heresy, original gifts — for being considered one in the eyes of society.

It would be too much to say, from the evidence of his autobiography, that T. S. Matthews feels like a failure; let us say that though he has had every reason to feel that the world is his oyster, he doesn't. His father was wealthy and Episcopal Bishop of New Jersey; his mother was a Procter (of Procter and Gamble); after St. Paul's, Princeton, Oxford, he went to the *New Republic* (the *old New Republic* led by Herbert Croly, which had probably the most distinguished editorial board in American magazine history); in 1929 he went to *Time* when it was still a bit of a college-boy stunt instead of the truculently smug organ that it is now; eventually he became its managing editor and for a brief period enjoyed the loftier but empty position of "editor." Eventually, after a series of disagreements with Luce starting from Matthews's opposition to a mean cover story on Stevenson during the 1952 elections, Matthews lost all power on *Time*, and after being sent abroad to investigate the possibility of starting a British version of *Time*, he resigned.

Name and Address, by T. S. Matthews. New York: Simon and Schuster.

« 2 »

In short, like another Henry Adams, T. S. Matthews would seem to have only American society to blame for his failure. And it is true enough that if Matthews lives in London today, more or less expatriated, writing acidly about newspapers and magazines, one reason for his dissatisfaction, an excellent reason, is that after working so close to the press most of his life, T. S. Matthews has come to doubt the usefulness of the press, thinks of it as an instrument of entertainment, not of information, "a sugar pill and not our daily bread." Moreover, like so many sensitive Americans brought up to believe in the revolutionary example of this Republic, he is increasingly disgusted with the example that we actually set. ". . . I shouldn't like to be compelled . . . to live in the United States. For this is not my day in America. . . . This day belongs to the '100 percenters,' the new-rich Texans, the Madison Avenue boys, the professional patriots, the organization men . . . the dogs that eat dogs. If they have really taken over America, and taken it over for keeps, then I think the American experiment has failed. The dinosaur, its tiny brain still dreaming of paradisal forests, is plodding witlessly towards the asphalt lake." He was scared by how much popular opinion in America McCarthy reflected. " 'McCarthyism' is not dead; it existed long before McCarthy and will long survive him, under different names and other auspices. Like the hysteria it feeds on, it lies, a quiescent but malignant growth, under the thin American skin."

There are good reasons to view things here with a fairly jaundiced eye, to enjoy in London a civilized withdrawal from "the dogs that eat dogs." Yet the greater part of Mr. Matthews's self-portrait — not only the disproportionate part on childhood and youth, but his account of working with Edmund Wilson on the *New Republic* and Henry Luce on *Time* — bears out my suspicion that Mr. Matthews's real struggle, most of his life, has been with authority, with those whom our current lingo has learned to call "father figures," with those who are not wicked, just stronger.

Mr. Matthews is a bit of an anachronism: he grew up in a world of religious orthodoxy, parental tyrants, horrid respectability. Nowadays so many parents look to their children for "friendship," are so utterly lacking in that sense of tradition whose authority parents used to represent to their children, that one recognizes among many young people the psychological stigmata of feeling lost rather than the old-fashioned neuroses that came from uncompleted rebellions against convention and authority. How can you rebel without stronger figures to resent, churches that you *had* to go to, schools that hazed you? Mr. Matthews had all that, and I read of his early life with sympathetic recognition, almost with gratitude to hear again of so much old-fashioned tyranny. I also had the uncomfortable recognition that the battles Tom Matthews lost to Edmund Wilson and to Henry Luce were lost first on the playing fields of Cincinnati and Princeton. The Bishop is straight out of Clarence Day's *Life With Father*, only harder, more powerful, and not funny. He made a scene every morning at breakfast; with tennis racket poised to serve, he would coldly wait at the base line for his son to bounce the balls exactly into his hand, and if he didn't catch a ball, he would wait until young Tom had retrieved it and bounced it back to him again. T. S. Matthews was sensitive and literary, and he certainly built up a lot of misery for himself in the unequal struggle with first the redoubtable papa and then old-fashioned teachers at a time when on Sunday a master at so fine a school as St. Paul's could take the boys to the lunatic asylum—*pour le sport*. It was perhaps not entirely the fault of Edmund Wilson and of Henry Luce that in his conflicts with them T. S. Matthews rather expected to lose.

The portrait of Wilson in this book seems to me weak in its spite, spiteful in its weakness. For as Matthews admits, he had been virtually a protégé of Wilson's on the *New Republic*. Matthews plays up Wilson's eccentricities of manner and speech, but on the *New Republic* or off it, Wilson upheld a standard of literary and intellectual distinction that, as Matthews certainly felt, made American writers proud of him. The other day I heard a present editor of *Time* say with admiration that Wilson was "the most uninfluenceable" writer he had ever known. And it is perfectly obvious that Wilson's staunchness, his refusal to knuckle under to anyone, his old-fashioned downrightness and exactingness, are more reminiscent of a bishop than of a literary finagler passing out compliments at a cocktail party. In his conflicts with Wilson, Matthews came out feeling small and injured. But it is interesting that he should write in so malicious a tone about a man whose external manner is the mark of an absorbed and dedicated intellect — the rarest of all virtues in this culture of "Madison Avenue boys" that Matthews claims he objects to.

When he was managing editor, Matthews sent to Luce and the top people on *Time* a devastating analysis of their magazine that Wilson had originally published in the Princeton University *Library Chronicle*. Matthews says that he sent this around "on the principle that enemies are better critics than friends," and adds, with the suspicion of a smirk, that he got no reply. I rather suspect that sending Wilson's essay around was a sneak attack on *Time* by Matthews himself, a man who felt intellectually superior to it but was helplessly fascinated by its perverse interest in style. And it is perfectly clear from the long account Matthews gives of his difficulties with Henry Luce that they arose because Luce knew his own mind and Matthews didn't.

Matthews worked more than twenty years on *Time;* for six of those years he was managing editor, the final clearinghouse for copy. He worked as much as seventy hours a week on a five-day basis, and he explains that just as it was the promise of uniting poetry with journalism that first brought him to *Time*, later, as an editor, it was his "problem writers" who kept him there. "It was mainly they who encouraged me to feel that, however prosaic the result, the effort we made sometimes approximated the poetic. I could never be proud of any particular number . . . but sometimes I felt that we had given it a first-rate try. There were more frequent occasions when, shuffling home to bed at three in the morning, I would ask myself, 'What am I killing myself for?' " As he himself indicates, the convulsive effort put into *Time* each week had conferred upon it the mystical American virtue of teamwork, "the first-rate try." And just as T. S. Matthews, like so many fine writers, found an odd sort of literary release in the mannered prose and editorial superiority of *Time*, so, as a lower boss reporting to a chief boss, he found his greatest pleasure in pulling "the team" to the finishing line each week. "What am I killing myself for?" For Henry Luce, for approval by Luce, for a chance to bask in the smiles of all those father figures, with umpteen millions of dollars and readers behind them, who can make their editors and writers feel that they are right to try and die for good old Siwash.

Matthews, painfully telling the story, says Luce's associates found it natural to become as Republican as himself. But he complains that in 1952, when Luce and his all-too-Republican underlings "sniffed victory in the air at long last, there was no holding *Time.* The distortions, suppressions and slanting of political 'news' seemed to me to pass the bounds of politics and to commit an offense against the ethics of journalism. The climax was a cover story on Adlai Stevenson . . . which was a clumsy but malign and murderously meant attack. As editor, I had taken over the editing of the cover stories, so I was able to scotch this particular snake — but Luce was appealed to, and that was the last political story I was allowed to edit."

Still, Matthews became "editor," and again was persuaded from resigning when Luce asked him to estimate the success of a British *Time.* He is plaintive about Luce's influence over him. "Why did I listen to him? Why didn't I stick to my resolve and quit, then and there? . . . Imperceptibly to me, during my years on *Time* I had gradually shed most of my original repugnance for it; or . . . [had I] grown a thicker skin? I had become so used to *Time's* ways, curt, snide, conceited as they were, that I hardly noticed them any longer." His final meeting with Luce is significantly described as a contest of unequals. "I remember bringing one haymaker right up from the floor: I told him that he was kidding himself about the power of the press; the press had no power of *accomplishment,* though it did have a negative power — to debase taste, harm individuals."

« 3 »

In describing his upper-middle-class childhood, Matthews says of himself and his sisters: "The fact that we were different was never absent from our consciousness. We were ashamed of our timidity and our lack of sturdiness, but we despised the rest of the world for all that; and looked down on everybody who was not like us. And we were sure that nobody *was* like us." It is not just the sense of failure that one carries away from this book — it is of well-bred failure, of the sensitivity and literary flair that made Matthews see a future for himself on a writer's magazine like *Time*, a sensitivity that now permits him to identify his own failures with the increasing materialization of our society. In all this he reminds me irresistibly of his friend Adlai Stevenson; the excessive sensitivity and loftiness bred into Matthews also explains why Stevenson lost to, and is not likely to prevail over, "the new-rich Texans, the professional patriots . . . the dogs that eat dogs." The strength with which some sons do take over is not in their muscle, but in their ideas. They are not just nice liberals; they think differently. Anyone who has ever worked for Luce knows that despite the "liberal" grumbling from the staff night and day, many of the people who write for him do not have convictions sharp enough to make them give up their bread, butter, and martinis. Intellectuals usually lack ideas far more than they do courage. More and more the nice people, the "better sort," praise themselves for their vulnerability and find distinction in their failure. Unfortunately, the nice people are not even nice all the way. They are petulant and resentful. They try to take advantage.

T. S. Matthews, who is almost sixty, wants his readers to know that when Edmund Wilson was a little boy, his parents, worried about his excessive bookishness, put him into a baseball suit and gave him a baseball outfit. Young Wilson promptly gave away the outfit and sat himself under a tree with a book. Brave Edmund Wilson!

[1960]

What's Wrong with Culture

I ONCE MET in a German university a professor of English literature who thought it "uncultivated" to discuss the concentration camps. Admittedly, this was an extreme case (though not untypical of German professors) of what "culture" has come to mean. But as Raymond Williams shows in this remarkable study of the different uses to which English writers have put this term since 1780, the dis-

Culture and Society: 1780-1950, by Raymond Williams. New York: Columbia University Press.

tinctly modern conception of culture as something "higher" than society is itself extreme — a desperate response to the Industrial Revolution and modern mass society.

Oddly enough, the term came into usage as a way of handling new social facts, not of escaping them. Romantic poets like Blake and Coleridge, who are now symbols for the cultivation of private fantasy, were concerned with every conceivable social abuse in a way that would stagger many American writers today. The great succession of literary salvationists in Victorian England — John Stuart Mill and Matthew Arnold, Carlyle, Ruskin, and William Morris — offered different gospels of what "culture" should mean; all of these were nothing but indirect reports on the ugliness, poverty, and despair of industrial England.

But these ideas of "culture" were always rivals to industrialism and democracy, alternatives to them rather than means of social change based on an acceptance of them. And step by step, this conception of culture as a rival party to society, as the ideal realm of value opposed to the dreary actuality of industrialism and mass literacy, has led to our present idea of culture — as a way not of creating a good society but of escaping from society altogether. Many intellectuals in America today doubtless find ridiculous that nineteenth-century hope to educate everyone which led Tolstoy to prepare his simplified version of the Gospels, or Emerson constantly to tour the country with set lectures on "Culture." Yet if the term "mass culture" means anything, it means the ever-widening social opportunity without which so many American intellectuals would have remained in the "masses." Mr. Williams reminds us that the vast new reading public that accompanied the rise of the novel in the eighteenth century provoked the same horror that intellectuals today profess of the audience for television or movies. Though the real vulgarity of *Kitsch* can be blamed more on the intellectuals who produce it than on the consumers who have no choice but to buy it, it is always this public that is blamed, for they symbolize "society" to intellectuals who, to themselves, personify "culture."

« 2 »

Mr. Williams's work is important, often brilliant, and a healthy change from the tiresome fear of our expanding society that is now so common among intellectuals. The book is uneven in style, and varies from a fairly stiff schoolmasterish prose to passages of remarkable passion and illumination. It is of real value, but it has one obvious limitation for an American reader. Mr. Williams, as he himself explains, comes from the working class, went to Cambridge on scholarships, and in his personal circumstances and general outlook is entirely typical of the first-generation of British intellectuals who have been educated at the expense of the state, have never felt themselves to be part of the Establishment or even of normal commercial middle-class society, and who have a profound and almost mystical attachment to the working class as a *community*. This feeling for community, for tradition, for local usages and settled habits (all of which represent the other meaning of culture, a total way of life), counts for much more in the ranks of British Socialism than does Marxist class antagonism. Although Mr. Williams, like so many intellectuals in Britain, calls himself a "Socialist," he is certainly no Marxist. The Marxist version of "class" is too abstract a term for someone with Mr. Williams's social experience to apply to the hearty realities of the British village and countryside, and the whole idea of radical and destructive opposition to "bourgeois" culture by an aroused working class offends his belief in society as a *common* culture. Besides, the Marxist idea also sets "culture," in the self-conscious and superior sense that Mr. Williams disapproves of, over and against existing society. Marx, as he shows, is on this side of his thinking very much a contemporary (as of course he was a neighbor) of the Victorian prophets of "culture."

What interests Mr. Williams is a national culture in which all classes can share. He does not want to revolutionize society but to see that the "masses" enter more and more into the common culture. He really believes in society as the solidarity of all classes within it. In this connection, it is interesting to note that he is much friendlier to a tradionalist idea of culture, like T. S. Eliot's, than one would expect from a British radical. And his essential disapproval of George Orwell is based on the argument that Orwell could not accept a relationship to any class in English society, that he had the essential point of view of an "exile." To many American admirers of Orwell, he has seemed for our time a peculiarly traditional English example of honesty and independence, and both Edmund

Wilson and Lionel Trilling have praised him for this. To Mr. Williams, however, Orwell is an outsider, and an irritating one at that, for of course Orwell was not from the working class, and while he spoke for Socialism, always attacked Socialists! During the war, I used to hear British Laborites complain of Orwell that "He's not one of us." But it has remained for Mr. Williams not only to give this objection meticulous critical definition, but to extend his disapproving term for Orwell, the "exile," into something even harsher, the "vagrant."

Mr. Williams, who is always fair-minded as well as intelligent, makes out a good case for the literary virtues of the "vagrant" as the observer from afar, the reporter and intermediary who comes fresh to every social scene because he is not really part of any. But the American who remembers how Orwell's gifts as a reporter served him in Burma and Catalonia, as well as on the road to Wigan Pier, is not likely to appreciate Mr. Williams's very provincial feeling that where "the substance of community is lacking, the tension, in men of high quality, is very great." What, after all, is so wrong about tension — especially when compared with the low pressure and pompous clichés of so much British prose? Even with D. H. Lawrence — a miner's son for whom Mr. Williams of course has much more open sympathy than for the Orwell who went to Eton — Mr. Williams has more a sense of class solidarity than a sense of the qualities that separate genius from the rest. In one way, Lawrence is a test case for critics with Mr. Williams's background. They can identify themselves with him up to a point; but his savagely uncontrollable gifts and his Messianic conception of himself actually irritate and estrange them far more than his class origin attracts them. Although he handsomely gives Lawrence points for his "instinct of community," and again is absolutely right in saying that Lawrence "was not a vagrant, to live by dodging; but an exile, committed to a different social principle," Mr. Williams ends up by complaining of Lawrence that what he always referred to as "the living, organic, believing community" will not be created by standing aside. "The tragedy of Lawrence, the working-class boy, is that he did not live to come home."

"Coming home" in this sense can only mean, to a writer of Mr. Williams's background, that ultimately culture and society may be the same. The very possibility of such a hope is the good fortune of a still traditional society.

Mr. Williams's real theme is that "culture," as the realm of value, must unite itself with social justice. He assumes, as people who think too much in social terms always do, that we all believe in the values passed down to us, that they need only to be shared, not re-established. But although "culture" may speak in the name of values, it does not always know what they are or even which are left. There is a purely creative side to the work of scholars and artists that seeks to define values, not just to save them from (or for) society. Ever since the decline of supernatural religion, which is perhaps the only realm where absolute justice and absolute value were one, we have become increasingly unsure of our ground—of that which gives importance to our values because it is prior to them and in some sense authorizes them. It is easy enough for an Englishman to identify his society with its traditional values—ultimately to be shared by all classes. But an American, who has made his nation rather than inherited it, is less likely to identify all value with his own society.

[1959]

Art Is Good for You

So far as I can tell, there is nobody in the great enlightened American middle class just now who is not an art lover. Truck drivers may sneer at art and old laundrywomen may be too tired even on Sundays to paint; but if you have enough money and enough leisure, it is safe to say that you would dare any heresy in America now except indifference to art. Art is the paradise of "fulfillment" and "creativity" that democracy grants each of its sons and daughters. Especially its daughters, for the confidence that an American woman has in her choice of clothes and her ability to furnish a room invariably extends to the confidence that she can paint. And why not, when the cultural humility of the hayseed American turned businessman and world traveler no longer allows him to ig-

Sight and Insight, by Alexander Eliot. New York: McDowell, Obolensky.

nore the money in painting, the cachet in painting, the splendor of museums and the tyranny of "taste"? If any wife can paint, every husband has to be artistic. These days, who cannot pay homage to art when one considers (*a*) how "everything else" has failed and (*b*) that the vague daily discontent which used to be equated with the experience of mortality has now been identified as the unrest of being "artistic"?

To perform in music, you at least have to learn the language of music, and it is manifestly more difficult to write a book than to "sketch" a picture. But painting, already allied in history with churches and palaces, with the furnishing and decoration of houses and the cultural authority of museums, has now become the principal embodiment of the "artistic," of "creativity" — all the more in that painting has now broken away from representation and *seems* to be as free and easy as a thought, anybody's thought. Music will always be a language, and whatever its purity of form, a book must have a subject. But the more abstract painting becomes, the more intellectualized and assimilable the nonartist's use of it becomes, the easier it is to feel "creative" in the presence of paintings rather than in the reading of books. André Malraux has pointed out that art now seems to be embodied not in works — objects originally made for a purpose not purely "artistic" — but in moments; works have become only moments in the experience of us who behold them.

« 2 »

The cult of art, the widespread illusion that everyone should feel creative and "artistic," has led to a literary invasion of the art of painting and of art criticism. The more we are pressured into liking what it is inherently impossible for everyone to like, especially at the same uniform pitch of enthusiastic perception, the more we are likely to take secret refuge in literary reverie. E. M. Forster once wrote a charming essay on "Not Listening to Music," and confessed that in the concert hall he often thought of "how musical" he was. Much of what I read by art critics these days seems to me merely impressionistic, reveries on how creative the experience of art makes them feel.

A flagrant example is this book by Alexander Eliot, the art editor of *Time*. It is the most unabashedly literary self-dramatization in the presence of painting that I have read in years. Mr. Eliot explains that art is really a "city," and that all sorts of people are treating the city as if they owned it, "and they do." But some of us are still afraid of art, which is why we need a guide through "battlements" that seem to be "walls" but are really "gates." (Surely no one who cares deeply about painting is this much worried that *everybody* should love painting.) Mr. Eliot, in order to sanction his own literary emotions, is careful to explain away the philistine specialist, the coldly destructive critic, and to establish what he calls the "personal" point of view:

> . . . The only way to begin to understand art is to accept it wholeheartedly on one's own, and then to enjoy it. The Spanish peasant drinking from a wineskin . . . never sips; he lets the wine spurt right down his gullet. Only afterwards will he reflect on its satisfying taste, the warm feeling in his belly and the new beauty of things round about. That is the way to enjoy art. Let questions of taste and scholarship . . . come later.

So much depends on the "personal" interpreter:

> Perhaps the path of free enjoyment and personal interpretation can help lead men back to the city. At least it demonstrates that art belongs to them. To all who have eyes, art offers a flashing multitude of insights. Some of these insights the interpreter shapes into words and offers over again. He does not work dogmatically but as a friend in conversation, exactly as if he were describing people or landscapes that had inspired him.

But Mr. Eliot's own conversation is confusing. The book consists of very short orphic chapters — "The Children of Light," "What Do Artists See?" "The Birth of the Invisible," "Mirrors of Death and Life," "How to Just Imagine," etc., which have no visible connection with each other; free-association phrases that sound as if they had come out of a notebook alternately with random reflections that sometimes, not very often, express shrewd remarks about differences of style. And Mr. Eliot's own style is marked chiefly by the lack of any sustained argument. He writes about paintings by Caravaggio: "A black clamor threads the stillness of these canvases, as comets thread the cold of outer space." He says that "at his easel

Monet was a frenzied athlete holding back the dusk. He begged mankind to witness a beauty on the edge of being lost. Not that he lacked faith in the morning: he knew the sun would arise again — and set again — but not for every man, not forever for any man, not very long for anyone." Does this say anything about pictures? Mr. Eliot's cult of the artist follows logically from his relative unconcern with the work itself, and at one point he even claims that great artists don't feel death as the tragedy that other human beings do:

> To pretend that artists of Titian's size are doomed to the same disappointments and eventual usefulness as other men is to deny the saving grace of art itself. The great creators are not momentary, white-capped waves, however towering upon the seas of history, but sailors, admirals indeed, masters of their voyages. They sail upon history, including the history of thought and style, as upon the ocean sea.

In short, anybody who is lucky enough to be a great artist has, it turns out, an easier time of it than other people. "Artists come into the world not to fill their own bellies but to bring new nourishment to mankind." I wonder, however, if even artists know why "artists come into the world." Admittedly, good artists are people who have the ability to create works of art that are more coherent and lasting than they themselves are; but despite the pleasure we take in these works or the quickening of our lives through them, we do not actually know much about artists and cannot actually learn anything from their lives about art itself. In the despair of politics and the inadequacy of romantic love as the solution to every personal problem, we have put the whole burden of our salvation on art. But we press art too hard, we are too greedy for it to perform miracles in our personal lives, and it is for this reason that it is now possible to despise people who do not seem to love art as much as "we" do: they threaten the theoretical foundations of our happiness. Actually, if there were more intimate experience of art and less self-conscious use of art, we might see that none of us can fully explain the effect of art, or correct it when it is unsatisfactory, or keep it up as an ecstatic experience all the time. If we in this country had an honest sense of the limits of art, we would have a more grateful sense of its power.

[1959]

The Village Today: or The Music the Money Makes

Bill Manville, who writes a column for the *Village Voice*, is an acute if perhaps too glibly rueful observer whose subject is New or Upper Bohemia. Whatever Greenwich Village may once have been or may now be supposed to have been, anyone who has recently strayed down MacDougal Street on a Saturday night knows that now it is a playground. What Coney Island was once to the honest workingman, Greenwich Village is now to the unmarried or ex-married young professional. The Village streets, pads, coffee houses, and bars are jammed with people who look a million times more sensitive, artistic, and "interesting" than William Faulkner or Igor Stravinsky, but who live by teaching economics, analyzing public opinion, writing advertising copy, practicing psychoanalysis, or "doing research" for political candidates. They are not intellectuals, but occasionally dream that they will be. That is their secret ambition. Meanwhile, being young and frisky, they are not yet the "managers" in our highly organized technical society. But they have the skills someday to become managers. Just now they don't want power any more than they want marriage. They want a good time, and a good time is what they go to the Village for, and a good time in the Village is what they get. The LeRoy Street Saloon, Chumley's, the San Remo, the White Horse Tavern, the Kettle, Minetta, O. Henry's, Louis's, the Riviera, Julius's, the Casa Allegra, El Faro. . . .

What I like most about Bill Manville's reports of conversations in these places is his honesty. He is aware of himself and his friends as the genuinely new fact the young always are, and he has the intelligence to notice what they want and what they miss. Maybe "honesty" in a writer is only a form that intelligence takes—perhaps this is why supposed rebels like the "beats" write so badly. But the vital difference is that the beat writers tend, on their own testimony, to

Saloon Society, by Bill Manville; photographs by David Attie, design by Alexey Brodovitch. New York: Duell, Sloan and Pearce.

be victims of mother and yearners after sex, and so write about sex as if it were the revolution. Manville's people are far more worldly than that. What the traveling salesman was once vis-à-vis the rural areas, these charming lechers and morning drinkers are now to all the humdrum and respectable marrieds in the suburbs.

The lines are carefully drawn: "Married and unmarried people should never mix. You can't be sentimental about these things; when your friends marry, you have to drop them, and they have to drop you." The same character says honestly, "God, I hate rent-payers, taxpayers, husbands, fathers, citizens, voters. I hate the *New York Times,* the Bronx, apple pie, motherhood, the forty-hour week, the Beat Generation, and Shirley Temple!" These are people who need just to support themselves and to pay the analyst, people (as Manville doesn't say) whose technical skills are automatic enough to leave them mentally free. They haven't moved to the Village because it's cheaper. But the blunt and concentrated pursuit of pleasure is still a vaguely subversive way of life in America. It is this that gives Manville's people their gallantry, charm, sauciness — and that touch of *tristesse* which Manville exploits like a musician sneaking in a few bars of Brahms.

« 2 »

But first things first. Manville has caught the delicious, the delirious, the whirligig music that money makes for so many people in New York just now. Here, at last, is a paean to good living by Greenwich Village as she is, not as she was when Edna St. Vincent Millay and Joe Gould burned their manuscripts to keep warm. "The cocktails came, so cold the gin smoked off the ice. Salad and steak, asparagus tender as love itself. Two kinds of wine cooled beside the table in silver ice buckets." On the wings of such food, sex follows swiftly. A young man named Phil confesses, "Wherever I go, I see magnificent women hurrying into saloons, stores, hotels, theaters, women so wonderful, so beautiful, so radiant and distant in their brilliance, they make me want to yell: 'Stop, stop, I don't want to lose you!' "

That is downtown today, and even when it laughs at uptown in the person of a brazenly cynical millionaire out of a play by Bert Brecht or a movie by René Clair, it's hard to see what the difference is. Maybe it's that downtown always has uptown to laugh at. Here is a Villager describing the millionaire who arrives "a little late, more than a little loaded. He has the standard uptown animal with him — taller than him, blonde of course, a certain dead-head serenity, a mink tent, and a Southern accent. Vanner himself is wearing an apricot-colored shirt and a tie that instantly lowers real-estate values for two blocks around. He glitters and winks with sharp metallic lights, and in fact he's encrusted all over with little bits of metal; gold cuff links, gold ring on the finger, a gold pin at the collar, another on the tie. . . . He's the kind of man who laughs a lot, you hip?"

Manville has a sure sense of style in his own writing. Sometimes, to be sure, he introduces names that remind you of Damon Runyon — George Garn, Lou the Ladies' Man, Perlman Pace, Maggie Singleton, and Big Mary; occasionally his interjected meditations on the world at large have the sentimental bitterness that reminds you of the pompous Broadway columnist. The very showiness and anxious cleverness of his obiter dicta tell you just how bourgeois and unintellectual the world of modern professionals really is. And this, I sadly discovered, is not a book to be read twice; it is journalism, not literature. But it has the great virtue of journalism — it brings news, it really informs us. And what makes these clever yet sometimes merely wistful conversations come alive is the fanaticism of people today trying to make a world entirely out of pleasure.

The "normal" world, the armed, busy, and political world, impinges so heavily that one has to blot it out to get a little privacy. But privacy is not enjoyable any more if it's experienced *alone;* hence the party in our age of the party — the party that starts Saturday morning ("Don't tell me about early in the morning, we'll pull the shades. We'll wear dark glasses") and that ends, really, never. Everything builds up and builds up all the time. The only question is the one Lou Manx discovered in his own mind when he fell ecstatically in love, and was ecstatically happy. "Then I thought: 'Is this all I will ever feel in my life? Is there nothing left now but the long, slow, peaceful walk, hand in hand, to the grave?' So I broke up with her. Love is not enough."

[1960]

Youth Is a Pressure Group

IN THE BOOK that first made him famous, Albert Camus spoke of the sense of the absurd that colors modern life for so many people nowadays, and identified it with the punishment of Sisyphus, who laboriously pushed a stone uphill only to see it roll down again. Camus's fable, based on Nietzsche's pronouncement that "God is dead," was really a complaint, such as naturally visionary intellectuals have been making since the eighteenth century, that with the grand mystery of supernatural religion taken out of life, the dimension of the unexpected had been taken out of life. But nowadays an equally painful predictability or ennui is commonplace among individuals whose material aims, at least, have been abundantly fulfilled, and who in the absence of any other positive social ideals for themselves find themselves paying a bitter price in boredom and exasperation of spirit for the materialism of their outlook. They have achieved a paltry goal that hardly expresses their longing as human beings. As a result, their secret ambition seems to them infinite and more frightening than it really is; they simply have no social tool or language to put it to. And still aiming at what they have already achieved, they understandably feel frustrated, and therefore "absurd" to themselves.

The great merit of Paul Goodman's book on "the problems of youth in the organized system" is that he is concerned constantly with human nature as it is frustrated by the society in which we actually live. The "absurdity" that many older people feel is the same one that many embittered, lost, and mutinous young people act on in incidents that get them into trouble, which indeed they often act on *in order* to get into trouble. No matter how high or low we put human nature itself, it has to be in excess of what society expects of it. Yet civic authorities constantly say that the trouble with youthful delinquents is that they don't sufficiently have a sense of "belonging." The only solution, as Goodman sees it, is to appreciate the still unrecognized capacity of human nature that

Growing Up Absurd, by Paul Goodman. New York: Random House, Inc.

has been proclaimed by all the generous intellectual and social revolutions that have brought us this far in the grand adventure of modernity but which have been frustrated in our day; our conception of human nature must be freed from the merely contingent goals of the society with which we have identified it. Goodman does not mean that human nature is independent of "culture," but that it is always superior to the existing values of society. Only as we are concerned with the demands of our human nature rather than with the loyalties imposed by society can we see what man has a right to expect of his society — and to what extent society frustrates this expectation and so becomes "absurd" in his eyes, unworthy of respect, and therefore a set of laws or conventions to be broken.

« 2 »

If you compare Goodman's deliberately utopian thesis with the two kinds of social criticism that are now in vogue — the merely descriptive sociology of a Vance Packard that exploits the present uneasiness of the American middle class, and the obstinate "position" taking that one sees in C. Wright Mills's self-consciously defiant "line" in favor of Castro and other unpopular causes — a book like *Growing Up Absurd* seems better than it is, since it is full of the intellectual dignity of the old-fashioned radical independent thinking things out for himself. Goodman is not only an extremely intelligent and acute social observer of troubled young men, delinquents, beatniks, Village apaches; he is also the last person in the world to take existing society as necessary and he is incapable of flattering it. He is free of the superficiality that seems to possess so many social commentators in America just now — writers who are no longer able to see their society from outside, and who, like Max Lerner and how many others, just now talk as if they were osteopaths and America were their patient. It is ridiculous to talk about the waste makers and the Mom complex, the lonely crowd and status symbols, without addressing oneself directly to the historic nature of the profit system, our middle-class culture, and the obvious imbalance between our wealth and the deprivations suffered by most other human beings. Too many Americans now want to remain fully attached to our social system and at the same time to draw the rewards of a little sophisticated (and wholly external) criticism of it.

Goodman, by contrast, is a thoroughgoing philosophic and intellectual radical. Not only is he able to see American society in perspective; he frees the reader, page after page, of the intellectual vagueness that comes from so much identification with our present scheme of things; the current alternative — identification with historical "destiny" in the shape of a Gomulka or a Castro — is equally impossible for him. Goodman thinks for himself; and in upholding the sanctions and demands of a human nature freed from contemporary American fears and shibboleths, he brings home the constant stimulus to independence of thought that lies in psychoanalysis (Goodman is a lay practitioner), which to the extent that it addresses itself to "nature" rather than "society" can help liberate the often anxiously conforming middle-class American from the disapprovals of a society which too often takes slogans for ideas and the national interest for all reality. I would even say that the very traditionlessness of America, which seemed such a blessing to philosophers in the eighteenth century, has under present mass conditions become a sanction of ignorance; we are so little aware that there are different philosophical approaches to reality that we feel compelled to choose only between accepted positions.

Goodman's tradition is that of the literary Romantics — the belief in a suppressed capacity in human nature that unites the Romantic poets to the psychology of Freud. His essay is often exhilarating in its independence and is full of penetrating insights into the intense quarrel with society that rumbles under the prosperous surface of our society. But I don't believe in his book as a diagnosis of youth in general. When Goodman talks about youth, he seems to be talking not about the suburban youth whose games he has never seen but about a whole class of consciously alienated young men in the city, Bohemian or excluded for all sorts of social or sexual characteristics, who understandably feel that the existing goals of society are boringly "square." When it comes to less consciously demanding young people, I think it is a fact that much of their pressure on society constitutes the demand of what is virtually a new social class — and when they attack society directly, it is not because they think society "absurd" but because they find its defenses weak.

To be young is often to find oneself in the position of the "barbarian" in the classic sense of the word — the stranger, the man from without, who does not know the ways of the capital but who longs for its prizes. Many different kinds of youthful rebellion and frustration — and above all ambition — enter into the social acts the courts call "delinquency"; it is only the constantly increasing pressure from many new groups that forces us, in order to keep the peace at all, to lump together the very different demands under the name of "delinquency." For myself, I don't believe that these pressures can be equated with "human nature" in general, or that this nature is either infinite in capacity or particularly hard to discover. Every day now new continents — whole populations — enter actively into society, demanding their share of life. Today youth definitely constitutes a social class, a pressure group. As soon as this group ceases to be wholly "barbarian" and alienated, comes into society and takes the measure of those presently in control, it takes over many of the same values it protested before. I have seen no evidence, as Goodman would suggest, that it is hatred of war and concern over the possible horrors of nuclear warfare that makes young people everywhere feel that our society is "absurd." Often enough they seem to accept war as the normal setup, no longer distinguishing between it and the scientific technology they admire. But war itself may become another part of the dismal routine of predictable social acts, and then the innumerable acts of gratuitous private violence come to symbolize only the self-indulgence, not the idealism, of people who are all too aware of how society can serve their wants — they never think, as Goodman does, of man *creating* society, of man the architect and utopian builder of his world.

"It is hard," Goodman complains, "to grow up in a society in which one's important problems are treated as nonexistent. It is impossible to belong to it, it is hard to fight to change it. The effect must be rather to feel disaffected, and all the more restive if one is smothered by well-meaning social workers and PALs who don't seem to understand the real irk. The boys cannot articulate the real irk themselves." Well, what is this "real irk"? In individual boys it is often a sexual and psychological problem in relation to the family rather than a conscious demand on society for a more meaningful vocation. I would guess that much of the "irk" that Goodman is concerned with in this book relates to the longings of unconventional sex; he quite airily overlooks the hideous satisfactions that very many people now find in made-up jobs, irrelevant research, the dissemination of mass culture, and thousands of other activities that represent very real employment to those who find an added purpose in life in setting their teeth against the new people making their way up from below.

Although Goodman ends his book with a list of the many modern revolutions whose frustration, he thinks, explains the impasse of youth today, it is noteworthy that he speaks always of "fellows," "lads," "boys," "kids," and never of the actual social, economic, and racial categories among youth who are in rivalry with the established order and who are now making their way up. His analysis virtually overlooks the disaffections of young girls, who he thinks always have a vocation anyway as mothers and housekeepers. This completely ignores the frustration, which we *can* study just now in America, of the many young women who have been educated for something better than being cooks and bottle washers. The revolutions going on today are always in behalf of races, groups, and classes seeking their share. It is only *when* they achieve their social goal, as so many middle-class Americans have achieved theirs, that the "rat race" and the "organized system" become problems — to people who have achieved all that they expect of life and have nowhere else to go. Goodman's analysis is most valuable, I think, as an articulation of what those who are actively independent of society really want for themselves. The acuteness of many of his observations articulates the radical energy and spiritual freedom of the kind of intellectual who is fast disappearing in favor of the organization-manager-turned-critic-of-himself and the nostalgic radical who has become desperate for a "position."

[1960]

Eichmann and the New Israelis

ON HOLY Mount Zion in Jerusalem, near the supposed sites of both King David's tomb and the Last Supper, there is a cave, Chamber of the Destruction, in which are exhibited some of the most gruesome relics of the Nazi fury against the Jews. You walk into a dark smoky room illuminated by the acrid flare of memorial candles; on the wall, so tightly joined together that in the uncertain light they look like hundreds of fallen tombstones, are rows of memorial tablets, black on white; each commemorates a community that was destroyed. The bearded young custodian, in full Orthodox costume, seems almost perversely eager to show his horrors — in the glass showcases are prayer shawls with bloody smears, prayer shawls with holes where bayonets went through, cylinders of the hydrogen cyanide crystals used in Auschwitz, the playthings of murdered children, Torah scrolls cut out by SS guards to make insoles for their boots.

The Chamber of the Destruction exhibition is deeply disapproved of by many Israelis, especially in the government, who view it as unnecessary and as a calculated effort on the part of certain small and fanatical religious associations to get support from emotional tourists. The government itself supports a magnificently organized research institute, Yad Vashem, devoted entirely to documentation of the Nazi campaign against the Jews. In row on row of air-conditioned vaults, trained scholars who were themselves prisoners in the camps collect materials on each of the concentration camps, still making every effort to locate Jews who may still be alive. It is from the files of Yad Vashem that the government will furnish the main proofs against Eichmann at his trial in Jerusalem's new "House of the People." It is in those spotless cool vaults, rather than in the cave of horrors on Mount Zion, that the full sweep of the Nazi attempt to exterminate all the Jews is displayed. Here, in file after file from the floor to the ceiling, are the names of the victims and, wherever possible, the manner of their death. By contrast, the Chamber of the Destruction seems contrived and useless. As soon as I walked into the smoky atmosphere of that exhibition, which seems bent, in Jewish fashion, on not giving up any of our dead, on not yielding or forgetting the memory of a single scream of agony, I found myself recoiling from the guide's voluble eagerness to show me everything. As he took me around from showcase to showcase, his voice rang out oratorically, and I felt that he was exploiting the dead, that although it was natural of him to praise the religious spirit in which so many Orthodox Jews had died, he was mechanically working on me to induce the hysteria in which he himself lived every day.

All calculation aside, who but someone for whom a Chamber of the Destruction represents normal Jewish experience could spend day after day in such a place? I imagine him constantly living with those bloody and punctured prayer shawls, those abandoned dolls, and, like a caretaker at Madame Tussaud's, adjusting with finicky perfection a cylinder of hydrogen cyanide, a desecrated Torah. There they all are — his heroes and his saints — and as he proudly tells you of the rabbi who calmly put on his *tallis* to die, you can see that on holy Mount Zion, near the (reputed) remains of King David and the (supposed) site where Jesus had His last Passover Seder with His fellow Jews, what the Chamber of the Destruction most honestly commemorates is the pre-Israeli Jew, the Jews who always expected to perish at the hands of European anti-Semites and who went to their death in community after community because even stronger than the Nazis was their own belief that, as Jews, they were destined to die en masse.

In Israel, I heard of how a deeply religious aunt of mine, my mother's younger sister, met her death in Poland in 1943. Her sons begged her for days to join them in going toward the Russian lines (where they were saved and joined the partisans; eventually they went to Israel). But my aunt refused to accept the transportation that was available, or even to leave her house. "It may not be God's will," she said. "I cannot go against God's will." She was shot on her doorstep. And, with equal certainty of what God wants for the Jews, whole communities of the religious, especially honored in the chamber on Mount Zion — very old men, wise men, saintly men — are remembered for not running away but for being in their place, village after village, when the Nazis pulled their beards, smeared excrement on their faces, and trod them in the mud before shooting them in layers.

There are many young Israelis and "new" Israelis, especially the most patriotic Israelis of all, the "Orientals" from North Africa and Yemen, who simply cannot understand these stories of the Nazi period. *Jews* died like that, like sheep, when *we* take on all the Arabs at once? Impossible! Look through the children's primers passed out in Israel. On every page there is a picture of a sunburned young boy staunchly standing guard, and everywhere you go in Israel people talk about "our war of liberation." A pretty young cousin of mine in the Army Reserve, whom I was meeting for the first time, perplexed me by her many references to "our King David," and when I discovered that she meant Ben Gurion, she responded to my teasing by saying calmly that there was no military force in the Near East that would challenge the Israeli Army.

Nationalistic militancy is always used as a challenge to those who, like me, are "relics of the Diaspora." At a reception in Jerusalem, Yigael Yadin, the celebrated Israeli chief of staff during the "War of Liberation," who is now professor of archaeology at the Hebrew University (he had recently dug up some amazing effects of Bar-Kochba, leader of the last great Jewish war against the Romans, A.D. 131-135), explained that he taught his children their national history out of the Bible, and insisted on knowing what I taught my children. General Yadin is an extremely charming man to talk with, and from the last World Orientalists' Congress in Moscow he had brought back some wonderful stories about Soviet cultural nationalism. He obviously did not recognize any resemblance to the cultural nationalism of Israel, but as a matter of fact, the ideological cocksureness and rasping dogmatism of a few "leading personalities" in Israel reminds me very much of many Soviet writers and intellectuals. The vital difference is that in Israel there is every shade of opinion, and one meets on every hand people who could not live by official slogans even if they wanted to; it is extraordinary how many people in Israel say that they are not Zionists, a form of cultural self-righteousness they apparently leave to "the Diaspora."

Most officials and intellectuals in Israel are "Westerners," tied by one link or another to the culture and traditions of Europe and the United States. It is the "new" Israelis, those growing up entirely under the cultural and political domination of the new state, who worry the authorities most. For as wards of the new state, they are so steeped in Israeli militancy that they are likely to view with disbelief the six million of their fellow Jews who went to their deaths.

To see the housing settlements made up entirely of new arrivals, who often enough owe their lives to the new state and certainly will not deny it their long-frustrated allegiance to a country of their own, is to have a glimpse of the enormous power of indoctrination the state possesses over its new citizens. Ben Gurion and his colleagues have talked constantly of the new type Israel would create, washed clean of the stains of the past. But if the new type will not accept or recognize the immediate past at all, he is not likely to feel deep kinship with even Ben Gurion and his militant colleagues. So deeply disturbing is modern Jewish history to the national vanity of Israel, so sharply does the Hitler period in particular challenge the mystique of Jewish militancy on which the state is built, that it obviously is necessary to make these "new" Israelis more sympathetic to the European Jews (especially the East Europeans), whose past they have never understood and whose fate they must now learn to respect. In short, Israeli leaders have come to recognize that Israel cannot divest itself of the Jewish past without destroying the *raison d'être* of Zionism itself.

So those who died, some no doubt "tamely" and even "shamefully," as writers once put it, now have their place in Israel. They have all been stepped up a grade in the golden book of honor. The official title of Yad Vashem Institute is now Martyrs' and Heroes' Remembrance Authority. The word "Heroes" was not there originally; it was added, as the director of the institute told me, in deference to the new conception that now prevails in Israel of the role of the Nazi victims. An official questionnaire the institute sends out in an effort to document resistance to the Nazis includes such questions as: "To which party or youth movements did you belong at the time of the war? . . . To which military unit did you belong before and during the war? . . . To what extent did you participate in the activities of the underground, ghetto, camp, or partisans? . . . Which Jewish officers and fighters are known to you?"

« 2 »

It cannot be said that Eichmann was tracked down and captured in Argentina solely in order to present, in him, a living proof of the Nazi war on the Jews. But it can be said that once Eichmann was captured and brought to Israel, certainly one very strong motive in putting him on trial was the desire to bring home, in full force from the lips of the principal organizer of the massacres, both how difficult it was for the Jews to resist their fate and how hard they tried.

In order to do this, the Israeli government faces appalling risks, for the main lines of Eichmann's defense, apart from the customary but ineffectual plea that he was obeying orders, are not likely to improve the already strained relations between Israel and the West. As one government official told me, Eichmann's copious pretrial testimony has taken the expected line that the Nazis simply wanted to get the Jews out of their territory; since none of the great powers would take them in sufficiently large numbers, the Nazis had no alternative but to kill them. This way of putting it, while not likely to endear the Israeli government to America or Britain, is of course not altogether unlike the Zionist claim that the Jews have ultimately no place to go but Israel. The recurring argument that I carried on with certain Israeli officials was over this dogma that Jews in America or England or France have no real future in their own countries. Although one official finally, and with great reluctance, went so far as to "admit" that America might be an exception, I must say that I find the extreme Zionist argument — that the Jews have no future except in Israel — catastrophically similar to totalitarian arguments about the "decline of the West" and dangerously shortsighted, since Israel is not likely to survive if the Jews do not survive elsewhere.

Eichmann's trial — every moment of which is to be "covered," photographed, filmed, and televised — will, it is expected, make it finally clear, through the person of the chief executioner, that six million Jews really were killed. And it will be clear who killed them. There he is; it all actually happened. Hard as it is to think that such things could have happened, it will also be clear that they took place outside of Israel — and that this is what happens outside of Israel.

[1961]

The President and Other Intellectuals

SOME YEARS AGO, when Sherman Adams was still grand vizier of the Eisenhower administration, a famous American poet and long-time friend of Adams's, while sitting in his office in the White House, expressed a desire to meet the President. Adams went in and came out again and tactfully explained that the President was not curious to meet the famous poet.

That same poet, however, was prominently displayed at the inauguration of John F. Kennedy. And although many of us who admire Robert Frost's poetry and enjoy Robert Frost's conversation and have not shared his political views may well be surprised to hear that he has *returned* to the Democratic fold, Frost's enthusiasm says a good deal about Kennedy's charm for some of the most interesting minds in the United States. During the campaign and afterwards, Kennedy certainly never hid his allegiance to the fundamental principles of the New Deal — which Robert Frost has always detested. Yet no sooner did the New Frontier get itself named (somewhat mechanically) than Robert Frost heralded "an Augustan age of poetry and power, with the emphasis on power."

For Robert Frost even to think of himself as Virgil to Kennedy's Augustus in this new age of American power shows how deeply Kennedy not only affected some writers but encouraged them to feel a new confidence about America's role in the world. During the campaign, the very literary and "socialist" columnist of the *New York Post*, Murray Kempton, confessed that although he was pledged to vote for Norman Thomas, his heart belonged to Kennedy, while Walter Lippmann must have carried many votes for Kennedy by certifying his faith in Kennedy as a thinking politician who promised to be a statesman.

It was particularly on the more intellectual and liberal correspondents with him that Kennedy seemed to make the greatest immediate impression. At Los Angeles, watching his first press conference before the nomination, Norman Mailer thought that Kennedy did not seem too popular with the general run of reporters; he was "too much a contemporary, and yet difficult to understand." But Richard Rovere in the *New Yorker* not merely testified with increasing warmth and affection to Kennedy's abilities, but that July was able to say "with a fair amount of certainty that the essence of his political attractiveness is his extraordinary political intelligence. . . . The easy way in which he disposes of the question of Church and State . . . suggests that the organization of society is the one thing that really engages his interest." In his recent book on the campaign, *The Making of the President, 1960,* Theodore H.

White describes Kennedy on tour as one "who enjoys words and reading, is a Pulitzer Prize winner himself and a one-time reporter; he has an enormous respect for those who work with words and those who write clean prose. He likes newspapermen and their company. Kennedy would, even in the course of the campaign, read the press dispatches, and if he particularly liked a passage, would tell the reporter or columnist that he had—and then quote from its phrases, in an amazing effort of memory and attention."

Norman Mailer at Los Angeles, preparing the article that *Esquire* was to insist on calling "Superman Comes to the Supermart," was staggered on interviewing Kennedy when the candidate said he had read "*The Deer Park* . . . and the others." The conventional remark on meeting Mailer is, of course, that one has read "*The Naked and the Dead* . . . and the others." But Kennedy, happily, was not conventional. The man who was very possibly the next President of the United States had read the scandalous hip novel about Hollywood doings in Palm Springs that had enraged and disgusted so many publishers and critics. Mailer's brilliant if overwritten article expressed the same hope for Kennedy that in their different ways Lippmann and Rovere and Kempton and even Robert Frost had openly felt. Given the "vacancy" in American life, as Lippmann had put it during the last days of the Eisenhower administration, the increasing divorce between private thought and the public realm, could it be that here at last was one of the "creative innovators" in politics, one man with brains and vision enough to pull our people to world reality, away from business as usual? Could it be, dared one hope, that with this rich, handsome, literate and courageous young man the sickening cycle of underground life and public inanity had at last been cut? *Esquire*, more hip than Mailer himself, advertised his article as "The Outlaw's Mind Appraises the Heroes' Dilemmas." But what Mailer said, with moving hope as well as concern, was that perhaps, with Kennedy, there might at last be some positive awareness of the ever-growing disrespect of intellectuals for politics. Too long, as he said, had politics quarantined us from history, and too long had we left politics to those who "are in the game not to make history but to be diverted from the history which is being made." Although the convention at Los Angeles was actually dull, full of seedy machine politicians, "The man it nominated was unlike any politician who had ever run for President in the history of the land, and if elected he would come to power in a year when America was in danger of drifting into a profound decline."

Mailer was stirred enough to romanticize Kennedy with faintly derisory analogies to Marlon Brando. Yet whatever Mailer's personal symbol of an American hero, what he said was no more than what so many intellectuals felt. "It was a hero America needed, a hero central to his time, a man whose personality might suggest contradictions and miseries which could reach into the alienated circuits of the underground, because only a hero can capture the secret imagination of a people, and so be good for the vitality of his nation. . . ."

And just recently there has come to hand the most moving expression of the wretchedness and the positive sense of unreality that political alienation can suggest to a sensitive mind. It is the brilliant excerpt, recently published in *Esquire,* from Saul Bellow's new novel, *Herzog.* The hero is a university teacher and writer, racked by the collapse of his marriage and by his spiritual loneliness, who wildly scribbles in his notebook letters to public leaders as well as to private individuals. At the end of this excerpt, he suddenly writes a letter to President Eisenhower, and this defines not only the ground of his private unhappiness but his feeling that it has a public source: ". . . it seems a long time since chief executives and private citizens had any contact. The President is briefed by experts or informed by committees on the problems of the nation. That is too bad. Sometimes obscure citizens are wildly intelligent, without the disabilities of special training. But we have to recognize that intelligent people without influence have a certain contempt for themselves. This partly reflects the contempt the powerful have for them, but mainly it comes from the contrast between strength of mind or imagination and social weakness or political impotence. . . . It seems to them that society lets them think everything, do nothing. The private resentment and nihilism that result are due to a private sense of failure which possibly comes from the intellectual's faulty definition of himself and his prospects. What should his thought do? What power ought he to have from it?"

The Russians speak of many disaffected and silent people in their country as "internal *émigrés*"; increasingly it has become natural for many American writers and scholars and intellectuals to think of themselves as "internal *émigrés*." In the very Thirties that now seem to some young people an unrecapturable time of *engagement* and public responsibility, Nathanael West said that we have no outer life, only an inner one, "and that by necessity." By the 1960 Presidential campaign, it was perfectly possible for writers like Robert Frost and Norman Mailer (who, whatever the outer life, are not so hilariously divergent as they seem) to herald, with varying tones of enthusiasm and private distrust, what Frost called "a new Augustan age" and Mailer an end to the "alienated circuits of the underground." I grant that writers welcome an audience in high places, that "the new Augustan age" is pure rhetoric — much more so (whatever the phrase) than Mailer's felt and even obsessive feeling that now there are "alienated circuits of the underground." But if the writer is good, even his egotistical affections are intelligent. And of course one reason for this pro-Kennedy feeling was the contrast he made with the General and the General's Westerns and the General's sentences — to say nothing of the General's party, which a year after the campaign announced a major new campaign to enlist "the specialized knowledge and experience of the nation's intellectuals," which has now drawn plans in every state "to facilitate the utilization of friendly academicians in party affairs at all levels."

Truman, even more than Eisenhower, showed himself to be intemperate in denouncing "advanced" American pictures that had been selected by museum officials for exhibition abroad, while F.D.R., whatever his spontaneous shrewdness in answering to immediate situations, had the landed gentleman's repugnance to excessive intellectual labor. No wonder that so many writers and scholars have felt that they can at least *talk* to Kennedy. He reads, he reads endlessly, his reading is constantly an amazement in a country where the strongest minds often on principle declare a positive contempt for the reading of serious books. Addressing a newspaper publishers' convention, the President of the United States recalled that Karl Marx had been correspondent for the *New York Tribune*. Before leaving for his talks with De Gaulle and Khrushchev, the President at his birthday dinner in Boston quoted

William Lloyd Garrison's famous thunder-cry from the opening number of the *Liberator*. When he was welcomed to Paris by De Gaulle, the President graciously replied by invoking Jefferson's love for France and Franklin's popularity in the *salons*. When Hemingway died, the President quickly issued a tribute in which he made reference to Paris in the 1920s, the lost generation and the fact that Hemingway had helped to end the old provincialism of American letters. The President, as James Reston has said, takes printer's ink for breakfast, and by now his bookishness and intellectual sophistication are so well known that one is no longer surprised to hear that C. P. Snow has been invited to the White House and that E. E. Cummings has been in to tea, or that at a certain juncture Kennedy alone, of all his intellectual entourage, knew the title of Churchill's first book. It did not seem at all pretentious to me that the First Lady, interviewed on her plans for redecorating the White House, should have spoken of her interest in antique furniture as natural to the wife of a "historian." Not only has "history" been the President's strongest intellectual interest, but so far as he has been trained to any profession, it has been to the study and the writing of "history." The son of the American Ambassador to Great Britain in 1940 had positive reasons to remember that during the Civil War the son of the American Ambassador to Great Britain was Henry Adams, and there learned a great deal that was to be important to the life of politics and the writing of history. President Kennedy, who before the war thought of becoming a newspaperman, reminds me, in the range of his sophistication, of a great many "intellectual" newsmen and editors. The author of *Why England Slept* and *Profiles in Courage*, the President whose favorite book has been given out as Lord David Cecil's *Melbourne* and favorite novel as Stendhal's *The Red and the Black* is in his personal interests alone far more of a "historian" than many who teach history rather than learn it.

Now it is also true that President Kennedy's anecdotes from American history tend to be trotted out rather irrelevantly to formal occasions, and that the punch line quoted in Paris from Samuel Adams is unaccountably accredited in Vienna to someone else. And if he cited a little-known detail from Karl Marx's biography to an audience of publishers, it was to joke that Marx had vainly asked the *New York Tribune* for a raise — look, said the President, what you fellows may get us all into by not giving a correspondent a raise! William Lloyd Garrison's "I will not equivocate and I will be heard!" is in excess of what a birthday dinner among Massachusetts politicians, even on the eve of his going to Europe to meet Khrushchev, seems to call for. And *Profiles in Courage*, perhaps because it was indubitably *written* by the author himself (as he replied to reviewers who doubted it), is certainly far more interesting for its personal emphasis on "courage," courage by *anybody* in the United States, whether Taft or Norris, than for any significant political ideas of his own. *Profiles in Courage* always reminds me of those little anecdotes from the lives of great men that are found in the *Reader's Digest*, Sunday supplements, and the journal of the American Legion. It is the kind of book that reads like a series of excerpts even when you read it through; and indeed it seems composed of excerpts — excerpts of reading, excerpts of anecdote. Nor, quite apart from his conventional public statements, am I impressed with the tales of a voracious reading that seems to be concerned largely with getting the "facts," the highly separable material and statistical facts that can be shoveled into the executive mind. And with everything that has been said about Kennedy's being a Catholic, almost nothing, so far as I can tell, has emerged about the personal and intellectual side of his Catholicism. Unlike Senator Eugene McCarthy and other American politicians whose thoughtfulness and sense of philosophical principles owe so much to the traditional teachings of their church, John F. Kennedy seems to have been more aware of Catholics as a source of political support than of the Church as a source of intellectual inspiration. And although Kennedy's narrow victory, which owes so much to Catholics, has caused many Catholic writers and intellectuals to rally almost defensively around him, some of them, before Kennedy was nominated, were positively bitter about his political exploitation of Catholic support.

Yet with all these limitations and conventionalities and sales tricks, it is interesting to see how much of an "intellectual" Kennedy wants to be and how eagerly his bookishness, his flair and sophistication, his very relish for the company of intellectual specialists, have been advertised to the public without any fear that it might dismay a people so notoriously suspicious of these qualities in others. Obviously in Kennedy's case an "intellectual" taste does not suggest a fastidious withdrawal from anything — not even normal passion. Adlai Stevenson in his two campaigns seemed to be running not only against the bluff, smiling General, but against the General's philistine supporters. It is interesting to learn from the autobiography of T. S. Matthews that when Matthews warned Stevenson against "Ohio" (meaning the Yahoos), Stevenson's advisers just stared at him, while Stevenson smiled and went back to work. The extraordinary identification that so many American intellectuals make with Stevenson has often struck me as loyalty not to a lost cause but to lostness as a cause. I have never been sure just how much of an "intellectual" Adlai Stevenson is, but he has certainly been cherished among intellectuals more for his obvious sensitivity than for the strength of his ideas. In 1956 even more than in 1952, and at Los Angeles in 1960 even more than in 1956, he seemed the peerless leader of intellectuals who boasted that they had never had a candidate before — and who warned that if he were counted out for positively the last time, they could never be that much concerned again: they would have suffered just too much. And since Stevenson's public style seemed to combine self-demeaning wit and vulnerability to such a degree that some of his closest friends condoled with him on having to face the public at all, perhaps it is no wonder that the candidate who publicly yearned that the cup might pass from him was defeated by the General who listens with particular respect to the head of any large American corporation.

By contrast, of course, Kennedy has not only surrounded himself with many of the liberal historians, economists and political scientists who were reputedly such a liability to Stevenson, but despite certain necessary political favors to be paid back he has made a point of appointing as Ambassador to Japan a professor of Japanese history, as Ambassador to India a John Kenneth Galbraith, as Secretary of the National Security Council the former dean of the Faculty of Arts and Sciences at Harvard, as one of his immediate advisers the author of a scholarly study of Presidential power, as another adviser a young man in his twenties who was first in his law class at Harvard. Although the Secretary of State obviously was chosen to be one of a team, it is interesting that his last previous job should have been as president of the Rockefeller Foundation; although the Secretary of Defense was president of the Ford Motor Company, he came to Ford and rose at Ford because he was a brilliant statistician; although the Secretary of the Interior necessarily comes from the West, the present one really is crazy about Robert Frost. Even the Postmaster General in this administration has written a novel; even the new Military Adviser to the President has written a superb book on American defenses. No wonder that Arthur Miller and John Steinbeck and W. H. Auden were asked to the inauguration as publicly declared assets of the Republic; that even the Kennedys' French chef is felt to be a compliment to their good taste rather than to their wealth — to say nothing of the *fête champêtre* thrown for the Pakistan President at Mount Vernon, which (it is safe to guess) irritated some congressmen not because of its reputed cost, but because, with its announced links to classic entertainments in the past, it represented a bit of intellectual swagger that not all Americans are likely to admire.

In short, the President has gladly let it be known that he is in fact a highbrow, an intellectual, an omnivorous reader. There was once a Tammany mayor of New York who, in private, talking with a favorite magazine reporter, confided that he indeed knew and enjoyed Joyce's *Ulysses*. But this was a secret, not a boast. President Kennedy's acquaintance with some minor details in the life of Karl Marx is rather more a boast than a secret, like his open espousal of Robert Frost, his invocation of William Lloyd Garrison in Boston and of Jefferson in Paris; all these and more are attempts to form his public style. As has often been said, Kennedy is the most "intellectual" President since Woodrow Wilson — some even say since Theodore Roosevelt. Hoover may have been a brilliant mining engineer on three continents and with his wife he did translate a medieval Latin treatise on mining; but in public he gave the appearance of suffering fools miserably, and stimulated no one. Wilson had been a political scientist and had written books; but he, too, tended rather to patronize and to moralize, and at Versailles in 1918 was hopelessly outclassed in wit and learning, to say nothing of his not knowing a single blessed word of French. (President Kennedy's French is primitive, but even on a state visit to Canada he was able to make a virtue of his limitations by likening it to

Prime Minister Diefenbaker's.) Like Theodore Roosevelt (also trained to no profession but that of "historian"), Kennedy has cultivated as his public style the bookman-in-office. Although Kennedy has not yet publicly found jobs for poets (as T.R. did for Edwin Arlington Robinson), he, like Roosevelt, has praised the strenuous life as if he were promoting a historical revival and, like T.R. again, he lets his literary opinions be known. He has helped to establish taste. And it is just this cultivation of the highbrow world as an executive taste and Presidential style, his turning the poor old suffering American egghead into something better than a martyr to popular culture, that I find most suggestive about Kennedy-as-intellectual. If during the campaign he grew on many thoughtful observers who distrusted his family background and despised his failure to say a single word about McCarthy, so in his first weeks, at least, he was able to persuade many cool observers that his was the necessary style of administration in these times — like Churchill, like De Gaulle. Before Cuba, one English joke was that Kennedy talked like Churchill but acted like Chamberlain; even after Cuba, it was said that there had been an *unaccountable* lapse of his dominant executive style. But Cuba apart for the moment, it is obvious that Kennedy's reputation as an "intellectual" has been an asset to him at a time when government operates on a scale of such complexity, requires so deft an ability at least to show a nodding acquaintance with many subjects. It has often been said that Kennedy turned the tide in his first television debate with Nixon by the precise answers he was able to supply to questions raised from so many different fields. Before his nomination, says Theodore H. White in *The Making of the President, 1960,* Kennedy astonished his own staff by analyzing without notes his chances in every single state of the union, and, in the "honeymoon" weeks of the administration, Vice President Johnson let it be known that he was positively awestruck by the President's ready handling of so many different subjects.

This smooth and easy assimilation of fact, this air of over-all sophistication, is what Americans have learned more and more to admire in journalism, in business, in conversation and on television quiz shows — whether the man in the dock is Charles Van Doren or the President of the United States being questioned mercilessly (and pointlessly) about everything from Laos to Tammany. The quiz show did not die out with the exposure that the contestants had been briefed; the candidates in the 1960 campaign were also briefed, as is the President of the United States today, and the show goes on. If the reporters sometimes act as if they wanted to trip the President up, the President knows that he can impress the country by way of the reporters. This over-all style, so much like the division of even the arts and sciences into departments of *Time* magazine, became a "research" style among the military during the war, and it has now invaded the big universities and "scientific research and development." It is our national style, *intellect-wise*. We now admire it — when it comes unaccompanied by personal stress. A recent article in a liberal weekly on "The Mind of John F. Kennedy" turns out to be an entirely admiring study of Kennedy's range as an administrator. This vocational or psychological use of the word "mind" is so typical of our time and place that it probably never even occurred to the author to extend the word to cover "beliefs." Instead we are told that Kennedy's "marshaling of related considerations" defines Kennedy's mind "as political in the most all-encompassing sense. The whole of politics, in other words, is to such a mind a seamless fabric, in which a handshaking session with a delegation of women is an exercise directly related to hearing a report from a task force on Laos." And this ability to assimilate on the jump necessary quantities of fact, to get statements of a problem that carry "action consequences" — this is what we have come to value as the quality of intellectual all-roundedness or savvy. It is a style that depends always on research done by other people, on a swift and agile reaction to the statement of the problem *set* by other people, on the professional politician's total recall for names and faces, the professional communicator's ability to wham the effective phrase right down the mass media to the great audience. The more complex and insoluble the problems become, the more intellectuals are needed to pile up research on them; the incoming trays are piled higher, ever higher, with Freedom Riders, Latin American poverty, education bills, recalcitrant congressmen, the Congo, obstinate Englishmen and offended Nigerian diplomats who were refused a cup of tea in a Maryland restaurant. The professors who coasted along on two courses and one committee now work from eight-to-eight before they go out to the big dinner every night: "I don't have time to put my shoes on in the morning." Since the boss is the man who takes his problems home with him, the boss proves that he is the boss by a certain air of tense vigilance and unsleeping physical resiliency and readiness. Never in any administration have we been told so constantly how little sleep the President gets.

The boss nowadays does not have to be an expert himself; in the normal course of nature he cannot be one and boss too. But he has to know who the experts are. So much is this executive style—with its dependency on batteries of advisers, experts, "researchers"—the admired "intellectual" style because it works with intellectuals, that the President of this nation of boastful pragmatists, in a public tribute to Robert Frost, told the story of a mother's writing the principal of a school, "Don't teach my boy poetry; he's going to run for Congress"—and affirmed: "I've never taken the view that the world of politics and the world of poetry are so far apart." No wonder that some who suffered with Stevenson in 1956 for being too good for the American public felt with Kennedy in 1960 that intellect was at last in touch with power. He had read the essential books; and the essential names, the principal formulae, the intellectual shorthand, were at his disposal. No wonder that, conversing with certain Kennedy advisers in March, one felt about them the glow of those who have not merely conceived a great work but are in a position to finish it. The boss *understood;* he was just as savvy as anyone else, but less "sensitive" (meaning destructible). It took half the time to explain highly technical problems to Kennedy that it had to Stevenson, and it turned out, too, that Stevenson actually wasn't much of a reader. During the Eisenhower administration, I heard a famous scientist say with some satisfaction that the President was "actually very intelligent." And Robert Frost, when he finally did get to an Eisenhower stag dinner at the White House, made a point of saying afterwards that President Eisenhower was extremely intelligent. I understood. When a really good mind, suffering from the natural loneliness of really good minds, gets the ear of a man smart enough to make his way to the very top, even to make the topmost pinnacle an attribute of himself, there is a natural sense of satisfaction. For when all is said and done, action *is* the natural sphere of a mind sane and hopeful, eager to revive the classic center of man's public activity. To real intellectuals, power means not Caesarism but right influence; and it must be said that the type of Henry Adams, who wants to be near power so that he can deride it but feels that he is too intelligent to influence it, is really the prisoner of his own despairing rationality. Adams did not want his private obsessions interrupted by any new dimension of experience. And while the *quality* of mind is not necessarily better among those who are more "healthy-minded," it is a fact that the capacity of certain intellectuals to wield influence, the belief that they not only can but that they should, is interpreted maliciously by those who are so alienated from the body politic (to say nothing of politics) that they must explain everything as self-seeking.

« 2 »

I would suggest that what drew certain historians, political scientists, economists and lawyers to Kennedy was the fact that he, too, was outside the business community, had grown up independent of the main influence, and that Kennedy's very adroitness and eagerness of mind, his sense that there were deeper sources which he could employ, pleased them as the style of a politician no more limited by the business ethos than they are. In many ways the current intellectual style brings together people who have nothing in common but their indifference to the conventional values. It is the style of labor lawyers from immigrant families; of university administrators with a family tradition of diplomacy and liberal Republicanism in the tradition of Stimson, not the shabby rhetoric of "free enterprise" set up by professional demagogues; of professors themselves brought up in professors' families; of economists who remember with bitterness what young men with brains had to fight in the way of prejudice and snobbery when they first made their way up the university ladder. Such figures, whether their background was too patrician or too scholarly or too radical or too foreign for the majority view, represent the accelerating war of the "specialists" (or the "engineers," as Veblen called them) with the "price system." They have grown up on ideas, they have made their way up on ideas, they live on ideas. And in some way that must be both exciting to them and yet frustrating, Kennedy is also not limited to business and by business. He shares with his advisers a certain intellectual freedom from the dominant prejudices and shibboleths. But what for them is often a positive article of belief may, for him, be only freedom from vulgar prejudice — and it is exactly here that Kennedy's use of his advisers has already proved so much more significant than their influence on him.

About Kennedy one *has* to make psychological guesses, for unlike his advisers, one does not know what he thinks by reading him — nor even by talking to him. His most essential quality, I would think, is that of the man who is always making and remaking himself. He is the final product of a fanatical job of self-remodeling. He grew up rich and favored enough not to make obvious mistakes or to fall for the obvious — he has been saved from the provincial and self-pitying judgments that so many talented Americans break their teeth on. He has been saved, not merely from the conventional, but from wasting his time on it. Even now there is an absence in him of the petty conceit of the second-rate, and a freshness of curiosity behind which one feels not merely his quickness to utilize all his advantages, but also his ability to turn this curiosity on himself. He turns things over very quickly in his own mind; he gets the angle. Yet all the while he stands outside, like a sculptor surveying his work. He is what a certain time has made, has raised highest, and he can see himself in perspective in a way that perhaps only Americans can — since only they have *made* so much of themselves. The father made a killing in liquor and even as ambassador managed to sound like a district boss; the son has as many European "connections" as royalty. The father worked it so that each of his children would have at least a million dollars; the son, starting out high above the economic motive, asked advice of fatherly gentlemen in New England as if he had all the world to choose from. The grandfathers in Boston still had to look at *No Irish Need Apply;* their grandson, as the Attorney General of the United States said with grim pride when he urged Negroes to fight more for their *political* rights, is now President of the United States. He is President of the United States, he is a millionaire, he has the sex appeal of a movie hero, the naturalness of a newspaperman and as much savvy as a Harvard professor — and whereas you and I would be scared even to imagine ourselves taking on such responsibilities as face him every moment of the day and night, the highest office is what he wanted, this is what he went straight for, this is what he has. He has learned so continuously, so brilliantly, even so greedily, that one observer, noting that the author of *Profiles in Courage* didn't show his profile on the McCarthy issue, dryly wonders "if the book didn't, on some very private level, instruct him in what to avoid." The determination to succeed, the guardedness against vulnerability of any sort, the constant vigilance not to show himself wanting (his health has been the only admitted "weakness") — this is so sharp that another writer has brilliantly compared Kennedy to the type of Whig who in the eighteenth century entered the rising House of Commons: "of large and comparatively recent fortune, intelligent, elegant, tremendously determined to make a place for himself, desiring above all to be effective and to succeed, contemptuous of the aristocratic condescensions and concerned not to be condescended to."

But unlike those Whigs, it is to be doubted that Kennedy represents a definite social interest. What has given him his influence, even over the "brain power," as he describes this resource passingly in *The Strategy of Peace*, is his sophisticated freedom from conventional prejudice. When one adviser, submitting a memorandum on Latin American problems, noted that certain recommendations could be highly irritating to American business, Kennedy waved the hypothetical objection aside. This elasticity makes him exciting to work for, and to pass from so detached a mind to the endless analysis of itself that Washington goes in for might well make an intellectual in Washington feel that "brain power" is at the center of things again, that the few have again the chance to do well by the many.

« 3 »

Yet as this is being written, nothing stands out so clearly about the Kennedy administration as its frustrations. The occasion is piled higher with difficulty than ever before, and "the most intellectual and idea-seeking President since Woodrow Wilson" must find it as hard to remember some of the ideas he came in with as it is to promote some he has acquired since. Only in the White House, it may be, will Kennedy know the "contradictions and miseries" that other men have always lived with. And perhaps it is only in the White House, too, that the intellectual advisers who have gone smoothly from academic success to academic success may for the first time experience rebuff, defeat, obloquy. The "decisions" get more and more "educated," to use the President's interesting word, but they do not grow more decisive. And when I think of the increasing ugliness of American "conservatives," the political stalemate that Kennedy is faced with by Russia, the impossible difficulty of getting Americans to limit their smallest economic privileges enough to create a new social sense in this country, the conflicting views of so many different groups of advisers who were meant to counteract each other but who can produce administrative chaos, I anticipate that so restless and so ambitious a man as Kennedy will want to cut through the ever-deepening morass.

The most striking side of the Cuban disaster, to me, was the virtually official apologia that since Kennedy inherited the invasion scheme from Eisenhower and found that the C.I.A. had been arming and training an invasion army that could no longer be "contained," the technical approval by the Joint Chiefs of Staff and the approval of a majority of his advisers were enough to make him approve not merely an immoral but an impractical scheme to invade Cuba. Even a literary man reading up on Castro and his revolution could guess that Castro was much too popular to be overthrown from a small landing at the Bay of Pigs. Yet, faced by so many conflicting and in a sense mutually canceling bodies of advice, Kennedy allowed the gun to go off. And nothing has been said by him since, or by his advisers, that indicates it was anything but the *failure* of the Cuban invasion that they regret. It has given a "bad mark" to the administration that wants so much to succeed. What is immoral and downright stupid about the invasion, what represents not merely faithlessness to our traditions but an executive temperament restless, tricky, irritable — this has not been understood by the administration and its advisers. And seeking out Hoover and MacArthur at the Waldorf in an effort to make a show of national unity at the first sign of national dismay! The only defense that I have heard against the frightening impatience displayed in the Cuban adventure has been that so-and-so wasn't in on the decision, and that intellectuals on the outside never recognize how many important decisions are improvised and uncalculated. Where, then, is the meaningful relation of intellectuals to power? Is it only to write memoranda, to "educate" the decisions that others make? History will not absolve them that cheaply. What troubled me about the Cuban adventure was that although its failure was attributed to "erroneous" advice, the essential philosophy behind it was perhaps uttered by the adviser who, when asked for a show of hands, said "Let 'er rip," and by another who said pompously that it was time to come to a power confrontation with Communism in this hemisphere. (Stewart Alsop reporting.) In short, actions may be excused as "improvised," but is the essential philosophy a longing to come to a power "confrontation" in this hemisphere? Is it possible that the very freedom from conventionality that I interpret as the essential mark of Kennedy's intellectuals and of his receptivity to them — that this may yet create an abstract and virtually ideological conception of American power?

The famous State Department "White Paper" on Castro, published before the invasion attempt, listed many distinguished Cuban liberals, democrats, intellectuals, who had fled from Castro after being part of the 26 July revolutionary movement against Batista. Various pro-Castro "progressives" in this country noted that the White Paper quite conveniently omitted mention of any of the privileges lost by American business in Cuba. But although it is not for me to prove this, I suspect that in the mind of the author of the White Paper was not so much the desire to overlook the resentment of American business against Castro as the intellectual bitterness of an American liberal democrat against a political adventurer (Castro), who began as a "reformer" and has since shown himself a cynical and dangerous ally of totalitarianism. Perhaps business just did not come into it for the principal author of the White Paper. Hard as it is for pro-Castro intellectuals in this country to take this, I believe that economic determinism seems to explain as little of our bellicosity as it does Russian bellicosity. Anyone who has studied Castro's political development can see that his gravitation toward totalitarianism has had nothing whatever to do with American economic policies in Cuba. Khrushchev's stated belief to Walter Lippmann that Kennedy takes orders from "Rockefeller" is as mechanical a piece of Communist rhetoric as Stalin's stated belief that Hitler's policies were dictated by German capitalists. Indeed, the Russian Revolution itself, launched entirely by intellectuals whose historic dissociation from the great mass of the Russian people explains the very structure of the Communists as a party of intellectual managers, offers the most devastating proof that, especially in our times of centralization, history is made not for material interest but out of intellectual fanaticism often divorced from the most elementary social interest.

After the invasion attempt against Cuba, Kennedy replied to Khrushchev's professed indignation by cautioning him not to support Castro militarily. He ended his message with this emphatic burst: "I believe, Mr. Chairman, that you should recognize that free people in all parts of the world do not accept the claim of historical inevitability for the Communist revolution. What your government believes is its own business; what it does in the world is the world's business. The great revoluton in the history of man, past, present and future, is the revolution of those determined to be free." This is stirring language quite different from the usual muddle of Eisenhower's public statements. But I find it hard to believe that for Kennedy the Soviet government's philosophy is "its own business"; I find it also hard to believe Khrushchev when he says (on alternate Tuesdays) that he himself does not plan to attack the socially backward nations and explains that the well-known law of Marxist development will take care of that. Of course Kennedy is not driven by a fanatical creed of political messianism that is taken as the only universal law of history; nor is he as driven as Russians have been by a profound resentment of the creeds and relative good fortune of the West. But to the extent that Kennedy has been liberated by his own good fortune from the intellectual torpidity of American business, he may have been thrown back on the intellectual's natural outlet in causes. And the most significant side of Kennedy-as-intellectual seems to lie, not in his public cultivation of the "intellectual" style that is now admired in the highest echelons, but in the fact that, as a would-be intellectual who happens to be President of the United States, his natural tendency may be to identify the United States with a crusade, a cause, with "liberty." It was exactly this accessibility to causes that now constitutes, retrospectively, the disagreeable and even false side of Theodore Roosevelt. Similarly, what one fears about Kennedy is the other side of what one admired and was prepared to admire more in him — that he has been left free by his immense power to adopt a cause forged out of his energy and the depths of his restless ambition. Hard as it is for most of us to imagine ourselves arguing the fate of humanity with Khrushchev, it does not seem to bother Kennedy. And when I ask myself, as I increasingly must, what it is in Kennedy's ambition to be an "intellectual" statesman that steels him for his awesome responsibility, what in his *convictions* can carry him over the sea of troubles awaiting all of us, I have to answer that I do not know. At this juncture, Kennedy's shrewd awareness of what intellectuals can do, even his undoubted inner respect for certain writers, scholars and thinkers, is irrelevant to the tragic issues and contributes nothing to their solution. To be an "intellectual" is the latest style in American success, the mark of our manipulatable society.

[1961]

IX
The Critic's Task

Writing for Magazines

CHEKHOV, who died at forty-four, would have been a hundred years old this year, and there have been suitable tributes to him from short-story writers, people in the theater, and scholars in the field of Russian literature. I am none of these things, and my feeling about Chekhov, though warm, is backed up by nothing more than what everyone else has read of him in English. And perhaps I would in this instance have had the grace to keep quiet had it not occurred to me that there was one significant but virtually unpraised side of Chekhov's genius that I could pay tribute to.

Chekhov began as a writer for magazines — he wrote jokes, sketches, fables, feuilletons, little articles, spoofs; he literally tossed them off, sometimes from the bath-houses where he happened to sit down and write them. And later, a bit mocking as he always was about the "Chekhovian" virtues, he nevertheless said proudly: "I wrote as a bird sings. I'd sit down and write. Without thinking of how to write or about what. My things wrote themselves. I could write at any time I liked. To write a sketch, a story, a skit cost me no labor. I, like a young calf or a colt let out into the freedom of a green and radiant pasture, leaped, cavorted, kicked up my heels. I felt gay myself — and, from the sidelines, the result must have been funny."

Do you realize how revolutionary this was and is — a magazine writer who did not think he had to be solemn in order to be serious? A writer of "pieces" who was glad that they were just that — fugitive as anything can be, meant to entertain, nothing more? The trouble with magazines is that they give you just enough space to impersonate wisdom. It is impossible to do full justice to your subject; but there is room to lecture, to sermonize, to create effects. Even in the nineteenth century, when an article was not yet called a "story" (a story was supposed to entertain, to distract, to enthrall, not to give information), Edgar Allan Poe took his own role as a contributor to magazines so seriously that he grimly conceived of every offering as a demonstration of intellectual genius. Poe, who virtually invented the detective story, created in the figure of Dupin, the intellectual *maudit* who figures as his detective, a figure who actually represents the modern writer far more than he does any detective. Dupin is a man who discovers what no one else can see, who has a special slant on the truth in all fields. For Poe, every tale, every essay, every review, represented not only the romantic virtue of originality, but Poe's particular need to unhinge the existing world of intellectuals and littérateurs, to sign himself Q.E.D. at the end of each demonstration by Edgar Allan Poe. Poe was a literary genius who thought that he was virtually the only first-rate mind in this country, and in having to make a living from magazines, he converted necessity into the virtue of omnipresent wisdom. Everything was turned not merely into a demonstration of his rightness but into a syllogism which readers could grasp. No wonder that in planting horror and suspense as deliberately as a movie director, Poe was able to impress his name sufficiently to keep attention to his ideas. He knew his public, and what he did not get in cash he made up in living power. For in writing for a public which then as now wanted to get information slanted to give the appearance of "the inside story," a public impatient for wisdom as well as for news, Poe turned himself into his favorite figure — the wizard, the intellectual giant, the man who from the podium of the American magazine was able to enlighten the American folk, open-mouthed and grateful for the facts.

Poe, whatever his personal anguish, did not lack a good opinion of himself, for as a writer for magazines he was always immediately in touch with his public, always in sight of their rapture or terror or humility when he made a point. In the same way, Dickens, through the constant serialization of his novels, was so much in touch with his public that he thought it necessary, in his own magazine, to explain his separation from his wife. Dostoevsky, though he complained bitterly of having to begin serialization of a novel before he had had a chance to think it out, adored playing weekly and monthly on the feelings of the inflammable Russian public. Perhaps because he was considered the most "abnormal" and uncharacteristic of the great Russian writers, he was eager to keep a column and to be constantly in touch with the Russian intellectual public.

« 2 »

The trouble with magazine writers just now is that we are put so quickly in touch with a large public, we have so obviously the brief but undeniable power to influence, to arouse, to change the thinking of people (who now as in the nineteenth century will buy dozens of magazines but grudge themselves the purchase of one book), that, often against our better selves, we become pompous, see ourselves as having to dislodge something with each article, to make a point or to contradict one. Magazine writers should be able to embody wittily the inconsequence which naturally belongs to many magazine pieces. Instead of admitting that an article may be only a small step forward in our thinking, like an entry in a notebook, or a sketch frankly meant to relieve, to lighten, to distract (even writers, when they get through with a day's hard work, would like to feel gayer when they pick up a magazine), magazine writers think that they must be pundits on all occasions, pundits in each piece of work. Each offering in a magazine is now so carefully deliberated, weighed, written, and rewritten that we have forgotten the *joy* behind Chekhov's life as a magazine writer—the joy of not writing for the ages, of the easy tone, the marginal comment, the social joke, the joy of being as unserious as one is brief, of knowing that one can be light *because* one is forced to be brief. Perhaps because one is read on Monday and can be forgotten the same day, there is an art in being inconsequent, an art which avoids the crashing and rhetorical final note, the art of appearing as light and easy as in one's heart one knows a "piece" must often be.

Of course Chekhov did not use a typewriter, and so was not tempted to clutter up his life and everyone else's with many "drafts." He, who wrote some of the most exquisite short stories ever written, did not have to *research* facts which he had absorbed as an individual. And after he had written a piece because he had a little something to tell and a little money to earn, his editors did not feel humiliated if, as it turned out, he had been off by two decimal points in reporting the annual rainfall in Minsk. Nowadays a magazine will very rarely quarrel with your opinions; it will check only your "facts." Yet Chekhov, who like so many great writers seized the immense opportunity that magazine journalism presented him with, was trusted to go out to Sakhalin Island, to write up his own report on the convict colony there, and to influence Russian public opinion.

Many of Chekhov's most beautiful things were written for magazines, and what I like most about them is the fact that, unlike so much American editorial practice today, Chekhov was allowed to be *easy*. He did not think of a story or of an article as a demonstration by a pedagogic mind in which, at the end, all themes were wrapped together and the point handed to the reader. "The open form," as one must call it, the classic style of the European feuilleton, the style of conversation, of intimacy, of pleasure and the cafés, was Chekhov's delight and his genius. He knew that a magazine writer, working not only against time but in time, with a sharper attention to immediate issues than other writers, should not pretend to iron things out, to settle all difficulties, to ape a logical perfection that his work cannot sustain. For Chekhov everything became what every good writer wants of a story — to make it truly "a slice of life." The phrase was used by the pseudo-scientific naturalists to make a slice taken out for analysis, as under a microscope. But for Chekhov it meant the moment seized in its actual and seeming insignificance. It was this, as everyone knows, which so influenced James Joyce, Virginia Woolf, Katherine Mansfield, Sherwood Anderson — writers who showed that it is because a story in a magazine must be brief that it can suggest the unexpected depth, the delicate beauty of life caught on the wing. O. Henry, like many a writer today, thought that the ending had to be "right," to give the reader a bang. The ending of a magazine piece should be a bridge to the next thought, the next issue, not a ceremonious wind-up. For a wind-up has to be planned, and the plan usually takes over the piece as a whole.

Chekhov, by not taking magazines or himself too seriously, by not thinking that he had to liberate the Russian mind every time he sent in a sketch to a journal, liberated the short story as a form from the prosiness of prose. He showed that prose could be as profound and touching and *felt* an intimation of human existence as poetry. Every writer of fiction who is any good has wanted that for prose: to give it at least *something* of the truth that is touched by poetry. But poetry is not only the oldest literary art but always the most personal, the one that most closely requires the writer to find that portion of language, of point of view, which is most solidly *his own.* It is in the art of "verse," which by its essence is quick and bright, that so many accomplished writers have learned to write prose. Criticism is interesting to me only when the critic is; when he writes easily and well and talks in nobody's voice but his own. The critics I read are those I read for pleasure. They are very often poets — Dudley Fitts, Conrad Aiken, Randall Jarrell. A poet like Auden, an old hand at writing for magazines, learned the deftness, the ease, the insinuating honesty, from writing verse. An unusually effective collection of magazine pieces, Harold Rosenberg's *The Tradition of the New,* is distinguished by the independence and wit of a man whose original language was poetry. The poet James Agee was in many respects the most eloquent magazine writer of his time, the only writer whose individual voice could be distinguished from the anonymous smoothness of *Time.* One of the reasons why so many academic scholars find it impossible to write effectively for general magazines is that they are not used to listening to their own voices, as poets are. They find their happiness in approbation, not in the English language.

Yet *Time* has incorporated the talents of many poets to create a corporate style for which the magazine gets the credit, never the writer himself. Too many magazine editors today see themselves as "creative," think of a magazine as having the stamp of an individual book. They want writers to make a product, *the* magazine, rather than to assist writers in finding their own voices. This is where the ever-increasing apparatus of rewriting, the many drafts, the copying machine, the proofs and the checkers and the researchers and the corrections, though all made necessary by the lack in this country of the corps of dependable writer-intellectuals who make possible the *New Statesman,* nevertheless serve the ambitions of the editor rather than of the writer. But only a magazine edited by a dominating writer, like Mencken, could be as much all in one tone as so many magazines now *try* to be (and the *American Mercury* displayed Mencken's passion for style, never exclusively his own opinions). The reason why such magazines succeed in this attempt, however, is that writers are often impressed by the editor's belief in his magazine, and are glad to lend their talents to his enterprise.

A writer for magazines must above all be interesting, for there is not enough of him in any one issue to justify boring the reader. Similarly, he must extract from the conditions of his work — the hurried deadline, the last-minute change — the liveliness of time itself. It is for his gaiety and ease, above all, that I honor Chekhov the magazine writer on this anniversary. A magazine is always a date, "an issue," a moment; it is created out of an exacting sense of time and it is about time. The spirit of occasion, the tone of conversation, the modesty of the passing moment, are what most belong to it. Let the magazine writer be faithful to this spirit of gaiety — and perhaps, like Chekhov, he may triumph over his own modesty.

[1960]

Saints for Our Time

In the continuing controversy about the literary merits of *Doctor Zhivago,* hardly anyone has admitted how peculiarly difficult it is to judge what in effect is a new kind of novel. Of course *Doctor Zhivago* is not anything like the great nineteenth-century Russian novels. It lacks the old-fashioned fullness of detail, the self-dramatizing "big" characters who struggle against an utterly provincial background to realize their freedom. At the same time, Pasternak deliberately rejected the finicky estheticism, the arrogant self-consciousness, that one identifies with founders of the "modern" movement — Joyce, Gide, Proust: writers who are sustained by a belief that creating beauty may suffice against a materialistic age. *Doctor Zhivago* is a problem novel of *our* period — a period when no intelligent novelist wants to keep up the elegance of form and style that dominates Hemingway's stories or Gide's *Counterfeiters.* Today a writer is more likely to be concerned with re-establishing principles than with his own freedom from convention. Doctor Zhivago is forced into an absolute moral position, a strange and private saintliness, when he realizes that his struggle is not against

The Picaresque Saint: Representative Figures in Contemporary Fiction, by R. W. B. Lewis. Philadelphia: J. B. Lippincott Co.

society but for a new teaching that will keep up the ties and commandments of our humanity.

But how does one judge a novel so inherently "problematical," full of abstractions, suffused with a nobility that may move us for accidental reasons, uneven in style, full of the typical "crisis" psychology of our period? Our canons for judging a novel derive either from the great social novelists of the nineteenth century or from the esthetes who after Flaubert put maximum emphasis on style. Old-fashioned readers still demand an absolute feeling of mundane "reality" in every novel they read, though the world we live in is actually less and less real to all of us. Literary intellectuals, who still judge all fiction by Joyce or Hemingway or Woolf, by symbolism and literary surface of style, are usually incapable of recognizing what is really new about a book like *Doctor Zhivago*. They are not prepared to judge on its own merits what is actually a new undertaking for a novelist: to describe a hero who has to make a world, to be the spirit of life itself to people fatalistically sunk in tyranny and subjection. The old-fashioned reader thinks he is back in Tolstoy, but he is not; the "esthetic" reader thinks that Pasternak is clumsy when he is being merely indifferent to esthetic concerns and leisurely ideas that are useless to his purpose. At the same time, we are now so likely to be in sympathy with Pasternak, to identify ourselves with his motive in writing the book, that we can be almost too eager to praise the novel and to overlook those sides of it that are merely doctrinaire, theoretical, and sentimental.

« 2 »

This problem seems to me fundamental to *The Picaresque Saint*, which describes with the greatest sympathy, tact, and fellowship the literary situation of novelists who are concerned with Pasternak's subject, but which does not answer, or even raise, the question of how to judge their novels. Mr. Lewis is concerned with six novelists —Alberto Moravia, Albert Camus, Ignazio Silone, William Faulkner, Graham Greene, André Malraux—who represent the "crisis" generation of novelists who succeeded Gide, Proust, Mann, Joyce. These are novelists for whom the esthetic solution is not enough; they are typically concerned with Communism, Catholicism, totalitarianism, political terror, war. They symbolize man's sudden feeling that he is his own predicament. The characters of Greene, Camus, and Malraux can hardly sit on a mountaintop discussing the future of Europe, as did Thomas Mann's characters in the world which is supposed to have ended in 1914 but which actually lasted through the Twenties. Novelists of this "crisis" generation cannot be concerned with André Gide's perpetual search for his own moral "freedom," with the typical overvaluation by the esthete of his own sexual idiosyncrasy; life presses too hard. To put it bluntly, Gide's generation worried about the individual's right to be "perverse"; today a novelist must cry out against the identification of perversity with all life itself.

No wonder that a strange kind of "sainthood" is seen in contemporary novels, for in the world of Hiroshima and Auschwitz and Karaganda the only revolutionary act has become charity. In a world in which not sexual repression but cannibalism has become the norm, only a "saint" can give hope, can give back belief in life, can act on the immortal words of Augustine: *I want you to be.* But of course such a saint is not likely to be the old-fashioned ascetic hermit. In a world in which no one is sheltered from anything, the "saint" in contemporary novels is likely to be not only an ex-Communist and a bit of a rogue but a restless wanderer over the face of the earth: a man pursued by guilt. Pietro Spina in Silone's *Bread and Wine* is an organizer who returns to Fascist Italy disguised as a priest, and in *The Seed Beneath the Snow* he sacrifices himself. The "whiskey priest" in Graham Greene's *The Power and the Glory* dies in a state of mortal sin. Nevertheless he is good, a symbol of faith, in the grotesque way that men in our time ever are good — in perfect surprise and in flight from themselves. Like Doctor Zhivago, who will undoubtedly come more and more to seem the representative hero of our time, Greene's priest is a man who becomes a "saint" not by abjuring the fierce demands of his sensual humanity but by thinking differently from the others around him, by setting up a new loyalty for men's hearts that may free them from their compulsive pessimism.

The problem of our time, Tarrou says in Camus's *The Plague,* is to be "a saint without God": which means only that, at a time when people do not know whether God exists, it is important to honor certain fundamental obligations in order to save humanity itself. This indeed is what Nikolai, the uncle of the hero, says in *Doctor Zhivago,* when he insists that the belief in "history," in man's struggle to abolish the meaninglessness of death, is open even to atheists. This is the feeling of Ike McCaslin in Faulkner's great story "The Bear," as it is even of Catholics like Graham Greene's heroine in *The End of the Affair* and Scobie in *The Heart of the Matter,* and of the humanist Vincent Berger in Malraux's *The Walnut Trees of Altenburg* (the fragment of a novel that was destroyed by the Nazis). More and more, in a world that seems not to exist in the old human terms, that cries out for human rebuilding, not for the old "revolt" against conventions that no longer exist, we have characters who are new to fiction, protagonists who are more like the founders of a new religion than like the heedlessly energetic middle-class characters of the old fiction; for these "new" people, who have been reborn to themselves, have discovered a fundamental truth and are now trying to think others back into life.

Mr. Lewis's description of this situation in contemporary fiction is excellent, and his book performs a most useful service in orienting us, in moving our historical attention and sympathy to the actualities of the present. There is probably no more sympathetic and understanding account in English of Silone's literary career than there is here, and Mr. Lewis has got to the heart of Camus's nihilism, of Moravia's eroticism, of Graham Greene's literary Catholicism, in a way that seems to me utterly admirable and thoroughly useful. In this respect he does what so few critics do nowadays: he is really thinking of the writer himself, from the point of view of another's spiritual plight; he is not, as so many professorial critics are today, so puffed up with the achievements of Joyce and Hemingway and Eliot that he is coldly superior to the creative problems of the moment.

Nevertheless, when we raise the fundamental question of how to judge these new books, Mr. Lewis does not really help us, for he thinks as a sympathetic moralist, not with the inner shrewdness of a creative writer. My objection is not to his actual judgment. It is that in describing books whose common theme moves him so much, Mr. Lewis, like all of us who have been moved by *Doctor Zhivago's* protest against Marxist materialism and Soviet cant, has to convert his approval of ideas into emotions of identification and participation which may signify gratitude rather than a genuine creative experience.

The only test of a "problematical" and "existentialist" novel is whether we, as readers, are made to feel that our own world has become entirely problematical. There are people to whom all literature of the human "predicament" is subjective and childish, as there are people to whom it can be as real as a blow or a nightmare. We cannot respond to *Doctor Zhivago* as we do to *War and Peace*, but we begin by recognizing its authenticity, and after a while we find ourselves in a world where the theme of the "reborn man," of the new vision, has been made palpable. In art there is either a tangible whole experience or there is not. Everything depends not so much on what is said as on the tone of voice in which it is said, on the force with which it is felt and the conviction that it instills in us. If we feel an obvious gap between the "problem" and its realization, if we sense that the approach is abstract, if we recognize that the author, in the fatal manner of non-art, has first raised a question and then simply answered it, we know that the "predicament of man" may be real, but not the book itself.

« 3 »

The danger of this new fiction is, of course, its own seriousness. What is merely intense and urgent tends to disguise itself as a creative emotion. But in art everything depends on the depth at which emotions are held. Thematic criticism can mislead when it brings together disparate writers linked only by their experience as contemporaries. Graham Greene is an absorbing, clever, talented writer, yet he seems to me fundamentally immature; I judge him by the lack of depth at which his world is created. His nightmares are real, his saints are real, his understanding is acute; he remains a clever English schoolboy with a gift of converting his personal anxiety into macabre fiction. (Mr. Lewis would have done better to choose Evelyn Waugh, who *looks* immature but actually possesses an extraordinary and obsessed imagination.)

One of the key words in Mr. Lewis's book is "conversion": he means not only the conversion to a new veneration of life, which everyone in our time needs, but a conversion into art. And here the very use of "conversion" as a term is wrong. Nothing is ever converted into art that is not felt inherently as art. The artist does not transpose, he realizes; he does not translate, he incorporates. Faulkner is a very great artist because he is a constant explorer and discoverer of his own thought. A *Fable* has many phony aspects to it without being phony; the single force behind the book has redeemed the shoddiness of some of its devices. Faulkner's artistic integrity is such that he could not write a "false" book if he tried. Camus's *The Stranger* is a wonderful book because it is entirely authentic in its own terms (Mr. Lewis's analysis of its "exasperating perfection" is excellent). But Moravia and Greene seem to me writers pursued by private nightmares which they "convert" into fiction, and I think that Mr. Lewis, despite his awareness of their faults, is misguided to group them thematically with Faulkner and Malraux. In a sense, he also overpraises Silone; he cannot leave himself the elasticity of judgment that a critic needs, for by confronting his subjects head-on, as examples of a contemporary theme, he has kept himself from the kind of particular background study which can distinguish the different shades in the common predicament. Silone receives a full and most sympathetic biography, and we can see how much the ex-Communist in him, the plight of the idealistic Marxist of yesteryear, helps to explain the strength and weaknesses of his fiction. But Mr. Lewis overlooks the role that politics plays in Camus's development, just as he ignores in Moravia the debilitating effect of the Italian bourgeoisie; he describes but does not evaluate the obviously neurotic background of Greene's fiction. The predicament which the novelist describes is in fact no less real when one realizes how much that has gone to shape it originates in social and personal pressures. The relative decline of Silone's novels is perhaps due to the very lack in Italy of those pressures which, growing fiercer and fiercer in Russia, helped to create *Doctor Zhivago.*

[1959]

Father Rexroth and the Beats

WHEN THE YOUNG BEATNIKS or literary hipsters became news in San Francisco a few years ago, an older poet and critic, Kenneth Rexroth, seemed to appear everywhere at their side like the shade of Virgil guiding Dante through the underworld. Rexroth — who had lived in San Francisco since the 1920s and had from early youth been connected with almost every "advanced" literary-radical-Bohemian movement, from the Wobblies and the John Reed Clubs to the objectivist movement in poetry and abstractionism in painting — suddenly became a public figure. He was an originator of the jazz-poetry readings and an extremely effective reader and teacher of poetry on the San Francisco radio. The enthusiasm of the hipsters for orphic art and poetry unfortunately went hand in hand with a professionally exploited ignorance. Rexroth, who had grown up in bitterest poverty and had never completed his high-school course, had the fanatical learning of the self-educated. He published translations from Chinese, Japanese, Greek, Latin, Spanish, French; he spoke as an authority on jazz and painting as well as on poetry. There was no subject within the range of interest of the new writers on which he disclaimed being an authority, yet by temperament he was a firebrand, a come-outer, a hundred per cent radical-anarchist — no compromiser with what he always called "the social lie."

In an essay for *New World Writing* called "Disengagement: The Art of the Beat Generation," Rexroth made out an extremely interesting case for Jack Kerouac before *On the Road* was published, and attributed the recent deaths of Dylan Thomas and Charlie "Bird" Parker, the great Negro saxophonist, to a social order so murderous and corrupt that the only possible recourse for the new writers had now to be "disaffiliation," absolute refusal to work "within the context of this society." This essay, though written in a showy style that did not inspire the reader's trust, nevertheless seemed to me the valuable

Bird in the Bush: Obvious Essays, by Kenneth Rexroth. New York: New Directions.

testament on the Eisenhower years of a veteran American radical who identified himself with all the old robust traditions of native protest. Although there was something about Rexroth's essay that suggested a man looking for a weapon, I recognized in his mordant comments on professor-writers and the decadence of big-city intellectuals a real old-fashioned American sorehead of the type of the old Populists screaming against the moneyed East. And I welcomed this not only because I prefer radicals — people who want to transform society — to the beatniks playing at poverty and drugs and looking for a "thrill," but also because Rexroth's smoldering violence against every surface of the American Establishment, his choked-up bitterness, made him, by the sheer momentum of his tendency to exaggeration, a humorist. Rexroth's unforgettable elegy on the death of Dylan Thomas ("You killed him, Oppenheimer the Million-Killer,/You killed him, Einstein the Gray Eminence. . . .") is in its sheer uncontrol one of the funniest as well as one of the angriest poems of our time. It takes a really unusual writer today to say a good word for science, but the usual romantic claptrap about science as the enemy reached in Rexroth's poem the positive pinnacle of outrage. Groucho Marx screaming "I'd horsewhip you if I had a horse!" is really not much funnier than Kenneth Rexroth screaming in one poem against Henry Luce, *Mademoiselle*, T. S. Eliot, the Statue of Liberty, the liberal weeklies, the cocktail habit, Brooks Brothers, and the university quarterlies — "the vaticides/Crawled off with his bowels to their classrooms and quarterlies." Those two clever night-club mimics, Mike Nichols and Elaine May, were right to parody Rexroth's poem as fashionable apocalyptic radicalism, and before long Rexroth was himself appearing in new Bohemian joints like the Five Spot Café in New York's Cooper Square.

« 2 »

Alas, "Disengagement: The Art of the Beat Generation" is not in this new book of Rexroth's essays. The reason, it seems, is that the beatniks, whom Rexroth seemed to be introducing and explaining to the American public, have became too ridiculous and disgusting to take seriously. "I will not take those would-be allies which Madison Avenue has carefully manufactured and is now trying to foist on me. . . . The Beat Generation may once have been human beings — today they are simply comical bogies conjured up by the Luce Publications . . . the trained monkeys, the clowning helots of the Enemy. They came to us late, from the slums of Greenwich Village, and they departed early, for the salons of millionairesses." (This is a fair specimen of Rexroth's usual moderateness of tone; I forget which Frenchman it was who wrote *"La vérité est dans la nuance,"* but he couldn't have discovered this from reading Rexroth. Rexroth writes even critical prose in the style of *New Masses* covers of the 1930s: slashing black-and-white, drawn with a knife. Down with the enemy! Down with "corn-fed metaphysicals" and "country gentlemen"! Down with "subway Neanderthals"! Down and down and damn and damn!)

It is a fact, however, that the beat writers whom Rexroth once heralded have now become rather famous in their own right, and it is striking that his appreciations in this book are devoted largely to established figures like D. H. Lawrence and Samuel Beckett, Henry Miller and Martin Buber and Yeats — plus the painters Morris Graves and Mark Tobey and J. M. W. Turner. But the bitter phrase in Rexroth's preface, "They came to us late," reveals the deep prejudice of a writer over fifty that there is an old radical-*avant-garde* tradition that the beatniks do not represent. This affirmation of "us" — what Rexroth and so many other ex-radicals fondly used to call "the movement" — is curious. Rexroth is a writer who will never make his peace with "the system," with what he unchangeably calls "the social life." He is so natural a romantic anarchist that a literary historian in the future could decipher all the secondary characteristics of today's romanticism from Rexroth's writings alone. He has the ingrained bitterness of those who have grown up in poverty, who have had to educate themselves in public libraries, who are constantly enraged by the attempt of university "New Critics" to divorce literature from life, by the attempt of our leading statesmen, with their pseudo-moral imbecilities, to evade the unsettling future. The best of his poems breathe an insatiable nostalgia for the insurgency of American literature before the First World War, for the moral freedom of the 1920s, for the early 1930s, when many an honest writer still thought that he could work with the Communists. His book is in part the intellectual autobiography of a whole generation of American writers born around

1905 — and more particularly of Western writers, writers attached to the Wobblies and the ideal of the free "working stiff," writers who to their own minds incarnate the manly democratic West against the wealthy decadent East.

However, Rexroth's belief that his experience constitutes the norm of American insurgency and literary radicalism, and that younger writers are to be regarded as "the trained monkeys, the clowning helots of the Enemy," is as trying as anybody else's nostalgia for the good old days. This country no longer attaches any spiritual value to poverty, and Rexroth's dear old "innocent Jewish mechanics and Italian peasants" are as bourgeois as the rest of us. When Rexroth proudly insists that unlike those who have sold out, "Life with us goes on just the same," he is talking through his hat. His book, though full of nostalgia for the radical past, has no radical content whatever. Rexroth is no longer interested in society, just in obtaining the largest possible freedom from it. He has nothing interesting to say about contemporary society, he merely denounces it:

> The contemporary situation is like a long-standing, fatal disease. It is impossible to recall what life was like without it. We seem always to have had cancer of the heart. . . . The first twenty-five years of the century were the years of revolutionary hope . . . Now the darkness is absolute . . . We have come to the generation of revolutionary hopelessness. Men throw themselves under the wheels of the monsters, Russia and America, out of despair, for identical reasons. . . . Writing this, sitting at my typewriter, looking out the window, I find it hard to comprehend why every human being doesn't run screaming into the streets of all the cities of the world this instant.

None of this is very enlightening about anything, and I suspect that what bothers Rexroth is not the despair but the gluttony and selfish ease, which cannot but enrage the man who has had to fight his way up with laborious suffering. One of Rexroth's very best insights in this book is into the capitalist psychology of Rimbaud — so often cited by Rexroth's friend Henry Miller as the rebel incarnate, but as Rexroth says, the very type of the entrepreneur, and never so happy as when he openly played the part. One can discount Rexroth's inverse snobbery about American neuroses being "actually, by and large, palpitations of behavior due to unsatisfied bourgeois appetites and lack of life aim." But he is in the path of truth when he says: "It is possible to mistake a demoralized craving for Cadillacs for 'revolt.' . . . Genuine revolt goes with an all-too-definite life aim — hardly with the lack of it." However, it must be admitted that while Rexroth as a critic always tries to stir up the Philistines, to agitate and to unsettle, he is actually not very interesting. He is a terrible show-off of his own learning, and though he calls himself a literary journalist in the tradition of Huneker, Mencken, and Wilson, he seeks to impress rather than to persuade. He is an impressionist of art, of all the arts, rather than a critic, and there is a certain solemn rapture about his attempts to put jazz and painting into words. But it is typical of Rexroth's lack of objective concern with ideas that although he profoundly admires Martin Buber, he thinks Buber sadly amiss in sticking to Judaism. "It is pitiful to watch a man of Buber's intelligence and goodness struggling in the toils of an outworn and abandoned social paranoia. . . . Why do people bother? If they must have a religion, the basic texts of Taoism, Buddhism, Confucianism need no such reworking."

A dilettante is someone who thinks that he can pick and choose from the world's arts and religions as if they were a department store. Again and again Rexroth betrays his fatherly place in the beat movement by his glibness of cultural allusion, by his admiration for sensation and violence, by his belief, so typical of all the culturally frivolous, that the Orient has transcended the intellectual torment of the West. A dilettante is a man who uses his anger to entertain society, not to change it. "I began to realize I was back in America, a place I try to keep away from." A dilettante is a man who writes that all the scientists in the universities are "genocidists," that "the practice of literature today is the practice of acquiescence," and that religion, any religion, may serve to stimulate the writer's imagination but should not involve tiresome considerations about God.

Mr. Rexroth is a dilettante. Mr. Rexroth, when all is said and done, is a beatnik himself. Let who will write the nation's laws, he says, so long as *he* continues to scorn them.

[1960]

Tynan's Theater

NO ONE who reviews all the specimens of an art regularly, by the day or the week, by the performance or the exhibition, can ever be better than, can really be *different* from, the stuff he works in. Just as it is impossible to tell which new book Orville Prescott is reviewing in the *Times* any longer, since they all sound as if he had written them himself, so all regular reviewers of drama, if they sit it out year after year, become performers as showy and adroit as any of the other theater fans who pump comic lines into sagging plays or revise lyrics in New Haven. Only an insatiable appetite for an art would ever get a man to absorb so much of it. To be that much of a critic, one must be essentially uncritical. What sustains the reviewer is his own performance. If he is good enough, he graduates into being a performer pure and simple, like Bernard Shaw. If he is not, he remains a glutton, consuming books or plays or pictures.

Kenneth Tynan, who after the death of Wolcott Gibbs succeeded (briefly) to the *New Yorker* job and is now back on the *Observer* in London, has never pretended to be anything less than passionate about the theater—and my guess is that he will never be anything more. When he likes something, he gets up from writing the review "on his knees," and there is almost nothing in the product, English, American, Russian, French, that he does not feel himself up to. Wolcott Gibbs, I recall, was always saying, on those pompous and funereal occasions when Shakespeare is dusted off for Broadway, that cripes, he hadn't looked at *King Lear* since high school and didn't know a decent chap at the Algonquin who had, either. But when Tynan, who began reviewing plays in his teens and who loves to read drama criticism as much as he does to write it, reports on Sir Ralph Richardson as Macbeth, you are certain that he has seen all the Macbeths since 1927 (when Tynan was born), has read up on all the performances before that date, has spotted all the divergences, omissions, and misquotations in the text, and has

Curtains, by Kenneth Tynan. New York: Atheneum.

studied the mind and vocal range of Sir Ralph to the point where he can relish all the fine points and spew forth all the bad ones.

« 2 »

"What, when drunk, one sees in other women, one sees in Garbo sober." Tynan sees the Garbo glow in the theater everywhere. The rave is equally for W. C. Fields and Ruth Draper, Jimmy Cagney and Tennessee Williams, what Stanislavsky said and what Brecht said, Maria Casares as Death in Cocteau's *Orphée* — "I have never seen the imminence of suicide more powerfully conveyed" — and *West Side Story*, which "compromises only on the brink of greatness; and that, surely, is triumph enough."

It isn't that Tynan likes everything, but that he is able so strongly to absorb and to respond to everything theatrical. He knows, from love, why French playwrights reserve their greatest parts for women and why the English have no "heavies." He knows to a decimal point what percentage of the box office goes for theater rent in London and Paris. And just as he is the only writer I have ever heard of who got to interview Garbo, so he is the only drama reviewer who has described himself as present at the frenzied rewriting of a play after a tryout. When he describes Michael Redgrave in *Richard II* as excellent but "still missing the real heights by an inexplicable inch," you recognize the sense of loss; and though he loves to make fun of Sir Ralph Richardson's personal manner, you can see that no one knows it better — "His feathery, yeasty voice, with its single spring-heeled inflection, starved the part of its richness; he moved dully, as if by numbers, and such charm as he possessed was merely a sort of unfocused bluffness, like a teddy-bear snapped in a bad light by a child holding its first camera."

Although Tynan is often glib in enthusiasm, he is never flip in condemnation; a virtuoso performer in journalism, a pro from the minute the curtain goes up, he never makes fun of anyone without establishing a valid point by it. His wisecracks are astonishingly accurate. He says of Orson Welles's production of *Moby-Dick* that "It is absurd to expect Orson Welles to attempt anything less than the impossible," which is so true that you can't imagine another way of saying it; and when he reports of *King Lear* at the Old Vic that

"A whole gamut of inaudibility is painstakingly run . . . listening to Stephen Murray's Lear was like lipreading Shakespeare by flashes of lightning," you can see that he may have lived the play better than the actors did.

So brilliant a critic is easy to read and fun to read, for Tynan throws himself wholeheartedly into the writing of a piece of critical prose. As he loves the theater, so he loves writing about it; and even though this is a very big collection of reviews, you can read him straight through with delight. He takes you on a tour of the contemporary theatrical world, and his reactions are so strong and intelligent that it is impossible not to enjoy the writing and to be grateful for the tour.

And yet, Tynan is exactly like the contemporary theater — as horridly professional, as glibly insurgent; everything is turned back into the usual sophisticated liberalism, the fatally self-conscious gesture. It is exactly to the extent that he mirrors the contemporary theater — in America he loves *West Side Story* and *Gypsy,* in France he adores Edwige Feuillière, in Russia he makes the perfect guest, and from East Germany he approvingly quotes back every piece of pseudo-Marxist *Kitsch* — that he displays the unlimited appetite of the reviewer rather than the free insight of the critic. Tynan can spot the pompousness in T. S. Eliot's verse plays and the hollowness in Christopher Fry's, but I am sure that he would rather die than confess himself to be baffled or bored or disoriented by a line of Bertolt Brecht's. Maybe he is equal to both *West Side Story* and Brecht, as Broadway itself always claims to be; but judging by the secondhand wisdom that Tynan circulates on Brecht, I doubt it. It took *Suddenly, Last Summer* and *Sweet Bird of Youth* to make him reproachful of Tennessee Williams, and though *Camino Reál* irritates him, he would like to take it seriously. Somehow he is unconvinced that there may not be a "big idea" in it; for Tynan, like many young writers who feel that they have been starved of big movements and "big" ideas, is sentimental only about abstractions.

The most combative point Tynan makes in this book is that he is a radical and a humanist, allied to the "angries" in Britain. This I value less than the fact that he is Irish (from Birmingham), for what the Irish react to instinctively in English institutionalized repression and gentility always makes them astringent and gay. But "humanist" and "angry"? These are labels, not a point of view. A point of view, especially for a critic, is like no one else's, and I do not find it reassuring for Tynan to parody Faulkner's *Requiem for a Nun* so viciously that one might suppose that Faulkner was a lyncher, while losing himself not merely over Lorraine Hansberry's *A Raisin in the Sun* but over the pro-Negro audience rejoicing in so rare a chance for a Negro playwright. And it puzzles me that in a book that is so roomy Tynan had no space for his shrewd appraisal of Lillian Hellman's overrated *Toys in the Attic*.

Like many young intellectuals in Britain, Tynan is much exasperated by America as the symbol of a dying social order, and I am sure that the outrageous way in which, before returning to England, he was summoned up before Senator Dodd's inquisitorial committee and rudely searched for his opinions did not further endear the United States to him. But too many of Tynan's running comments on this country reveal that last resort of snobbery — the British determination to like only our "low" culture. There is something too much of the tourist in Tynan's mental make-up. I once read a marvelously giddy piece by him on New York and was astonished that there was not a thing in it that a native would recognize. He quotes a Russian theater director as saying that "In our society there may be occasional collisions, but there are no defeats." Tynan adds: "That is the attitude, and the theater reflects it." How does he know? He can't know that much from a quick tour and the constant intervention of interpreters. But on the basis of a slogan, Tynan goes on to suggest that "The pressures which produce lyric artists, passionately affirming their own selfhood, are inexorably being removed. Collective art is taking their place, for how can one *épater les bourgeois* when there are no *bourgeois* to *épater*?" The ignorance of Soviet society that is displayed in this passage is really shocking.

Tynan looks at the social facts in England and America with pitiless eyes, like a man who cannot be deceived. But he would *like* to believe that the slogans retailed to him in East Berlin or Moscow are true. He too is looking for a placard to march under, and one can't blame him. Life in the bourgeois democracies is dull, dull,

dull, and older people seem to have had all the fun of trying to change it.

[1961]

The Poet against the English Department

As I sat down to write this review, I noticed in the paper that a critic who has had more than the usual experience of academic life has just published a satiric novel about academic life. There are so many novelists, poets, and critics teaching in America that it sometimes seems as if the only human activity they can write about *is* the academic life. Whenever the writer has had to repress, to tone down, to meet with, it has become routine for him to bite the hand that has just fed him (and that in time will feed him again).

But the deeper complaint that a creative writer is likely to have against the English departments is that they are so sophisticated. The rebels of 1910-1925 — Eliot, Pound, Joyce, Yeats — have become the "modern" tradition and supply all the canons. The writer who knows himself to be an odd duck, who is engaged in finding the language for *his* sense of things, can be so exasperated by the intellectual togetherness of critical opinion, by the self-satisfied airs of those for whom T. S. Eliot has supplied all the answers, that he is tempted to turn into the court jester, the department fool. Where everyone is solemnly concerned with "order" and "orthodoxy" and discovering the marvelous "tenderness" in one stanza of Ezra Pound's delirious *Cantos,* the writer is driven to attack all criticism, to play the part of the wild man, the primitive, the *naïf*.

This seems to me the situation behind Karl Shapiro's *In Defense of Ignorance,* a collection of lectures delivered under academic auspices whose purpose is to attack the cult of "modern" poetry as personified by Eliot-Pound-Yeats and to bring up, as a corrective, the more lyrical, spontaneous, and romantic work of Dylan Thomas, William Carlos Williams, and Henry Miller. Shapiro has for some

In Defense of Ignorance, by Karl Shapiro. New York: Random House.

time been professor at the University of Nebraska; before that he edited *Poetry* in Chicago. Since poets tend as naturally as Marxists and psychiatrists to divide into hostile factions, Shapiro found himself under constant pressure from those neo-orthodox, always anxiously correct people who as a matter of course identify the "modern" tradition in poetry with fear of what Eliot likes to call "heresy."

I well understand Shapiro's exasperation with the cult that has set itself up in English departments as *the* tradition of modern poetry. And yet, sympathetic as I am with many of his literary opinions, much as I admire his specific judgments on individual poems and poets — the best feature of his book — I think that he has fallen into the trap of playing literary factions that has been set up for him by his life in the university. The answer of a free and spirited writer to the intellectual neo-classicism of Eliot should not be the *other* intellectual line of anti-intellectualism. This is a crude and emotional way of discharging the resentment that a creative writer can feel in the university — especially when he is an outsider, an original, an old-fashioned American nonbeliever or non-Christian. It is exactly the "liberal," easy, conciliatory sophistication which sees literature only as a clash of positions that we have most to fear just now, and as a "position" Shapiro's is likely to attract support from both old fogies and the lunatic fringe. The first are against any poetry that they have to think about, the second are interested not in poetry but in being taken for poets.

Shapiro's book is a mixed bag. Insofar as it is a defense of "ignorance," an attempt to set up an attack on criticism and intellectualism, it seems to me weak, bitter, and, worst of all, ineffective. The way to defend "ignorance," if *that* is what needs defending just now, is to stay away from the language of reason, not to tackle Eliot on his own ground of critical argument, and to *be* a naïve genius. Shapiro is anything but this. He has never seemed to me even a passionate poet; his own work is striking for its concrete but detached insights; it is witty and exact in the way it catches the poet's subtle and guarded impressions, and it is a poetry full of clever and unexpected verbal conceits. It is a very professional poetry — supple, adaptable, by no means Dionysian. Like much contemporary lyric poetry, it seems to me imprisoned in "sensibility," muscle-bound except in relation to the poet's specific rendering of a place, a time, a mood. Shapiro's essays are full of the same excellent and detached insights. He is often brilliant in his judgment of particular texts, as luminous and witty then as he is unnaturally programmatic and self-defeating and even a bit hysterical on Eliot as the evil genius of modern literature:

> Eliot is untouchable . . . The enemy . . . searches his citadel for an opening and cannot find one. Eliot has long since anticipated every move; he and his men can prevent ingress or exit. Eliot resembles one of those mighty castles in Bavaria which are remarkably visible, famed for their unsightliness, and too expensive to tear down. Life goes on at the bottom; but *it* is always up there.

Yet when Shapiro lives up to his own prescription that the critic should do nothing but judge works of art, when as a fellow poet he takes up those pieces of Eliot's which in university classes are often read only as a puzzle to decipher or as necessary condemnations of contemporary society, he is exhilarating. Criticism *is* discrimination; the only real use a critic often has is in sticking his neck out, on choosing between those works which so many people are afraid or unable to choose from.

There is no better critic than a professional judging in his own field. Much of what Shapiro has to say about particular works by Eliot and Pound seems to me absolutely first-rate. His criticisms of Auden are cruelly shrewd. But the reader of such passages is likely to wonder why so intelligent and witty a critic should, in order to attack the programmatic criticism of Eliot, identify it with *all* criticism. Shapiro has a strong appreciation of William Carlos Williams, but many of his affirmative judgments are really based on Williams's critical pronouncements. He says roundly that Dylan Thomas "was a tremendous talent who stung himself into insensibility because he could not face the obligations of intellectual life, which he mistakenly felt he must. He could not take the consequences of his own natural beliefs." But *why* couldn't Dylan Thomas do that? Why can't any Romantic poet do it? It is because every work of literature *is* a criticism of life — of human destiny, of society, of history. To pretend that these things no longer exist, to mistake oneself as a *naïf*, a primitive disengaged from the society that our intellect and sympathies judge all day long, is just self-defeating. It is because Dylan Thomas could not or would not justify his "natural beliefs," because he would not grow up to them as a poet and thinker, that he gave up. Circumstances now press so hard on all of us, the earth is getting so overcrowded and over-organized, that it is perfectly possible to get lost in the shuffle, and there at the bottom to pretend that nothing exists but oneself.

But every writer — every "beat," every disengaged anarchist — criticizes life and society with every word he writes. The better the writer, the more this criticism and his imagination will fuse as one. Shapiro is emotional and unjust on the reasons for Eliot's fame. Eliot from the first made it his responsibility to offer us a constant critique of our society; one can quarrel with the quality of his concern but not with this concern itself. He has been faithful to the human community in our time, to the necessity of saving society from self-destruction. It is this concern, in art, that made Eliot's fame.

And if Shapiro wants to know why Whitman has ceased to mean as much to American writers, the answer is in his own book. He says that Whitman "is the one and only poet of America who has attempted to adumbrate the meaning of America. The twentieth-century poet avoids this commitment, by and large; he considers it fitting and proper to take refuge in History against the horrors of progress . . ." I agree with Shapiro's account of Whitman as a great poet and prophet. But Whitman at his best is identical with faith in America as a political proposition, and you cannot plead for "ignorance" without turning Whitman over to those who see him as just another self-centered homosexual. To believe in Whitman you must believe in his revolutionary politics, in his concern with the masses, in the spiritual leaven of democracy.

It was the decline of this faith that opened the gates to Eliot's Anglomania and Ezra Pound's Fascism, to Allen Tate's celebration of the Old South. There was no conspiracy in this, as Karl Shapiro suggests; the triumph of these writers resulted from the despair of those who gave up Whitman's ideals, who no longer trusted in Whitman's America of "great souls," who doubted that out of our mass society would come the spiritual triumph of the ordinary man, Whitman's "forgotten." It was exactly those poets who agreed with Henry Ford that "history is bunk," who thought that Dylan

Thomas could escape "the obligations of intellectual life," who opened the gates wide to the new medievalists, the dreary croakers whose despair of democracy has always fastened on *The Waste Land.*

But such is Shapiro's own value as a critic, as a celebrant of what he truly loves, that he ends his book with a perfectly splendid appreciation of Henry Miller. Miller—the Miller who in the "*Tropic*" books felt himself one with Emerson and Whitman—*is* the poet of real life, the Romantic anarchist that so many rebel writers now try to be, out of disgust with the organized society. This is because Miller at his best is powerfully in love with what he writes about. He really accepts life, all of it, in the enchanted and singing style that Whitman hoped the man in the street would find for his life. Very few writers in the Romantic, now "beat," style actually feel so strong a love for the facts of ordinary existence. They are afraid of our world. But like all true poets, Miller gives us a taste of the actual joy, energy, and freedom we are starved for. He makes one happy. No wonder that after reading Miller with so much pleasure, Shapiro is convinced that

> . . . Combatting the "system" is nonsense. There is only one aim in life and that is to live it. In America it has become impossible, except for a few lucky or wise people, to live one's life; consequently the poets and artists tend to move to the fringes of society. . . . The American way of life has become illusory; we lead the lives of prisoners while we boast about free speech, free press, and free religion, none of which we actually enjoy in full. The price for security has become too great; abundance has become a travesty.

I like this passage; it speaks that criticism of our lives which reminds one of Chekhov: "You live badly, my friends!" We do live "badly" in this country just now, and the writer who does more than say so, the writer who brings this home to our blood and nerves, as Miller does on occasion, shows us what life can be like. He proves that the critic and the poet are in the true writers always indissoluble—as they are in Shapiro at his best, when he is writing not against the English department but out of himself.

[1960]

The Function of Criticism Today

SOME YEARS AGO, in a course I was giving on European novels, a student handed in a paper in which he described Emile Zola's *Germinal* — that powerful but old-fashioned novel of French miners struggling for their rights — as characterized by *paradox, tension,* and *ambiguity*. Since these terms were brought into modern criticism to characterize the tensely wrought and ambivalent verse of the seventeenth-century metaphysicals, and then the poetry of those (like T. S. Eliot) who absorbed a style, a manner, from these Hamlet-like literary intellectuals, I explained that Zola's rather large and florid prose style — the style a French naturalist needs to get himself through a shelf of documentary novels describing the ravages of alcoholism and syphilis on all the descendants of a French family — could not possibly be compared to those highly artful poets. Zola's style certainly has its share of grandiloquent poetry, and Zola liked, in the manner of the epic-writing Romantics, to sign himself *poète*. But *Germinal*, in both its crudity and its passion, its violent sexual metaphors and its indignant description of the oppressed, is so far from the language and subject of an Eliot that, properly speaking, it makes no sense to find in nineteenth-century naturalistic fiction the attributes of what is, even for our time, only one kind of poetry.

My student insisted on his point. He had been instructed in *paradox, tension,* and *ambiguity* in a course called "Introduction to Literature," and with the very text of *Germinal* before him, he was so concerned with showing that he knew how to read his book with a modish approach to literature that he simply could not recognize the most obvious quality of Zola's great novel — which was its force. He felt no necessary connection between his experience and that described in the novel, but he had brought in wholly arbitrary connections, couched in a critical vocabulary that he had learned by rote, whose historical applications and limitations he did not understand. He was like a tourist in a foreign country; he could imitate the language but he did not understand it. There was no community of interest between himself and the novel, but he did not even realize this; he was not even thinking of the novel he was reading, so busy was he plastering *paradox, tension,* and *ambiguity* over Zola's astonished face.

Now this quality of making arbitrary connections, this lack of historical awareness, often of historical information rudimentary enough to supply guideposts and danger signals in going through the country of Zola, this false sophistication — this is what troubles me about many students who have been taught to read critically, as the saying goes, but who do not really read at all, who do not enjoy reading, who have no interest in literature. But equally, I'm troubled by the editors who print my essays but are utterly unconcerned with my ideas and values, with the readers who come up to say how much they have "enjoyed" a piece but who never discuss the argument in it. There's something wrong, some basic element missing, in the relationship of the audience to the critic in America today, and I see this wrongness in the professional journals for which you don't have to take the trouble to write well and in the Sunday book supplements that exist only to sell books; in the lack of general magazines publishing serious criticism and in the very absence of any responsible and authoritative evaluation of contemporary literature. There are a great many rewarding and fruitful sides to being a literary critic, but one of the things that we don't talk about, that some of us never even notice, is the absence of echo to our work, the uncertainty of response, the confusion of basic terms in which we deal. It's not that we lack an audience; it's that the audience doesn't know what it wants, is not sure of what it thinks, is fundamentally uneasy with literature, even afraid of it, and wants to control the beast rather than to live with it.

This situation is what characterizes criticism in a mass society — mass communications in themselves have changed nothing and determine nothing. As soon as you get people who do not, themselves, read but who feel that they need criticism to make contact with literature, as soon as the educated public (which used to test its own opinions on the critic's) breaks up into the self-declared mass that wants things to be explained, then you get the critic-as-popularizer, the critic consciously mediating between the work of art and the public. But no critic who is any good sets out deliberately to enlighten someone else; he writes to put his own ideas in order; to possess, as a critic, through the integral force of his intelligence, the work of art that someone else had created. Of course he will elucidate, he will analyze, he will define and locate and explain, but all the things he does for his reader he does first for himself.

« 2 »

What the critic does for his reader, for the public, he does on the flood tide, so to speak, of his excitement with a particular book, a brave new insight, an evaluation, a theory. A critic is not an artist, except incidentally; he is a thinker, and it is the force, the exactness, the extension — perhaps the originality — of his thinking that gets him to say those things that the artist himself may value as an artist, the reader as a reader. To the true critic insights are valuable for themselves, and different members of the audience may use them in different ways. But no critic who works for the pleasure and excitement of his task writes just to instruct the writer he is reviewing and for the sake exclusively of the public that reads him. For the interest of criticism lies in itself, in the thinking that it practices.

Criticism affects the artist only as the artist is himself a member of the educated public that reads criticism. A writer will often get better advice about a book from his editor or his wife, or his literary agent, than from a critic. But the critic, if he is interesting and deep enough, will affect the writer far more profoundly than would specific technical criticism of a book — by making him see the significance of his efforts. At its best, true literary criticism may actually suggest new subjects, can enliven the imagination. This is the great tradition of criticism, a part of the general criticism of established values which must go on in every age. Its greatest single attribute is its force, its passionate declaration of the true nature of man and what his proper destiny must be. In America itself, this was the kind of criticism that Emerson wrote in his great essay on The Poet and that Whitman created in *Democratic Vistas,* John Jay Chapman in his essay on Emerson, and the young Van Wyck Brooks in *America's Coming of Age* and his much underrated book on Mark Twain. The greatest examples of such criticism in modern times were Arnold's essays on poetry and culture, Proust's attack on

Sainte-Beuve, and Nietzsche's on Wagner. To me this is the most valuable kind of criticism — the kind that Baudelaire wrote in dealing with art, Shaw in dealing with drama, and that before them had been practiced by Goethe in his remarks on the Age of Prose, by Schiller in his letters on esthetics, by Blake in his personal manifestoes, by Wordsworth in his preface to *Lyrical Ballads*. It is the kind of criticism that I always think of as *histoire morale*, that sums up the spirit of the age in which we live and then asks us to transcend it, that enables us to see things in the grand perspective, and that, in the way of Marx on Greek philosophy, of Kierkegaard on Mozart, of Nietzsche on the birth of tragedy, of Shaw on Ibsen, of Lawrence on American literature, asks us — in the light not only of man's history but of his whole striving — to create a future in keeping with man's imagination.

It is precisely because he once wrote criticism of this kind that Eliot has had his influence. Eliot, when asked by Paul Elmer More why his poetry and criticism were written in such different tones, replied that poetry deals with the world as it is, criticism with the world as it ought to be. It is because of his grounding in the historical ideals of self-liberation which we associate with Marx and Freud that Lionel Trilling has remained so steadily a moral influence, an Emersonian teacher of the tribe, and it is because of his constant awareness that books make revolutions in the public history as well as in the private sensibility of men that Edmund Wilson has been able to write with equal insight of Proust and John O'Hara, Michelet and Edna St. Vincent Millay, Tolstoy and Lincoln, the Hebrew Bible and the Marquis de Sade. The Van Wyck Brooks who, at least in 1915, wrote with such verve and exhilaration against the plaster gods of American life worked constantly with this sense of being sent forward by an irresistible movement of social criticism in all fields. And as I write I seem to see this image not in any young American critic but in the young British drama critic, Kenneth Tynan, who before he left this country was summoned up before a secret congressional session for his dangerous thoughts. Tynan's rule for drama criticism is, "Rouse tempers, goad, lacerate, raise whirlwinds," and I must say that his sense of art as something dramatically and effectively involved in the affairs of men is one which any serious critic of drama must have, for on the stage, at least, the passions of men as makers of history are inescapable.

The essence of such criticism is that it is concerned explicitly, fightingly, with an ideal of man, with a conception of what man is seeking to become, with what he must become. The dynamic sense of values, the electric and constantly demanding sense of his age which such a critic has — this is the quality that makes him a particularly keen and demanding analyst of concrete values, of esthetic differences. For there is a significant distinction between what I would call passive "taste," as a social category concerned only with success of execution, and the critic's judgment, which says that so-and-so is a good writer, but not good enough, or that it is because he is a good writer that he is also a dangerous writer, such a narrowing or stultifying influence. By keeping alive the spirit of criticism in the sense in which the Enlightenment gave it to us — the "modern spirit," as Matthew Arnold called it, which subjects everything handed down to us, all institutions and beliefs, to critical examination — we no longer limit our esthetic categories to the beautiful, the sublime, the merely correct. Goethe, says Erich Heller, identified the modern age with what he called the age of prose, and lamented that "the all too radical attempt of the age of philosophy (eighteenth century) at a 'humanization' and rationalization of the mysterious ends in a perverted miracle. The mystery, cheated of its rightful place, goes underground, reverting to its primeval, unholy and barbarous stage. No center holds the human world together and men must lose their bearings." This is virtually the language of Yeats's "The Second Coming," and in one form or another of most of the criticism that has been modeled on Eliot's well-known laments for Catholic order. But Goethe himself, as a poet, a dramatist, as a speculative free-wheeling scientist, found his new forms, new interests, a brave new future for himself, in exactly this modern spirit. And criticism, in our modern sense of it, examining works not for their classic theory or neo-classic correctness, but for their fulfillment of the goals which they have independently set, has led to an awareness of esthetic possibility and of individual vision which unites *all* modern poets, novelists, and painters, whether they acknowledge it or not, whether they want it or not, as children of the Romantic movement. The point of this modern spirit in art is not that everyone agrees on the value of the modern movement, but that everyone must work in its atmosphere of freedom and individual discovery — Catholic artists as well as secularist artists, the haters of the modern spirit as well as its most pragmatist admirers. There are no longer any esthetic goals which we can name outside the individual works of art that give us our fertile and experimental sense of esthetic achievement.

Marcel Proust wrote an essay attacking Sainte-Beuve's naturalistic conception of art, and in the middle of this essay virtually began to sketch the first pages of his famous novel. He had discovered his own necessary vision, his artistic credo, in attacking as a profound danger to the imaginative life of humanity Sainte-Beuve's "neo-scientific" view of life. But out of this necessary "chaos" of positions, as Goethe thought of it, had come not merely Proust's discovery of himself as an original and major artist but his discovery, through the profound revelation afforded by the inner consciousness, of the new vision of the eternal open to modern artists. The possibilities opened up to us by creative memory became Proust's idea of the future.

« 3 »

To use Jacques Barzun's significant phrase, the "energies of art" are revealed to us, and so can be described and judged, only when they are seen against the background of man's striving, man's belief that *he* can help create the future he wants. There is no energy where there is no hope — no energy, no wit, no passion, no involvement, no lightness. Our individual sense of the future is the dimension in which we breathe, or as Emily Dickinson put it: "I dwell in Possibility — / A fairer house than Prose." We can judge what things are like because in our hearts we know what we really want; we judge by the direction, the vector of forces, along which life seems to be moving. If a writer believes in his own vision of things, no matter how idiosyncratic it may seem, that is all the future he may need. But he must believe in it, as Blake believed in his visions, Dostoevsky in the redemption of sinners, and Marx in the holy city that would be created by Communism. This sense of the eventual vindication of life by the imagination is what gives meaning to every great artist's life, and it is the critic's job to support this belief, to delineate it, to fight for it. Through this dimension of the imaginative future alone can we understand what literature is for. And to bring this kind of imagination, this historical sense of what has been, of what is now, of what must be — to bring this into play, in the immediate confrontation and analysis of works of art, is to make evaluation significant — one might almost say, possible. There is in every true work of art a tendency pressing for recognition, pressing a work of art together, and if we do not recognize what the work of art is itself striving to be, in the light of what man himself is always striving to become, our evaluation becomes a question of frigid correctness.

So strongly committed are we by now to the idea of a work of art as created from a wholly individual standpoint, and measurable by the goals which the work itself has set, that anyone who really practices critical judgment, who constantly deals with new and unforeseen works of art, actually finds his own physical energies challenged and changed by the energies of art. He cannot save himself from the sometimes painful new experience that a new work presents. This does not mean that he is an impressionist, taking his own prejudices and limitations as the only values. It means that his skill begins by noticing his intuitive reactions and building up from them; he responds to the matter in hand with perception at the pitch of passion, as Henry James put it; the unity of thinking and feeling actually exists in the passionate operation of the critic's intelligence. Judgment can be a very physical matter indeed. A false or strained work of art can make you literally sick. Anyone who is serious about criticism, for whom judgment is an active factor in his daily awareness, will have an intensely sensory and tactile response to poems, stories, novels, dramas, essays. In some way, the critic's sense of his existing balance is challenged by that new balance of forces that is a work of art, and in this downright challenge to our physical being that a new work of art can represent, the critic will recognize how much he has been advanced, and how much not, by a work that can be as real to him as sex and his daily bread.

There is no discrimination without partisanship to an ideal. It is undesirable to have a perfect taste, to respond properly to all the masterpieces. Unless we approach literature demandingly, as I say, unless we respect it for its influence, we fall into the attitude of the dilettante, the epicurean, on the style of the late Bernard Berenson, who by trying to prove that his taste was equal to the best that has been thought and said, made culture look like a table set with tidbits. The critic who has the equipment to be a force, the critic who can set up standards for his age, must be a partisan of one kind of art and a bitter critic of another. Like Johnson, he will be unfair to the metaphysicals; like Goethe, to Hölderlin; like Sainte-Beuve, to Flaubert; like Arnold, to Whitman; like Emerson, to Dickens; like Henry James, to Tolstoy; like Eliot, to Shelley; like Wilson, to Kafka; like Trilling, to Dreiser. Such a critic will be not only unfair, he will pursue his prejudice to the point of absurdity, setting up a straw figure that will serve to bear all his dislike and even his hatred of a certain kind of art. And significantly, the critic who sees himself setting standards for his age may stimulate new works of art by helping to create the climate of discussion, by revealing the hidden issues that give a writer a hint of new subjects.

Above all, the critic who works with this sense of the age in his bones, who sees himself working toward the future that man must build for himself, is always a writer. He writes for the public, not to a few imagined cospecialists; he writes to convince, to argue, to establish his argument; he writes dramatically, marshaling his evidence in a way that pure logic would never approve and pure scholarship would never understand, but which is justifiable, if it succeeds, as moral argument in the great tradition of literature. The critic who writes well is the critic who lives in literature, who is involved himself and therefore sees the involvement of literature in our conduct, our thinking, our pleasures, our human fate. Some of the best criticism has been communicated in talk, like Hazlitt's, Goethe's, Alfred Whitehead's, but we know this only because someone wrote it down. Criticism that is not *written*, in the best sense, communicable as literature, is only advice — and if you read the letters to authors of such famous editors as Maxwell Perkins, you see immediately the difference between editing and criticism. Some striking criticism has been written in private letters, like Ezra Pound's to Laurence Binyon on the latter's translation of *The Divine Comedy;* some as inserts in novels, as in Goethe's *Wilhelm Meister* and Joyce's *A Portrait of the Artist as a Young Man;* a good deal of really valuable criticism has, of course, been written in the form of verse. But it has to be written so that we can read it — that is, like Plato's philosophy and Marx's sociology and Freud's psychology, it has to explain itself and be read for itself. Criticism should never be so professional that only professionals can read it, for the trouble with writing for professionals is that you don't take the trouble to write well. I have been staggered lately by the absolutely worthless essays in so many recent academic journals devoted to modern literature and criticism. Eliot and Faulkner and Salinger haven't smiled on their anxious elucidators at all. The scholarly journal, in this sense, is no more an organ for criticism than is the *Saturday Review*.

Criticism exists as literature only when it has a great argument to present, and to this I would add that the critic knows his argument in full only by writing it, by coming to grips with his own mind. Arnold's essays are a prime example, and indeed Arnold's essays are far greater than his poetry precisely because even his best poems give the effect of a mind too quickly made up against the modern age and lamenting its loneliness, whereas in his essays, those incomparably noble essays on the study of poetry, on translating Homer, you feel that the subject under discussion has taken him in hand and is directing and searching him out. Eliot's essays seem to me most valuable not for their general prejudices but for the thinking that goes on in them line by line. I have always found it hard to understand how people who dislike Eliot's general line, and I myself certainly do — people like F. R. Leavis and Kenneth Rexroth and Karl Shapiro — can overlook the exciting and moving quality of concern, the level of actual critical thinking, that goes on in Eliot's essays. Eliot, in his essay on Blake, managed to say exactly the right things about Blake's imaginative independence, and to draw the wrong conclusions. But who cares about Eliot's disapproving conclusion so long as we have his exhilarating analysis of Blake's mind? Like everyone else, Eliot has changed his mind about so many things that his conclusions, as such, have no more authority than has Henry James's ignorant assumption that Russian writers never have any style. But Eliot working out a line of critical thinking about the character of Othello, or the conflict between Pascal and Montaigne, creates superb criticism by thinking, how shall I say, not conclusively, as a philosopher might, but critically — making us see all the elements of the literary experience before him.

This has always been Edmund Wilson's special gift, and it is because of the excitement that a particular essay by Wilson can generate, not necessarily by the taste that he upholds, that he can give so much pleasure to people who distrust his opinions. For ironically, it is because Wilson is *not* the mediator between artist and public (except incidentally) he often declares himself to be, it is because in his best work he thinks and thinks, almost desperately, to put his own thoughts in order, that the resulting tension and passion make him effective to the general reader. Similarly, Lionel Trilling's *The Liberal Imagination* comes out of a deep personal drive to set in order the underlying conflict that must possess a radical mind that has seen so many radical values abandoned, misused, and converted into the very opposite of these values. Any critic who is any good is going to write out of a profound inner struggle between what has been and what must be, the values he is used to and those which presently exist, between the past and the present out of which the future must be born.

This struggle with oneself as well as with the age, out of which something must be written and which therefore can be read — this is my test for a critic, and it is for this reason that I admire critics in themselves so different as Shaw and Mencken and Chesterton, Santayana and Eliot, Wilson and Trilling. Of the newer critics writing in English, I admire the dramatic criticism of Kenneth Tynan and Eric Bentley and Lionel Abel, the essays on Whitman and Frost by Randall Jarrell and on the American novel by Richard Chase. W. H. Auden's poetry seems to me terribly impoverished in recent years, but his critical essays are often profound — yet always written in the great English and Continental tradition of the feuilleton, the weekly article. I once heard Professor Harry Levin say disparagingly of the English critics that they have the amateur spirit; but I would reverse the term and say that a critic should be able to write well enough to get paid and so lose his amateur standing.

I like criticism to be as serious as possible in content, but as personal and even idiosyncratic in style as possible — thus reversing the usual academic recipe of the trivial point and the heavy style. Have we forgotten under what conditions so much of the most powerful criticism has originated? Poe wrote his greatest critical essays for general magazines, in the same way that Coleridge and Hazlitt wrote for newspapers. Arnold lectured to audiences so large that many could not hear him. Sainte-Beuve wrote his greatest pieces week after week for newspapers. Eliot wrote his best early essays as a reviewer for English weeklies. Proust wrote his own first essays for frivolous Parisian papers. In our time perhaps the most valuable new interpretation of Lincoln appeared in the *New Yorker*. It was the *Seven Arts*, the old *Nation* and *New Republic*, the *Freeman*, the *Dial*, the *Liberator*, *Poetry*, the old *Masses*, that published the essays of Randolph Bourne and Van Wyck Brooks and Edmund Wilson, Conrad Aiken and Santayana, William Carlos Williams and Ezra Pound. It was the *American Mercury* that made Mencken one of the prime critical influences on the Twenties, and it was in such magazines that Eliot and Pound, Frost and O'Neill, were defended, explained, established. Go back and recall that Emerson's great essays were popular lectures, that Henry James's famous essay on "The Art of Fiction" appeared in a popular magazine, as did his best fiction, that Howells's essays on realism and his marvelous essay on Mark Twain all came out first in magazines. In England, the most significant essays of Beerbohm, Shaw, Wilde, were written as dramatic criticism for magazines, just as Virginia Woolf and Orwell, Lawrence, Chesterton, Ford Madox Ford, and more recently C. P. Snow, Angus Wilson, V. S. Pritchett, have been read in the *New Statesman*, the *Spectator*, the *Sunday Times*, the *Observer*, the *Manchester Guardian Weekly*, the *Times Literary Supplement*, the *Tribune*. This kind of critic sees himself not as a hack, but as a man seizing the largest possible audience for his ideas, and in the weekly dialogue he holds with his readers he establishes standards, and sets up a forum around which ideas gather, where neglected important figures can be revived and new writers recognized.

Behind this tradition of criticism lay the common conviction that there were issues to be fought out, that terms might be shared and understood but that there was no agreement over the solutions. Criticism was still seen as part of the general debate over the ends of man in our age. This was the struggle between Chesterton and

Shaw, and earlier, between Wells and Henry James; in America, between the new experimental writers of the 1920s and the bitterly resisting old guard represented by the New Humanists. Criticism cannot live without dispute over the terms of art and the significance of certain kinds of art, and dispute was possible because the critic and *his* critics — and the audience which criticized them all — were somehow alive to the same issues and shared the same culture, so they were free to disagree about the necessary ends to be reached.

« 4 »

Now it is my impression that for some time critics in America have had too easy a time of it, that their readers no longer make any great demand on them. And I believe the reason for this is the growing assumption that literature cannot affect our future, that the future is in other hands. It is my impression that there is not much belief that literature can exercise its classic functions of providing ideas central to social policy and moral behavior.

Literature no longer seems to exercise much influence. The reason for this, I think, is the pervasive feeling that our freedom is being taken away from us, that the new society now being built up by the technological revolution and collectivism may no longer leave room for the old-fashioned individual in literary pursuits. C. P. Snow, in *The Two Cultures*, insists that so long as our most sensitive poets and distinguished literary intelligences refuse to become literate in science, the prime maker and shaper of our lives, literature must continue to dwindle into insignificance. Last summer, when I visited the Soviet Union in a delegation of American writers, I discovered that in *that* science-worshiping society, delegates at the Congress of Soviet writers applauded Khrushchev's open contempt for their efforts, and that, in public at least, the only function of literature in a totalitarian and technological society was journalism and propaganda. If the Russian literature of the nineteenth century made the revolution possible, the new Communist society has turned literature into advertising. Gomulka's Poland even grants *avant-garde* poets and writers artistic latitude, permits them to write like Wallace Stevens or to paint like Jackson Pollock, so long as they do not tamper with politics. And to speak here only of our own country, you can see that the enormous increase in our population, the predominating influence of an inflationary prosperity, the widespread leisure so often absorbed by television and the cheapest magazines, have accelerated the division into classes that are culturally haves and have-nots. You have more and more people who are indifferent to literature, who positively prefer cheap or bad literature, who are certain that literature has nothing to say to our age. Then you have all the people who, though they profess an interest in literature, know very little about it and cannot make up their own minds about a book. Yet at the same time, those who in a sense are most intimately involved with literature, who care most about it, are in such despair over the future of our society that you have, in the most prosperous and still relatively the most open society in the world, whole battalions of what the Russians call internal *émigrés* and what we call the beat movement — people who simply don't see the connection between their personal striving and the country at large, and who have holed up in their pads, made a fetish of external spontaneity, in order, even if they cannot write, to live like writers and so preserve what they think of as the last possible portion of their freedom.

Much of this seems to be a phenomenon of economic prosperity rather than of political despair, yet it cannot be denied that the kind of intellectual élan which we now associate with another expansive period, the 1920s, and which has always been characteristic of imperial wealth and influence like ours, tends to be muffled in anxieties of one kind or another. I myself believe that we, like everyone else, are now going through such a constantly accelerating historical advance that we are unable to seize the moment properly, to see all that is happening and where it will end. Our whole sense of time has to be changed, but since the only real measure of time is our daily biological cycle, we feel ourselves being constantly exploded into the sky like rockets. We are rushing into our future so fast that no one can say who is making it, or what is being made; all we know is that *we* are not making it, and there is no one, no matter what his age is, who does not in his heart feel that events have been taken out of his hands.

Yet, ironically enough, the great idea systems of the past have been so outdistanced by events that very often the only check we have on events at all is contemporary literature. Often enough now it is not Marx, or even Freud, but Eliot, Hemingway, and Faulkner, and more recently J. D. Salinger, by whom an American undergraduate tries to read the plight of the individual today. The literature that we have come to think of as modern literature, the literature that began in the idealism of the early twentieth century and that perished only in the depression, the literature of 1914-1935 that now seems to us as almost the last proud assertion of man's will in a still liberal and confident society — this literature has become the great text of our teaching. From it we compose our introduction to literature for students who are separated from the last modern generation not by frustration but by the irresistible momentum of a continually changing society. As English schoolboys once learned history from Homer, so American undergraduates now learn it from Eliot and Hemingway and Faulkner.

The enormous interest in contemporary literature that one finds everywhere in American colleges today stems from this awareness that contemporary literature somehow records our fate — that not only *The Hollow Men,* "The Bear," but, pressingly now, "A Perfect Day for Bananafish" and *Augie March* and *The Deer Park* provide a text in which we still read our hopes and our fate. No matter how negative Augie March or Seymour Glass or Charles Frances Eitel may seem to be, these heroes of contemporary American literature are still human in the classic manner — they suffer, they are comic, they aim at a world in which human beings can live. I would even say, from my experience as a teacher, that probably nothing else in the liberal curriculum now so much touches on the lives and the real thinking of American students as these stories and novels and poems which have kept the unforgettable impression of man's effort to apply his understanding and to assert his will. In many American colleges and universities just now we have virtually no other way of approaching fundamental questions except through the materials furnished by contemporary literature.

And it has been my experience that the critic who teaches literature is now the focus for values and influence that in other cultures are furnished by the family, religion, political ideologies. Randall Jarrell once said that in America today many intellectual couples turn to criticism for the sort of guidance they used to get from a minister. Look at the way the stories of Salinger have been taken up by students, at the frenzied interest in the beats, at the way various paperbacks become the Bible of the student intellectuals. Students in America are starved for what one can only call enlightenment, for the literature that will bring the hidden issues out into the open. Just as America alone has turned psychoanalysis from a clinical method into an ethical system for living, so we fasten on contemporary literature with the same avid need.

Yet the most obvious thing about criticism in America today is that it is not consciously related to any literary movement. It does not consciously work toward a future. Look at much of the criticism that concentrates on Joyce, Eliot, Faulkner, Stevens. Are these essays written so as to suggest new possibilities for art, to welcome new writers, or are they written to explain a point in *Ulysses* that no one else has mentioned? The rebels of the little magazines, the crazy men of *transition* and the *Dial*, have become the staple of the curriculum. If you take the kind of essay defending Faulkner that Conrad Aiken wrote for the *Atlantic Monthly* in 1939, to justify him when he was being ruthlessly attacked, and compare it with the latest essay on Faulkner's orthodoxy of sensibility, indistinguishable from other essays on the same subject, you will see that criticism of modern authors likes to regard them as safe authors, classic authors, and often misrepresents the rebelliousness and iconoclasm that gave these authors their force. Faulkner, like everybody else, is a moralist, but he should not be used year after year to buttress Southern nostalgia. No one has ever shown quite so conclusively how dead the old South is. When Faulkner's profoundly heretical and important book, *A Fable*, came out in 1954, I was struck with how much the advanced critics joined with the professional philistines of the daily book reviews to attack it. The remarkable appreciation of the novel published by the poet Delmore Schwartz stands out in interesting contrast both to the attacks on the book and to the fawning and derivative essays still being published on *The Sound and the Fury*. *A Fable* is a fantastic book, literally a fantasy, for it is about peace in our time, a peace that very few really now believe in. No one accustomed to moving in the safe grooves of literary criticism was prepared for a book about the First World War by an author whose experience, like that of his generation, is attached to the last time when men went from peace to war knowing they could never return.

The trouble with all of us who teach and explain so much of modern literature is that we are too far from the kind of historical confidence, the *élan*, the historical swagger, that made it possible. A critic like Edmund Wilson has a kind of independence, constitutes a personal resistance movement in himself, that critics who come after him can hardly understand. Once, when I heard a professor at the Salzburg Seminar explain in good English-35 fashion that *The Great Gatsby* represents a search for the Holy Grail, I thought of Fitzgerald and Zelda diving into the Plaza fountain in New York, and was ashamed to think that no one roughly of a later generation, not even Allen Ginsberg, would do it just for fun. No one could ever confuse a poem by Eliot with one by Stevens, or an essay by Wilson with one by Kenneth Burke. These writers are all originals, and you always know where you are with them. But when, as critics and teachers, we pass on to our students, with all the latest modern methods, *The Waste Land*, *In Our Time*, "Sunday Morning," "My Father Moved through Dooms of Love," we can't help distorting such works by omitting something. What we omit is our own experience of the unself-conscious individuality, the relaxed independence, the natural sauciness and sassiness and exuberance of style that gives these works still — as Fitzgerald said of his own — the stamp that goes into them so that we can read them like braille. Step by step the great confidence that man could understand his time and build from it, the feeling that provides the energy of modern art, has gone out of us, and we are left teaching such books as if they were models of correctness rather than rare moments of spirit.

This is why, properly speaking, there can never be a consciously ignorant, a mass psychology, in regard to modern literature. For the essence of the modern movement is that it represents a permanent revolution of consciousness, an unending adventure into freedom. In the deepest sense, we can never study modern literature or art; we can only be part of it. That is why criticism is important. We must practice criticism on the older writers lest they harden into the only acceptable writers. We must learn to practice criticism on the newer writers, in order to bind them more truly to our own experience. We must practice criticism on our age while it is still here to show us its possibilities.

Index